THE MIND ALIVE ENCYCLOPEDIA
THE EARTH

CHARTWELL
BOOKS INC.

THE MIND ALIVE ENCYCLOPEDIA
THE EARTH

Edited by Thomas Browne

Published by Chartwell Books Inc.,
a division of Book Sales Inc.
Distributed in the United States by
Book Sales Inc., 110 Enterprise Avenue,
Secausus, New Jersey 07094

©Marshall Cavendish Limited 1968, 1969, 1970, 1977

Printed in Great Britain

This material has previously appeared in
the partwork *Mind Alive.*

This volume first published 1977

ISBN 0 85685 303 8
Library of Congress Number 77-73849

Pages 2 and 3: Sheep graze in the Plain of
Jezreel, Northern Israel. In the distance is
Mount Gilboa, mentioned in the Old Testament,
and this pastoral scene has probably changed
little since biblical times.

Pages 4 and 5: This photograph was taken at
the Swiss mountain resort of Unterwasser,
3000 feet up in the St. Gallen canton. It shows
the majestic mountain ranges of Oesterreicher
and Bundner Gebirgsketten.

Page 6: In the immense empty spaces of the
world's deserts, dawn can be an awe-inspiring
sight.

Introduction

As we read more widely and travel further afield, the thirst for knowledge about the world we live in increases. The Earth gets smaller — and our horizons expand. And here is a valuable compendium of knowledge for the student, traveller and armchair explorer alike, a book which takes the reader on a journey back in time to the very formation of the Earth, and around that Earth as we know it today, through equatorial jungle, savanna, tropical island and desert.

The Encyclopedia of the Earth traces the life history of our continents and seas, and explains how volcanic action, glaciers, wind and water have built and sculpted the world's mountains, valleys and coastlines. It tells the fascinating story of the early explorers and map-makers, and describes how their modern counterparts chart the Earth from space using unmanned satellites with highly sophisticated instruments.

We live in a world rich in agricultural and mineral resources. Some, such as our oceans and the agricultural potential of deserts, remain largely untapped: others, such as our mineral resources, have been ruthlessly exploited. This book describes their distribution, and issues a timely warning of how our greed may in time destroy the delicate balance of the Earth's ecology, a subject of vital concern to all who wish to retain the beauty and bounty of our planet for future generations. A consistently interesting and informative text, hundreds of maps, photographs and diagrams, and a comprehensive index, combine to make this a thoroughly enjoyable book.

Contents

Picture Credits

Dating the dawn of time

For centuries Man has tried and failed to establish the Earth's age. Now modern science has solved many mysteries of its turbulent past and learned much about the monsters that roamed its changing surface.

THE EARTH has long been thought of as something permanent and changeless, a symbol of firmness and stability. Until about 300 hundred years ago, most people in the Western world assumed that the landscape was here to stay, that the hills were eternal, and the rivers kept their appointed courses. In fact, all good Christians believed nothing had really changed since Creation a few thousand years ago and then only as a result of catastrophes, such as Noah's Flood, which were caused by supernatural forces.

These accepted views were based on a literal interpretation of the Old Testament, and any attempt at a more scientific study was considered heretical. The French Comte de Buffon who suggested in the mid-eighteenth century that the six days of creation in the Bible must represent six long periods of time, was forced to recant such a revolutionary opinion.

Non-Christian cultures in Asia, unaffected by belief in the literal interpretation of Genesis, had more realistic ideas of the Earth's age. The Hindus, for example, believed that the Earth was about 2,000 million years old.

At the end of the eighteenth century scholars in the Western world began to look more closely and curiously at the world around them and found many clues to indicate enormous and continuous change: coasts were advancing or retreating; the edge of Niagara Falls was wearing away at the rate of a few feet a year; some hills were decaying while others seemed to be rising; valleys were widening and deltas forming. It was not until then that a few pioneers, including James Hutton, recognized the enormous age of the Earth and the constant changes which have occurred on its surface. Rain, snow, rivers, the sea, earth movements and volcanic activity are all agents of this constant change, and in one person's lifetime may be barely noticeable.

Devil's work

To understand how the landscape is gradually transformed, some knowledge of historical geology and the time scale of the history of the Earth is necessary. Geographers need to understand the immense amount of time involved in geological eras, periods and epochs, before they can appreciate the slow rate of erosion and deposition which is causing the Earth's surface to change.

Until the last few years of the eighteenth century the evidence of fossils was generally misunderstood or disregarded. Some scholars affirmed that fossils were the Devil's work, put in rocks to confuse mankind. Others believed that they were evidence of the Biblical Flood. A tooth, nearly six inches long, belonging to a

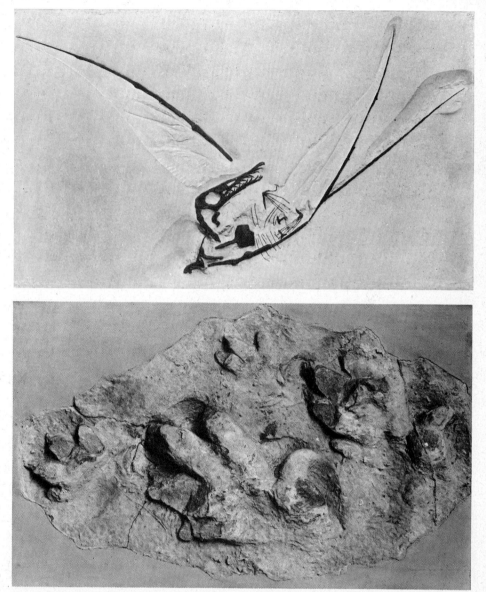

This fossilized pterodactyl, *top,* was one of a species of flying reptile which dominated the skies during the Jurassic and Cretaceous periods about 135 million years ago. Found in southern England, Bavaria and elsewhere, their wing-span ranged from a few inches to 25 feet. *Above,* these footprints of a prehistoric reptile were buried by sedimentary rock during the Triassic period.

mastodon (an extinct elephant-like animal), was discovered in the United States in 1706. After serious consideration, the Governor of Massachusetts concluded that this was a human tooth belonging to a giant who had been drowned in the Flood. Such were the fantastic notions which serious students of the Earth had to contend with.

Apart from James Hutton and Sir Charles Lyell, who established the theory of uniformitarianism – that the landscape has constantly been changed by the same natural forces that operate today – another British geologist, William Smith (1769–1839), made an important contribution. Smith was a surveyor and civil engineer and was also a keen collector

of fossils. During the excavation of canals in Britain, Smith had many opportunities to study fossils and the rocks which contained them. He discovered that the sedimentary rocks of southwestern England followed a logical pattern. For example, he found that chalk outcrops always lay above coal seams, never under them, unless the rocks had been disturbed by earth movements. From such observations, Smith advanced the *Law of Superposition* which simply means that providing sedimentary rocks have not been disturbed or deformed, the more recent rocks will always lie above the older rocks. Intrusive igneous rocks, which form when molten material solidifies underground, do not fit into this law because they may be injected into layers of sedimentary rock at any level.

Smith also discovered from his study of fossils a close relationship between them and the layers of rock in which they were found. Each layer of sedimentary rock contained certain characteristic fossils. Some fossils tended to occur in one rock formation after another but others were found in only one rock layer. Smith had no idea why this should be so and the mystery was not solved until 1859, when Charles Darwin's *Origin of Species* was published. But, despite his ignorance of evolutionary processes, Smith recognized the importance of fossils, especially those called *index fossils* which occurred in only one layer of rock. From them, it became pos-

Time Scale of Earth History
To grasp some sense of the vast time scale of this chart, remember that a million *days* would only take us back from the present to 800 years before the birth of Christ – when even imperial Rome was no more than a few mud huts on a hillside. Yet this chart covers many millions of *years*.

sible to deduce that two layers of rock, perhaps miles apart, were formed at about the same time in the history of the Earth, because they contained the same index fossils.

The Law of Superposition greatly assisted geologists in establishing the relative age of rocks in a particular region. But no one knew the rate at which sedimentary rocks accumulated. The rate of deposition may vary greatly depending upon such factors as crustal instability, and climatic and sea-level changes. Also, no region on Earth contains a complete record of rocks formed during its history. In most places, the sequence of sedimentary rocks has been disturbed by folding, faulting and erosion which has worn away great thicknesses of sedimentary rock before the next layer was deposited. Discordances of this kind are called *unconformities*. It is, therefore, not surprising that estimates of the lengths of geological periods and epochs based on the thickness of sedimentary rocks have varied greatly.

The texture and character of rocks is no

guide to correlation. Rocks laid down in one area may contrast sharply with those laid down in another area during the same period. The Cretaceous period gets its name from *creta*, the Latin word for chalk, because chalk is the main rock formation built up during this period in Britain. But, in the United States, a wide variety of Cretaceous rocks occur, of which chalk is certainly not the characteristic formation. It was, therefore, impossible to correlate the periods of geological time from one continent to another without reference to fossils.

Death and preservation
Geologists have largely based their division of rocks on the fossils contained in each division. Fossils are in fact the ancient remains or imprints of plant and animal life which once flourished on Earth but which has been buried and preserved in sedimentary rocks. Many fossils are the remains of extinct forms of life.

Some complete bodies of extinct animals have been found, but such discoveries are rare. When a plant or animal dies, it

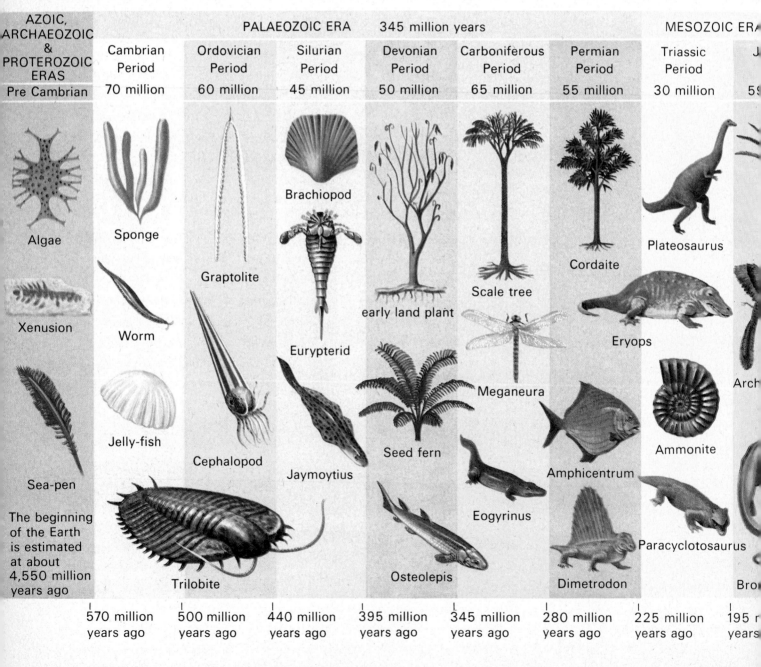

AZOIC, ARCHAEOZOIC & PROTEROZOIC ERAS	PALAEOZOIC ERA 345 million years						MESOZOIC ERA	
	Cambrian Period	Ordovician Period	Silurian Period	Devonian Period	Carboniferous Period	Permian Period	Triassic Period	J
Pre Cambrian	70 million	60 million	45 million	50 million	65 million	55 million	30 million	5

Algae
Xenusion
Sea-pen
The beginning of the Earth is estimated at about 4,550 million years ago

Sponge
Worm
Jelly-fish

Graptolite
Cephalopod
Trilobite

Brachiopod
Eurypterid
Jaymoytius

early land plant
Seed fern
Osteolepis

Scale tree
Meganeura
Eogyrinus

Cordaite
Amphicentrum
Dimetrodon

Plateosaurus
Eryops
Ammonite
Paracyclotosaurus

Arch
Bro

570 million years ago	500 million years ago	440 million years ago	395 million years ago	345 million years ago	280 million years ago	225 million years ago	195 r years

rapidly decays and is liable to be damaged by weathering or partially dissolved by the sea. To form a fossil the animal needs some hard parts, such as a skeleton or shell, and to be rapidly buried to avoid destruction by the elements. Traces of soft-bodied creatures, such as worms, are therefore far less common than fossils with shells or backbones. The hard parts of organisms are often dissolved away over a period of time but sediment may fill the cavity, leaving a cast.

Sometimes substances such as silica or pyrites replace the hard parts of the organism. Other fossils are moulds showing the external details of the organism. Footprints and tracks of animals have also been found. They were probably made in soft sediment, then baked hard in the sun and finally covered by a new layer of sediment. Geologists have even discovered fossilized animal droppings, which have provided information about the eating habits of now extinct creatures.

Fossils of land organisms are generally much less common than fossils of animals which lived in the sea, where dead organisms are quickly covered by sediment. Fossils of sea organisms are also important when geologists try to correlate rocks found in different parts of the world, because sea life generally spreads over a much wider area than land organisms. From fossils, we can also deduce much about the geography at earlier stages of the Earth's history, because some creatures were adapted to live in warm water rather than cold, or in deep water rather than shallow seas.

Signs of old age

The study of fossils gives a means of establishing the relative age of sedimentary rocks, but it does not, of course, enable us to fix their *absolute* age in terms of years. Scholars in the second half of the nineteenth century realized that the Earth must be incredibly old, but they had no accurate way of measuring the age of the Earth or of the rocks in the crust.

These trilobites, dating from the Cambrian period, some 500–570 million years ago, were then the dominant and most highly organized animals.

160 million years		CENOZOIC ERA		65 million years			
Cretaceous Period 71 million		Tertiary Period 63·5 million					Quaternary Period 1·5 million
	Palaeocene Epoch	Eocene Epoch	Oligocene Epoch	Miocene Epoch	Pliocene Epoch	Pleistocene Epoch	Holocene Epoch

Pteranodon

Phenacodus

Brontotherium

Proconsul

Pithecanthropus

Australopithecus

Ichthyornis

Diatryma

Heart urchin

Cynodictus

Homo sapiens

Smilodon

Uintatherium

Baluchitherium

Alticamelus

Trilophodon

Tyrannosaurus

Eohippus

Mesohippus

Merychippus

Pliohippus

Equus

| 136 million years ago | 65 million years ago | 54 million years ago | 38 million years ago | 26 million years ago | 7 million years ago | 1·5 million years ago | 10,000 – 25,000 years ago |

11

William Smith (1769–1839), an engineer, became interested in geology and fossils during the excavation of canals. He found that sedimentary rocks always lie over coal seams and older rocks, *top right,* unless disturbed. He also recognized the importance of fossils for identifying layers of rock of the same age. *Right,* fossilized remains of the Stegosaurus, which lived about 150 million years ago, are found in England, Portugal and America.

Some scientists tried to compute a figure from the maximum known thicknesses of sedimentary rocks. Others tried to estimate the length of time by dividing the total salt in the oceans by the amount added each year. The results of these and other attempts varied greatly but they all fell far short of the figures accepted today.

The discovery of radioactivity around the turn of the century, and especially Rutherford's announcement that each radioactive substance disintegrates at a fixed rate, made possible measurements of absolute age. Uranium disintegrates at a constant rate, leaving lead as the end product. In 1906, an American radio-chemist suggested that, in any sample of a uranium mineral, there was a certain amount of lead, and so if the percentage of lead was great, then the age of the rock was proportionally great. Scientists have found that other elements, such as potassium and rubidium, also disintegrate and can be used for dating rocks.

From such methods it has been established that the Cambrian period, the first that contains rocks rich in fossils, began about 570 million years ago. The Earth itself was consolidated, according to lead isotope studies, some 4,550 million years ago.

The rocks identified

We know almost nothing about Earth history until about 3,500 million years ago. The table *Time Scale of Earth History* shows that the last 570 million years have been divided into three main *eras:* the *Palaeozoic* (old life), the *Mesozoic* (middle life) and the *Cenozoic* (new life). Each of the eras is subdivided into *periods,* which can be further subdivided into *epochs.* Some of the names used for the periods

refer to places where such strata were first identified. They include the Cambrian period, named after *Cambria,* the old name for Wales; the Jurassic period, named after the Jura Mountains on the French-Swiss border; and the Devonian, named after Devon.

Other periods, the Silurian and Ordovician, refer to the names of ancient tribes who lived in Wales, called the Silures and Ordovices. Other periods are named after the dominant rock of the period – Cretaceous (chalk) and Carboniferous, after the coal measures contained in this system in Britain. Another classification divided the last 570 million years into four eras called Primary, Secondary, Tertiary and Quaternary. The Primary and Secondary are the equivalent of the Palaeozoic and the Mesozoic, but, rather confusingly, Tertiary and Quaternary are used as subdivisions of the Cenozoic.

It is one of the great mysteries of geology that Cambrian rocks contain many fossils of highly organized creatures, whereas the Pre-Cambrian strata immediately below are almost devoid of traces of once-living organisms. But remains of algae and bacteria have been found in many Pre-Cambrian formations as far back as 3,000 million years ago.

Although we can identify many great events, such as mountain-building and volcanism, in the Pre-Cambrian, there is much evidence that can be pieced together to tell the story of the evolution of living species and the constantly changing face of the Earth since the beginning of the Cambrian period. The Palaeozoic era was a time when invertebrates and, in the latter part, fishes and primitive amphibians and reptiles flourished. The Mesozoic era was the great period of the reptiles when huge monsters, the dinosaurs, roamed the land – some harmless herbivores, others terrifying carnivores. The giant reptiles had largely disappeared by the end of the Mesozoic, and the Cenozoic was the period of mammalian dominance.

Where does Man fit into this process? It has been calculated that if we imagine the entire history of the Earth compressed into one year, the first known living things, bacteria, would have appeared about 120 days before the end of the year. Early Man would have appeared some two hours before the end of the last day, and modern Man some five minutes before midnight.

Creation's six long days

Was the world born in 4004 BC? This was the accepted view in Europe until the eighteenth century, when scholars began to suspect the Earth's great age and the natural forces shaping its surface.

ABOUT 300 YEARS AGO, most European scholars accepted the general view that Heaven and Earth were created in 4004 BC. It was universally agreed that the features of the land had not changed substantially during the Earth's short history. The fossil shells found embedded in rocks high in mountain ranges were often attributed to the Flood, which had occurred, according to the theologians in 2348 BC.

Today most people accept that fossils in sedimentary rocks are of enormous age, that the Earth was formed about 4,500 million years ago, and also that land forms, instead of being static, are in fact constantly changing. Rainwater causes some rocks to decay; rivers and glaciers erode deep valleys; and the sea is constantly wearing away parts of the coast. Eroded material from mountains is spread over plains, builds up deltas, or is swept into the sea, where it piles to great depths forming new rocks which may be uplifted into mountain chains.

The continuous process of change may be almost imperceptible in one man's lifetime but, spread over millions of years, the forces of nature can plane down the highest mountains. We therefore appreciate that the forces of erosion and deposition active today are a key to the understanding of the Earth's geological history. But how has this profound change in our thinking come about?

Some Greek and Roman philosophers speculated about the nature of land forms, but their studies were limited and had practically no influence on later scholars. The Arab philosopher and physician Avicenna came nearest to the modern view when, nearly 1,000 years ago, he argued that landscapes did change largely as a result of the action of running water. But Avicenna's views were ignored in Europe in the Middle Ages, where scholars influenced by the Christian Church based their explanations of the creation of the Earth on *Genesis,* and it was not until the beginning of the sixteenth century that any opposing ideas were suggested.

Evidence of the Flood

During the fifteenth, sixteenth and seventeenth centuries, most people believed that land features were either formed when the Earth was created or were the result of sudden, violent catastrophes, such as the Flood, which were usually caused by supernatural forces. Called *catastrophism,* this concept could scarcely be challenged by those who believed that the Earth was only a few thousand years old. Even if rivers could wear away land, the rate of erosion was clearly very slow indeed, and

Until the mid-eighteenth century, most European scholars believed the Flood, *above,* and other catastrophes, caused by supernatural forces, were responsible for the only changes in the Earth's landscapes since the Creation in 4004 BC.

therefore deep valleys could not possibly have been formed in a few thousand years.

But inevitably there were scholars whose curiosity and personal observation led them to contradict the apparently water-tight catastrophist philosophy. Leonardo da Vinci, the great Italian artist and scientist, was convinced that fossils in land rocks were not remnants of the biblical Flood, but relics of creatures living in seas once covering the area. He also came to the conclusion that rivers could wear away deep valleys, carrying material from one place and depositing it in another. Other later scholars advanced similar views, but they were often in conflict with the theologians. Such a scholar was the French Comte de Buffon, who, in the eighteenth century, became one of the first people to argue that the Earth's history was much longer than was generally supposed. He suggested that the six days of creation in the Bible were not days as we know them, but long periods of time.

From the mid-eighteenth century research into geology rapidly increased.

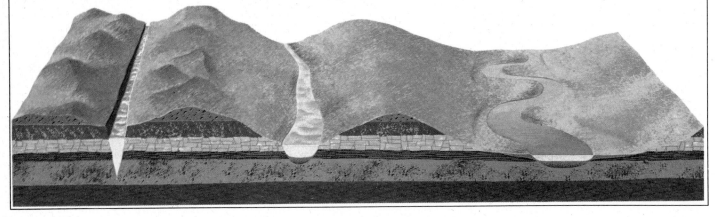

An uplifted block of land in its *youthful stage* with fast rivers cutting deep valleys.

Maturity is reached when still-vigorous rivers cut a complex network of steep-sided valleys.

Finally, in *old age*, the land is worn down to a broad level plain with meandering rivers.

In his *Cycle of Erosion, above,* W.M. Davis suggested that a landscape evolves through three main stages before it is reduced to a *peneplain,* the lowest limit of land reduction. The Bowder Stone in Cumberland, *top right,* is an *erratic,* or boulder transported a long way from its source by glaciers during the last ice age and left stranded when the ice melted. The Stone, of Borrowdale volcanic rock, weighs 1,971 tons and stands on soft glacial drift material of different origin. *Below right,* the river Tees at High Force in County Durham shows the erosive forces always at work on the Earth's surface. The Yellowstone river, *below far right,* is a remarkable example of water, wind and weather as landscapers. The canyon is 1,540 feet deep.

Two main schools of thought emerged: one led by a German, Abraham Gottlob Werner (1750–1817), and the other by a Scot, James Hutton (1726–97). Werner eventually became an inspector and teacher of mining and mineralogy at the Freiberg Mining Academy, where his outstanding lecturing and striking personality attracted many young students. Werner's views on the origin of rocks did not conflict radically with those of the catastrophists, because he believed that rocks were precipitated from the waters of a vast ocean. For this reason, his followers were called *Neptunists.*

Rocks from the sea

Werner argued that the heavier masses in the water settled to form *primitive* rocks such as granite, and above these primitive rocks other formations were deposited. Werner recognized that river valleys cut across layers of rock, but he believed that the sea and not rivers had eroded the valleys. Werner's ideas are largely discredited today, although he was a fine mineralogist. But at the time the Neptunists offered what appeared to be the most scientific explanation of rock formations.

At the time that Werner was enjoying enormous popularity in Germany, James Hutton was evolving a new and vitally important theory concerning the Earth's surface. As a young man, Hutton settled in Berwickshire on a farm he had inherited from his father, where he developed his interests in chemistry and geology. In 1768, he returned to his birthplace, Edinburgh. There he became involved in the

scientific circles in the city and also managed to travel widely. In 1785, he read a paper summarizing his views about the Earth to the Royal Society of Edinburgh. Three years later, the paper was published under the title *Theory of the Earth, or an Investigation of the Laws Observable in the Composition, Dissolution and Restoration of Land Upon the Globe.*

Hutton owed much to the work of contemporary French geologists and also to the work of Horace-Bénédict de Saussure, the Swiss geologist who did much to popularize mountain climbing as a sport. De Saussure supported Werner's views on the under-water precipitation of rocks,

including granite. But, unlike Werner, de Saussure believed in the power of glaciers and rivers to erode valleys.

Hutton extended de Saussure's arguments, stating that the landscape was constantly changing as a result of natural, not supernatural, forces. He clearly perceived how weathering caused the decomposition of rocks, rain carried away soil, and running water eroded deep valleys, accepting the implicit assumption that the Earth must have had a very long history. He correctly deduced that sedimentary rocks were either formed from material eroded from the continents and deposited in bordering seas, or by the shells and other

continued to defend his theories. Sir James Hall conducted laboratory experiments to demonstrate the effect of great heat on rock, but Hall did not accept Hutton's views on erosion. On the other hand, John Playfair (1748–1819), an outstanding mathematician, replied to Hutton's critics on practically every point. Five years after Hutton's death, Playfair's *Illustration of the Huttonian Theory* appeared and won considerable acclaim. Hutton was a poor writer, but Playfair's elegant style brought life to Hutton's ideas, and he enlarged on many points that Hutton had underemphasized.

Playfair also added much new material to support Hutton's arguments, including the observation that large boulders called *erratics* which are scattered around parts of Europe were transported by glaciers. Between them, Hutton and Playfair had introduced and popularized a theory that existing processes had uniformly and continuously acted throughout the Earth's history. This theory was known as *uniformitarianism*. But uniformitarianism was ahead of its time, and it was not until towards the end of the nineteenth century that its implications were fully understood.

Biblical story in doubt

Between the publication of Playfair's book in 1802 and the 1830s, a great debate developed between the uniformitarians (Huttonians) and the catastrophists. Prominent among the catastrophists were clergymen and other devout Christians who passionately believed in the biblical account of the Flood. Such men as the Reverend Dr William Buckland in Britain, and the French naturalist Baron Cuvier, abandoned Neptunist ideas but vigorously opposed Hutton's concept of river erosion. They attributed the formation of river valleys either to the action of the Flood or to major catastrophes or disruptions in the Earth's crust. Some geologists also argued that erratics were in fact transported to their present location during the Flood.

The *diluvialists,* as Flood theorists were called, undoubtedly represented the majority of contemporary opinion until the publication of another landmark in the history of geology, Sir Charles Lyell's *Principles of Geology,* which appeared in three volumes between 1830 and 1833. Lyell (1797–1875), who became known as 'the high-priest of uniformitarianism', had originally been a supporter of Buckland. But Playfair's book impressed him greatly, and in the 1820s he devoted himself to geological research in Britain and France. His book contained much new information gathered by himself or by other Huttonians, and it received widespread attention.

Lyell dealt a death blow to the ideas of the diluvialists. He tried to avoid offending religious scruples, and he did not deny the existence of the Flood. He simply cast doubts on its universality, arguing that it could have been a localized flood. He also attacked those who believed that the Flood was responsible for a great many features of the landscape. But although diluvialism was quickly abandoned and most of its advocates soon admitted they were wrong, catastrophism persisted for some time.

remains of sea creatures. Fossils were therefore evidence of the constant process of change, although he did not recognize any evolutionary process. He argued that heat deep in the Earth's crust consolidated these sedimentary deposits into rocks and also raised them above the sea, an understandable over-generalization in view of the limited knowledge of chemistry and physics at that time. But Hutton's great contribution was to establish the relationship between erosion and deposition, and to recognize that the present is the key to the past. To use his own memorable phrase, he discovered 'that we find no vestige of a beginning – no prospect of an end'.

The differences between solidified lava and molten rock which solidified underground under great pressure were also noted by Hutton, and he identified basalt, and later granite, as rocks of this type. This observation contradicted Werner, and followers of Hutton were dubbed *Volcanists* or *Plutonists*. But despite the importance of Hutton's theories, his work met with little response and might well have been lost were it not for attacks from catastrophists and Neptunists. Hutton replied to his critics in 1795, when he published a revised two-volume edition of his *Theory of the Earth*.

After Hutton's death, two of his friends

Even Lyell, who passionately argued the cause of uniformitarianism, could not accept that river erosion was in itself sufficient to wear away some of the world's largest valleys and he thought that, in some cases, underground sinking of rocks must have contributed to their formation.

Another important contribution to our understanding of land forms came from Europe. In the 1820s, French, Norwegian and Swiss investigators advanced the view that, at some stage in the Earth's history, the Alpine glaciers must have covered a far greater area than they do now. In 1834, Louis Agassiz (1807–73), a professor of natural history at Neuchâtel in Switzerland, became convinced that, during a great ice age, when the climate differed greatly from conditions today, ice sheets and glaciers had covered much of northern Europe. His findings, published in 1840, slowly gained acceptance and were generally agreed before his death. Study of land forms continued throughout Europe during the mid-nineteenth century and, by 1875, there was general agreement on river erosion, glaciation, soil formation, and some other topics.

American pioneers

From about 1875 to 1900, the spotlight shifts to the pioneer research accomplished in the United States, which had a profound influence on our present thinking about *geomorphology* (the science of land forms). In the first half of the nineteenth century geological thinking in the United States was dominated by the latest controversy in Europe. But the nineteenth century was also the time of westward expansion, and geologists often explored routes for pioneers.

One explorer-geologist, John Wesley Powell (1834–1902), is worthy of note if only for his intrepid journey by boat through the rapids of the Colorado Canyon. After the American Civil War, in which he lost an arm, Powell tried to settle down as a professor of geology, but soon his wanderlust prompted him to begin a series of expeditions. In the course of his studies, he carried the concept of landscape erosion further than his predecessors. He considered that, if erosion continues indefinitely, the land will eventually be planed down to a *base level,* the lowest limit of land reduction – a concept later used by W. M. Davis, who called it a *peneplain.* Powell also studied the Grand Canyon, noting that there were *unconformities* (breaks) in the sequence of rocks. These unconformities were, he inferred, the base levels of past periods of erosion.

Probably the first true American geomorphologist was Grove Karl Gilbert (1843–1918), who was at one stage an assistant to Powell. Gilbert not only wrote descriptions of land features, but he also deduced the natural laws that affected them. He examined, for example, the connection between the amount of material carried by a stream in relation to the water volume, gradient and velocity of the current.

Such men and others paved the way for William Morris Davis (1850–1934), who

Gordale Scar in Yorkshire shows the effect of water on soluble carboniferous limestone. The stream has cut down and back into the plateau, eroding its bed into a gorge 200 feet deep.

has been described as 'the great definer and analyst'. He brought together all the information available and formulated it into a general theory, the most famous part of which is his concept of the *cycle of erosion:* after a block of land is uplifted, it passes first through a *youthful stage* with fast-flowing rivers cutting deep valleys. Eventually, the area reaches *maturity,* when many still-vigorous rivers flow through a network of steep valleys. Finally, in *old age,* the landscape is characterized by sluggish rivers and broad plains. This concept has been criticized by later geomorphologists who argue, among other things, that the final stage of the peneplain is never reached. Further uplift always takes place before the end of the cycle. But Davis's general concepts still form the basis of much of modern geomorphology.

James Hutton (1726–97) was one of the first European geologists to believe that the Earth is of very great age and is constantly changing.

Sir Charles Lyell (1797–1875), called 'the high priest of uniformitarianism', preached that the landscape's changes are due to natural forces.

The drifting continents

Land and ocean have not always been distributed as they are today. Recent findings seem to confirm the theory that the continents were once clustered together and have since drifted apart.

WE ARE all familiar with the intricate pattern of land and sea set out in a modern world atlas. Yet probably very few of us have any clear idea about the origins of this pattern.

Francis Bacon commented in 1620 that the two sides of the Atlantic Ocean appeared to match each other. Three centuries later this same fact led F. B. Taylor in America and Alfred Wegener in Europe to postulate the theory of Continental Drift. In this scheme it was envisaged that all the present land masses of the world had once formed a single vast continent, called *Pangaea*, a Greek word meaning 'all earth'. Pangaea, it was thought, had fragmented during the previous 200 million years, and its parts had drifted to their present positions.

Wegener assembled a very impressive amount of geological evidence to show that the continents of today were once much closer together. In particular he showed that extensive glaciation had once affected all the present southern continents (South America, Africa, India and Australia) and that the age of this glaciation became younger from west to east across the continents.

The Earth's floating crust

Wegener believed that these continents were once in the position of the South Pole and that they had since moved radially outwards and northwards. He thought that the increase in gravitational attraction caused by the bulge of the Earth at the equator would cause this movement, which he called *Polflucht*, or flight from the poles. Physicists have since shown that this force is far too weak, millions of times too weak, to have caused Continental Drift in the manner outlined by Wegener.

It was, in fact, this lack of an effective system of forces to move the huge blocks of the continents across thousands of miles of ocean that led to the controversy that surrounded the theory until very recently.

There were two schools of thought. There were those who saw in the theory a neat solution to the distribution of ancient land masses and climates, and there were those who pointed out that there still existed no convincing account of the drift mechanism.

Not until submarine exploration had revealed the topography and structures of the ocean floor, could any real progress be made. These advances have taken place in the last few years and have helped to suggest the mechanism by which continents can be displaced. In order to explain this mechanism it will be necessary to outline a few facts about the structure of the continents and the sea.

The Earth consists of a liquid *core* (which may have a small solid core), with

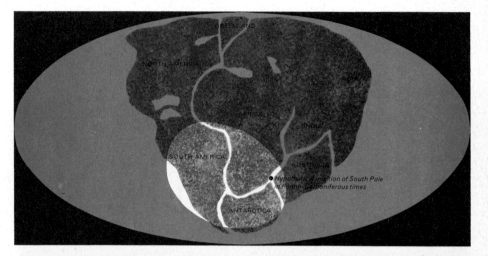

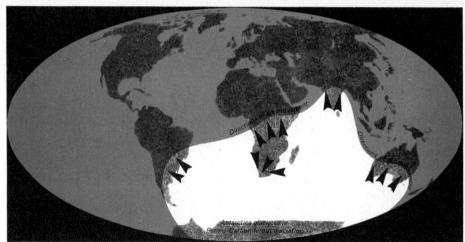

The theory that the continents were once very much closer together has recently gained new impetus. It is now known that about 300 million years ago a polar ice cap covered parts of South America, Africa, India and Australia. These land masses must have been grouped roughly in the positions suggested *top*, for if they were at that time already in their present positions, *above*, the ice cap would have been impossibly large. Earth has not enough sea to account for it.

a radius of about 2,170 miles; a *mantle* (about 1,800 miles thick) and a *crust*. The crust differs in thickness and composition below the oceans and continents. The continental crust is on average 20 miles thick and is rather acidic in nature, with a high proportion of silica. There is a thin layer of more basic material at the base and it is this layer that forms the crust beneath the oceans, where it averages only five miles in thickness. Considered as a whole, the crust is lighter than the mantle and therefore tends to ride over it.

Investigations of the age of the rocks found in the continents and in the oceans show that the oceans contain no rocks older than about 120 million years, although the adjoining continents show ages as great as 3,000 million years. This appears to be true for all the major oceans of the Earth and suggests that there is some truth in the idea that the continents have reached their present positions quite recently in geological time. For the oceans have apparently not

had time to accumulate the sediments of the earlier periods.

However, there remains the question of where the ocean beds of these earlier periods have gone. We do not yet know the answer to this question. There is a theory that sediments were in some way pushed up from the deep ocean trenches, to form the sedimentary rock which is now welded on to the edge of ancient continents as greatly-eroded mountain ranges.

The mountainous areas of Scotland and Wales, for example, are much older – really the roots of mountain ranges that towered to Alpine and Himalayan heights some 400 million years ago.

This still does not explain how the continents are moved and to answer this we need to look in detail at the ocean floors. The most surprising features of the oceans are the mid-ocean ridges that run along the floors of most of the major oceans of the world. Measured from their base, these ridges are composed of mountain chains rising on average to heights of 6,000 feet

CRUST
(hardly noticeable
at this scale)

MANTLE

'LIQUID' CORE
(Metallic in nature
rather like iron/nickel)

SMALL SOLID CORE (?)

Seismologists, who study the behaviour of earthquake shock waves as they pass through the Earth, have detected three levels of major 'discontinuity' and this has led scientists to visualize the interior of the Earth as shown *left*. The Earth could not consist entirely of surface rocks, for, in that case, its total density would be far too slight to account for its gravitational pull. Expansion of the inner core may be one cause of Continental Drift.

and to nearly twice that height when they break the ocean surface as volcanic islands.

These ridges are displaced along their full length by faults that divide them into segments studded with volcanic islands. The ridge in the North Atlantic runs through the middle of Iceland, and here it is possible to measure the rate of displacement of Europe from North America. The rate seems to be as high as two inches a year, or nearly 17 feet in 100 years.

This adds up to a displacement of 3,150 miles in 100 million years, a rate which matches the known age of the oldest rocks in the North Atlantic basin and the present scale of the basin. The presence of volcanoes clearly indicates an abundance of subterranean heat that must have a source in the mantle. Moreover, oceanographers have shown by careful measurements that

there is a heat loss through this ridge higher than in the deeper ocean basins on either side.

This suggests that heat is concentrated below the ridge and is heating up the entire area to such an extent that volcanoes can break through and erupt. It is the actual addition of new lava into vertical fissures on the Earth's crust, known as dykes, that accounts for much of the crustal distension in Iceland.

Activity in the Red Sea

The Mid-Oceanic ridge is also known to be an area where shallow earthquakes originate, and these would result from the crustal movements caused by the injection of lava into the crust and the displacement in the existing crust that this would require. The lack of earthquakes originating deep in this zone is taken to indicate

that the sub-crustal mantle material rises very close to the surface.

Although not liquid in the sense that water, oil, or even tar is, it is nevertheless insufficiently rigid for stresses to accumulate and to be released as earthquakes. If, therefore, new material is being added to the crust at the Mid-Oceanic ridges we must assume that it is being brought up from the mantle, by what amounts to an upwelling convection current.

A further assumption is that the ocean floor must get older as we go away from the ridge on either side, until eventually we reach the continental margin and the ancient rocks of the land masses. In a crude manner it has been shown that the age of volcanoes in the oceans gets older as we go away from the ridge, and this also seems to be true for the sediments on the ocean floor. The depth of sediments also increases away from the ridge (as would be expected if these areas were older and had had more time to accumulate them).

We are, therefore, led to the inescapable conclusions that the continents seem to have broken in the region of the Mid-Oceanic ridges, and then to have moved sideways away from these features. The abundant faults which cross the ridge at right angles do indeed suggest that the ocean floor moved away from the ridge in the form of huge slabs of oceanic crust.

Most obviously this is true for the Atlantic, and the way coastlines correspond with each other is very clear. Greenland is separated only by long, narrow seas from the Canadian land mass. The separation of the North European area from Greenland is marked very clearly in Iceland, where active separation can be measured at the rate of 0·4 inch a year, and

The highest mountains in the world, the Himalayas, were formed when the Tibetan Plateau was forced up to a great height as India and Asia collided. This is a view of Kanchenjunga, from India.

Oceanographers believe the continents broke apart near the Mid-Oceanic ridges. The North Atlantic ridge runs through Iceland, where the separation of the north European area from Greenland is measured as 0·4 inch a year. The faults crossing the ridges indicate that huge slabs of crust moved away from them. Some crustal rocks still remain in mid-ocean, like those which form the Seychelles Islands.

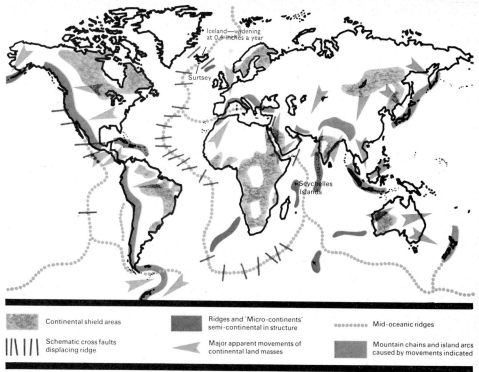

Continental shield areas	Ridges and 'Micro-continents' semi-continental in structure	•••••••• Mid-oceanic ridges
Schematic cross faults displacing ridge	Major apparent movements of continental land masses	Mountain chains and island arcs caused by movements indicated

the creation of new volcanoes testifies to the upwelling of hot new basic matter from the mantle. The new island of Surtsey near Iceland is the best example of this.

A very recent area of continental splitting, has recently been identified in the Near East, where the entire Arabian Peninsula is rotating away from Africa. Careful mapping of the Red Sea showed that along the centre of the sea there was an area where very few basic rocks were present and where heat flow through the crust from the mantle was exceptionally high.

The area is a continuation of the East African Rift System and the movement away from Africa began about 25 million years ago in Miocene times, and is still continuing. As a consequence of this movement, the Gulf of Aden is also being pulled away from the African block. The Jordanian side of the large fault runs through the Dead Sea, and the Sea of Galilee is being dragged north relative to the Israeli side. A break in the continuity of this fault meant that a gap was left behind which became the Dead Sea.

Birth of the Himalayas

Finally, on the front edge of this moving block, a mountain range was created by the compressive movements as the block crushed against sediments in a former extension of the Persian Gulf; and so the Oman Mountains were folded and created in Miocene times.

In the south of this area, in the Indian Ocean, physicists and oceanographers have discovered several blocks of rock standing in the ocean as major shallows or island groups, but which, despite their oceanic position, consist of typically con-

tinental rocks. The Seychelles Islands are such a group and the crust beneath them has been identified as having the same characteristics as the crustal rocks to be found in the African mainland.

This is interpreted to mean that as the continents drifted apart, the split between them was not made cleanly, and as a result a piece of crust was left behind. This now forms the shallow part of the Indian Ocean from which rise the Seychelles Islands.

Meanwhile, India in its drift northwards encountered the continental block of Asia. The two blocks not only collided but the Indian portion was forced to thrust under the Asian block and in doing so forced the Tibetan Plateau to rise to tremendous heights, so that it forms the highest plateau in the world today (12,000–

18,000 feet), and caused the intense folding of rocks that then reared up to form the towering ranges of the Himalayas.

We can see, therefore, that the distribution of the continents today can be explained only by studying the geography of the past. About 250 to 120 million years ago, nearly all the land masses of the Earth were closely united and since then they have been split asunder and dispersed to the corners of the Earth thousands of miles apart.

The pattern that this creates can vary greatly. In East Africa the great rift systems of the Eastern and Western Rift Valley are potential areas where a continent could split. In fact the crustal movements lie along this weakness, not across it, so splitting is not taking place. A little

On 16 November 1963 a spectacular volcanic eruption on the ocean floor occurred off the Icelandic coast and the island of Surtsey was born. *Left,* plumes of smoke indicate its position

on the third day of eruption. *Right,* an aerial view of the island showing rivulets of lava flowing to the sea. In the spring of 1965 another island, Surtling, appeared in the same area.

to the north in the Red Sea, where the lines of weakness in the crust lie athwart the tensions caused by the rising convection currents from the mantle, continental blocks are being dragged apart.

During the process some continental blocks may be left behind, and the centre of the process at the Mid-Oceanic ridge is likely to be a focus for volcanic activity as has happened in Iceland. Thus the result may be continents separated by thousands of miles and with no obvious present connections: such as India and Africa; Africa and America.

The only known process to account for this behaviour is the heating of the Earth's interior, and some physicists say that the molten core of the Earth is growing at the expense of the overlying mantle, and this is leading to the expansion of the Earth as a whole. Such an expansion could account for the obvious displacement of the continents with respect to the oceans, which, as we have seen, are growing by the addition of new, basic, mantle material at the centres.

Legends of a Great Flood

A growth of the diameter of the Earth and the consequent slowing in the rate of the Earth's rotation can probably be demonstrated by counting the number of daily growth rings in the structure of fossil corals. This indicates that there might have been about 400 days in a year about 370 million years ago, and so helps to confirm the theory. Nevertheless, the entire subject is fraught with difficulties and scientists are not unanimous in their interpretation of these facts.

One other factor needs discussion in this broad analysis of the distribution of land and ocean. Although we may have accounted in broad outline for the pattern of land, we need to explain why the intricate coastal patterns of, say, western Europe, exist. Here the reason is that the actual coastline does not mark the limit of continental blocks. The continental shelf is that part of the continental crust which is submerged below the sea.

As the continents are dragged apart they are left unsupported and so tend to sink and become submerged. In addition to this, since the Ice Age, when so much water went to form ice in the ice sheets that the sea level was depressed by up to 500 feet, the sea has been rising constantly and submerging the shallow, gently sloping continental margins.

Where the topography has been carved out by glaciers or deeply eroded by rivers, the sea has flooded the lower end of these valleys to form the sort of intricate coastline that we find today in western Scotland, Norway, Patagonia and New Zealand. Indeed, almost all the coasts of the world have been flooded in the measurably recent past and it was probably this effect that led to the innumerable local legends of catastrophic floods submerging the lands of prehistoric peoples.

The best known of these legends is the Great Flood of the Bible, but the folk stories and myths of many ancient nations, including the Hindus, the Sumerians who lived between the rivers Tigris and Eu-

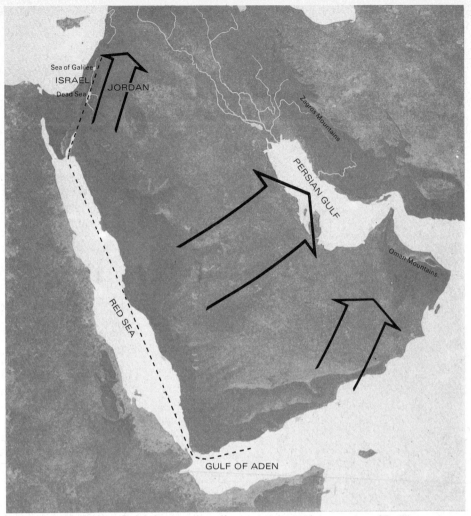

This map shows the Near East, where continental splitting has been identified very recently. It has been found that along the centre of the Red Sea there is a large fault. Movement away from Africa began about 25 million years ago and is still continuing. The Oman Mountains were formed as the moving block encountered sediments in a former extension of the Persian Gulf.

phrates, the ancient Greeks and the Celtic tribes of Wales preserve records of similar catastrophes. From the North Sea there are records of peat containing animal bones and teeth being dredged up by the fishing boats of today, and even finely fashioned Mesolithic spears made of antler bones have been recovered.

Similarly, the tremendous volcanic erup-

tions of the prehistoric Mediterranean and of early historic Iceland are enshrined in the memory of Man by way of classical mythology and the Icelandic Sagas. We can see that the complex interaction of land and sea has affected Man since prehistoric times. Who can say what fundamental influence these continuing changes will have in the future?

Since the Ice Age the sea has been rising and has flooded the lower ends of valleys carved out by glaciers and eroded by rivers. Intricate coastlines have been formed all over the world, including Patagonia and New Zealand. *Above*, a typical example is this fjord in Norway.

Why mountains move

The rise and fall of the world's mountains is the interplay between immense natural forces. Far from permanent features on the map of Earth, nature still works to sharpen and sculpt them.

THE GRANDEUR and beauty of mountains have always held for Man a fascination unequalled by any other land feature on Earth, although this has sometimes been blended with fear. To the mountaineer, the highest and most precipitous peaks present a challenge, inviting him to risk exposure and death in their conquest. Magnificent scenery, crisp, clean air and facilities for winter sports draw many tourists to mountains.

But mountaineering and tourism are comparatively recent developments. Not long ago, men generally avoided mountains, associating them with danger and discomfort. Travelling across them was difficult, sometimes impossible. Landslides or avalanches often blocked the few rough roads that existed, and travellers were often robbed by armed bandits.

Mountains have traditionally been places of mystery. To the ancient Greeks, Mount Olympus was the home of their gods. It was on Mount Sinai that Moses received the Ten Commandments from Jehovah. Many East Africans believe that God dwells on the snow-capped peak of Mount Kenya, and Fujiyama in Japan is a holy mountain visited by thousands of pilgrims every year. Even to geologists, mountains are mysterious, because such a number of problems about their origins continue to remain unanswered.

The highest point on Earth

What is a mountain? No scientific definition exists. Dictionary definitions are generalized, often describing mountains as prominent land features which rise considerably higher than the surrounding land. We can all agree that Everest, the highest point on Earth, is a 'prominent' feature and, by definition, a mountain. It is also clear that volcanoes rising 30,000 feet from the ocean floor in the Pacific are also mountains. But sheer height does not qualify a land prominence to be called a mountain. Some plateaux are higher above sea level than many mountains. How, too, can we distinguish between mountains and hills?

For practical purposes geographers classify mountains as prominent land features which rise to a considerable height, say 2,000 feet or more, and which have a noticeably different character from the surrounding area. Mountains vary a great deal in character, but one feature is common to them all. The higher you climb upwards, the colder it becomes. The temperature falls at a rate of about 1 °F. for every 330 feet. Different kinds of plants and animals are found in each successive temperature belt, giving each level of a mountain its own distinctive character.

Several types of mountains have been classified by geographers. The only mountain building which we can trace during historical times or actually witness today is the growth of volcanoes. Although volcanic activity accounts for a fairly high proportion of the world's mountains, it is not responsible for the great mountain ranges, such as the Rockies, the Alps and the Himalayas. These ranges arose as a result of intense folding and fracturing of rocks in the Earth's crust, caused by powerful forces originating from within the Earth.

Fold mountains are, in their simplest form, large ripples in the Earth's crust. The Jura Mountains, which form part of the Swiss-French frontier, are an example of simple fold mountains. The folds are comparatively gentle, and if stretched out

A slow-moving river of ice, this glacier in the French Alps is carving out its valley. It plucks rocks from the walls and deepens the floor by grinding it down with debris caught in the ice.

straight would increase the present width only by about three miles. The Himalayas, by contrast, were compressed by some 400 miles and in consequence the folds are much more complicated. Sometimes one huge fold topples on to another. A low angled break or *fault* may develop within a fold. The top section is then thrust over the lower section along the fault, and sometimes it is pushed miles away from its previous position.

Most fold mountains are formed from *sedimentary rocks* (rocks which were laid

21

down millions of years ago in shallow seas). Such rocks contain *fossils,* the remains of marine and other life. Rocks containing traces of creatures which once lived in the sea are found even on the upper slopes of Mount Everest. What gigantic force heaved these fossil-bearing rocks from the sea floor to become the tops of mountains? Do such forces still operate today?

We know that earth movements cause earthquakes, but the nature of *orogenic* (mountain-building) forces in the Earth remain a mystery. Geologists, from their study of Earth history, know that mountain-building has been going on for millions of years. Old mountains, once of enormous height, have been almost completely worn away by the processes of erosion. Geologists estimate that the original mountain-building forces which buckled and folded the Rocky Mountains in North America operated for perhaps ten to 15 million years. Their formation was therefore very different from the rapid development of volcanoes. Normally, mountain building is an extremely slow process. Many geologists think that the Alps and the Himalayas are still being pushed upwards, but if this is so, the movement is too slow to measure.

Shattered rock faces

We do know, however, that the Earth's surface is constantly changing. Even while mountains are being slowly pushed up, they are simultaneously being worn down. In the cracks of high mountain slopes, water freezes and expands continuously, shattering rock faces. The broken rocks and boulders tumble down the steep slopes, forming a pile of scree at the bottom.

Glaciers and swift-flowing rivers carry boulders downhill, smashing them into smaller pieces and cutting deep valleys in their path. Rivers carry huge loads of material into the sea every year. Geographers estimate that the Mississippi and its tributaries sweep more than 440 million tons of material into the sea each year. Some of this river-borne material builds up along the coast to form new land areas. The rest is carried under the sea, where it piles up as sediment.

When a vast quantity of sediment builds up, it is compressed into sedimentary rock. The pile of sediment in the Gulf of Mexico has now reached a depth of 40,000 to 50,000 feet. This does not mean that the sea was originally a very deep one; there is evidence that the floor of the Gulf has been sinking.

Is it possible that the sediment in the Gulf of Mexico may eventually be uplifted into a chain of folded mountains? This we do not know, but geologists think that the history of the great fold mountains began when sediment was piled up in great, long troughs formed by movements in the Earth's crust, called *geosynclines.* A shallow sea flooded the geosyncline and rivers began to flow into it in much the same way as the Mississippi flows into the Gulf of Mexico. The rivers brought down eroded sediment from ancient mountains, piling up layer upon layer of material in the geosyncline.

The floor of the geosyncline sank slowly, but the increasing layers of sediment ensured that the sea occupying the geosyncline was never deep. Such a sequence of events began during the early Jurassic period, about 180 million years ago, when a geosyncline began to form in what is now the western United States. The geosyncline, which was several hundred miles wide and about 2,000 miles long, was gradually filled by the sea. Over a period of about 100 million years, a great thickness of sediment filled up the slowly sinking geosyncline. Late in the Cretaceous period, which followed the Jurassic period, the depressed floor of the geosyncline began to buckle and the orogenic phase began.

The layers of sedimentary rock were pushed up into a great folded mountain range, and simultaneously the forces of erosion began to wear it down. In less than 30 million years after the end of the orogenic phase, the mountains were worn down to a plain broken only by a few stumps of old mountains. The final stage then occurred, when the area was gently uplifted to form the mountains we know today: the Rockies. Most fold mountains had a similar history, although the evolution of no two ranges is identical. The Alps and the Himalayas began their development much later than the Rockies and may still be in the orogenic phase.

In addition to fold and volcanic moun-

22

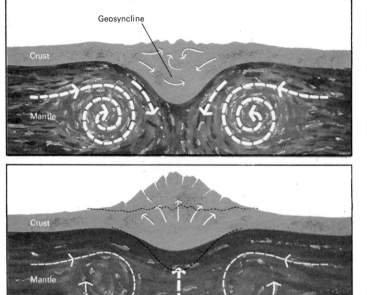

Symbol of purity, *far left,* Fujiyama is the holy mountain of Japan. Volcanic in origin, it built upwards to its height of 12,388 feet in the remote past. *Left,* natural erosion sculpted this landscape in Dakota's Badlands, so called because they are so difficult to cross. *Below,* the Matterhorn in Switzerland bears a name which means 'sharp peak'. Geologists use the term *horn* to define a mountain that has been worn to a sharp point by the abrasive action of glaciers. The massive story of a mountain's rise and fall is still argued among scientists. But experiments re-creating the kind of currents that may be at work in the Earth's mantle suggest, *centre top,* that convection currents could drag the crust into a geosyncline which would eventually buckle, squeezing the sedimentary deposits in the trough into a folded mountain range, *centre middle.* Erosion planes down the lofty range until the eroded mass rises again, *centre below,* restoring isostatic balance.

tains, geologists have identified another important category of mountains – block mountains. These mountains are huge blocks of land uplifted by vertical Earth movements along fault lines in the Earth's crust. The faults may be vertical or steeply slanted, giving the uplifted block one or more precipitous sides. The enormous African Rift Valley, which runs from Mozambique in the south to Jordan in the north, and contains the Red Sea and the great lakes of eastern Africa, may have been formed by the same Earth movements.

Compression does not explain such vertical movements. In block mountains or rift valleys, it is possible that the crust was stretched, so that blocks of land could sink between two major faults. Block mountains have been identified in Mongolia, Libya, southern Algeria and the Basin and Range province of the western United States.

We must not, however, imagine at this point that mountains can be fitted neatly into one classification. Most mountainous areas contain evidence of several types of mountains. For example, the Rockies contained active volcanoes during the final stage of uplift, but these are now extinct. On the other hand, the Andes, which is a folded range of similar age to the Rockies, contains several active volcanoes.

Geologists have identified four basic movements in the Earth's crust which are associated with mountain-building: upward and downward vertical movements, and horizontal compression and stretching. Of these four movements, by far the most important is horizontal compression.

The energy required to compress millions of tons of sedimentary rocks and lift them into a mountain chain must be colossal, and certainly beyond the imagination of most of us. But scientists have advanced several theories about its cause. Until fairly recently, a popular theory suggested that the Earth was shrinking, possibly because it was getting colder. Gradual cooling and contraction would wrinkle the Earth's surface into fold mountains, in much the same way as the skin of an apple wrinkles as it dries up. This theory was never supported by much real evidence and, since the discovery of radioactivity, it has been discredited. Scientists now believe that heat produced by radioactive substances in rocks fully compensates for any heat lost by the Earth at its surface. Some scientists have even suggested that the Earth might be getting warmer, and perhaps expanding in size.

Another theory was related directly to the formation of geosynclines. It suggested that the sheer weight of sediment which accumulates in shallow seas was sufficient to depress the Earth's crust and form these great troughs, in the way that a raft sinks when swimmers board it. According to this theory, the geosyncline is continually depressed until it reaches a point when it is so arched downwards that its sides are pulled together like a vice, squeezing the sedimentary rocks into folds and forcing them up into mountains.

Convection currents

Most scientists, however, now believe that while the weight of sediment in the geosynclines probably contributes to the sinking, it is not the main cause. The deep ocean trenches, which appear to be similar to geosynclines, were not depressed by the accumulation of sediment. Some other factor or factors must be at work.

One theory, advanced as recently as 1948, suggested that geosynclines were caused by movements in the Earth's mantle called *convection currents*. To understand this theory, we must first recall certain facts about the nature of the Earth. The mantle lies under the Earth's crust and consists of much denser rocks. It is about 1,800 miles thick. The average thickness of the crust, on the other hand, is only ten miles, but the thickness varies from place to place. Under the oceans, it averages five miles in thickness, but the submarine rock is much denser than the rocks of the continents. The continents are much thicker but, because they are lighter, they appear to be floating in the denser material that underlies them, in much the same way as an iceberg floats in water. Only the tip of the iceberg shows above the water: a much larger amount is submerged.

In the same way, a large mass of rock is concealed under the continents, and it is especially thick under the mountains, where it sinks deep, perhaps 50 miles, into the mantle. The balance between the visible part of the mountain and its deep root is called the *isostatic balance,* or state of equilibrium. If this state of equilibrium is disturbed, then changes will occur. When some of the ice on the top of an iceberg melts, the whole iceberg rises a little in the water. Because of isostasy, the mountains will be gently uplifted to restore the isostatic balance if their tops are worn away.

The temperature along these Mid-Ocean ridges which 'run through the centre of most oceans is markedly higher than elsewhere; volcanoes and earthquakes are

Forty million years ago the earth moved in what is now the county of Cumberland in England, thrusting a dome-shaped mass skywards. Its contours survive in High Peak, seen *above* in spring.

One day, erosion may strip Everest, *top*, of pre-eminence as the world's highest mountain. Its summit was first conquered on 29 May 1953 by Edmund Hillary and his guide, Tensing Norgay.

common. The heat and volcanic activity suggest that there is a source of heat deep in the mantle, causing an upwelling or current to rise upwards towards the ocean ridges.

It is difficult to imagine dense' rocks flowing, even if they are subjected to enormous heat and pressure. But geologists have demonstrated that this is possible. For example, they have discovered evidence of flow in *metamorphic rocks* (rocks changed in character and appearance by heat and pressure). Scientists have suggested that as the hot mantle rock rises close to the Earth's crust it spreads out laterally on either side. During its horizontal flow, it gradually cools, and eventually sinks. It is reheated at a lower depth, and then rises again. This movement sets up an enormous *convection cell.*

The mountains wear away

Once we have accepted the possibility of convection currents in the Earth's

mantle, we can imagine that in places where the mantle rock is sinking, the Earth's crust may be pulled down to form a geosyncline. The movement of flow must be very slow, perhaps an inch a year, and so the formation of geosynclines would take millions of years. At a much later stage, according to this theory, the geosyncline is weakened by heat deep in the mantle, and both sides of the trough are compressed by converging convection currents. The sedimentary rocks filling the geosyncline are crushed and pushed up into folds. After the forces of erosion have worn away the mountains, and the convection currents have ceased, the entire block is lifted up to restore the isostatic balance.

This theory has been successfully demonstrated in laboratory experiments; although it is by no means proven, it does fit most of the little evidence we have and does suggest possible solutions for other geographical mysteries, such as the origin of the deep oceanic trenches.

When the Earth shakes

Volcano and earthquake, twin terrors for Man's frail cities, unleash their violence with scant warning. But we now know that our planet is circled by a 'ring of fire': the earthquake zone.

IN APRIL, 1902, the people of St Pierre, a gay, bustling port on the island of Martinique in the French West Indies, were preparing for the municipal elections which were due to be held on 10 May. Five miles from St Pierre stood Mt Pelée, a mountain of volcanic origin which was noted for two minor eruptions in the previous 250 years. Neither eruption had caused any loss of life, and the mountain was regarded as a scenic attraction for visitors.

On 23 April 1902, Mt Pelée began to rumble. Smoke and occasionally ash and cinders exploded into the air. The volcano's stirrings aroused considerable interest but little concern. On 27 April, several visitors climbed to the rim of the crater, and later reported that a lake had formed there, and that to one side there was a small cinder column emitting steam. In the days that followed, activity in the volcano increased. Falls of ash on St Pierre made this tropical town look as though it were covered by a blanket of snow. Conditions were becoming decidedly unpleasant. The ash blocked roads, and poison gas from it killed birds. Businesses closed, and some people decided to leave town. But people from the countryside and nearby villages were by now alarmed, and they poured into St Pierre for refuge, more than replacing those who had decided that greater safety lay in flight.

Thirty thousand died

In early May, the French governor arrived to assure the people of St Pierre that there was no cause for panic. But on 5 May, there was real concern when news arrived that a torrent of boiling mud had swept down from the crater, burying a sugar mill and killing at least 30 workers. Some accounts put the death rate as high as 150. On 6 and 7 May, violent explosions shook the volcano, but also on 7 May, some apparently good news arrived to cheer the people of St Pierre. A volcano had erupted on St Vincent, another island to the south. Believing that this volcano was connected underground to Mt Pelée, the people thought that the eruption on St Vincent would probably relieve the pressure on Mt Pelée.

On 8 May, however, at 7.50 a.m., Mt Pelée exploded again. From a hole in the volcano emerged an enormous black cloud, consisting of superheated steam, gas and intensely hot dust particles (mainly tiny fragments of lava). The cloud swept towards St Pierre, burning everything in its path. In two minutes, it had reached the town and, a few moments later, some 30,000 people perished in the heat. The temperature was sufficient to melt glass. Stocks of rum caught fire, and a burning river of rum flowed down the streets into the sea, which hissed and boiled with steam.

The cloud hit St Pierre with the force of a hurricane. There were two survivors from the town. One, a shoemaker, incredibly escaped on foot through the blazing city. The other, Auguste Cyparis, a 25-year-old Negro, had been locked in a dungeon, charged with murder. He was badly burned, but survived for four days before attracting rescuers with his cries for help.

Volcanologists call clouds such as these *nuées ardentes* (glowing clouds). Mt Pelée was the first place where this phenomenon was recorded, but the *nuée ardente* of 8 May was not the last. Several followed, including one on 20 May which completed the destruction of those buildings still standing in St Pierre. Another at the end of August struck five villages and killed 2,000 people.

By October, the eruptions had almost ceased, but another phenomenon had begun. A large mass of almost solid lava was being pushed up through the crater, rising tower-like above the volcano. Even while it was forcing its way upwards, it was disintegrating, but, by the end of

The results of local tremors in Japan: *top,* the railway lines and embankment at Kisoqawn demonstrate the earth's buckling movement. *Above,* an upheaval collapsed the supports of the Nagara-Gawa bridge on the Gifu-Ogaki railway line. For days after a severe earthquake the earth vibrates; the vibrations are detected by seismographs all over the world.

May 1903, this gigantic column soared more than a thousand feet above the crater floor.

Gradually the tower of lava was worn down and Mt Pelée was quiet once more, but in 1929, it entered another period of eruption lasting until 1932. *Nuées ardentes* poured forth from the crater, but people were quickly evacuated and no lives were lost. Lava now seals the vent of Mt Pelée, but no one knows when the next active phase will begin.

Mt Pelée has lent its name to a certain kind of volcano, the *Peléean* or *explosive* volcano. The biggest known volcanic explosion took place on Krakatoa, a large volcanic island reaching 2,600 feet above sea level, between Java and Sumatra. On 27 August 1883, at 10.00 a.m., a deafening explosion destroyed practically the entire island. Left behind were three tiny islands, small parts of the rim of the volcano, and a hole 900 to 1,000 feet deep. The noise of the explosion was heard 3,000 miles away and a cloud of ash rose 50 miles into the atmosphere. Following the eruption, a *tsunami* (big wave), reaching in places a height of 120 feet, battered the coasts of Java and Sumatra, killing about 36,000 people.

Volcanic explosions are generally caused by gas in the magma, which is underground molten rock existing in pockets under the surface of the Earth. Most of the volcanic débris hurled out of the explosive or Peléean volcanoes is highly fragmented. The cones built up by explosive volcanoes are composed not of lava flows but of ash, cinders and other fragmented material.

Blacksmith of the Roman gods

If the magma contains little gas, or if the gas can escape easily, then lava will pour out of a volcano relatively quietly and explosions are less common. Volcanoes of this kind, called *quiet volcanoes,* are found in the Hawaiian islands. But most volcanoes are *intermediate* between the explosive and quiet types.

Examples of the intermediate type include Vulcano, an island off the coast of Sicily, and Vesuvius, which towers over the Bay of Naples. The word *volcano* comes from the Latin name for the island, Vulcano, which many Romans thought was the site of the forge of Vulcan, the blacksmith of the Roman gods. The intermediate type of volcano begins with a phase of activity similar to the explosive type. The seal of solid lava is burst open by violent explosions caused by gas, and a great cloud containing much ash rises above the volcano. But the explosions are not followed by *nuées ardentes*. Instead, lava often flows from the crater.

Vesuvius has been quiet since 1944, and many visitors make the ascent to the crater every year. The volcano probably began life under the sea, emerging as a volcanic island. The mass of material which it ejected eventually filled in the gap between the island and the mainland. The famous eruption of AD 79, which was preceded by a series of earthquakes, led to the destruction of Pompeii and Herculaneum. Neither was destroyed by a *nuée ardente* like St Pierre. Pompeii was covered by a thick layer of hot ash and pumice, while Herculaneum was buried by an avalanche of hot mud, probably caused by heavy rains falling on the ash which had accumulated on the upper slopes of the volcano. About half of the original dome of Vesuvius was destroyed in this eruption, but a new cone was built up, the beginnings of the one we know today. Lava did not flow during this eruption, but since the eruption of 1036, lava flows have accompanied most of the eruptions of Vesuvius.

In the so-called *quiet volcanoes,* gases in the magma are liberated quietly rather than explosively, and the main product of such volcanoes is lava, which, at the time of the eruption, is extremely fluid. These volcanoes have extremely broad bases and gentle slopes and are sometimes called *shield volcanoes*. At the time of eruption the word 'quiet' seems inappropriate, because fountains of lava may shoot up from *fissures* (cracks) in the ground – the result of exploding gases. Lava then pours out of the fissures and flows downhill at speeds up to 12 miles an hour, sometimes reaching the sea.

Several other kinds of volcanic activity occur in addition to those mentioned above. They include the fissure eruptions which have built up such great lava plateaux as the Columbia-Snake River Plateaux in the United States, and the Deccan Plateau of western India. Such lava flows are not erupted by a volcano, or even several volcanoes. Instead, the lava has welled up from extremely long fissures, perhaps several miles in length. Such lava flows can completely obliterate the original landscape over large areas. A fissure eruption in Iceland in 1783 spread lava over a great area, filling valleys and covering ridges. The heat of the lava melted the snow and ice, causing floods and a great loss of human and animal life.

Perhaps the most celebrated of all recent volcanoes is Parícutin, in Mexico. On 20 February 1943, volcanic activity began in a small hole in a cornfield. By 4 March 1952, when volcanic activity ceased, the cone was 1,345 feet higher than the original field. Equally dramatic are new islands formed by submarine volcanoes. Some of them are quickly eroded by the sea, but others become permanent. A recent example occurred when the island of Surtsey appeared off the coast of Iceland in November 1963. In 1965 another island, called Little Surtsey, emerged close to Surtsey.

We know far more about the behaviour of volcanoes than we do about their origin. Where does magma come from and how does it move upwards? These questions and many others still await satisfactory answers. We know that rocks in the lower part of the Earth's crust would melt were it not for the pressure of the overlying rocks. If this pressure were relieved in some areas, then the rocks would melt, expand and rise to the surface.

Volcanoes have their uses

The relief of pressure may well occur in regions of crustal unrest, because most volcanoes occur in such regions, namely along the edges of continents with mountainous coastlines, such as border the Pacific Ocean; in ocean basins, such as along the Mid-Ocean ridges; in areas where major fractures or rift valleys occur; and in some inland areas bordering inland mountain ranges.

No discussion of volcanoes would be complete without some reference to their usefulness. Not only do they build up new islands, which eventually support human life, but life on Earth may only have been possible because of their activities. Some scientists consider that volcanoes may be

This cross-section of a volcano shows the fissures in the Earth's stratas of rock, topped by a cone of solidified lava. Internal pressure has forced molten rock and gases upwards through cracks deep enough to traverse the Earth's crust from top to bottom, causing a violent eruption.

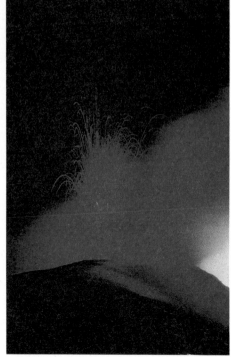

Europe's highest volcano, Mount Etna in Sicily, puts on impressive displays of glowing rivers of lava and fireworks of red-hot rocks from the crater. Covering more than 500 square miles, its height of over 10,000 feet is constantly changing, and is capped with snow for much of the year.

responsible for much of the Earth's atmosphere and its water. Some of the gases released from the Earth's crust by volcanoes are poisonous, but others, such as carbon dioxide, are basic to life on our planet. Volcanoes also create water by combining hydrogen and oxygen to form steam.

Many suggestions have been advanced about the harnessing of the power of volcanoes to produce electricity, but success seems unlikely in the foreseeable future. But some countries such as Italy and New Zealand are producing electricity from volcanic steam. Probably the most important benefits Man gets from volcanoes are the rich soils which form from lava and ash, which explains why such large communities often farm on the slopes of dormant volcanoes.

27

Despite the benefits they bestow, volcanoes are still feared. Today vulcanologists can forecast fairly accurately the start of an eruption from a study of changes in temperature, pressure and the composition of gases within a volcano. But they are still unable to predict the intensity and duration of an eruption. Each volcano has its own peculiarities and, today, active volcanoes, especially in advanced countries, are closely observed. If volcanologists discover that an eruption is likely, the local population can be evacuated in time. After an eruption, volcanologists can also advise on the likelihood of destructive mudflows, which they call *lahars*. The great danger that still exists is that some volcanoes, generally believed extinct, may suddenly erupt. Our knowledge of the activity of volcanoes is only based on historical records, and in many areas historical records have only existed for a very short time. Some mountains not even identified as volcanoes may suddenly erupt. A recent example occurred in New Guinea in 1951 when Mt Lamington, hitherto always peaceful, suddenly erupted, killing 3,000 people.

San Francisco earthquake

Areas associated with volcanic activity are often earthquake zones, too, but volcanoes do not, as was once thought, cause major earthquakes. Both features are characteristic of areas of crustal instability. Small earthquakes can be caused by volcanic eruptions, landslides, or even nuclear explosions. But major earthquakes are generally associated with areas where there are active *faults* (fractures in the Earth's crust). In the San Francisco earthquake of 1906 a fault line, called the San Andreas fault, was shifted horizontally along about 250 miles of its total length of 600 miles. Near San Francisco, the ground was displaced about 15 feet along the fault. The displacement was seen most clearly where such features as roads and lines of trees cross the fault.

The greatest earthquakes, called *tectonic* earthquakes, originate from move-

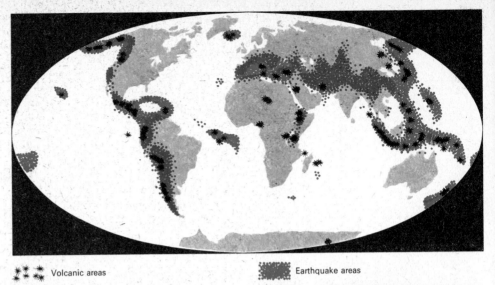

✳✳✳ Volcanic areas   Earthquake areas

Most of the world's major earthquakes and volcanoes occur in an area which encircles the Pacific Ocean, known as the 'ring of fire'.

ments of rock within the Earth, caused by great stress. Sometimes the movement is along a fault that appears at the surface, but most fractures are concealed underground. Seismologists (those who study earthquakes) call the point of origin of the earthquake the *focus,* and the point on the Earth's surface directly above it the *epicentre*. Most earthquakes are *shallow-focus* in that they originate at depths of ten to 30 miles below the epicentre. *Deep-focus* earthquakes have originated from depths of 400 miles below the surface, but their effect at the surface is far less devastating than that of shallow-focus earthquakes.

Natural disasters caused by earthquakes can be even more devastating than volcanic eruptions. At 11.58 a.m. on 1 September 1923, a severe earthquake shook Tokyo and Yokohama. Many buildings collapsed, and only the most modern remained standing. Great fires raged throughout the area, destroying two-thirds of Tokyo and almost all Yokohama.

About 100,000 people perished as a result of the earthquake and the fires.

The famous Lisbon earthquake of 1755, mentioned by Voltaire in *Candide,* generated a tsunami which swept up the river Tagus and greatly added to the death toll. The vibrations or *seismic waves* of even small shocks in the Earth's crust are recorded at seismograph stations all over the world. With data from several stations, both the focus and the epicentre can be accurately determined. But as yet it is impossible to forecast earthquakes. What can then be done to diminish their effect?

A great loss of life caused by earthquakes occurs when buildings collapse, crushing those unfortunate enough to be inside. Engineers have now established that buildings on firm foundations, such as hard rock, withstand shocks far better than those on waterlogged or unconsolidated ground. They have also learned that a building should not be too rigid, and should vibrate as a single unit. Engineers are engaged in research, especially in the United States and Japan, to find the best building materials and designs to withstand both earthquakes and fire.

Left, about 100,000 people were killed and the survivors made homeless when a severe earthquake struck Tokyo in 1923. Strong winds fanned the fire which swept through the city. *Right,* the ruins of San Francisco after the earthquake of 1906. This disaster was caused by the ground shifting (near the city about 15 feet) along 250 miles of the San Andreas fault – one of the largest shifts recorded for a single earthquake.

Beneath the scene

What accounts for the enormous variety of ups and downs of the world's landscapes? The answer is found in the underlying rocks, their formation and the erosive forces which have shaped them.

ANYONE WHO TRAVELS AWAY from his own town or village with its familiar scenery, soon notices that the landscape differs from place to place. Every country in the world has this variety in scenery, although in some regions vast plains stretch for hundreds of miles without any change to break the monotony. In other areas roads and railway lines run across plains, through valleys, over hills, round mountains, past lakes, streams and rivers.

The changing scene is largely determined by three factors: the nature of the underlying rocks; the structure of the rocks caused by convulsions in the Earth's crust; and the action of weathering, running water, ice and the sea in sculpting the land. The special shapes of hills, valleys, cliffs and plains which give regions a distinctive character were not the result of chance. With a trained eye, the traveller can increase his pleasure by understanding the age and the nature of the rocks beneath his feet. He can also appreciate that the landscape is constantly changing, a process which has been continuing throughout geological history over vast periods of time which make Man's brief occupation of the Earth seem puny and almost insignificant.

The British Isles has an enormous variety of scenery over very short distances that is scarcely rivalled by any other country in the world. A journey of just over 100 miles from the Malvern Hills to London would take only a few hours but, in geological time, it covers a vast span of millions of years – from a time when life barely existed on Earth to the threshold of the emergence of Man. The rocks underlying the journey are chapters from the history of the Earth, marking some of the episodes in the long story of the evolution of England and the evolution of living things.

The milestones of evolution

The Malvern Hills, which rise more than 1,000 feet on the borders of Herefordshire and Worcestershire, are of Pre-Cambrian rock, which were laid down over 570 million years ago, and are amongst the most ancient in England. Travelling eastwards from the Malverns towards London, more easily dated rocks are crossed which were formed between 225 and 65 million years ago – the Cotswolds, the Oxford clay vale and the Chiltern Hills. These rocks were largely laid down in seas which covered the area during the long Mesozoic era when the giant dinosaurs were the dominant living things. From here the Chilterns slope gently eastwards to the London Basin, which is composed of rocks which accumulated after most of the ferocious giant reptiles had perished, and mammals had taken over the leading

The famous Carrara quarries in Italy have been a source of pure white statuary marble for many centuries. Marble occurs when limestone is subjected to great heat from *magma* or molten rock.

role among living things in England.

Rocks are divided by geologists into three main types: *igneous*; *metamorphic*; and *sedimentary*. Igneous rocks, such as the dark-coloured basalt and the tough, resistant granite, are formed when molten rock called *magma* wells up from deep down in the Earth's crust to solidify at or under the surface. Although it is hard to imagine, the British Isles have been the scene of much volcanic activity during periods of geological history, especially during mountain-building phases. Several examples of old volcanoes occur in Scotland. Edinburgh Castle stands on the neck of an ancient volcano, and Arthur's Seat nearby is a more complicated structure with two *vents* (outlets), the remnant of a volcano which was active more than 300 million years ago. The tough, solidified magma of such volcanic remains have resisted erosion and stand out even today as steep hills.

Some lavas, such as basalt, are extremely fluid when they reach the surface through cracks in the ground. Flowing over large areas, they blanket the original hills and valleys to form plateaux, including those of Antrim, the northern Isle of Skye, and a large part of the island of Mull, in Argyllshire. Basalt has a tendency on cooling to contract into six-sided columns, forming on the surface a checkered pavement and, at the edge of the flow, steep-sided cliffs. Such jointed basalt surfaces are found at Fingal's Cave on the Isle of Staffa, and at the Giant's Causeway in County Antrim.

Sometimes magma does not reach the surface but solidifies underground. The large granite masses of the southwestern peninsula of England, and large areas in Scotland including the Cairngorms originated in this way. Magma often forces its way between the beds of sedimentary rock and spreads horizontally. When great quantities of lava are forced between the layers of rock, the top layers may be pushed up into a dome. Horizontal *sills* of igneous rocks may later be exposed by the forces of erosion to form tough ridges on the surface, such as Whin Sill in Northumberland, which the Romans followed for many miles when building their famous wall. When the tremendously hot magma comes into contact with other rocks, the heat, together with gases and liquids given off by the magma, often changes completely the character and appearance of the neighbouring rocks. Such transformed rocks are called metamorphic, and the area surrounding the magma is called a *metamorphic aureole*. Metamorphic rocks often contain veins of valuable minerals, such as the tin and copper of Devon and Cornwall, which is found in metamorphic aureoles. Metamorphism also occurs when rocks are subjected to great heat other than contact with hot magma or to pressure. The heat can transform limestone into marble, and great pressure can turn fine clay into slate.

Rocks from sand, mud and clay

Sedimentary rocks are originally deposited in lakes or seas and represent fragments of eroded land, the remains of formerly living organisms, chemicals precipitated from sea water, or the remains of organic material, as in coal beds. For example, the sand on the sea shore, when consolidated into rock, becomes sandstone, a common building stone, and muds and clays are compacted into mudstones and shales. Sometimes layers of sedimentary rocks are extremely thick, such as the chalk deposits of the Cretaceous period which reach depths of 1,000 feet in places. But more often, layers of rocks are much thinner and sandstones, clays, shales and limestones follow in rapid succession, with beds only a few inches thick in places.

Variations in scenery are often caused by the degree of resistance of different rock layers to the forces of erosion. Running water, the sea and glaciers are naturally most effective in wearing away the least resistant rocks. The loose glacial drift which borders parts of the coast of eastern England is being worn back by the sea at a much faster rate than the massive, resistant granite cliffs of Land's End. But many sedimentary rocks, though tough in themselves, contain structural weaknesses which expose them to attack.

Most sediments are deposited in horizontal or nearly horizontal levels, and each bed of rock is separated from the one above by a *bedding plane,* a surface which usually indicates the end of one period of deposition, and the beginning of another. Sometimes currents in the water during the process of deposition cause bedding planes to lie at angles to the general level of deposition. The bedding planes in sedimentary rocks are lines of weakness. Where layers of sedimentary rock have been sharply tilted, landslides may occur

along bedding planes. Thick layers of rock which can be quarried and fashioned easily into building stones without danger of shattering are called *freestones*. The freestones of the Portland limestones have been used for many of London's greatest buildings, including St Paul's Cathedral. In addition to horizontal bedding planes, many rocks are riven by vertical cracks or joints, lines of weakness also exploited by the forces of erosion, and evident in many cliffs which have been fractured along the joints.

Rocks dissolved by water

Limestone is an interesting rock from a scenic point of view, because it is the only rock occurring on a large scale in the British Isles which is soluble in weak acid – that is, rainwater which has dissolved carbon dioxide from the air. Most rain tends to seep into the ground and follow the joints and bedding planes in the rock until it re-emerges at a lower level in a spring. In limestone country, surface streams are not common. Even where large streams flow, they often disappear into deep pits called *swallow holes,* in areas of Carboniferous (or Mountain) limestone. Such outcrops occur in the Mendip Hills, parts of South Wales, and large areas in the Pennines. A good example of a swallow hole is Gaping Gill in the West Riding of Yorkshire. There, water plunges 365 feet to the bottom of the pit, where there is a cavern about 110 feet high and 500 feet long. Water from this cavern flows through a maze of tunnels before finally reaching the surface. Some caves are adorned with icicle-like structures called *stalactites* and *stalagmites*. These are formed by drops of water, charged with soluble calcium carbonate, seeping through fissures in the roof of a cavern. Successive drops build up stalagmites from the floor and stalactites down from the ceiling, the two sometimes meeting in a complete pillar from the floor to the roof of the cave.

When underground caves collapse and the debris from the roof has been removed by natural forces, a narrow gorge remains. On the surface of Carboniferous limestone, bare rock outcrops often occur and they are often patterned with a criss-cross of dissolved grooves called *clints* or *grikes*. Impurities in the limestone, not soluble in rainwater, also cover parts of the surface. They include pockets of clay. The Karst region of Yugoslavia has lent its name to this characteristic countryside.

But not all limestones weather into a karst landscape. In Britain, the other chief types of limestone include the more recent Jurassic limestone of the Cotswolds and the North Yorkshire Moors and, most recent of all, Cretaceous limestone or chalk which occurs in such planes as the Chilterns, and the North and South Downs of southeastern England. In both the Jurassic and Cretaceous limestones, underground channels are rare, because rainwater seeps through the many fissures in the rock. The light-coloured Jurassic limestones are resistant to erosion, but their character varies from place to place. Soil covers most of these rolling uplands,

Mammoth Cave in Kentucky, *top left,* is one of many huge caverns eroded by water in deep beds of limestone. Rain, containing weak acid, seeps into the ground, dissolving the rock. Mineral-rich water dripping from the ceiling has formed the 75-foot stalactites and stalagmites. *Left,* the rugged peak of Snowdon in Wales is all that remains of glacier-worn downfolded volcanic rock.

Legend says that the Giant's Causeway in County Antrim, Northern Ireland, *top right,* was built as a road to the Scottish Isle of Staffa by a race of giants. In fact, the six-sided columns, some 20 feet high, were formed by rapidly cooling lava flowing into the sea. *Above,* looking across Worcestershire from the 1,000-foot Malvern Hills, one stands on some of England's oldest rocks.

and bare rock is generally only exposed in quarries.

The *colitic* limestones of the Jurassic, named after the Greek word for *egg,* consist of small round grains of calcium carbonate. In cross-section, the colites look like onions, each successive skin being a layer of soil, chemical precipitated from sea water around an original nucleus. The colitic limestones of Portland and Bath are among the finest of all building stones. The pleasant chalk uplands are covered by a thin layer of soil, supporting enough grass for pasture. But farms are few, usually confined to valleys, in this rolling, green land. The chalk is composed almost entirely of organic remains and is very pure. Broken layers of flint, that substance so important to Prehistoric Man, occur within the chalk.

Hills in retreat

When earth movements raise sedimentary rocks from under the sea to form new land areas, the layers sometimes remain horizontal. After considerable erosion, the more resistant rocks remain, in places capping the less resistant rocks to form structures called *mesas,* which rise like tables above the surrounding area. If the uplifted rocks are tilted gently, as in southern England, a feature known as a *cuesta* develops, consisting of a steep escarpment and a gentle dip slope.

Most of the gently-dipping resistant limestones of southern England slope to the east, southeast, or south. Their escarpments therefore face west, northwest and north. Gradually, the escarpments are cut back as rivers wear away the less resistant, underlying rocks. Evidence of such recession in the Cotswolds can be seen in the small, attractive hills that dot the Severn plain. Such hills are in fact outliers or remnants of the Cotswold escarpment. In some cases of uplift, layers of resistant rock are steeply tilted to form ridges called *hogbacks,* such as the Hog's Back in Surrey and the ridge in the centre of the Isle of Wight. Hogbacks have steep slopes on both sides.

Where rocks are folded, the upfolds are called *anticlines,* and the downfolds *synclines.* One might imagine that anticlines would form mountains and synclines valleys but the reverse is often the case. A newly uplifted anticline may be rapidly cut down by the forces of erosion, whereas the neighbouring syncline might weather into a mountain range, as in the case of Snowdon. The most studied of all English anticlines is the Weald in Kent and Sussex. Here a dome has uplifted, sloping away to the north and the south. Rivers flowing off the dome soon cut through the top layers, exposing the underlying rocks and the inward-facing chalk escarpments of the North and South Downs.

Often accompanying earth movements are the developments of great *faults* (cracks) in the surface rocks. The Central Lowlands of Scotland is a rift valley lying between two sets of fault lines, one bordering the Highlands to the north and the other bordering the Southern Uplands. The valley of Glen More was also formed along a fault. There a horizontal movement displaced rocks on either side of the fault by 65 miles. Similar faults also occur in Newfoundland, and recent research suggests that the faults were linked at a time when Europe and North America were close together.

The effects of erosion

But most of the rugged mountain areas called Highland Britain owe little of their character to either the structure or the nature of the rocks. They are still predominantly areas shaped and moulded by the great power of glaciers and ice sheets which occurred during the Pleistocene Ice Age. Regardless of structure, the highlands are largely typical glaciated regions with deep hollows, ridges, U-shaped valleys and sharp peaks. The features of many low-lying areas are also the result of ice action, because the rocks lie under deep blankets of glacial drift. The ice, which extended as far south as a line joining the Severn estuary and the lower Thames valley, had an especially profound effect on Britain's scenery.

At The Buttertubs in Yorkshire, *left,* a mountain stream has disappeared underground through the surface limestone. *Below left,* one of the largest slate quarries in the world, Dinorwic Quarry in North Wales, is still in active production. The purple-grey slate was laid down 500 to 570 million years ago by tremendous pressure on beds of fine clay. *Below right,* at Portland in Dorset the famous limestone is quarried. Easily cut, it has been used for buildings all over the world.

When the Earth's surface moves

The landslides, avalanches and mud flows which sweep down into the world's valleys often cause terrible disasters. Now efforts are being made to detect them and give advance warnings.

ON THE NIGHT of 9 October 1963, a 230-foot-high flood wave, carrying millions of tons of mud and rock, engulfed the little alpine holiday resort of Longarone in the Belluno province of northern Italy. More than 2,000 people died and many of the bodies were never recovered. Whole families disappeared and, in hundreds of cases, there were no survivors to identify the bodies of the victims. The first thought of many Italians when they heard of the disaster was that the Vaiont Dam, up the valley from Longarone, had burst. But when rescue parties arrived, they found that the 875-foot concrete wall was still intact. Only a road along the top of the dam had been washed away. The tragedy was caused not by a dam burst but by a tidal wave triggered off by a landslide, which brought several million tons of rock crashing into the artificial lake behind the dam.

This appalling disaster might have been foreseen. The dam, the second highest concrete structure in the world, was built in 1960. Within a few months of its completion, a landslide on the slopes of Monte Toc, one of the alpine peaks surrounding the Vaiont valley, had hurled a million cubic tons of earth and rock into the lake. The tidal wave created by this landslide was contained by the dam and no one was injured. Having been alerted to the danger, the Italians kept a careful watch on the movement on the slopes of Monte Toc. A line of stakes was hammered into the ground and their position was accurately measured every day.

Mountain on the move

Between 1960 and 1963, an average movement of ten to 12 inches a week was noted but was no cause for alarm. Similar landslides are common on the steep slopes of the Alps and no one imagined that the 1960 slide would be repeated. Deep boreholes were sunk at several points to determine the nature of the underlying rock. But the holes did not penetrate deeply enough and failed to reveal a layer of clay and marl below the surface limestone. This layer was steeply inclined towards the valley in which the dam was built. The landslide of 1963 occurred along the *plane of contact* between the limestone and the underlying clay and marl.

After a period of torrential rain which began on 28 September 1963, the downward movement of the stakes increased to several inches a day. Cracks began to appear in the surface layers and several small Earth tremors were felt. Perhaps sensing the danger, the animals which grazed on the pastures of Monte Toc moved away on 1 October. At 10.43 p.m. on 9 October, the whole mountain side slipped into the lake with a thunderous roar, creating a gale of hurricane force down the

valley. The landslide took only 30 seconds. During the next ten minutes, a wall of water ricochetted across the lake, rebounding from the steep valley walls, until it eventually overtopped the dam. By 10.55, all was again quiet, but for Longarone and the neighbouring villages it was the quiet of the grave.

What had happened was that, over a period of several days, the exceptionally heavy rain had percolated through the joints and cracks in the limestone. On reaching the underlying, steeply sloping beds of clay, the rainwater had lubricated

1 Below the Vaiont Dam, which was built across an alpine valley in northern Italy in 1960, lay the town of Longarone.
2 All that was left of Longarone after a landslide,

the plane of contact between the two layers of rock. The whole mass of overlying rock and soil had slid over the layer of wet clay with the speed of an express train. Such geological conditions occur in many parts of the Alps and are the cause of many landslides. Often the people who live in alpine valleys where such conditions exist receive sufficient warning of an impending landslide and can be evacuated in time. In 1927 the Valle d'Arbedo, north of Lake Maggiore, was blocked by a landslide but sufficient prior warning enabled the authorities to evacuate people

in October 1963, sent millions of tons of rock crashing into the lake, causing a huge wave which swept over the dam and down the valley, destroying everything in its path.

from the threatened villages and farms.

Earthquakes can also trigger off landslides but there is little hope of any warning. In May 1960, an Earth tremor in Chile set off a series of landslides in the mountains east of Valdivia. Tens of thousands of people were killed by the earthquakes themselves. Others were victims of the tidal waves that were caused by the upheaval along the Pacific coasts of Chile. Landslides added to the death toll but their effect was partly delayed, striking after the main earthquake shock. The entrance to the Riñihue valley in south-central Chile was blocked by 40 million cubic yards of sand, gravel and clay which slid into the valley. This loose material, which had lain at rest on the valley slopes since the end of the last Ice Age, was disturbed by the earthquake shock and slid into the valley floor, blocking the flow of the stream at the bottom. Trapped behind this material, the waters of the stream rose to a level of 80 feet in a few weeks. Finally the water burst through this natural dam, in a huge flood. Some 80,000 people were made homeless in the Valdivia area, 60 miles downstream.

Dammed by a landslide

An even more dramatic example of the havoc caused by landslides which block the valleys of mountain rivers occurred in 1840. An earthquake near the Himalayan mountain of Nanga Parbat, which is 26,630 feet above sea level, caused a landslide in the valley of the Upper Indus where the river flows through a gorge more than 15,000 feet deep. The landslide of rocks, stones and soil blocked the valley, and a lake formed which was 40 miles long and more than 1,000 feet deep. The weight of this huge mass of water was too heavy for the loose material which was holding it in check. Eventually it burst through and the lake emptied in two days. The sudden release of the pent-up water created disastrous floods hundreds of miles downstream and swept away an army camp near the banks of the Indus, with a loss of thousands of lives.

Sometimes the slipping of the surface occurs in regions where the rocks are not dipping steeply and where there is no inclined plane of contact between rock layers. But, in cases where the material making up a slope is loose and unconsolidated, *slumping* may occur along curved planes. On a small scale, slump can produce narrow ridges in the surface which run parallel to the line of the contours. Such ridges are the so-called 'sheeptracks' which are found on many hills. Sheep may use them and hikers may walk along them, but these features, called *terracettes,* are caused by soil slumping. In tropical regions which have heavy rainfall, large-scale slumping often occurs. Still-growing trees are sometimes carried down a slope because the soil which holds the trees' roots moves them bodily downhill, exposing bare bedrock on the upper slope.

The same process which causes soil creep of this kind also affects *screes* or *talus* (accumulations of rock fragments which pile up at the foot of rocky slopes in

mountain regions). The scree is made up of material which has been dislodged by frost action and weathering from the face of a steep slope. It is always unstable and rocky fragments continually slide downwards. New material is constantly added from above and fragments tumble further down the hillside. In normal conditions, the scree, like any loose material which is piled up, lies at a natural angle of rest. But this comparative stability can be upset if heavy rain or melting snow penetrates the mass. In some cases, the entire scree becomes cemented together by ice. When

1 In 1966 heavy rain saturated a slag heap which looms above Aberfan in Wales. A sheet of loose material flowed downwards and engulfed part of the village, causing tragic loss of life.
2 Rescue workers shovel the wet coal-pit waste out of a house window in Aberfan.
3 At Wast Water in Cumberland, screes of small loose fragments of rock, broken up by frost and weathering, continually slip down the steep mountainside into the lake.

set the whole hillside flowing down into the valley. After heavy rain, such movements may occur in railway cuttings which are dug through clays. In the same way, great sheets of material, called *earth flows*, slide downwards. A flow of this kind occurred on the coal-pit heap of Aberfan in south Wales, causing the terrible tragedy in which so many school children of the village perished.

Similar to earth flows are *mud flows*. Mud flows, however, occur mainly in the normally dry valleys of arid or semi-arid regions, filling them temporarily with rivers of mud. Large quantities of sand and dust accumulate in the dry valleys. After an occasional violent storm the rainwater mixes with this material, creating a porridge-like substance which flows downstream, sweeping away everything in its path. When it reaches flatter ground, it fans out, littering the lowlands with a sheet of rock waste, sand and mud.

Conditions similar to those which produce mud flows also explain the *bog bursts* which occur in Ireland. The peat beds cover large areas in central Ireland, sometimes filling in a former lake basin. The floor of the basin must be made up of some *impervious material* (a rock layer through which water cannot flow), which originally caused the accumulation of water to form the lake. Rainwater seeps through the peat, but it cannot percolate downwards through the old, impervious lake bed. In normal conditions, the underground water percolates horizontally

4 In Rogers Pass in Canada, where the rumble of trains may start an avalanche of snow sweeping down the slopes, sheds are built over the railway lines to prevent blockages.
5 Where avalanches threaten houses or roads they are sometimes set off deliberately. Here Canadian engineers fire a mortar to dislodge snow before it reaches avalanche proportions.

the ice thaws, it becomes unstable and moves suddenly. Sometimes the whole scree slips downhill, burying the pastures on the slopes below under layers of stones and rocks. If the hillside is furrowed by valleys, the scree will slide into these channels, which may become rivers of

stone. In high mountains or in polar regions, such rivers of stone include blocks of ice.

Rocks such as clay or shale, which are composed of finely grained material, sometimes become so saturated with rainwater that the slightest tremor or vibration can

along the old lake bed and drains away through a channel which may follow the course of the stream which originally drained the lake. Sometimes, however, the outlet for the underground water gets blocked. The water level inside the peat then rises, mixing with the powdery particles of the decayed material below the surface. The bog begins to swell up, until it can no longer hold the black, watery mass which then bursts out at its weakest point. If there is a downward slope, a flood of the black, muddy, evil-smelling mixture sweeps

35

down, covering the countryside with a thick layer of slime.

Mud flows sometimes sweep down the sides of volcanoes, causing enormous destruction. Some volcanologists believe that such mud flows may well have taken a greater toll of human life than volcanic explosions and outpourings of lava. The fine ash, sand and dust that accumulates on volcanic cones, is transformed into liquid mud by water. Such mud flows are fairly common in Java and, for this reason, they are known by the Indonesian name *lahar*. The water may come from a crater lake, or from snow and ice that has accumulated on the top of the volcano during a long, quiet period. Most lahars, however, are caused by heavy rainfall, particularly in tropical regions.

Floods of ash

Irazu, a volcano in Costa Rica, erupted in May, 1963 and several feet of ash piled up on the slopes of the cone. In the following December, heavy rains transformed the ash into a lahar, which swept downwards causing great damage, killing 30 people. Lahars greatly increase in volume as they rush downhill; they uproot trees, tear boulders from the ground and are swollen by any loose material in their path. On reaching the foot of the volcano, they spread out over the flatter land, burying the original surface. Today, volcanic eruptions can be predicted fairly accurately, but little research has been done on the prediction of lahars. In 1964, a UNESCO team visited Irazu and set up a warning system, which included taking rainfall measurements in areas considered to be likely sites of lahars. As a result, people can now be evacuated in time if lahars are imminent. Possibly the most famous lahar in history occurred in 79 AD at the Roman town of Herculaneum which lay at the foot of Mount Vesuvius in Italy. A lahar of hot mud engulfed the entire town. When

An avalanche of dry snow swirls down a mountain in Switzerland at tremendous speed, destroying everything that lies in its path.

the mud cooled, it set hard, completely sealing off the town which lay beneath.

Mud flows and landslides are movements of loose rock and mud which slide downhill under the force of gravity. Similar movements occur in the banks of snow which blanket high mountains in winter. In the case of avalanches the snow produces its own moisture and its own planes of sliding. Avalanches sweep down boulders and other rock fragments, shattered by the action of frost or by the weight of the overlying snow. They can strip a slope bare of its trees and plants and bury villages in valleys. The spring season, when the thaw begins, is the time for avalanches.

Landslides, like this one which crashed into an Italian valley, often occur in parts of the Alps. Watch is kept so that the threatened villages can be evacuated in time.

In Switzerland avalanches of wet snow are most frequent in spring when sudden thaws set off many, but often predictable, snow slides.

The people who live in mountain regions can often predict avalanches well in advance and make preparations to protect life and property, but a sudden unseasonal rise in temperature, an explosion or an Earth tremor can set off an unexpected train of avalanches. Such a situation occurred in the Swiss resort of Davos which was cut off for several days in the spring of 1966, when avalanches blocked the road and railway. The new Felber Tauern road tunnel, opened in 1967, was specially built to permit travel throughout the year through the heart of the Austrian Alps and links Munich with Lienz in the Tyrol.

In fear of the white death

Many Alpine roads are closed for several months of the year because of avalanches. Occasionally avalanches occur as a result of Man's activities, sometimes accidentally and with disastrous effects, and sometimes deliberately with the object of saving life. When a mass of snow is perched precariously above a steep cliff or rock face, it may reach a condition in which the slightest vibration can start an avalanche. The rumble of a train, the sound of a siren, the crack of a rifle shot, or even a shout can be sufficient to set the whole mass moving. Matthew Arnold in his poem *Sohrab and Rustum* described how travellers in a caravan train through the mountains on the borders of Afghanistan and Russia 'stop their breath for fear they should dislodge the o'erhanging snows'. When small avalanches threaten to block mountain roads, engineers sometimes deliberately precipitate them by setting off loud explosions, having first, of course, cleared the road of traffic and made sure that the snow will slide harmlessly down the mountain-side away from houses.

Although landslides, mud flows and avalanches cannot be prevented, Man is learning what causes them and where and when they are likely to occur. With prior warning, people and property can be saved from the destruction of these sudden slips and movements on the Earth's surface.

How the coasts were carved

Smashing into a rock face with a force of up to 6,000 pounds per square foot — enough to shift a 1,000-ton stone block — waves are the world's fastest and most dramatic landscape shapers.

EVERY WAVE that breaks on any shore in the world either gnaws away or builds up the coastline. Unlike the slow geologic changes that sculpture a continent, the effect of the sea can be seen in a few years or, during storms, in days. During a North Sea storm in 1953 the sea vented its full force on the low cliffs that border parts of the east coast of England. Towering waves lashed against a 25-foot cliff near Lowestoft, undercut it, and ripped away 35 feet of land in two hours. Nearby on the same night, the raging seawater cut back about 90 feet of land that had stood behind a six-foot high cliff.

In much of eastern England, especially in East Anglia and along the Holderness coast of Yorkshire, the coast is formed of glacial materials–sand, gravel and boulder clay – that offer little resistance to the pounding force of the sea. Since Roman times, the Holderness coast has been cut back by two to three miles by the constant action of the waves especially by the on-slaught the coast receives during great storms. A map dated 1786 lists many towns and villages that now lie under the sea.

Not all coastlines are composed of such easily eroded material. In Britain the tough rocks that border parts of western Scotland and the granite outcrops at Land's End stand as bulwarks against the encroaching sea. Erosion in such places is extremely slow. But sometimes apparently tough rocks are composed of materials that are soluble in seawater. Other rock stratas have joints and faults, lines of weakness that are fairly easily opened up by the battering force of storm waves. The sea often cuts into the less resistant rocks, forming bays and coves and leaving the harder rocks jutting into the sea as head-lands. The chalk outcrops of southeastern England, however, offer generally uniform resistance to erosion. There the White Cliffs of Dover form a smooth wall extending almost unbroken for several miles along the English Channel.

A wave's battering force

Storm waves, the most destructive agents that assault the coast, are generally caused by two factors: strong prevailing winds that drive them towards land, and a large stretch of uninterrupted water, called the *fetch,* where waves build up to a considerable height and great velocity. Storm waves, particularly at high tide when their effects reach furthest inland, batter coastal cliffs, lighthouses and marine promenades with tremendous force. The force of Atlantic waves are estimated to average about 2,000 lb per square foot, but when gales whip the sea into a fury, this force may be three times as great. Engineers building light-

The cliffs at Etretat in France, *top,* are being undercut by waves which grind pebbles against their base. When a mass of rock is undermined the overhanging cliff will fall on to the beach, to be broken up and washed away by the sea. *Above,* all loose material on a beach, shells, pebbles, driftwood and sand, are moved by the waves and currents, constantly changing shore profiles.

houses and breakwaters have to allow for this great force, which can shift blocks of stone or concrete weighing more than 1,000 tons. When storm waves crash against a rocky coast, the seawater traps air in all the cracks and crevices in the rock face and compresses it. When the pressure is released, the expansion of the air has an explosive force which can enlarge cracks and blast out chunks of rock.

An even more powerful erosive force occurs when storm waves churn up shattered material, varying in size from sand and pebbles to boulders, and hurl the entire load at the coast. Such crashing blows hollow out the bases of cliffs, under-mining huge masses of rock until they break away and the cliffs recede. The constant grinding of rocks and boulders causes *attrition* (the jagged material is rounded into smooth pebbles by impact and friction, and pebbles are worn into grains of sand). Erosion by the sea operates in four main ways: the hydraulic action of the water itself; *corrasion* (when the sea is armed with rocks and other material); attrition; and the solvent action of seawater.

Some of the most impressive features of coastal scenery are associated with the erosion of cliffs. In some places waves eat out caves along lines of weakness. Inside the caves the pressure of air and rushing water may continue the erosion upwards through the roofs to the surface forming deep pits called *blowholes*. Clouds of spray spout out when the sea is rough and breaking waves roar into the underlying tunnel. When the tops of such caves collapse and the material that formed their roof is swept away, long, narrow sea inlets remain. Sometimes caves hollowed on both sides of a headland meet and form a natural arch. When the top of the arch collapses, the seaward support of the arch is left as an isolated pillar, called a *stack*. Such stacks form the Needles, the chalk islets that fringe the western coast of the Isle of Wight. Constant erosion of cliffs causes them to recede further and further inland.

Moving cliffs

Wave-cut platforms (rocky shelves) flank the seaward side of cliffs. Gradually, as the cliffs recede and the platform is extended, the power of the waves diminishes and marine erosion decreases in effect. In some areas in northern latitudes, the cliff faces continue to recede at a relatively rapid rate owing to the action of weathering, mainly in the form of frost action. Shattered rock falls to the base of the cliffs as *scree,* and this material is broken down and removed by the constant ebb and flow of the sea. In parts of Norway, wave-cut platforms have widths of up to 37 miles.

On all beaches, eroded material from the land is gradually broken down into smaller and smaller pieces. The finest material, including the tiny particles carried in suspension by rivers into the sea, is swept out some distance before it finally comes to rest on the sea floor. All the loose materials on the beach are moved by seawater. The surge of waves pushes pebbles and sand up the beach, while the *backwash* (the return of seawater down a beach after a wave has broken) or, in some cases, underwater currents pull the material down the slope. During storms and high tides, pebbles may even be flung high out of the water to build up quite high *shingle* (pebble) beaches which form natural barriers against the sea. Natural barriers are also formed by coral reefs which fringe many islands and parts of continents in and near the tropics. Separated from the shore by clear, calm lagoons, the reefs are quickly repaired by the corals when damaged by storm waves. The Great Barrier Reef of northeast Australia, 1,200 miles long, is the most famous coral reef.

Movement of material up and down the beach ensures that the profile of the shore is constantly changing. There is a tendency in normal conditions for the sea to produce a smoothly graded slope or profile, erosion of the landward side being balanced

by deposition on the seaward end of the slope. Such graded slopes can be ravaged in a single night, which occurred when the beaches of Lincolnshire were washed away in 1953. But even after such extreme disturbances, the sea slowly readjusts the shore line, building up once again areas that were torn away. Sometimes the natural process is upset artificially. Around the turn of the century, dredgers began to remove shingle from the coast of Devon to supply material for a new harbour at Plymouth. But the dredging upset the shore profile and, as a result, the erosive power of the waves and their backwash was quickly and considerably increased. The sea began to erode the land, dragging back material to restore the balance. Eventually the danger was realized and the dredging stopped, but it was too late to save the fishing village of Hallsands, which was undermined and destroyed by the sea.

Most people regard the sea's destructive power as the most dramatic aspect of

The fishing village of Hallsands in Devon, *top,* was undermined when the sea slowly readjusted the shoreline after dredgers had removed shingle from the coast. When the effect of dredging was realized, it was stopped, but too late to save the village. At Beesands in Devon, *above,* the south-west longshore drift has swept sand and pebbles along the coast to form a bar across an inlet.

changing coastlines, probably because erosion often involves loss of life and property. But the sea also plays a constructive role. Much of the material washed away in one area is transported elsewhere to build up new land. The processes by which the sea transports material up and down and also along the shore are complicated, and some of the mechanisms are still not fully understood.

Waves are the most important agent in transporting material. *Longshore drift,* the movement of shingle and sand along a coastline, occurs when the wind and the waves strike a shore at an angle. In southern England, the prevailing wind and

Fingal's Cave, *top left*, the most famous of many sea caves in Staffa, the Inner Hebrides, runs 227 feet into the basalt lava cliffs. The hexagonal pillars of the arch, which reaches 66 feet, were formed by cooling in a deep lava flow. *Top right*, Durdle Door in Dorset is the result of the waves wearing away caves in the headland until they met and formed an arch.

A blowhole at Oahu, Hawaii, *above left*, formed by the constant action of the sea eating out a cave along a line of weakness in the cliff. Air and water pressure built up by the waves have torn a hole in the roof which spouts spray with every wave. This *stack*, or isolated pillar of rock at Orkney in Scotland, *above right*, remained when rough seas caused the cliffs to retreat.

rocky scree, whereas small crescents of sand lie at the head of coves.

The sea builds other land forms apart from beaches. When material is being shifted along a coast by longshore drift, it often reaches headlands or estuaries where the direction of the coast changes quite sharply. The longshore drift, however, continues straight on and the load is carried into deeper water, where the coarser material slumps to the bottom.

Longshore drifts and spits

Ridges of sand, gravel and pebbles pile up in this way and material is added from the land. These narrow ridges, which extend the general direction of the coast across inlets, are called *spits*. Spits are seldom straight because, as they increase in length, waves deflect them towards land so that, from the air, they appear curved or hook shaped.

Spits are common features along the coasts of Norfolk and Suffolk. The largest spit in this area has grown southwards

consequently the main direction of the waves is from the southwest. The waves sweep the loose material up the southward facing shores at an oblique angle. The backwash then generally pulls it back down the steepest slope. The pebbles and other material therefore move in a zigzag course from west to east along the shore, building up beaches further along the coast. Further out, longshore currents move material in deeper water along the coast. Other currents also play their part. When storms drive huge waves against the coast, a great volume of water piles up. To relieve the pressure, underwater currents flow seaward, scouring the beach with

considerable power. Tidal currents move material seaward, especially in areas such as estuaries where they are forced into bottlenecks.

Another important agent in coastal scenery is the wind, which drives grains of dry sand inland. In fact, a typical beach on a lowland coast is bordered by sand dunes which extend up to the band of shingle at the top of the beach. Beyond the shingle lies a large area of sand, exposed at low tide, and sometimes rocks covered by seaweed rise just above the low-tide mark. But beaches vary widely in character. In places where erosion is proceeding quickly, there is no beach, only piles of from the fishing town of Aldeburgh in Suffolk. It first sealed off the estuary of the river Alde and deflected it southwards for several miles to join the river Butley. Its estuary was later also blocked by the ever-advancing spit. United, the rivers flow into the sea some way south of the old estuary of the Butley. The growth of this spit has been rapid. The inland town of Orford, which now lies north of the junction of the two rivers, was a port facing the open sea in the Middle Ages.

Sometimes spits extend from headland to headland sealing off large areas of water, which eventually become marshland or shore-line lakes. More commonly, however, the spits do not completely seal a bay. A deep, narrow channel often remains through which excess water can escape into the sea. Such is the case with the *Nehrungen* (sand spits) that border parts of the southern Baltic Sea. Spits have also inched forward from the mainland to provide natural bridges with islands. The best known example in Britain is Chesil Beach which has linked the Dorset mainland to the former Isle of Portland. In Italy, such natural bridges are called *tomboli,* after the two spits, Tombolo di Feniglio and Tombolo di Gianetta, which have united the former island of Monte Argentario with the mainland.

Two spits built up from opposite headlands may converge in an angular point. Behind them, cut off from the sea, marshes may develop which can later be reclaimed. Such areas are called *cuspate lowlands.* Many spits and bars occur off the Atlantic and Gulf coasts of the United States. Some bars, called barrier islands, are not connected to the mainland at either end, and there is still some mystery and much argument about their origin.

Swanbridge, South Wales, *top,* was battered by storm waves in 1962 which broke through the sea wall and flooded the front. During such storms the force of the waves is so great that entire beaches are ripped away in hours. At Worthing in Sussex, *above,* stout wooden groynes protect the beach against winter waves, driven by the prevailing wind, which sweep shingle along the coast.

Erosion and deposition are constantly changing the coastlines of all land masses, but another factor of considerable importance in this change is the level of the sea itself. Geologists have established that, since the end of the last Ice Age, water from the melting glaciers and ice sheets has emptied into the oceans, steadily raising the level of the sea by up to 400 feet. Most, though not all, of the world's coasts have therefore been submerged in the past 20,000 years. Some areas, which were depressed by the great mass of ice that covered them, rose at a faster rate than the sea level when the ice melted. Earth movements have also raised some regions and caused subsidence in others. Because of such changes, geographers sometimes distinguish between *coasts of submergence* and *coasts of emergence*.

Submerged coasts have several distinctive features. In hilly regions, submergence has led to the flooding of gently sloping river valleys which form long, but generally shallow, sea inlets called *rias,* good examples of which occur in southwestern Ireland. In glaciated regions, seawater has gradually filled the steep-sided valleys that were gouged out by the abrasive action of glaciers. Such deep inlets are called *fjords*. They occur in many parts of the world, from Norway and Greenland to Chile and New Zealand.

Mountain-top islands

Where the mountain ranges of a country run roughly parallel to a coastline, submergence causes the flooding of the longitudinal valleys to form sounds or straits. The mountain tops remain above the surface of the water in lines of offshore islands, running parallel to the coast. They are called *Dalmatian* or *longitudinal coasts,* and the best example is probably the Adriatic coast of Yugoslavia. Submergence is still continuing in this region, and archaeologists have found fairly recent traces of human settlement a few feet below the present sea level. Submerged lowlands form large shallow seas, such as the Great Australian Bight.

Striking evidence of submergence is provided by the tree stumps and roots of former forests that are now below high-tide level, and sometimes even below low-tide level. Coasts of emergence are much less common, but they are generally characterized by raised beaches, often bounded by cliffs, but now situated well above the present sea level.

Man's struggle against the sea has led to considerable research in recent times into the mechanics of coastal changes. Marine engineers study the way in which the sea transports material, so that they can prevent the silting up of harbours, and select the best sites for new ports. They also conduct research into techniques to prevent the destruction of popular holiday beaches, or sea flooding of lowland areas. They build *groynes* (low walls) at right angles to the shore to slow down the rate of longshore drift of shingle and sand. The construction of dykes or sea walls that will withstand the pounding of storm waves is enormously important for the protection of all coastal lowlands.

At odds and evens with the sea

Placid, prosperous, well-watered – the world's lowlands are the favourite dwelling places for the world's peoples. But sometimes an eye-level view of the sea is a dangerous viewpoint.

ON THE last day of January 1953 weather forecasts indicated that a severe storm was moving southward from the northern part of the North Sea. During the day, high waves began to batter the coasts of eastern England and the western coast of the Netherlands, especially in the southwestern delta region of the rivers Rhine, Maas and Schelde. The people who lived on the islands in the delta were not concerned, knowing that the dykes, those sturdy protective walls of earth and stone, had withstood the pounding of the sea for centuries.

But this was no ordinary storm. Winds reaching 115 miles an hour combined with a high tide and raised the level of the sea to a completely unforeseen height. That night, after most people had gone to bed, gigantic waves smashed against the dykes. Under the incessant battering, the dykes were breached, and the angry sea water surged through the shattered defences, submerging great areas of low-lying Dutch farmland and villages. For example, on the island of Tholen, the sea remorselessly hammered the dyke near the village of Stavenisse. Some villagers dashed towards the dyke hoping to reinforce it, but they were too late. The dyke broke and a wall of water crashed through, destroying farmhouses near the dyke. The fierce current, armed with the debris of the shattered farmhouses, swept into Stavenisse, smashing the buildings and drowning 200 people. Some people were asleep when the rising water overpowered and drowned them. Others woke to find water reaching their beds. With difficulty, they scrambled through the windows to rooftops in the hope that help would come.

Closing the breaches

The sea seemed victorious. It flooded an area of about 375,000 acres of farmland, about 4·3 per cent of the Netherland's land area, destroying or damaging more than 30,000 houses, and killing 1,800 people and great numbers of livestock. In the days that followed, the Dutch people worked swiftly, saving lives and evacuating the homeless. They then faced the task of repairing 67 major and over 500 minor breaches in the dykes, and reinforcing those which showed signs of crumbling.

They proved once again their energy in combating the sea, always the main threat to their national survival, and by November all the major breaches were closed. Over the centuries, the Dutch people have literally wrested their land from the sea. Some 140 disasters have occurred since 1287, when floods in Friesland drowned 50,000 people. But the Netherlanders have achieved much. Two-fifths of their land would be under the

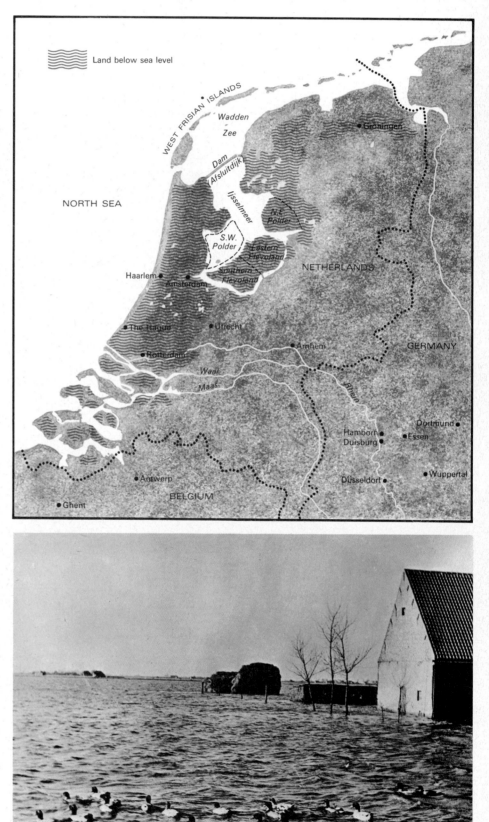

The Netherlands, *top,* shows the great delta built up on the continental shelf by sediment deposited by Rhine, Maas and Schelde rivers to form a lowland of salt marshes and sandbanks.

Disaster in Holland, *above:* strong winds and a high tide have breached a defending dyke, flooding low-level farmlands, destroying the villages and causing a great loss of life.

sea at high tide were it not for an elaborate system of dykes and dams, and pumps to rid the land of water. Their task is made more difficult because the coastal region is sinking and the sea level is rising. Experts estimate that the total submergence of the coast is about eight inches every 100 years.

The Dutch response to the catastrophe of 1953 was typical. Not only did they quickly repair the damage but, within three weeks of the disaster, they established a commission of inquiry which recommended a new project for protecting the delta region. The Delta Plan envisaged a series of dams closing the four main sea inlets in the delta, leaving open the waterways to the ports of Antwerp and Rotterdam. The project is due for completion in 1978. The first dam linking the islands of Walcheren and North Beveland was opened in 1961, and a second, the Haringvliet dam, is in its final stage of construction.

The Delta Plan is not merely a defensive measure. By blocking the sea inlets, the salt waters of the delta will be replaced by fresh water, and land now infertile because of the high salt content of the soil will be reclaimed. The linking dams will provide road contacts between the islands, giving the entire area a much greater economic potential. The whole of the Netherlands is in fact a great delta formed by sediments deposited by the Rhine, Maas, Schelde and other waterways. Deltas are areas of flat land formed at a point where a river enters a lake or sea.

Banking the deposits

On entering flat deltas, rivers generally split into a series of smaller sluggish streams called *distributaries*. Each time a distributary overflows its banks and floods the surrounding marshland, it deposits a layer of *alluvium* (sediment). Gradually the level of the land is built up around the head of the delta, and alluvium deposited near the mouth gradually extends the marsh area into the sea. When a distributary overflows, the accumulation of alluvium is generally greatest along the banks of the stream.

After the flood waters subside, the borders of the stream are raised higher than the surrounding delta plain, and gradually narrow ridges are built up on both sides of the stream. These ridges, which are called levees, can be reinforced or raised to prevent flooding. In the Netherlands, the Dutch began to reclaim land by building dykes, which are in effect artificial levees, around a marshy area between two streams. The enclosed area, called a *polder,* was drained by ditches, and the water was pumped from the ditches into the streams. This same principle is now applied over much greater areas, as in the Zuider Zee.

Although some deltas are badly drained and unsatisfactory for settlement, others grow food and provide territory for a great many people. For example, in the Ganges-Brahmaputra delta disastrous floods sometimes occur, but generally the flood water rises slowly enough to

keep pace with the growth of rice in the flooded fields. The delta is therefore a major food-producing region and supports one of the densest populations of Asia.

In northern China, another great and densely populated plain has been built up by the Hwang-ho (Yellow river) and some other streams. The delta has extended far into the Yellow Sea, linking a hilly island to the mainland. This former island now forms the Shantung peninsula. The Hwang-ho carries an enormous amount of alluvium which consists largely of a fine soil called *loess*. This soil is yellowish in colour – accounting for the name of the river and the Yellow Sea. In winter the river is generally at a low level but in summer, swollen by heavy rains, it may overflow its banks.

Chinese historians have recorded more than 1,500 floods in the past 3,000 years. To prevent flooding, the Chinese have built artificial levees along the river, but the level of the river is always rising, because a great deal of the sediment piles up in the river bed. As a result, the levees must be constantly raised in height to hold back the rising river. The Hwang-ho now occupies a channel which in many places rises ridge-like above the surrounding countryside. In the past, the Hwang-ho has several times broken through the earth levees and completely changed its course, sometimes flowing north to its present outlet, and sometimes south of the Shantung peninsula.

Called 'China's sorrow', the Hwang-ho has caused many great disasters and enormous loss of life. Nearly 900,000 people perished in 1938, when the Chinese deliberately broke the banks of the Hwang-ho and diverted it southward in a desperate attempt to stop the advance of the Japanese army. The river was diverted northward once again in 1947 by a United Nations team.

Deltas in arid regions present different problems. Flooding is not a serious hazard and the main problem is how to use the

An intricate network of canals, **1**, lined with traditional windmills for pumping water, drain the low-lying fields of Holland. **2** The coastal plain of Lincolnshire, once covered by the sea, is now one of Britain's most cultivated and productive agricultural areas. Spalding is noted for bulb growing. **3** The marshes and shallow lagoons of Camargue in southern France, dwindle during the dry summers. Formerly of little use, the introduction of rice cultivation has turned the sparsely populated delta of the Rhône into a productive region. **4** For centuries water from the summer monsoons in the East African and Ethiopian highlands has carried fertile silt across 1,200 miles of arid desert to the delta of the Nile, building a broad, flat, marshy area, intersected by tributaries which drain into the Mediterranean. This annual flood is fed into the irrigation system and when it recedes crops are planted in the mud. **5** The Everglades in Florida are part of a continental shelf which has been raised up comparatively recently to form a swampy coastal plain. The southern region is now a national park to protect wild life. Alligators, manatees and snakes haunt the tidal mangrove swamps.

water from the distributaries to water the crops and spread fertile silt over the land. This is achieved by irrigation systems, and such regions as the Nile delta, which has been irrigated for centuries, support enormous populations.

Not every river has a delta at its mouth. In many cases, off-shore currents and tides sweep away the river sediment, spreading it evenly over the continental shelf. But many rivers, with or without deltas, are bordered by alluvial flood plains in their lower courses. Alluvial plains are similar in many ways to deltas. They are caused by rivers overflowing their banks and spreading great depths of alluvium over adjoining areas. A prominent feature of many flood plains are levees, some of which are natural and some artificial, to prevent flooding. Swampy areas often lie beyond the levees but, when drained, they can become rich and fertile. This has happened in the Nile valley, which is bordered on both sides by desert and

where every possibility of agricultural land must be exploited. But in other areas, the land is so flat that drainage is difficult and costly.

River valleys containing swift-flowing streams are often V-shaped in cross-section and may contain no flat areas, whereas large rivers in their lower courses generally occupy broad, shallow valleys. The lower Amazon has a flood plain slightly less than 30 miles wide, and the Mississippi flood plain around Cairo, Illinois is about 75 miles wide. Other prominent features of flood plains include channels which the river has abandoned, leaving behind *oxbow lakes* which gradually fill up with silt and become swamps. The levees of the river may block the entrance of tributary streams and, on many flood plains, tributaries may run parallel to the river for miles before they join the main stream.

Apart from deltas and flood plains, there is another important type of alluvial lowland. *Piedmont alluvial plains* often

occur at the foot of steeply-rising mountain slopes in generally arid areas. They consist of a series of *alluvial fans* (fan-shaped deposits) formed around points where swift-flowing mountain streams suddenly reach a broad flat area and lose their velocity. Larger material carried by the stream in floods, such as rocks and boulders, is deposited at the head of the fan, near the point where the gradient of the river changes. Finer material, such as silt, is carried to the edge of the fan. Where several such fans coalesce, they form a piedmont alluvial plain. Such plains generally have a steeper gradient than does the otherwise similar delta.

Old alluvial plains

Some of the world's largest plains are made up of old alluvial deposits. The characteristic features of alluvial flood plains have largely disappeared, and swift-flowing rivers which have smaller flood plains of their own now dissect many of

these plains. Alluvial material reaches a depth of about 2,000 feet on the Pampas of Argentina. Geologists consider that such ancient alluvial deposits of such depth must have accumulated on a slowly sinking plain. Such plains are now dissected by rivers with greatly increased velocity and volume, caused possibly by uplift of the land or by a change in the climate.

Another type of plain borders many coasts, varying greatly in width. Such plains are often parts of the continental shelf which have been raised above sea level, and they slope gently down under the sea. For this reason, such coastal areas are usually flat and badly drained. Parts of the coast of the Gulf of Mexico have been raised above sea level comparatively recently and now form marshy lowlands. The swampy Everglades of Florida is a particularly good example of a new coastal plain. Such areas are of little use for agriculture even when drained, because

Carried by strong tidal currents, silt brought down by Italy's eastern rivers has formed long banks at the head of the Adriatic just above sea level, parallel to the shore. On these banks stands Venice, *above,* surrounded by lagoons.

the sandy soils are often infertile. In many arid areas, sand dunes cover the coastal plains. Except for settlements around ports and seaside resorts, people generally settle on inland lowlands which offer more opportunities for agriculture.

Some interior lowlands often resemble hill country rather than flat plains. As we have seen, the rivers of many lowlands are eroding the landscape by cutting broad valleys. Erosion may expose certain features of the geology of a region. The tilted sedimentary rocks of lowland England have been eroded to form *cuestas* (belts of hills) separated by undulating plains.

Other lowland plains which have distinctive features include those affected by the action of ice sheets and glaciers which, during the last Ice Age, covered large areas in northern Europe and northern North America. The great ice sheets spread southward, picking up soil and other weathered loose material. The eroded material became embedded in the base of the ice, giving it an abrasive surface which scoured the tops of hills bare, gouged out rock basins, and generally rounded any sharp angular features. Its effect was much like sandpaper on wood. After the ice sheet melted, it left behind a landscape characterized by bare rock outcrops, small lakes filling the rock basins, and irregular drainage. Such ice-scoured plains occur in Sweden, and also in Finland where tens of thousands of small lakes dot the country.

Some glacial plains are covered by thick layers of eroded material called *drift* or *boulder clay,* which was left behind when the ice melted. Such deposits, which may be as deep as 500 feet, smoothed out the features of the original plain which was covered by the ice. Other deposits include rocky ridges, called *terminal moraines,* which pile up along the fringe of ice sheets and glaciers. Beyond the ice sheets, streams from the melting ice carried material and spread it over the *outwash,* or alluvial plain. The undulating glacial plains form much of the best agricultural land of Canada, the northeastern United States and northern Europe. But not all glacial plains are fertile. Lüneburg Heath in Germany is covered by infertile sandy and gravelly soils deposited as outwash material.

Densely populated plains

Lowlands have other disadvantages, apart from areas of infertile soil. Broad, flat plains are exposed to the wind, and crops can be ruined by gales. Farmers often plant rows of trees which separate the fields and also act as windbreaks on many cultivated lowlands. Some plains are too arid for extensive cultivation while others, such as some deltas and coastal plains, are too swampy and poorly drained for farming. The Arctic lowlands are too cold to support large populations, while tropical lowlands can be unpleasantly hot and humid.

But apart from the temperate tropical plateaux, most of the world's people live on lowland plains. The gentle slopes afford easy cultivation, and flat, well-watered, and well-drained lowland plains have the greatest food-producing capacity. Travel is much easier on the plains than it is on steep mountain slopes or on high plateaux, which are often dissected by deep canyons. On the plains, railways can easily skirt hills, and forests can be cleared without much difficulty. The concentration of people on lowland plains and the ease of travel ensures contact between one group of people and another, a contact which has been important in the spread of ideas and the development of civilizations.

The ice sheet which spread southwards over Finland, *left,* during the last Ice Age, scoured the tops of hills, gouged out basins and smoothed sharp features. When it melted it left a plain of bare rocks, thousands of small lakes and a litter of glacial debris. The piedmont alluvial plain of Yorkshire, *right,* formed when swift-flowing streams from the Pennines reached the vale and deposited deep fans of rich, fertile sediment.

Frozen frontier

Survivors from the last Ice Age, the world's glaciers and ice sheets are still in retreat. Fortunately, the frozen frontier is shrinking only slowly – a sudden thaw would flood all lowlands.

IF ALL THE ICE in the world melted, the level of the sea would rise by between 100 and 200 feet, flooding some of the most thickly populated lowlands of the world and submerging the great seaports. Most of this potential flood water is locked in two great continental ice sheets, Antarctica and Greenland.

A continent covering a larger area than the United States and India combined, Antarctica is a desolate plateau around the South Pole. Except for a few *nunataks* (mountain peaks projecting above the ice) and some isolated coastal strips, the continent is covered by great depths of ice, reaching 14,000 feet in parts of Marie Byrd Land. In places, the ice overruns the land and projects into the sea. The Ross Ice Shelf is about 1,300 feet thick and ends in the Great Ross Barrier, a line of ice cliffs 100 to 160 feet high. The ice is constantly moving outwards from the centre, and would continue pushing further into the southern oceans were it not for the action of the sea in cutting back the ice cliffs, the *calving* (breaking off) of gigantic icebergs, and underwater thawing. Since the early part of this century, the forward spread of the ice has been balanced by the loss of ice caused by such factors, whereas, during the late 1800s, the front of the ice had been receding.

Greenland, the world's largest island, is only a sixth of the size of Antarctica. Ice covers about 85 per cent of the island, the northernmost point of which lies about 450 miles from the North Pole. Near the centre of Greenland, the ice reaches a depth of 10,000 feet. It spills outwards from the centre, finding gaps in the mountain rim to form valley glaciers overlooking the green coastlands, or, in some places, flowing into the sea in ice shelves. The iceberg that holed the 'unsinkable' steamship *Titanic* in April 1912, drowning 1,500 people, broke off from the Greenland ice shelf and had drifted southwards probably for about two years before the fatal collision.

Born in the mountains

Ice-caps are smaller areas of ice than continental ice sheets, but they are similar in that they often spread outwards in valley glaciers. Ice-caps occur in Spitzbergen, on some islands in northern Canada, in the Norwegian highlands, and also on Iceland where they cover about an eighth of the country. Mountain glaciers originate in permanent snow fields which are found throughout the world, except in Australia. They even occur on the high slopes of equatorial mountains. Glaciers form in areas above the *permanent snow line,* where accumulations of winter snow do not melt completely in summer. At the Poles, the permanent snow line is at sea

A huge melting iceberg, which has broken off a glacier in Greenland, floats slowly south towards Newfoundland, moved by currents. A danger to shipping, only about one ninth is above water.

level, in the Alps at 9,000 feet, and on the equatorial mountains of Africa and the Andes at 17,000 to 18,000 feet. No permanent snow fields occur in Britain but it is estimated that Ben Nevis, where the snow on the summit melts during May, is only a few hundred feet below what would be the permanent snow line in that latitude.

The formation of glaciers depends on low temperatures, heavy snowfall, and slopes on the mountains gentle enough to permit the accumulation of snow fields. On precipitous slopes, the snow often cascades downwards in destructive avalanches. But, providing some snow remains on a slope or in a hollow every year, the depth of the snow will gradually

increase, and layer upon layer will be compacted into glacier ice. The compacted snow is called the *névé* (in French) or the *firn* (in German). Compaction is caused by pressure, but the ice crystals are also cemented closely when surface snow melts and water seeps downwards only to freeze again. In the névé field, the compacted snow is white, but as all pockets of air are gradually squeezed out, the deeper snow is transformed into clear blue ice.

Gravity forces a tongue of ice downhill along valleys, the least line of resistance, until the snout of the glacier is sometimes thousands of feet below the permanent snow line. The flow of ice was dramatically demonstrated in 1863, when parts of the bodies and bits of the clothing and equipment of three mountain guides emerged at the base of the Glacier des Bossons on the slopes of Mont Blanc. These men had been hurled by a sudden avalanche into a deep crevasse some 43 years earlier. Their bodies, encased in the ice, were transported some two miles at a rate of about 240 feet a year. In 1933, a well-preserved carcass of a mountain ram appeared at the base of the Lyell Glacier in California. Such sheep had been extinct for some 50 years, but experts believe that this refrigerated ram probably fell into a crevasse at the head of the glacier about 250 years ago and had been carried nearly the entire length of the glacier by the flow of the ice.

The Black Rapids Glacier of Alaska made a dramatic advance of four miles between September 1936 and February 1937, possibly as a result of an avalanche caused by an earthquake which piled up a great volume of snow on the glacier's source. The fastest rate of advance during this spectacular flow was more than 200 feet a day.

The rate of flow of glaciers can therefore vary greatly. In general, glaciers move only a few feet a day and, in Antarctica, the ice sheet moves only a few feet a year. Like rivers, the fastest movement is in the centre of a valley glacier. If the surface of the ice slopes downwards from its source or centre, glaciers can flow uphill, even riding over and covering ridges. Why, then, does it appear that the snouts of glaciers are stationary? The end of a glacier is where the rate of *ablation* (loss of ice due to evaporation, melting, or the calving of icebergs) balances the rate of accumulation at its source. But if the snowfall increases, then the glacier will thicken and its snout will move forward. Fluctuations in glaciers provide evidence of climatic change. An advancing glacier is an indication of increased snowfall, or generally colder conditions lowering the permanent snow line. Although exceptions exist, the rate of ablation has exceeded accumulation in most glaciers during the past 100 years and their snouts have been retreating. The average thickness of the ice which covers the Arctic Ocean has decreased by about a third during the 1900s.

The flowing ice

Since scientists first realized that ice could flow, much research has been conducted to discover the causes of flow in what is a solid substance. Even today, all the processes involved, especially in the movement of the gently-sloping ice-sheets, are still not fully explained. We do know that below the brittle crust the ice has plastic properties. The ice is really a mass of interlocking crystals which, under pressure, are recrystallized in the direction of the flow of the ice. Pressure and stress also lower the temperature at which ice melts. Molecules of water liberated in this way form a lubricating film between the ice grains, and crystals glide over each

other. An example of the lowering of the melting point of ice under stress occurs when a skater glides over an ice rink. The skater is really skimming through narrow grooves of water which form under the stress of the skates' blades but which freeze over as soon as the skater has passed. Mechanical slipping of ice down slopes, and stress caused by shearing in the ice, also contribute to the flow of glaciers.

On the surface of a glacier, yawning crevasses in the ice often open up – a great danger to climbers, especially when filled with snow and not easily seen. Some crevasses develop laterally across the glacier at points where the slope increases. Marginal crevasses occur as the ice drags against the valley sides, and longitudinal cracks split the ice where the glacier broadens out from its constricted valley course. Sometimes, when the slope increases sharply the ice is shattered into a jumble of crevasses and *séracs* (icy pinnacles). Such areas, which are very difficult to cross, are called *ice falls*. After an icefall, the blocks are soon reunited and continue their downward flow. At the top of the névé field, there is often a special type of crevasse called a *bergschrund,* which develops at a point where the glacier pulls away from the steep slope or ice wall at the head of the glacier.

The surface of the glacier is strewn with debris called *moraine.* Rock fragments shattered by frost tumble down the valley slopes on to the margins of the ice to form *marginal moraines.* When two glaciers from separate valleys unite, two of the marginal moraines combine to form a *medial moraine,* which may be as high as 50 feet. Heated by the sun, small fragments on the ice melt the underlying ice and sink below the surface. Large rocks sometimes protect the underlying ice from the sun's

rays. The ice around the rock melts but the rock itself remains as a *glacier table,* supported by a pillar of ice.

During the summer, the surface of the glacier may be covered by many streams which cut deep runnels before they flow into holes in the ice and through tunnels, perhaps to emerge as streams at the snout. The streams wash debris into crevasses or other holes to form *englacial moraine. Sub-glacial moraine* is embedded in the base of the glacier. When the load is too much for the glacier to shift, some material slumps to the floor of the valley as *ground moraine.* Around the snout of the glacier much of the material, varying in size from 'rock flour', the finest fragments, to large boulders, piles up as *terminal moraine,* sometimes forming a curved ridge.

Hanging valleys

Glaciers not only transport material, they are also powerful agents of erosion. Ice at the glacier head and along the valley sides freezes around jointed and faulted rock. As it moves forward, the ice plucks out these ice-engulfed blocks. Embedded in the base of the ice, rocks from the size of stones to huge boulders give 'teeth' to the moving ice, turning it into a gigantic flexible file, that abrades the sides and floors of valleys. The floors are worn down to great depths and the characteristic river valley spurs are blunted and removed. The gentle slopes of the pre-glacial, V-shaped river valleys are cut away as the ice gouges out deep, trough-like, U-shaped valleys. The overdeepening of the main valley often leaves the tributary valleys 'hanging'.

Sometimes a tributary valley may itself contain a glacier but, because it is small and less powerful, the rate of erosion is much less than in the main valley. When

ATLANTIC OCEAN

NORTH SEA

Inverness

Aberdeen

Dundee

Glasgow Edinburgh

Londonderry

Carlisle Newcastle

IRISH SEA

Leeds Hull

Manchester

Dublin Liverpool Sheffield

Lincoln

Norwich

Birmingham

Cambridge

Harwich

Cork

ST. GEORGE'S CHANNEL

Swansea

Cardiff Bristol London

Dover

Southampton

Portsmouth

Plymouth ENGLISH CHANNEL

The Aletsch Glacier in the Swiss Alps, *top left*, flows down a glacial valley from the flanks of the Monch and Jungfrau. It carries wide bands of *marginal moraines*, rock fragments from the walls of the valley. Pressure ridges in the pack-ice of Antarctica, *top centre*, occur when the constantly moving ice sheets collide and one slides on top of another. The surface of the Joestedal Glacier in Norway, *top right*, is broken by an ice fall. *Above*, The Rhône Glacier in Switzerland is about eight miles long and is the source of the Rhône river. Flowing down an eroded valley, the ice is coloured with ground-up rock and split with deep crevasses. *Left*, This is what would remain above sea level of the British Isles if all the ice in the world melted. The sea would rise by between 100 and 200 feet, drowning major cities, flooding coastal plains and making islands of higher ground. Throughout the world, densely populated lowlands and ports would disappear.

the ice melts, the tributary valleys end in the steep, almost vertical, main valley walls high above the valley floor. A stream in a hanging valley plunges over the precipitous edge in a waterfall. Glaciated valleys often descend in a series of steps. They cut into the least resistant rocks, deepening such sections to a far greater extent than sections where the rocks are more resistant. Such *overdeepened* sections often become the sites of lakes after the ice withdraws. In regions where glaciated valleys reach the sea, they are often flooded to become fjords when the ice disappears.

Steep-walled valleys are not the only sign that a region has been sculpted by ice erosion. The mountain regions of large parts of northern Europe and North America show many signs of the glaciation which occurred during the Pleistocene Ice Age. Among the most dramatic features are *cirques* (armchair-shaped basins) that once contained névé fields. From a chance hollow, the freezing and thawing of snow eats into the rock, wearing out a basin where snow can accumulate, forming the source of a glacier. Cutting back increases when the ice plucks at the walls of the basin, which rise as sheer cliffs. When two cirques are eroded back to back, a knife-edge ridge called an *arête* is formed between them. When three or more cirques converge, a sharp pointed peak, called a horn, is carved from the rock. The Matterhorn in Switzerland is the best known example, but horns are characteristic features of many glaciated uplands. After the ice disappears, cirques often contain lakes called *tarns.*

Glaciers and ice sheets strip the soil cover to expose the bare rock below. The ice embedded with fragments of rock scratches the bedrock leaving *striations* (narrow grooves) which indicate the direction of flow. Sometimes glaciers gouge deep basins in the bedrock, which may become lakes after the ice has gone. Other rock formations carved by ice erosion include *roches moutonnées,* which are hillocks of bare rock over which the ice has flowed. The upstream side is smooth but marked with striations, whereas the downstream side is jagged as a result of ice plucking. Roches moutonnées were so named in the early 1800s after sheepskin wigs placed face downwards, which they were supposed to resemble. Sometimes a glacier encounters a particularly tough outcrop of rock, such as the neck of an ancient volcano. The ice erodes the less resistant rock on the upstream side, exposing the obstruction. It then flows over the resistant rock and deposits waste material on the downstream side. Geographers call such formations *crag-and-tails,* and a good example can be seen at Edinburgh, where the castle, which dominates the whole city, rests on the crag.

Glaciers as landscapers

Most glacial erosion occurs in upland areas, whereas land features associated with glacial deposition are found most often on lowlands or, in the case of terminal moraines, at the edge of glaciers and ice sheets. A series of terminal or *recessional* moraines usually marks the stages in the retreat of the ice. The main glacial deposits are called *drift* and consist of *boulder clay* (unsorted clay, sand and stones) and *glacio-fluvial deposits,* which are carried by melted ice issuing as water in streams from a glacier or ice sheet. Glacio-fluvial deposits are sorted by the streams in that the coarsest material is dropped near the glacier and the finest material is carried some way across the outwash plain. Hummocks of boulder clay, rounded and elongated in the direction of the ice flow, are called *drumlins.*

Among distinctive glacio-fluvial deposits are narrow winding ridges called *eskers,* which were possibly built up by sub-glacial streams. Esker ridges provide natural routes for roads and railways in flat, waterlogged plains. Another feature found on glaciated plains are kettle lakes formed where chunks of stagnant ice are covered by glacio-fluvial deposits. The ice later melts and a pond or lake fills the depression.

With a knowledge of features associated with glacial erosion and deposition, geologists have been able to chart the area which was covered by the Pleistocene ice sheet over a million years ago, and even the area covered by the Permo-Carboniferous Ice Age, 225 million to 345 million years ago, in the southern hemisphere during the Palaeozoic era. Glaciers have carved, and are still carving, some of the world's finest, most rugged scenery.

The melting snout of the Athabaska Glacier, *top,* in the Canadian Rockies is the source of the Athabaska river. The glacier has deposited a dam of moraine through which the river cuts its way.

Above, the glistening ridges of a moving glacier in Austria. During the summer, water from melting ice cuts deep runnels which flow into holes and tunnels. Streams also wash debris into crevasses.

Oceans and seas

Our planet is wrongly named Earth. Other planets are dry. But seven-tenths of the Earth's surface is in fact water. Today, Man is beginning to explore the oceans' 330 million cubic miles.

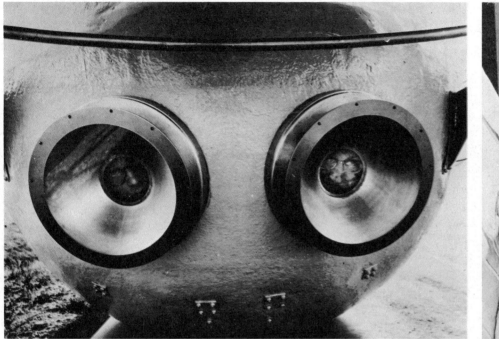

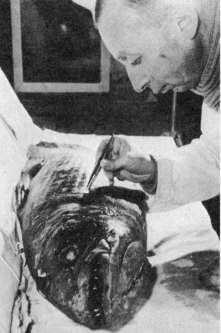

This strange vehicle with owl-like eyes, *left*, is *Deepstar*, one of the United States submersibles. Safely inside, scientists survey the dark, mysterious landscape of the ocean. Untold wealth in minerals exists there, but it will be a long time before we find methods of exploiting this. Through the development and use of such craft, it is known that life thought to be extinct for 50 million years still exists in the vast deeps of the ocean. *Right*, a professor of the French Natural History Museum is examining a marine monster, the coelacanth, the first of which was caught in 1938.

WE CALL the planet on which we live Earth, the same word that we use for dry land. In early times, this seemed a suitable name for the world. The Babylonians and the early Greeks thought of the Earth as a flat disc consisting largely of dry land, surrounded by water. They were totally unaware of the extent of the waters that bordered their known world. The great explorers of the past used the seas and oceans as highways. Their objective was to discover and open up new land areas.

Today our perspective is changing, and the oceans are being explored for their own sakes. Most land areas have been explored and their coastlines charted, and we now know that dry land covers less than 30 per cent of our planet. If we look at a globe, we can see that the continents are large islands in a vast area of water. The Earth is the only planet of the solar system with a large cover of water. Those planets nearer the sun are too hot to have oceans, those farther away are too cold. In fact, Ocean would be a more logical name for our planet than Earth.

Until recently, our knowledge of the oceans was confined to practical matters concerned with their surface and the problems faced by seamen and fishermen. There was no way of finding out much about the world that lies under the sea. But in recent years many scientists, aware of the problems caused by the rapid growth of the world's population, have come to the conclusion that Man's future on Earth may depend on his knowledge of the oceans and their potential resources of minerals, power and food. 'Aquaculture' may in time become as important as agriculture. In the past 15 years we have enormously expanded our knowledge of the oceans, and we are now in the middle of a new age of exploration: discovering what lies beneath the watery surface of seven-tenths of the globe.

Echoes from the deep

Some of the most surprising information to come to light has resulted from the mapping of the ocean floor. Before the First World War the ocean floor was generally thought to be a broad, flat plain. Up to that time, the only device used for measuring ocean depths was a weight attached to a line. This method was inaccurate, and only of real value in shallow coastal waters as a guide to shipping. Understandably, few measurements of deep ocean waters were attempted. The echo-sounder, which replaced the line and weight after the First World War transformed our knowledge of the landscape under the sea. This device measures the depth of the ocean by the time it takes for a sound to travel to the bottom and return to the form of an echo.

Continents are mostly bordered by a shallow sea covering a gently sloping ledge called the *continental shelf*, which is part of the continental crust. The width of the shelf varies and in some places, such as parts of Chile, it is non-existent. Off western Europe it covers a large area, and extends for about 200 miles west of Land's End. The continental shelf ends and the ocean really begins where the gradient suddenly becomes much steeper in the continental slope, which falls sharply to the ocean floor.

A dramatic feature of some continental slopes is that they are crossed in places by deep underwater valleys called submarine canyons. Scientists still differ in their views on the origins of these canyons. Some argue that they are submerged river valleys, formed when the level of the sea was much lower than it is today. Others claim that the canyons were formed by powerful underwater currents.

A much greater mystery surrounds the origin of ocean trenches, in the floor of the ocean proper. In these trenches the greatest depths of water have been measured. The maximum depth discovered so far is 36,198 feet below sea-level, in the Mariana Trench off Guam in the Pacific Ocean. Most of the ocean trenches lie at the base of the continental slope in the Pacific Ocean, near land or groups of islands, and not in the centre of the ocean, as might be expected. The trenches, many of which seem to have depths around 35,000 feet, also occur in regions of great volcanic and earthquake activity.

Right, a diagram of the ocean depths. The deepest descent, to over six miles, was made by two men in a bathyscaphe in 1960. Figures on the left denote pressure in terms of tons per square inch.

Study of these trenches may in fact yield information of great value concerning the forces which move the Earth's crust.

Although scientists have little information so far, many believe that the trenches are among the most unstable parts of the Earth's crust, and were formed by gigantic forces inside the Earth dragging the crust downwards. There is also some evidence that, when eventually the trenches are filled with sediment over millions of years, forces in the Earth push up the bottom of the trenches until the sediment rises above the ocean in a chain of new offshore islands.

Beyond the continental slope or the ocean trenches, scientists have discovered a great variety of underwater landscapes. There are indeed flat areas called *abyssal plains* but, apart from the Mid-Ocean ridges, there are hundreds of mountains called *seamounts,* most of which are of volcanic origin. Some of the underwater mountains are called *guyots.* These have flat tops, which suggests that they once rose above the surface of the ocean, their tops were planed off by wave action, and they were then totally submerged. Other features adding to the variety of the topography are great cracks in the sea floor, along which lie deep valleys.

Seven miles below

Our knowledge of the features of the ocean bed is based on information supplied by advanced instruments. Most of us cannot descend nearly seven miles to the bottom of the Mariana Trench to see what it is like, although this feat was accomplished by two Frenchmen in a bathyscaphe in 1960. Our awareness of the sea begins along the coast where we can watch the constant motion of waves breaking on the shore, and the rise and fall of tides.

The wind generates most waves and the effect of waves is therefore felt mainly near the surface. On the open sea, while the crests of the waves move, the water itself remains almost stationary. From a boat, we can watch a corked bottle rise and fall with the passing of waves, but the bottle remains in more or less the same position. Movements of water by waves only occurs in coastal areas where the water drags against the bottom. Many stories have been told about the size of waves, but most waves in the open sea are in fact less than 12 feet high – although

Parts of the ocean floor have been explored and mapped out. This is a section of the bottom of the Atlantic from the United States to Gibraltar. It was produced by American marine biologists.

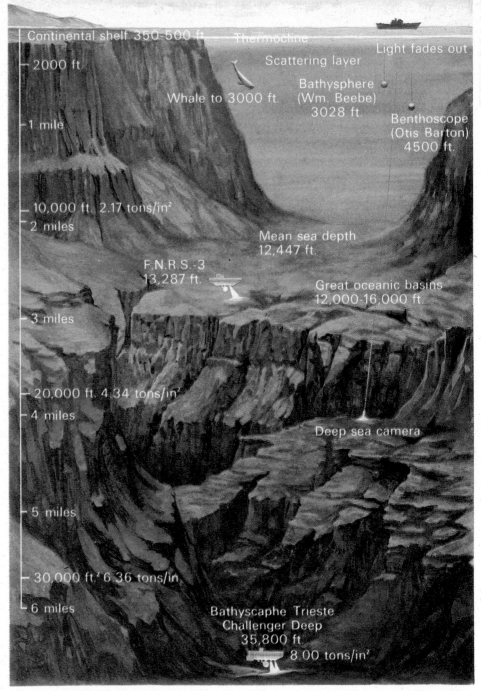

Continental shelf 350-500 ft.
2000 ft.
Whale to 3000 ft.
1 mile
10,000 ft. 2.17 tons/in²
2 miles
3 miles
F.N.R.S.-3 13,287 ft.
20,000 ft. 4.34 tons/in²
4 miles
5 miles
30,000 ft. 6.36 tons/in²
6 miles

Thermocline
Scattering layer
Light fades out
Bathysphere (Wm. Beebe) 3028 ft.
Benthoscope (Otis Barton) 4500 ft.
Mean sea depth 12,447 ft.
Great oceanic basins 12,000-16,000 ft.
Deep sea camera
Bathyscaphe Trieste Challenger Deep 35,800 ft. 8.00 tons/in²

in 1933, a watch-keeping officer of an American tanker measured a wave of 112 feet, the highest so far recorded.

During a storm, we can watch large waves pounding the shore, dislodging pebbles and rocks and sometimes smashing breakwaters. But the most destructive waves are not caused by winds. The *tsunami,* named after the Japanese word for a 'great wave', is usually generated by underwater earthquakes or volcanic eruptions. Tsunamis, often misleadingly called tidal waves, can inflict terrible destruction of life and property. The 1883 eruption of

Krakatoa, in what is now Indonesia, generated a tsunami which killed 36,000 people, and was recorded as far away as the coast of England. In the open sea, tsunamis are not high waves, but they travel at enormous speed. As they reach the coast, they lose their speed but increase their height and may break on the shore with terrifying force at heights of more than 20 feet. Most tsunamis occur in the Pacific, but the Atlantic is not free from them. In 1755, an earthquake in Lisbon generated a tsunami which destroyed the city.

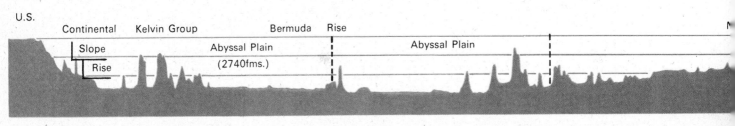

U.S.
Continental   Kelvin Group   Bermuda Rise
Slope   Abyssal Plain   Abyssal Plain
Rise   (2740fms.)

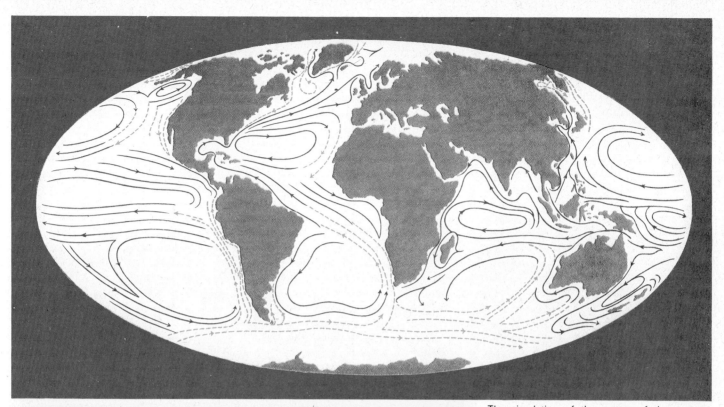

The circulation of the waters of the oceans, caused by currents, is of fundamental importance to Man. As the Earth swings round the sun it spins on its axis so that seas near the equator receive the direct rays of the sun and therefore more heat than polar seas. Water warmed in this way flows from the tropics to northern latitudes, thus moderating the climate. Water from the Poles, heavier because it is colder, flows northwards and southwards under the warm water to the equator. The Earth's rotation causes winds and currents to be deflected to the right in the northern hemisphere and to the left in the southern hemisphere. On the map, warm currents are shown in red and cold currents in blue.

Left, a whole world to be explored, an enchanting panorama under the sea. We now know that fish can live at depths where humans, even submarines, would be crushed by the pressure of the water.

Knowledge of tides and the currents associated with them has always been important to fishermen and people who live by the sea. The connection between the moon and the tides has been known since classical times, although it was not until the work of Sir Isaac Newton (1642–1727) that the forces causing tides were properly understood. The sun and moon exert a gravitational pull on the Earth and its waters. The pull is greatest when the Earth, the sun and the moon are in line. This is the time for the *spring tides* and the greatest tidal range. when the

high tides are at their highest and the low tides at their lowest. The *neap tides* occur when the sun and moon form a right angle with the Earth and their gravitational pull tends to be cancelled out, producing the lowest tidal range. Other factors complicate this simple pattern, including the variations in distance between the Earth, the sun and moon throughout the year.

Tides occur over the entire Earth, but their effect varies according to the shapes of the sea bed and of coastal land forms. In the open sea, the tidal range may be

only one or two feet, but at the coast it is much greater. For example, an average high tide at London Bridge is about 23 feet higher than low tide. The highest tidal range ever recorded, 70 feet, occurred at the Bay of Fundy in eastern Canada.

As we have seen, waves and tides are comparatively limited movements of the ocean's surface. The general circulation of the waters of the oceans is caused by ocean currents. These currents are of enormous importance to Man. Warm currents flowing northwards from the tropics moderate the climate of northern latitudes. Around Newfoundland, the warm Gulf Stream collides with the cold, iceberg-carrying Labrador Current. The icebergs, which are a danger to shipping, soon melt in the warm waters of the Gulf

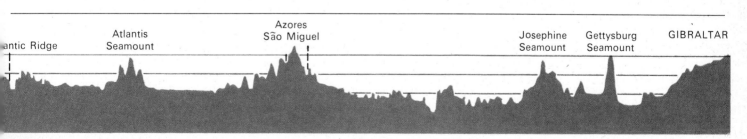

Stream. Vertical movements of water are also important. Many of the world's richest fishing grounds are in areas where water containing the chemicals needed by marine life wells up from lower levels.

How then does the water of the ocean circulate? The movement of currents is affected by the density of the water. Denser water tends to sink and less dense water rise to the surface. Around the equator, the water on the surface is heated by the sun. It becomes less dense and tends to flow northwards and southwards towards the Poles. In the polar regions, cold and therefore denser water flows southwards and northwards under the lighter warm water.

The *salinity*, or amount of salt in the water, also affects the density of sea-water. The average salinity of ocean water varies between 33 and 37 parts of salt per thousand parts of water, or, in the oceanographer's shorthand, 33 to 37 per thousand. Variations in salinity also produce current movements. In the Mediterranean, for example, the water generally has a high salinity because there is little rain and much evaporation. For this reason a dense current with a high salinity flows into the Atlantic across the Straits of Gibraltar. Above it, another less saline and therefore less dense current flows into the Mediterranean from the Atlantic.

A submarine current

The rotation of the Earth also affects ocean currents. In the northern hemisphere, currents are deflected to the right; in the southern hemisphere the deflection is to the left. The effect of this deflection is to set up a clockwise movement of water in the northern hemisphere and an anticlockwise movement of water in the southern hemisphere. The general circulation of water in the North Atlantic follows the same pattern as in the North Pacific. The currents in the South Pacific, South Atlantic and the Indian Ocean south of the equator are also similar.

The landscape of the ocean floor and the shapes of land masses have an important bearing on ocean currents. The Gulf Stream is the most celebrated of all currents affected by land masses. The origin of the Gulf Stream lies in the movement of the North Atlantic Equatorial Current towards the West Indies. Some of the water is deflected, but most of it flows into the Gulf of Mexico. Turning from land it veers north-east and is channelled between Cuba and Florida, where it bursts into the Atlantic Ocean.

Surface currents have been observed and charted for some time, but little is known about the movement of underwater currents and the waters of the deepest parts of the ocean. In 1951, a major eastward-flowing submarine current was discovered in the Pacific directly under the westward-flowing South Equatorial Current. During the International Geophysical Year, 1957–8, scientists discovered a large current flowing under the Gulf Stream and in the opposite direction.

The oceans are far more than moving masses of water. They are home to an

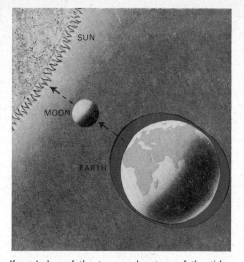 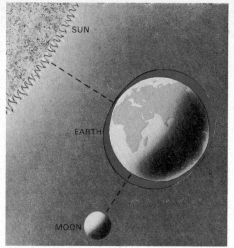

Knowledge of the type and nature of the tides has always been essential for those whose living depends on the sea. Spring tides, those with the highest range, occur when the Earth, the sun and the moon are in line, thus exerting a strong gravitational pull, *left.* Neap tides, those with the lowest range, happen when the sun and the moon are at right angles to the Earth, *right.*

enormous range of living things, both plant and animal. Oceanographers have established that few areas are without some form of marine life. Until recently, textbooks informed us that there was no life in the dark ocean deeps. Scientists based this belief on the fact that sunlight, the source of life, does not penetrate beyond about 1,000 feet and that the pressure in the deepest parts is immense, about seven tons per square inch in the ocean trenches. Recently, however, living forms have been found in the ocean trenches, and we have the eye-witness account of the men who made the record descent into the Mariana Trench that they saw fish 35,800 feet below the surface. Other intriguing discoveries have brought to light creatures that were thought to be extinct. Almost every marine expedition brings back evidence of strange and

previously unknown forms of life.

Most marine life, however, is to be found on or near the surface of the ocean and in the coastal waters that surround it. At this level live the small plankton, the *phytoplankton* (plants) and the *zooplankton* (tiny animals that feed on the phytoplankton). Many of the swimming creatures, even those as large as blue whales, live mainly on plankton. Other predatory creatures eat the animals that consume plankton. Hence the distribution of plankton is essential to marine life and therefore also to Man, who every year seeks a richer harvest from the sea.

The study of the teeming variety of life in the oceans is now of great importance in a world where the population is expanding rapidly. As the late President John Kennedy once observed, Man's survival may depend on knowledge of the oceans.

This havoc of wrecked cars and smashed buildings was caused by a tsunami. The most destructive of waves, they can move at incredible speed. Generated by underwater earthquakes or volcanic eruptions, they are not high waves when out on the open sea, but near the coast they lose their speed and gain in height, sometimes reaching 50 feet or more.

Water's way to the sea

Worshipped as gods, the centres of civilization, the bringers of life and death, rivers have shaped the history of the world. Unopposed, running water would reduce the whole Earth to sea level.

RAIN BEATS DOWN on mountain slopes and hillsides, sinking into the soil and bringing life to trees, shrubs and grass. Some raindrops seep into the earth, through layers of rock to dark underground caverns, while others soon reappear further down the hillside as springs. But some rainwater stays on the surface, collecting into tiny streamlets which merge into clear, glittering brooks, and finally into rivers flowing down to the sea or, sometimes, into inland lakes.

Underground sources

Until the seventeenth century, scholars doubted that *precipitation* (rain, snow, sleet and hail) could possibly account for all the water that fills the rivers of the world. They thought that great underground reservoirs constantly supplied water to rivers on the surface, maintaining their flow. But, in 1674, a French scientist, Pierre Perrault, calculated that, in the valley of the upper Seine, enough rain fell to account several times over for the volume of water in the rivers. Rivers do, of course, receive water from underground which surfaces in springs, and some rivers flow from the snouts of melting glaciers. But underground water and the ice of the glaciers are also derived originally from precipitation.

In the second half of the nineteenth century, geologists came to realize that, in all areas except deserts and frozen polar wastes, rivers were the main agents responsible for planing down great mountain chains, reducing them after millions of years to flat plains. They accepted that the thin ribbon of water flowing at the bottom of the Grand Canyon was the destructive agent which had carved out

Hindu pilgrims bathing in the holy river Ganges at Benares in India. Draining from the central Himalayas to the Bay of Bengal, the river brings water and alluvial soil to a vast fertile plain.

that spectacular valley. Even more important, they realized the tremendous power which rivers possess to transport eroded fragments of land downhill to the sea, where it piles up in deltas or in thick layers on the ocean floor which consolidate into new strata of sedimentary rock.

Against the vast background of Earth history, the American geomorphologist William Morris Davis advanced the theory of the cycle of erosion. He described how, in humid regions, rivers etch narrow valleys in a 'young', recently uplifted land mass, and how these valleys deepen and broaden until a 'mature' hilly landscape evolves. Eventually the steep slopes of the mature landscape are planed down until the area is reduced to a lowland where sluggish rivers wind slowly across the land, which is only a little above sea level. This final stage he called a *peneplain* (almost a plain).

Erosion is a slow process, scarcely noticeable in one man's lifetime. Geomorphologists estimate that, in the United

England's river Wye cut deep meanders when the slowly uplifting land increased the gradient and the flow of water. *Left,* the Wye wearing away the outer bend of a meander while dropping small pebbles on the inside, building shallows. *Right,* Mongolian sheep and camels search a dry river bed for grass in the Gobi Desert. Water flowing into the desert from Tibet is seasonal and ends in salt lakes or sinks into the sand.

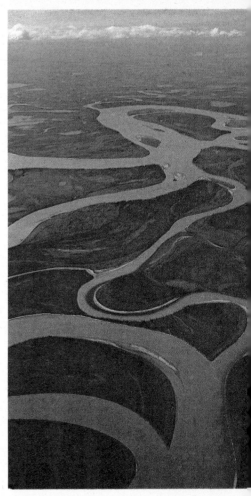

States, erosion wears away about one foot of land every 9,000 years. But the rate of erosion varies from place to place, depending on such factors as the height of the mountains or hills and the climate of a region. In the Irrawaddy-Chindwin basin of Burma, the estimated rate of erosion reaches about one foot in every 400 years, whereas in the Hudson Bay lowlands, it is as slow as one foot in 47,000 years.

Geologists have discovered that the average rate of erosion today, which is also about one foot of land every 9,000 years, is much faster than it has been throughout most of the history of the Earth. The speed of present-day erosion is probably explained by the greater area of the continents, by the pronounced relief of many areas – the result of recent mountain building – and also by greater climatic contrasts. Other factors probably include human interference with nature, such as bad farming which has led to soil erosion, scarring large parts of the surface of the Earth.

Eroded valleys

In a mature landscape most rivers flow through broad valleys with gently sloping sides. But the river itself cuts out only the central section of a valley. Most river valleys would be steep-sided gorges were it not for the action of weathering and other factors which constantly broaden the valley's profile. Except in extremely dry areas, rainwater is an important agent, washing soil down the valley slopes into the river. It also causes chemical weathering, by dissolving carbon dioxide from the atmosphere and other substances from the soil to become a weak acid. Rocks on the valley sides are shattered by another weathering process. When water fills crevices and freezes, it exerts an enormous bursting pressure, because the water expands by about nine per cent of its volume when it becomes ice.

Top left, Bangkok, the capital of Thailand, developed on the river Menam, once the only means of transport and communication. Now the city has roads as well as waterways, but the busy river life still continues. *Top centre,* the Shotover river, Otago, New Zealand, has scoured deep ravines through historic gold-mining country. *Top right* The American Falls of the Niagara complex flow over a very hard layer of limestone and are wearing away the softer layers underneath. From time to time great slabs of rock crash down into the river nearly 200 feet below, and the Falls recede about three feet a year towards Lake Erie. *Below right,* the river Yukon flows across Alaska to the Bering Sea, its many channels winding round low islands and sand bars. *Far right,* the Colorado river meanders through the Great Goosenecks of San Juan in Utah. Scouring away layers of rock, the water is brown with gravel.

The roots of trees and shrubs prise large boulders loose, and even earthworms and burrowing animals play their part in breaking down the soil, which eventually slides, or is swept by rain or wind, into the river.

The rivers carry the fragmented rocks and soil downstream. Some material is dissolved in the water, and fine material such as sand is carried along in suspension. Stones, pebbles and boulders slide or bounce along the river bed, borne along by the swirling currents. In fact, about 70 per cent of a river's load is usually made up of solid material, and the rest is dissolved.

The energy of a river depends on several factors, which include the velocity and volume of the water. When sudden floods increase both velocity and volume of a river, its carrying capacity is increased out of all recognition. In the Devonshire floods of 1952, nine inches of rain fell in 24 hours in the catchment area of the East and West Lyn rivers. The West Lyn burst its banks and a torrent roared through the town of Lynmouth, killing 23 people and making more than 1,000 homeless. After the floods subsided, the town was littered with thousands of tons of boulders, striking evidence of the power of a river in flood.

Geomorphologists have estimated the effect of velocity by measurements showing that a river flowing at 0·3 mile an hour can transport fine sand. Small stones are

smooth pebbles. Eddies whirl pebbles and stones in hollows in the river bed, cutting deep potholes. The downhill movement of the bed load and the constant grinding of rocks and pebbles cause the low, rumbling sound that characterizes many mountain streams.

The scenery associated with rivers varies greatly along its course. Just as W. M. Davis gave the human attributes of youth, maturity and old age to stages in the development of a landscape, so the same terms can be applied to the evolution of river valleys. The earliest stage is the *infant* stream which occupies a small gully and may only be filled with water after heavy rains or when snow melts. For the rest of the year, it is dry.

The *youthful* valley contains water most of the year, although the level fluctuates from season to season. The main feature of the youthful valley is its steep gradient. Flowing quickly downhill and armed with eroded debris, its river cuts deeper and deeper into the underlying rock, forming a sharply V-shaped valley. Its course is seldom straight because it generally follows lines of weakness in the rocks, and its bed is by no means smooth. It is frequently interrupted at points where it flows over resistant bedrock. Waterfalls and rapids which occur at such breaks in the river's profile are among the most attractive of river features, but they are not permanent.

Waterfalls in retreat

The Niagara Falls occur where the river draining Lake Erie flows over a tough, horizontal layer of limestone, which caps other layers of far less resistant rocks. The turbulent water which thunders over the limestone cliff constantly wears away the less resistant layers, undermining the limestone. From time to time, great slabs of limestone crash down into the swirling waters nearly 200 feet below. In this way, the waterfall is gradually receding at the average rate of about three feet a year.

If this process continues without interruption, the Falls will eventually be cut right back to Lake Erie, and the entire contents of the lake will pour out through the escape channel. But this will not happen for many thousands of years. Not all waterfalls recede: some rivers cut downwards through the resistant rocks at the heads of falls, reducing them to rapids, and ultimately eliminating the break in the gradient altogether.

The *mature* valley, the middle part of the river's course, has a smooth profile, a more gentle gradient and a broader valley. Down-cutting, the process associated with the youthful stream, is less pronounced, and *lateral* (sideways) erosion becomes important. A mature river follows a winding course with large *meanders* (bends). Erosion is most powerful on the outside of the meanders. On the inside of the bends, the river drops material, building up banks of shingle and sand. The lateral erosion constantly cuts back the sides of the valley, lining the valley floor with *bluffs* (low cliffs). The river also cuts its channels down as well as sideways, and eventually it occupies a trough-like

swept along the river bed when it reaches 6 miles an hour and, at 20 miles an hour, a river can move large boulders. If the velocity increases, the size of the material shifted downstream is greater. If the velocity decreases, when the stream enters a flat area or flows into a lake or the sea, the largest material is dropped first, and the finest material last. In this way, the river deposits are graded.

The stones and rocks rolled and pushed along the bed of the river give it the 'teeth' to cut downwards into the underlying rock. Running water has the power to dissolve some soluble rocks, such as limestone, but otherwise is has practically no erosive power unless it is armed with fragments. The currents swirl jagged rocks against each other until, by a process called *attrition,* they are worn to stone-littered valley floor.

The *old age* stage is usually identified when the flat valley floor is several times wider than the *meander belt* (the widest extent of the river's loops). The river flow is sluggish, except when the river is in flood, and much of its load is deposited along the flat valley. The old age river is usually dark and murky in appearance, because it carries so much fine material in suspension. In times of flood, the fine material is swept across the flood plain, covering the area with a thin veneer of sediment. The coarser material piles up along the edges of the river channel to form *levees* or natural banks.

Old age rivers often change their courses. Great loops are abandoned when the river cuts through the narrow neck of a meander. The deserted channel forms an *oxbow* lake, which soon silts up to become a swamp. Sometimes Man takes a hand in this process. The Mississippi River Commission has cut through the necks of many great meanders of the Mississippi river to straighten the river's course, and so reduce greatly the distance that river boats must travel. Many rivers have had their courses changed in this way over the centuries.

Old rivers made young

The development of most rivers does not, however, follow this simple progress from infancy to old age, because the cycle is often interrupted. A change of climate, bringing more rain, can increase the volume of water in river channels. A fall in sea level or the slow uplift of a land mass can steepen the gradient and therefore increase the velocity of rivers. Such changes rejuvenate rivers, giving them new power to cut deep valleys. The spectacular gorges of the upper Indus, the Brahmaputra and the Ganges, which in places are more than 15,000 feet deep, were caused by rejuvenation resulting from uplift of the land.

The great springtide bore, 15 feet high, roars like a wave up the Ch'ien Tang river at Hangchow in China. It is caused by normal tides reaching shallow water and meeting the river current.

River terraces (parts of former flood plains) border some river valleys and are evidence of rejuvenation. Successive stages of rejuvenation have been identified in the terraces which border the present valley of the river Thames in the London Basin. Rising some 50 to 100 feet above the present level of the Thames is the Taplow terrace, and 50 feet higher is the Boyn Hill terrace. Both terraces are the remnants of former flat flood plains occupied by the Thames, which was rejuvenated in stages, cutting out new valley bottoms at lower levels. Sometimes rejuvenation causes great meanders, associated with maturity or old age, to be cut deeply into

the surface. The impressive *incised* meanders of the lower course of the River Wye in Gwent are good examples.

As rivers flow towards the sea, they are joined by tributaries which create a pattern of drainage. Geographers call the rivers which flow directly downhill off a rising mass of land *consequent* rivers. Tributaries which join the consequent rivers at an oblique angle are called *insequent*. Geographers describe the resulting drainage pattern, with its many branches, as *dendritic,* from the Greek word *dendron,* meaning a tree. Dendritic drainage occurs when rivers are flowing over rocks of generally similar hardness, which therefore wear away at the same rate. But many tributaries make their courses along rock strata that offer less resistance, often joining the consequent rivers at right angles. Such tributaries are called *subsequent* rivers.

A drainage pattern characterized by right-angled river junctions is described as *trellised*. All river systems occupy basins surrounded by higher land called *divides* or *watersheds*. The divide separates one drainage basin from another, but some rivers back at their source, break through the divide, and capture the headwaters of other river systems.

Men and land animals need supplies of fresh water, and river valleys have therefore played an important part in evolution and in the development of civilizations. Some of the great early civilizations were based in river valleys. Men learned to control the waters of rivers, using them for irrigation and, as a result, developed the sciences of surveying and mathematics, and advanced social organization to a considerable degree.

Use and control

Rivers also play an important part in the economy of the world today. Most of the world's older cities were built on rivers for easy communication. Although river transport is now generally less important than it was, on such rivers as the Rhine it is still of major economic significance.

Today the power of rivers can be converted into cheap supplies of electricity, and recent industrial developments in many parts of the world have been constructed around hydro-electric plants. Rivers such as the Nile have many times caused great devastation and tragedy by sudden floods. But now much has been learned about flood control. Storage dams have been built to hold back flood water, which is released to irrigate the land during the dry season.

The channels of some parts of rivers have been greatly enlarged to lower the level of the rivers and to reduce their velocity. This method of flood control is expensive, because a river tends to silt up its enlarged channel. In a 12-mile-long section of the Thames which has been enlarged to prevent flooding in London, about 250,000 tons of sediment must be dredged out from the channel every year. But engineers are increasingly taming the waters of the world's chief rivers and utilizing these great natural resources to the advantage of Man.

In 1952 torrential rain drained into the West Lyn river, which broke its banks, changed course and roared through Lynmouth, Devon, causing great loss of life and devastation. When the river subsided the town was littered with thousands of tons of rock carried down by the floodwater.

Down to Earth

The soils beneath our feet are the product of decomposed rock and decayed plant and animal life. On the productive top few inches depends the vegetation and agriculture of the world.

SOIL CAN BE DESCRIBED quite simply as the stuff in which plants grow – a storehouse of water, heat and food and a support for plants' roots. Soil is also an incredibly complex substance which is studied by many different scientists – the geographer, the chemist, the agronomist, the biologist – and by its own scientist, the pedologist. The results of all their researches must be understood and made available to the users of the soil, the farmer, engineer and gardener. To an engineer, the soil can, or perhaps cannot, provide a stable basis for a road, a tall building or an airport runway.

In planning, enlightened nations pay close attention to areas of high soil fertility and conserve them by placing industry and housing on land of low agricultural productivity. Although the economic yield from urban use is much greater than the most intensive horticulture, land of good quality once built on is useless for crop production.

The great pioneer of soil science in Britain, Sir John Russell, in his book, *World of the Soil,* claimed that soil was among nature's greatest marvels. It contains mineral particles partly derived from some form of rock in times past, but many of the minutest particles, the clays, are of a most elaborate and complex composition. Far from being inert, they react with the films of water which surround them. The water contains high concentrations of dissolved material which is the living space for countless micro-organisms. By no means as solid as it appears, soil is about 40 per cent air space, partly or wholly filled by water. In this underground network of tubes and channels, pores and hollows, move countless forms of organisms and roots, preying on each other or deriving nutrients from the minerals and products of organic decay.

Changing, evolving soil

Soil is not static but is changing and evolving through the action of percolating water and organic action. In wet climates it is being constantly *leached,* or washed, and easily soluble substances are leached downwards. This paves the way for more resistant materials to be subjected to greater alteration and breakdown; much of the clay and colouring matter is then removed from the surface soil, which usually receives its dark colours from vegetable debris or crop residues, and its reserve of nutrients from the ashes of plants.

In the late nineteenth century, various Russian pedologists led the way in showing that soil was not just a mass of earth but that it was a surface formation with its own characteristics which changed both vertically down to the rock beneath and horizontally over the land surface.

Now rarely seen in England, a splendid pair of horses pull a traditional plough in Kent, *top.* Ploughed-in straw from a previous crop will decay and provide nutrients for future crops.

A worker in the hot, dry fields of Lanzarote in the Canary Islands, *above,* spades the *andept* soil. This highly productive grey-brown soil is formed of broken-down volcanic material.

For the vertical changes they coined a term which can be translated as *soil profile,* which means a sequential change downwards from the surface of distinct but interrelated soil horizons, which have a specific origin and mode of development. If one were to dig a pit at least three feet deep (an exercise not lightly undertaken as it might take all day) one would soon see such a profile, which will hardly ever be uniform in colour, structure or degrees of wetness from top to base. The uppermost soil – the *A horizons* – will be darker in colour, and show the most densely and uniformly distributed results of organogenic activity. Mineral material will be mixed with this organic matter and there will be many fine rootlets at this level.

Such a surface soil may be rich in wormcasts.

Gradually, or perhaps quite sharply, this surface soil gives way to one or several central *B horizons,* which are usually brighter coloured, may have much more clay, show well-developed structural forms, blocky or nut-like in shape and size. The number of roots, pore spaces and cracks may have decreased and in turn this part of the soil is obviously different from the soil at the base of the hole, which in pedological terms is called the *C horizon* but is often commonly called mineral soil or subsoil. Normally it is much more moist in temperate climates and very dry and calcareous in dry climates. Often it varies only very slightly from the rock beneath and shows little, if any, sign of modification by biological agents.

Tropical red soils

The agents of change, static or active, which are responsible for the formation of soil profiles vary in their effects, but the most important is rainfall. In relatively dry climates water supplied by rain or by irrigation is largely used by plants, and little drains to any depth. Therefore only the most easily dissolved substances, soluble salts, are leached away to the drainage water. Soils in such areas may have high reserves of plant nutrients near the surface which can only be used on irrigation.

Slightly more intensive leaching in a moister climate promotes a more advanced form of soil formation, corresponding to the brown soils of temperate areas, which are mainly devoid of lime. These soils have a quite appreciable clay formation in their *B horizons,* with potash-rich clays derived from the breakdown of rocks rich in mica. Such soils have stable structures, are well drained and readily respond to applications of commercial fertilizers. More intensive leaching breaks down nearly all the original mineral. Only the relatively resistant metallic oxides, quartz grains and rare earths are left in the soil, forming the typically red and deep soils of low fertility which are found in tropical areas.

The vast areas of tropical red soils are divisible into two major groups. The ferruginous tropical (ferritic) soils which receive up to 50 inches of rain a year, usually with a definite dry season, have a small reserve of weatherable minerals and therefore of plant nutrients. They are never very deep, up to 10 feet, and are not markedly sandy. Some have a high iron content or ironstone layers, called *laterite,* near the surface. Usually vulnerable to wind erosion in the dry season and to water erosion in the wet season, most ferritic soils are used for annual crops in the wet season by village subsistence economies. Possibilities of improvement include the use of fertilizers, the rotation of crops, the introduction of grasses and legumes, and measures against erosion.

In the perennially humid tropics, with rainfalls greater than 50 inches, are the *ferrallitic* soils. The most extensive soils of South America and Africa, they represent the ultimate stage of weathering and soil formation. Dominated by iron and aluminium oxides they may be termed *ultisols* and *oxisols.* These soils are very deep and have a complicated profile with a sandy surface layer, while lower down they are mottled red and yellow, looking rather like 'corned beef'. Usually thought of as clayey, these soils are *permeable,* porous, and well structured, for the dominant clay, *kaolinite,* is relatively inert. They are entirely devoid of rock fragments to a great depth; only quartz has survived the weathering processes. Such soils are of low agricultural value, the only nutrients coming from forest debris, which can be burned.

Local cultivators prefer the sandier surface soils which have a lower density of vegetation and are easier to till, but these are quickly exhausted. The more clayey soils, often related to clayey sediments or basic *igneous* rocks (molten rock from deep down in the Earth's crust which has solidified), are favoured for plantation crops of rubber, cocoa and other commercial crops such as the oil palm. Generally the growth potential of the climate exceeds that of the soil and remedies for the soil's deficiencies are urgently sought, especially for the rapid decline in organic matter caused by cultivation.

Mountain soils occupy about 16 per cent of the land surface of the world. Though usually shallow and stony, or peaty and perhaps eroded, they support valuable forests and indirectly conserve moisture and regulate the natural supply of water to reservoirs and lowlands. Many mountain areas, such as in Indonesia, Japan, New Zealand and East Africa, have extensive volcanic areas with *andosols,* highly productive dark grey-brown soils with a good reserve of nutrients in the unweathered minerals. Problems of erosion are great here and spectacular measures against erosion have been evolved in many areas.

The tundra lands of arctic latitude are found mainly in North America and cover about 18 per cent of the continent. Such soils have a permanently frozen subsoil and the surface is peaty, and, when thawed, often wet, sticky and unstable. Of little use for agriculture, the difficulties of road and house building are very great.

Fertile river valleys

In many river valleys and delta areas extensive tracts of *aquic soils* are found, which often support intensive agriculture and dense rural populations, especially in the sub-tropics, the lower Ganges, Canton and Mekong, as well as the lower Rhine, Po and the Hwang and Yangtze areas. In tropical areas year-round availability of water promotes continuous crop-growing, though the alluvial soil of these areas, derived by the erosion of much weathered soils, is inherently infertile. In temperate areas alluvial soils are generally rich in mineral nutrients, though micro-climates and the salinity of ground water impose many limitations on crops.

Together andosols and alluvial soils seem to support at least one third of the

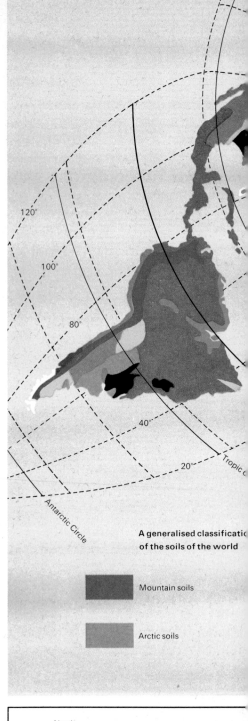

A generalised classification of the soils of the world

Mountain soils

Arctic soils

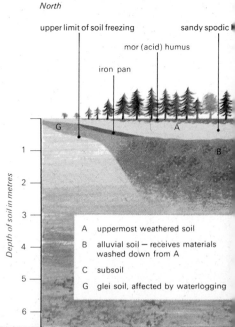

North

upper limit of soil freezing

sandy spodic

mor (acid) humus

iron pan

Depth of soil in metres

A uppermost weathered soil

B alluvial soil – receives materials washed down from A

C subsoil

G glei soil, affected by waterlogging

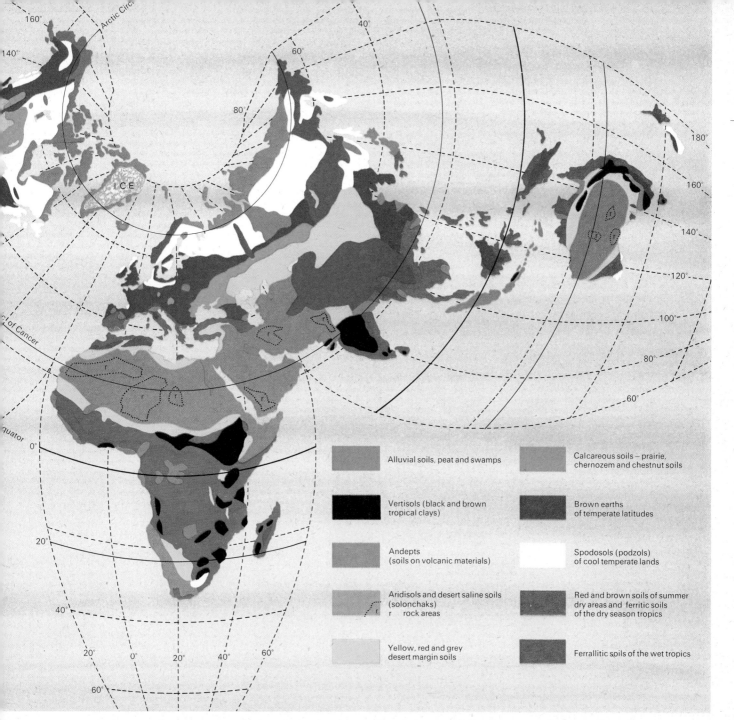

Alluvial soils, peat and swamps	Calcareous soils – prairie, chernozem and chestnut soils
Vertisols (black and brown tropical clays)	Brown earths of temperate latitudes
Andepts (soils on volcanic materials)	Spodosols (podzols) of cool temperate lands
Aridisols and desert saline soils (solonchaks) r rock areas	Red and brown soils of summer dry areas and ferritic soils of the dry season tropics
Yellow, red and grey desert margin soils	Ferrallitic soils of the wet tropics

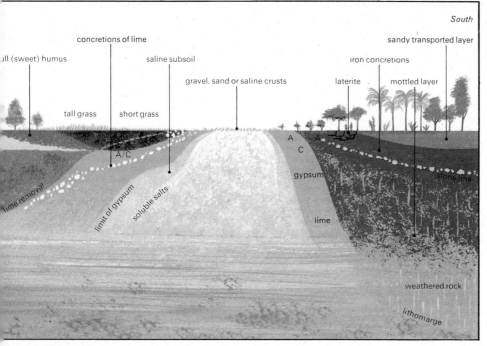

Soils of the World

This map shows that vast regions of the world have largely similar soils but the work involved in the survey and correlation is so great that very few maps of the soils of the various huge continents have, as yet, been compiled. Even in an area of only a few square miles, brown loams, reddish sands and dark, ill-drained soils may be found. Soils of badly drained or upland areas may also vary from the regional type. Nevertheless, the map of the soils of the world provides a very generalized, if provisional, reference.

Soil and Vegetation

This diagram represents the relationship of soil and vegetation, as affected by climate, from the Arctic tundra to the rain forests of equatorial latitudes, in the northern hemisphere. The growth of trees and grass is directly related to the amount of rainfall, the mean annual temperatures and amount of evaporation in the regions. Below the few inches of productive top soil, on which agriculture depends, the layers of soil are constantly changing through the action of water percolation and decay of plant and animal life.

world's population and much international effort is being devoted to the survey and study of these soils in many development schemes. Tropical alluvial plains form attractive regions for the future development of agriculture now that their great drawback of disease has been largely mitigated.

Soils of deserts, *sierozems, solonchak* (saline) soils and *aridisols* form one of the most extensive of the world's soil types, covering almost 20 per cent of the land surface, mainly almost half of Australia and over a third of Africa. What little rain falls is heavy, and rarely drains into the soil. Desert margin soils are based on wind-blown silt which is often reddish or slightly weathered in tropical areas. Such soils can support intensive pastoral farming, ground nut cultivation and intensive cropping with irrigation and the use of refuse, as in the closely settled zone around Kano and in the Gambia. There is danger of crop failure in dry years, of soil salinization or erosion, but soil and water conservation, and the introduction of grains and *legumes* (plants of the pulse family) have done much to safeguard the livelihood of these areas.

Though very limited in distribution, to about 3 per cent of Africa and 10 per cent of Australia, but also found in India and South America, one of the most interesting and promising forms of soil are the *vertisols*, the black and brown clays of sub-humid warm areas. Such soils, found in lowlands or on plateaux, are formed from basic igneous rocks or calcareous clays. They are rich in nutrients, potentially very fertile and, in lowlands, easy to irrigate. Unfortunately, they have very unusual physical properties. They have a high content of very reactive montmorillonite clays which swell on wetting and become very unstable. In contrast, on drying they harden and crack. It is almost impossible to maintain permanent roads, buildings or tree crops on them, or to use them for high-grade pastures. Formed in a climate very favourable to agriculture, most could be developed for grain, sugar cane, tobacco and cotton, but vast areas are still uncultivated or used for grazing low-grade stock.

Wheatlands of the world

The great wheatlands of the world are based on limy soils, rich with *humus* (decomposed organic matter of animal and vegetable origin) in sub-humid temperate climate areas – the steppes of Russia, the Prairies of central North America and in Argentina. Covering about 12 per cent of the world, they are the most extensively cultivated of all soils, with 65 per cent of their total area in Russia under the plough, perhaps more in North America. The soils grade from a dark brown *brunizem,* or Prairie soil in the most humid parts, through blackish *chernozem* into markedly lighter and calcareous chestnut soils in the semi-arid plains. In moister areas the soil is rich in humus and nitrogen, and earthworms completely mix all the soil materials. The subsoils may be paler owing to a high lime content. These wheatland soils have many desirable pro-

The sand dunes of the Sahara, *above,* considered typical of deserts, are, in fact, exceptional and cover only ten per cent of the area. The rest is bare rock, coarse gravel or a lime or saline duricrust. Desert soils, one of the most extensive of the world's soil types, occupy almost 20 per cent of the land surface. *Left,* a mud soil cracks as it dries in the hot sun.

perties for continuous cultivation; good aeration, stable structure and high nutrient reserve. The only measures needed to maintain them as productive systems are rational crop rotation, moderate additions of fertilizers and deep ploughing to promote water conservation after the spring thaw. Similar in productivity but different in origin and appearance are the brown earths of temperate areas, often cleared of deciduous woodland in historic times. These, too, support intensive cropping as long as cultivation techniques maintain soil structure, and fertilizers are added to replace nutrients removed by high yields.

Two forms of infertile soil are among the most widespread of the world's soils; the *spodosols* of cold temperate lands forming 10 per cent of the world surface, and the red and yellow ferritic and ferrallitic soils of hot humid tropical lands which take up 20 per cent of the world – the latter with 60 per cent of South America and 30 per cent of Africa as their realm. Although the

soils with *spodic* (sandy and ashen-looking) surface horizons are inherently infertile, various measures can be used to improve them: the addition of clay, marl (clay and calcium carbonate), organic manure, and the use of sprinkler irrigation.

In some regions, the relatively productive brown earths and *calcareous* (limy) soils of Europe and North America are largely used, but even then much of the plant mass is unused and wasted – straw, leaves and fine roots. In these and other areas there is much waste due to pests or inefficient marketing, but the greatest problem is the fuller use of the remoter areas; settlements and routes leading to and from many areas of the world are sparse, or local and selective, especially in the areas of *spodosols* (coniferous forests), *ferritic soils* (the savanna lands), and on the desert margins and drier steppe lands. The same is also true of many parts of the tropical forests. There is tremendous scope for the more rational use of the world's land. Only about ten per cent is cultivated.

Starvation and famine is most frequent in the most productive lands, in the alluvial lands and in the intensively tilled lands near to cities. If farming land can be extended to areas yet unused or underused, and if soils now in use can be persuaded to give higher yields, there is no reason to doubt that world production of food can match the needs and demands of a rising population.

Deserts at the world's dry heart

One-fifth of the Earth's surface is covered by dry, sparsely inhabited deserts. How did these areas develop, and what are the characteristics which distinguish them from the rest of the world?

FOR CENTURIES deserts have captured the imagination of Europeans. To the Greeks the fiery wilderness of Arabia and the Sahara marked the end of the inhabitable world and the beginning of the torrid lands where the heat was thought to be so intense that no man could survive. This illusion was gradually dispelled as knowledge of the great deserts of Africa and Asia increased, but the idea of the desert as a barren wilderness devoid of life persisted through the Middle Ages and into modern times. Only in the last few decades has there been a shift of attitude. Many people now look on deserts as lands of promise which offer vast untapped mineral resources, unlimited supplies of solar energy for desalination and other purposes, and fertile acres awaiting only water to yield ample harvests.

Both these mental pictures arise from a vague and overgeneralized view of desert land and life. Their landscapes are usually thought of as uniform and monotonous, but the world's deserts actually consist of a complex mosaic of different environments which offer varied habitats to plants, animals and Man. It is, in fact, difficult to define a 'desert' at all precisely. But we need a clear idea of what deserts really are before we can understand their distribution and natural characteristics.

What is a desert?

The word desert derives from the Latin *desertus* (abandoned), and its literal meaning is a deserted place or wasteland. Certainly large areas within the desert are uninhabited or only very sparsely populated, but if we were to define deserts by the number of people who live there we would have to include huge tracts of the tropical rain forests, the northern coniferous forests, the tundra and the polar regions which have populations of less than two per square mile. Although the overall population of deserts is small in comparison to the area, the people tend to be extremely unevenly distributed and very large settlements often cluster around sources of water.

The lack of vegetation is also sometimes regarded as a defining characteristic of deserts. But large areas of bare surfaces of rock, sand and silt occur all over the world from the poles to the equator, while some deserts support many different types of plant life.

A third problem of defining deserts is provided by climate. Most people think of deserts as hot, dry places, and the study of their climate enables us to measure just how hot and how dry they are, to classify them into different types and to select appropriate boundaries. Temperature and rainfall are the most significant climatic elements because together they

1 Sheep graze on the stony desert of Iraq where the summer temperatures rise to well over 100 °F. and frosts occur in winter.
2 A giant suguaro succulent cactus grows up to 50 feet high in the desert of Arizona. It has a large shallow root system which quickly soaks up rain water, and its fluted surface expands when it drinks and contracts as it dries.

set limits on plant growth, animal life and the possible occupation and exploitation of deserts by Man. Temperature alone is less significant than rainfall. Although the highest shade temperatures in the world have been recorded in deserts – for example, 136·4 °F. (58 °C.) at Azizia in Libya and 134 °F. (56·7 °C.) at Death Valley, California – extreme heat does not prevent plant growth if there is sufficient moisture available for the plant to *trans-*

pire (lose water vapour through leaves). Although intense heat does limit the possibilities of animal and human life, it has not prevented the occupation of the deserts by animals and Man. Many specialized natural and social adaptations have evolved; nocturnal and burrowing habits, special clothing and house designs allow animal and human populations to extend their occupation of deserts.

Deserts far inland away from the cooling influence of the sea have very cold nights and winters which check plant growth but do not prevent it altogether. It is *precipitation* (rain, snow, hail, fog and dew) which has the most direct control over all forms of desert life, since lack of water is much more critical to plant and animal life than heat or cold.

The amount of water available is governed by the relationship between supply by precipitation and dispersal, which is the combined result of evaporation, transpiration of plants, drainage into the soil and surface run-off in streams and rivers. The 'water balance' between supply and dispersal provides us with a theoretically satisfactory way of defining deserts or arid lands as those areas of 'water deficit'. But it is difficult to apply this theoretical definition because meteorological and hydrological records for most parts of the

world do not provide the necessary information.

Many geographers have tried to define and map the world's arid lands by using climate statistics. But the recognition of dry climates as a definite type was long delayed by the ancient Greek idea that the world was divided into latitudinal temperature zones which grew progressively hotter from the poles to the equator. Dry climates were not even recognized as such when Henri Berghaus published the first world precipitation map in 1845. It was not until 1900 that they were first given equivalent importance to the traditional temperature zones by Vladimir Köppen who devised a simple empirical formula which related average annual temperature to average annual and seasonal precipitation. Köppen proposed a major division of the dry climates into the hot, dry deserts and the cooler, moister steppes, and devised a special category of coastal deserts which had frequent fog.

Defined by climate

Then, in 1910, Albrecht Penck introduced evaporation into the definition of dry climates and came closer to an accurate definition of deserts: those areas bounded by a line along which evaporation equals precipitation. But the lack of evaporation measurements prevented the general application of Penck's scheme.

In recent decades many other climatologists have tried to define dry climates by relating precipitation to temperature and evaporation. The most successful attempt was made by the American climatologist C. Warren Thornthwaite when he proposed a world classification of climates in 1948, and in 1953 the part of the classification which dealt with dry climates was revised by Peveril Meigs for the UNESCO Advisory Committee on Arid Zone Research. The result was a world map which distinguished between arid and semi-arid

1 In Death Valley, California, where Bad Water reflects Telescope Peak, less than three inches of rain falls throughout the year.

2 A village clusters around an oasis in the dry Moroccan desert. Here wind-blown palms send their roots deep underground to the water table.

areas. It also introduced a new category of 'extremely arid', based on stations where no rain fell for 12 consecutive months and, for the first time, pin-pointed the world's most forbidding deserts.

The most striking feature of the map is the great extent and uneven distribution of the deserts. Dry climates occur over approximately one fifth of the world's land surface. They are most extensive and

extreme in the great Saharo-Arabian desert belt which stretches from the Atlantic coast of North Africa to the Persian Gulf and includes the waterless waste of the inner Sahara and the 'empty quarter' of southeastern Arabia. This belt is part of the 'dry heart' of the Old World which, briefly interrupted by the better-watered mountain ranges of southwest Asia, continues east across the arid lands

offshore which cause coastal fog and unusually large amounts of fish.

Although the world map shows no orderly pattern of dry climates, their distribution can be broadly explained by the general circulation of the atmosphere and the existence of coasts and mountain ranges. With the exception of the west-coast deserts – where there is little precipitation despite cloudy skies – the scanty rainfall and high evaporation of deserts is normally associated with clear skies and burning sun. These conditions are the result of high atmospheric pressure and stable air so that we can expect to find deserts where major high-pressure systems or anticyclones persist. This explains why there are no deserts in the atmospherically unstable equatorial zone, although *insolation* (radiant energy from the sun) is at a maximum there, and why they do occur over sea and land in the subtropical high-pressure belts of the northern and southern hemispheres. These high-pressure belts are caused by the subsidence of air which, having risen from the surface along the equatorial 'doldrum' zone, because of intense heating and convectional uplift and then cooling at high altitudes, descends and forms domes or cells of persistent high pressure. As the air descends it is warmed and able to hold water vapour so that there is little chance of rain falling, and the major latitudinal deserts result.

Circulating winds

The fact that the latitudinal arid zone is not continuous but is broken by areas of abundant rainfall, particularly over the eastern sides of the continents, is due to the cellular structure of the subtropical high-pressure belts. These persistent high-pressure cells tend to form over the oceans, and because of the deflective effect of the Earth's rotation (the Coriolis force) they circulate in a clockwise direction in the northern hemisphere and an anti-clockwise direction in the southern hemisphere. The subtropical highs of the northern and southern Pacific and the North and South Atlantic cause warm moisture-laden winds to blow off the open ocean across the east coasts of Asia, Australia and the Americas; whereas along the subtropical west coasts of North and South America and Africa the direction of circulation induces coast-parallel winds, which increase the general aridity. Over the Indian Ocean a high-pressure cell of equivalent intensity fails to develop because of the huge Asian land mass to the north. This creates its own monsoonal circulation which draws moisture-laden air in over much of the continent and brings summer rains to the subtropical west coasts of India and southeast Asia which otherwise would have dry climates.

The subtropical dry area is dependent on the Earth's general atmospheric circulation and is a major permanent feature in the pattern of world climate. Local land features, such as coasts and mountain ranges and cool water offshore, do, however, account for variations in the extent and intensity of dry climates.

The dryness of the west-coast deserts,

1 In central Turkey a road winds through the dry valleys where sparse vegetation and thin crops cling to the wind-blown soil.

2 Hundreds of cacti species grow in the Oaxaca Desert in Mexico. After a few drops of rain the desert becomes green.

of southern Russia to the Takla Makan desert sheltering in the barren Tarim basin and on across the Mongolian steppe and the Gobi desert into northern China. Nowhere else in the world do such intensely dry climates occur over such huge areas. Dry climates are also very extensive in Australia and in the southwestern quarters of North and South America and Africa where there is a distinctive type of

extremely dry west-coast desert.

These west-coast deserts, which include the Namib in southwest Africa, the Atacama in Peru and northern Chile, the fringes of the Sahara in Mauritania and Western Sahara, and the Sonoran Desert of northwest Mexico, are particularly interesting because they are affected by the winds which blow parallel to the coast and by cool currents and upwelling water

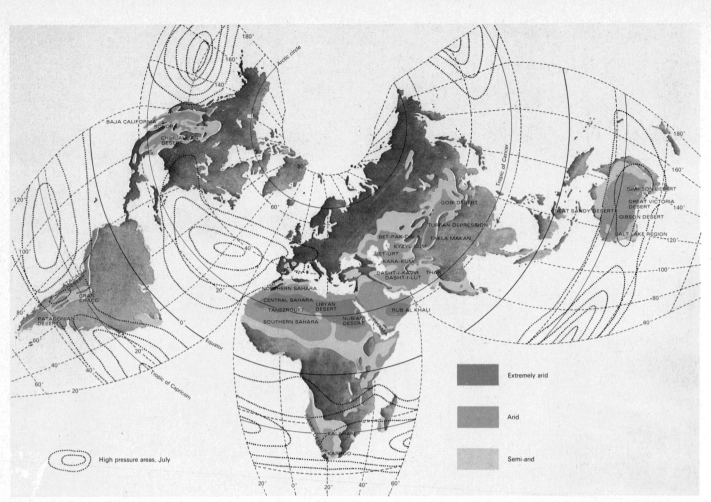

High pressure areas, July

Extremely arid

Arid

Semi-arid

for example, is related to the angle at which a coastline projects into the winds and currents which circulate around the eastern margins of the oceanic high-pressure cells. Where coastlines run parallel to these stream-lines, as they do in the Atacama, Namib and Mauritanian deserts, atmospheric stability is enhanced both by the tendency of winds and currents to diverge at the surface and by the temperature inversions which are caused by warm air being cooled as it flows over cold water offshore. In parts of all these deserts the average rainfall is below two inches a year. On the west coast of South America extreme aridity runs to within 5° of the equator because the Peruvian coast swings west along the lines of atmospheric and oceanic circulation as far as Cape Blanco.

By contrast, the subtropical west coast of North America constantly trends south-east away from the stream-lines and consequently, although the peninsula of Baja California has less than five inches of rainfall a year, arid conditions do not extend nearer the equator than 22 °N. Western Australia, too, is less arid than the other west-coast deserts because its coast is not influenced by the eastern margin of a circulating ocean high and because it lacks a cool current offshore.

Sheltered by mountains

In the interior of Asia and of North and South America dry climates reach polewards well beyond the subtropical high-pressure belts. Arid climates occur in Patagonia, the Great Basin of North America and the Russian deserts east of the Caspian Sea, and semi-arid conditions extend still further polewards to about

55 °N. in the Canadian prairies and the Siberian steppes.

These poleward extensions of dry climates are restricted to the interiors of the major continents and they all lie on the lee side of major mountain systems – the Andes, the Rockies and the Central Asian ranges – which block the westerly rain-bearing winds. The dryness of the 'rain-shadow' areas is accentuated, particularly in the Central Asian deserts, by their remoteness from the sea. These continental interior deserts suffer extreme heat and cold; in winter temperatures drop well below freezing and in summer they soar to over 100 °F. The annual range of temperature is even greater than in the subtropical deserts, and in spring and summer violent winds cause dust-storms so thick they blot out the sun and sometimes last several days.

Arid and semi-arid climates are so widely distributed about the Earth that they embrace an astonishing variety of landscapes. The popular metaphor of the desert as a sea of sand is drawn from limited European experience of the Arabian and North African deserts and even there the picture is misleading. Most of the Sahara consists of bare rock (hamada) and gravel-strewn (reg) surfaces; the sandy areas are restricted to occasional massive dunes (ergs) and to large flat plains. There is very little sand on the other deserts of the world where there is more plant life than the Saharan and Arabian deserts.

The North American deserts, where plants flourish even in the driest areas, are a striking contrast. Here the vegetation displays all the ways plants have adapted to their inhospitable home. Many

The map shows the world's main deserts and the areas of high air pressure which affect them. In the extremely arid regions no rain falls for over 12 consecutive months.

perennial trees and shrubs resist desiccation by storing water in succulent leaves and stems and growing small leaves, or even developing spines instead of leaves, to check transpiration. The cacti are the most spectacular examples of such adaptation. They are native to the Americas and many of the same adaptations have also been evolved by the remarkably similar but unrelated euphorbias of the African deserts.

Life and death after rain

As well as the true *xerophytes* (drought-resistant plants) there are many perennials which endure aridity by very extensive root systems. These desert *phreatophytes* usually grow along dry water-courses where their roots reach down, sometimes over 50 feet, to tap the sub-surface water-table. The drought-evading annual plants complete their life cycle after a sudden desert rainstorm. They grow in great variety and, following rain, bloom in a brief but brilliant mass of flowers. Then they set seed and die.

The size and diversity of the world's deserts defy generalization about their physical resources and potential use. But as world population is increasing much faster than available food supplies, there is a pressing need for more research into the economic possibilities of the dry fifth of the Earth's land surface on which, at present, only about five per cent of the world's population lives.

High and level living

Does a lost world survive on the high plateaux of South America? What secrets lie unexplored on Tibet's savage Chang Tang plains? Such are the mysteries of nature's tabletops.

MYSTERIOUS, REMOTE, Tibet has long intrigued the imagination of armchair travellers. But much of its mystery is based not on romance but the harsh facts of its place on the world map. Too high, too cold for trees, the icy expanse of the Chang Tang plateau, that immense and desolate region also called the Northern Plains, is among the grimmest of the world's plateaux. Only a short grass clings to life on these wide horizons. Mountains that ring the plateau give no protection against the cruel winds that sweep it in winter, for even the level land lies between 10,000 and 15,000 feet above the sea.

The earth, frozen hard most of the year, thaws to a swamp in the brief, almost rainless summer. Indeed, here, on a midsummer's day, only a moon-dweller might find some hint of home, for the intense heat of noon can plummet down some 80 degrees on the Fahrenheit scale after nightfall. And in winter, up to 72 degrees of frost have been known. This land of Tibet is the home of a population only a little larger than that of Birmingham, scattered thinly across an area, some five times greater than that of the United Kingdom. Moreover, most Tibetans keep to the sheltered valleys of the south and east. Very few venture to live in that two-thirds of the country taken up by the terrible plateau.

In thin air

Most high plateaux in northern and mid-latitudes are avoided as places for human settlement, although few are as bleak as Chang Tang. Plateaux are generally cold because, throughout the world, the mean temperature of the air falls by about 1 °F. for every 330 feet above sea level. Further, although the *insolation* (energy and heat received from the sun) is intense in the thin and pure air of the high plateaux, the heat radiated from the Earth's surface is not retained in the atmosphere, in the way that it is at sea level. This is why it can be unpleasantly hot at noon but frosty at night on high plateaux.

The thinness of the air at considerable heights above sea level causes other problems, because people from lowland areas are quickly tired by any physical exertion. At heights above 10,000 feet, some people find it difficult to breathe. Scientists have established that the local inhabitants of high plateaux or mountainous regions have larger lungs and hearts, and also more blood, than people who come from the lowlands. In other words, they are better adapted physically to live in the rarefied atmosphere.

Many of the world's highest and largest plateaux are, like Chang Tang, situated within folded mountain ranges. These mountain ramparts form a climatic barrier,

The bleak monotony of grass and scrub of the Pamir plateau on the China-Afghan-Kashmir border, *top,* is relieved by flowers during the short, dry summer. *Above,* a children's playground on the flat, salt shores of Great Salt Lake in Utah. Streams drain into this *intermontane basin,* from which there is no outlet, deposit sediment and build up the level plateau.

as well as a physical obstacle, to travellers. The winds that blow down the mountain slopes on to the plateaux are generally dry, because most of their moisture has fallen as rain or snow on the mountains. But plateaux are not always hostile environments for human life. In the tropics, the lowlands are often unbearably hot, and people choose the relatively cool plateaux as the best areas for settlement.

How do geographers define a plateau? Like many descriptive geographical terms, the word plateau has no precise meaning. Some geographers even avoid using it, preferring the term *high plains,* but this is not really a satisfactory alternative. Most authorities define plateaux as *tablelands* or generally level areas of elevated land, so as to distinguish them from mountains and hills, which are characterized by steep slopes, and plains, which are generally low-lying.

Some geographers argue that a definition of plateaux should include reference to the steep-sided river valleys which distinguish plateaux from low-lying plains, which have broad, shallow valleys. Providing that a plateau is well watered, rivers will eventually erase its plateau-like character. The so-called Appalachian plateau in the eastern United States is dissected by such deep river valleys that it has the character of a mountain range. The same process has occurred in the Massif Central of France, and the south China hill country.

High plateaux which lie between folded mountain ranges are more properly called *intermontane basins.* They include plateaux in the North and South American *cordilleras* (groups of mountain systems) as well as in Anatolia, Armenia, Iran and Tibet. Rivers that flow into intermontane basins often tend to deposit sediment eroded from

the mountains in deltas and flood plains, thus building up the level of the land. Gravel, silt and clay may cover existing land forms. Sometimes, as in the Great Basin of Nevada and in western Utah in the United States, intermontane basins may be regions of interior drainage (regions where water drains from the surrounding mountains into the basin and where the inflow is balanced by the loss due to evaporation). Other intermontane basins have outlets leading ultimately to the sea, but are covered by hundreds of lakes and marshes, both fresh and salt.

Some huge blocks of land have been uplifted to form plateaux which have a level surface because the rock strata have remained horizontal. Examples include the Table Mountain of South Africa and the Colorado Plateau of the southwestern United States. The Colorado Plateau is partly bounded by mountains, but in some places it descends in a series of steps called *escarpments*. Geologists estimate that, one or two million years ago, the Colorado Plateau was a flat low-lying plain, not much above sea level. Slowly, large parts of the plain were uplifted by more than 7,000 feet. The gradual increase in height speeded the rate of flow of the slow, meandering Colorado river and its tributaries, rejuvenated them, and gave them the erosive power of swift mountain streams. As the gradient increased, the rivers cut deeply into the plateau and carved out deep gorges in the sedimentary rock, including the Grand Canyon, which

South Africa's flat-topped Table Mountain, *left,* broods over Cape Town. Rainfall on the summit is heavy and southeast winds cause a thick cloud. Known as 'the table-cloth', it is forced down the northern face but never reaches the lower slopes.

is more than a mile deep in places.

From photographs of the canyon, we can see clearly that the layers of rock are not folded but almost horizontal, more or less as they were when they were formed as sediments under the sea. From the rims of the canyon, thousands of square miles of level plateau remain, relatively untouched by erosion in this arid area.

Theories and mysteries

How could such an enormous area be uplifted to such great heights? The convection current theory of mountain building suggests that currents may operate within the dense rock of the Earth's mantle to form geosynclines and folded mountains. But this theory does not seem to account for the uplifting of the Colorado Plateau, where there is no evidence of compression or the folding of the sedimentary rocks, which would result from such compression. Another theory advanced recently in the United States is based on the fact that substances in the Earth's crust change in form when subjected to great heat and pressure. For example, carbon is transformed into diamonds in such conditions. Dense rocks are changed into less dense forms by this process. In other words, the changes of

A butte of Navajo Tribal Park in Arizona, *right,* stands like a natural monument. Characteristic of this arid plateau region, buttes are produced when hard rock tops protect the underlying soft layers of strata from being eroded by water.

density in a mass of rock will increase its volume, and this increase in volume may cause vertical uplift. This process, called the *phase change* theory, may well explain how rocks have been uplifted without folding or any other deformity. But present theories concerning mountain building are based on little evidence, and the great forces within the Earth remain a mystery and a challenge to scientists.

Some smaller plateaux are formed by the uplifting of blocks of fairly level land between roughly parallel *fault lines* (fractures) in the Earth's crust. Such blocks are often called *horsts*. Examples of horsts include such areas in Europe as the Black Forest, the Harz Mountains, the Massif Central and the Vosges. These horsts were once worn down into low-lying plains but, during the Hercynian mountain-building period, which occurred at the end of the Carboniferous period, these blocks of rock were uplifted between fault lines, and other blocks, called *graben,* were downfaulted – that is, they sank between fault lines. For example, between the uplifted blocks of the Vosges and Black Forest is a graben which now forms the valley of the river Rhine.

The horsts of Europe vary a great deal in character, depending largely on the

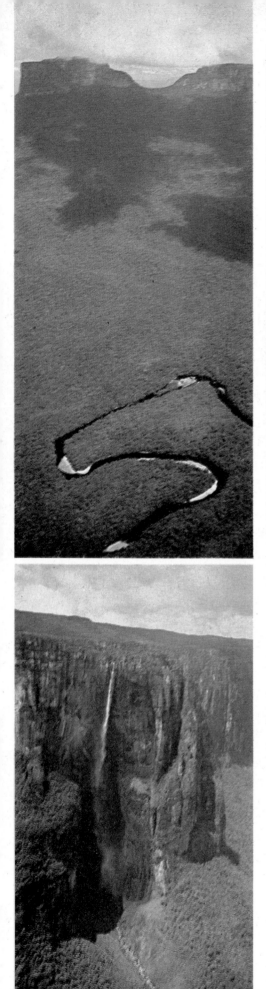

High inaccessible plateaux have inspired tales of lost tribes and huge monsters and snakes. The Gran Sabana in southeast Venezuela, *top left,* is the least known area of all South America. Believed to be the highest waterfall in the world, Angel Falls, *below left,* discovered in 1935, cascades over 3,000 feet from the Gran Sabana. The river Tarn in France, *above,* has cut a deep bed in the *horst,* or uplifted rock between fault lines, of the Massif Central.

height they attained after uplift. In areas such as the Massif Central, the uplift was considerable in the south, and the rejuvenated rivers occupy deep, narrow valleys. In the northern part of the Massif Central, the valleys are shallow and broad, because the uplift was not great. But although their plateau character is evident in places, most of the Hercynian horsts are dissected uplands. But, as is characteristic of many plateaux, they are largely infertile, and in consequence are thinly populated.

Levelled by lava

In such places as the centre of the Massif Central, the uplift was associated with lava flows and other volcanic activity and the highest point on the Massif is an old volcano, the Puy de Sancy. The lava has decomposed to form the most fertile soils of the Massif Central, but the main occupation on the horsts is animal raising. On a much larger scale, some major or continental blocks consist largely of a series of plateaux, which rise steeply from surrounding areas. Such major plateaux occur in Africa (especially in the east-central and southern parts), Antarctica, Arabia, parts of Australia, Greenland and Spain.

Volcanic activity also accounts for some extensive plateaux. Great outpourings of lava from hundreds of long fissures in the ground have built up such great plateaux as the Columbia Plateau in the northwestern United States, the Deccan plateau of India, parts of Ethiopia, and Antrim in Ireland. Lava flows can totally obliterate an existing landscape, blanketing a rugged hilly area until it is levelled into a high plain. In places on the Columbia Plateau, the lava is about a mile thick.

As we have already seen, the land features of the Earth are constantly changing. Even while great blocks of land are raised by tremendous Earth movements, rivers and other agents of erosion simultaneously wear them down. Sometimes remnants of the original plateau remain, forming small, flat-topped uplands. In dry regions, the main agent of erosion is the flood water from sudden storms. The water occasionally fills the network of canyons, sweeping away everything in its path. The canyons are deepened around relatively small isolated steep-sided plateaux. Where the rock strata are horizontal, these plateaux are called *mesas* (the Spanish word for tables). Mesas and *buttes* (small mesas) are striking features of dry plateaux that have been severely eroded. They are

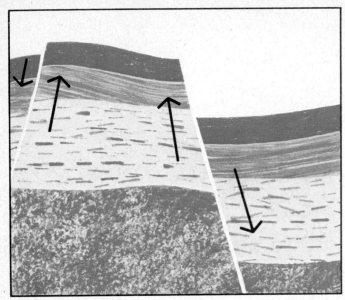

Left, the making of a plateau. This cross-section shows blocks of fairly level strata being uplifted between vertical fault lines in the Earth's crust, leaving *escarpments,* or steep cliffs, on either side. On the 'roof of the world', *right,* nomads struggle through icy snowstorms which constantly sweep the high, grim Tibetan plateau. Ringed by mountains, it covers two-thirds of the country.

common in the western United States.

Most people throughout the world live in low-lying sheltered areas and plains. Plateaux are generally drier and colder than the lowland areas, and, for this reason, are thinly populated. The chief economic activity is usually the breeding of cattle and other animals, and the few small settlements are confined to sheltered river valleys, or built around wells and springs. On the dry plateaux, crops are grown only in irrigated areas, which are usually limited in extent. Forestry may be important on plateaux that are neither too high nor too cold for tree growth. Manufacturing industries are not of great importance on most plateaux largely because of the sparse population and the inaccessibility of such areas, which causes high transport costs.

Ravines and rapids

The precipitous canyons on many plateaux are lined by a series of sheer cliffs and rocky slopes, and pose serious problems. Usually, at the bottom of the canyon is a deep ravine which must be bridged. Road construction is therefore expensive, and often unjustified in these generally unproductive areas. To cross the Grand Canyon, tourists must drive about 250 miles, although the canyon is only about 12 miles wide from rim to rim.

The rivers which flow in the deep canyons of dry plateaux, and also those which descend over the steep edge of a plateau, are usually unnavigable. The plateaux of Africa delayed interior exploration until the mid-nineteenth century. Waterfalls and rapids blocked the way of explorers who tried to sail inland along the rivers. Until the advent of air travel, the river and rail journey from the coast to Bogotá, the capital of Colombia in South America, took eight days – a distance of about 210 miles as the crow flies.

Many plateaux are therefore isolated

The Great Rift Valley, *right,* runs from the Jordan Valley to Malawi and was formed when level rock sank between fault lines.

regions, and the people who inhabit them are sometimes backward because they have no contact with outside, modernizing influences. Some historians argue that the remoteness of the plateau of Judea ensured the survival of the ancient Hebrew religion and language. The people of the more fertile lowlands, in contrast, modified and changed their beliefs as a result of their contact with other Middle Eastern peoples. Christianity survived in Ethiopia partly because the Moslems from Arabia and from the plains of the Horn of Africa found it difficult to penetrate the high Ethiopian plateau.

The disadvantages of life on plateaux count for far less in the tropics, where the high plateaux are the temperate zones. The coolness of the plateaux is far more comfortable than the hot, humid conditions of the lowlands. The coffee-growing plateau of Brazil is clearly a much better place for human settlement than the tropical forests of the Amazon lowlands.

Outside the tropics, most large cities are built at heights of less than 1,000 feet above sea level. Exceptions, including Madrid, generally have a severe climate. On the other hand, in the tropics a relatively high proportion of cities lie above 1,000 feet. The people of much of central

and southern America live in the highlands. The Andean plateaux were in fact the centre of a great civilization which had its capital at Cusco, which stood at about 11,000 feet above sea level. Ruins of the ancient Inca civilization are found at high altitudes in Ecuador, Peru and Bolivia.

During the age of European colonization, most settlers made their homes on plateaux where the temperate climate contrasted with the oppressive heat of the lowlands.

Tableland transport

In eastern Africa, British engineers constructed a railway from the coast into the Kenyan highlands in the 1890s. Nairobi, the capital of Kenya, was built at a height of more than 5,000 feet above sea level. The railway was essential to the development of the region because it provided the only transport for trade with the outside world. Transport facilities are in fact the key to the future development of tropical plateaux. Air services have recently helped to open up many remote areas, but real economic progress will depend largely on the extensive development of roads and railways, which can provide cheap transport services.

Mysteries of the savanna

Vast rolling plains of tall grasses, dotted with trees and shrubs, lie between the forests and deserts of the world. Geographers are still puzzling out the role played by fire, animals and Man in their creation.

YOU ARE STANDING in tall, waving grass, beneath a tropical sun. On all sides, the grass rolls on beyond the horizon, broken only by trees and shrubs. You could be in Africa, or South America; in the West Indies, India or Ceylon; in South East Asia or North Australia. For this is one type of *savanna*, a kind of countryside found across the globe. For geographers, it is a landscape of some mystery; a mystery of why savanna is there in the first place. Was it caused by natural fire, man-made fire, grazing wild animals, grazing domesticated animals or shifting cultivation? Geographers have not fully solved the problem yet, although they know that these factors as well as the climate, the soils, the rocks under the soils, water drainage, and the shape of the landscape all influence the vegetation.

The definition of savanna is also a problem. The word probably originated in the West Indies where, in the sixteenth century, it was used to describe 'land which is without trees, but with much grass, either tall or short'. Since then the term has been applied to tropical, subtropical and even temperate grasslands, with or without trees and shrubs. In 1956 an international meeting at Yangambi in the Congo cleared up the confusion by deciding to use the term savanna to describe tropical vegetation in which perennial grasses with flat leaves grow at least 80 cm high forming a more or less continuous ground layer. This distinguishes between savanna and the other grasslands which have a more open grass cover, usually less than 80 cm high, and with many more annual plants.

Tall grasses and short trees

Within this definition, there are many types of savanna and they can be classified according to the vegetation, especially the height and density of the woody vegetation and the height of the grasses. Woodland savanna has trees and shrubs which make a light canopy; tree savanna has scattered trees and shrubs; and some areas are covered by shrub or grass savanna. The dominant type of woody vegetation, such as pine or palm savanna, or the Latin names of the dominant trees, such as *Combretum* or *Acacia* savannas in East Africa, give a more accurate description of the woodland and tree savannas.

In some countries the savannas have been given a variety of local names, such as the *llanos* of Venezuela, which are huge, almost flat plains of tall rank grass, once roamed by herds of half-wild cattle. In Brazil the savannas, which lie about 2,000 feet above sea-level, are called the *cerradão*, *campo cerrado*, *campo sujo* and *campo limpo* and are divided by deep river valleys into separate uplands.

In the tropics, the savannas usually lie

1 In Zaire, on the higher land surrounding the tropical rain forests of the Zaire River Basin are large expanses of savanna, with a vegetation of grass, shrubs and low trees.

2 New shoots will soon spring up through the fire-blackened grass of a savanna in Uganda. Trees with tough barks and protected roots, such as palms, survive the frequent fires.

1

1 In the drier savannas of Uganda, only grass, a few trees and thorny acacias can survive the long dry season.

2 Many of the herds of wild deer, antelope and other game, which once roamed the savanna of Kenya, are now restricted and their migratory routes cut off. Large numbers are limited to reserves, like this zebra in Nairobi National Park.

between the tropical rain forest and the drier steppe and desert areas. An irregular rainfall, a long severe dry season, dry soils and dry air limit the potential spread of the forests. In regions of very low annual rainfall and very long dry seasons, the luxuriance of the savanna also changes. At one extreme grasses grow 10 to 12 feet high, whereas in the drier areas there is often only a scatter of low thorny trees in short grass.

Although climate lays down a framework, a mosaic of savanna types may be generally related to the varied relief, drainage and soils. In particular, the proportion of grass to woody vegetation is often influenced by the properties of the soil. In relatively moist areas, for example, alternating waterlogging and drought conditions seem to impede tree growth. The extensive level of plateau surfaces of Brazil and Rhodesia support only a grassy savanna where ancient, infertile soils are poorly drained. In the same climatic regions, on the steeper slopes with good soils and drainage, the savanna has more trees. Similarly, in moist areas of undulating landscape, the seasonally waterlogged valley soils only support grassland. But in the valleys where termite

2

70

ants build mounds, the more fertile and better aerated soils above the level of waterlogging often support dense thickets and tall trees. These islands of woody vegetation are a striking feature of the valleys, and stand out as large dots on aerial photographs, while the shrub savanna and savanna woodland approximately reflect the lower and upper valley slopes and ridges.

Fire and soil

The depth and texture of the soils may also affect the distribution of types of savanna. Shallow *lateritic* (rich in iron or aluminium) soils often prevent or reduce tree growth, and clay soils are also unfavourable to tree growth in the drier savannas. This has been shown in the Sudan where moisture-loving acacia trees extend further into dry areas on the sandy soils. The resistance of the vegetation to fire is often partly dependent on the soils; very open vegetation on nutrient-deficient or shallow soils may provide a natural point of entry for fires caused by lightning.

The influence of fire is one of the most controversial problems in the origin of savanna vegetation. Apart from its occasional natural occurrence from lightning,

it was one of Man's earliest tools, for hunting game and gathering honey. In Africa it has probably been used for some 50,000 years. With the introduction of cultivation and iron-smelting, fire must have been used more intensively and regularly for vegetation clearance, and since the domestication of animals, fire has undoubtedly been frequently used over large areas.

Pastoral farmers burn the vegetation to prevent bush encroachment and to obtain an early flush of grass growth in the dry season. Fires vary enormously in their intensity and extent, and under-populated regions may remain untouched by fire for variable lengths of time, while other areas are burned up to three times a year. But, even occasional fires can have very long-lasting effect on the vegetation, and it is probable that frequent fires also impoverish the soils. Burning reduces the amount of leaf litter and plant and animal remains which decompose to produce soil humus. The ash may add nutrients to the soil, but large amounts of nitrogen, carbon and sulphur are lost to the atmosphere in smoke. The loss of humus may reduce the soil's ability to hold water and nutrients, and nutrients may be also lost by water

drainage. The opening up of the vegetation by fire changes the *micro-climate* (local climate caused by variations of landscape) and exposes the soil to more sunlight and evaporation. The structure of the topsoil and the number of microorganisms within it may also be affected by the heat of a fire. But the extent to which the possible long-term soil impoverishment affects the savanna vegetation is unknown.

Frequent and prolonged use of fire seems to have three direct effects on the vegetation, influencing its structure, composition and pattern. The structure is altered by fires which prevent seedlings from establishing themselves, causing a more open vegetation. When the growing buds of trees are damaged, the trees are dwarfed and stunted. Many savanna trees survive because of their protective, often corky bark, and their ability to produce new shoots from dormant buds beneath the bark or below ground. But, this often leads to bushy, gnarled and contorted growth, and simpler structure of tree and shrub layers.

The composition of vegetation is also affected by a process of 'fire selection' over a long period of time, as only fire-tolerant plants can survive over wide areas. The savanna vegetation shows many apparent adaptations to fire survival. Sucker-forming trees and shrubs and tussocky perennial grasses produce new shoots from buds well protected from the heat of fires, and many savanna herbs have underground food-storage organs. One widespread grass weed, *Imperata cylindrice,* produces many more seeds if it is burned, and some grass seeds germinate better in heat equivalent to that of a fire. Such attributes may help them to compete with other plants when fires are relatively frequent, but if fires were eliminated, other plants sensitive to fire might well invade, and even dominate, savanna areas.

Changing boundaries

There are many clues to indicate that much of the present forest-savanna boundary is artificial. It is often abrupt and apparently unrelated to any physical environmental change; isolated trees surrounded by grass savanna suggest that the forest will spread if left undisturbed by Man. Rapid advances and retreats related to land-use within a man's lifetime have occurred in some areas. The type of savanna vegetation may give a clue to the possibility of being degraded forest if the plants present are typical of forest clearings and include many of the weeds of cultivation or even some planted trees or shrubs. Reports from early explorers, missionaries and government officers have helped to trace the former wider extent of forest in some areas.

But the problem remains of assessing the probable potential limit of forest, in the present climatic conditions, and in the absence of Man. In many areas intensive cultivation over long periods of time may have altered the micro-climate and reduced soil fertility, removed any nearby source of forest seeds, and encouraged the spread of more fire- and drought-resistant

1 Huge herds of cattle graze the unfenced grass and woodland *llanos* or savanna which lies between the forests of Venezuela. The alluvial plain, with outcrops of granite and watered by the Orinoco river, is very dry for four months of the year and flooded from June to October.

2 The curious mound, beside a *Mauritia* palm, is one of many which dot the savanna of Venezuela. They are built by termites and help to aerate the soil of waterlogged areas.
3 The *Gloriosa* climbing lily is one of the many flowers of the savanna in Uganda.

savanna plants. In such cases there may be no signs of forest relics left, and only fire-protection experiments suggest that the area was once covered by forest.

In a moist savanna area of Southern Nigeria, a fire-protection experiment was begun in 1929. The results showed remarkable changes in the vegetation. The experiment involved three plots: one was severely burned late every dry season, the next was only lightly burned at the beginning of the dry season, and the third was completely protected from fire. After 28 years the severely burned plot remained as typical savanna vegetation with gnarled, stunted savanna trees and a good ground cover of grasses. The lightly burned plot gradually developed two clumps of closed woodland where savanna grasses disappeared and some fire-sensitive plants invaded. In the protected plot the number of savanna species was reduced by more than half, the remainder grew taller and straighter, there was a definite increase in forest species and practically no grass.

This experiment illustrates the importance of fire as an agent in the replacement of mixed deciduous forest or woodland by moist savanna vegetation. In such cases the vegetation is called 'derived' or 'secondary' savanna. In drier areas, however, fire protection has produced fewer striking changes: grass is not eliminated, and the present savanna seems to be only a modification of what would be, even without Man's influence, a fairly open vegetation.

Penalties of overgrazing

This does not imply, however, that the drier savannas are little altered by Man. Although fire may be less important here, grazing has often been more important. Where the amount and distribution of rainfall is very irregular, cultivation is hazardous and the main livelihood of the people is their livestock. Where the quantity of animals, rather than their quality, was a sign of wealth, these areas have often been overstocked and overgrazed. The pasture has decreased in density and

A leopard stalks through the grasses of the Serengeti National Park in Tanzania. Here in the Ngorongoro Crater exists one of the most perfect examples of savanna wild life left in Africa.

the number of weeds increased. In some areas the bush has encroached and in others the soil has been eroded. In both cases the attractiveness and usefulness of the savanna is almost irretrievably lost.

In the moister savanna there is a tendency to introduce more cattle into many areas. This is being made possible by better management of the grasses and disease and pest control, especially the tsetse fly which has been, and still is, a scourge of vast savanna areas. In East Africa, the tsetse, the carrier of sleeping sickness, is sometimes eliminated by destroying most of the game whose blood provides a food supply for the fly. In this way, the large range of plant-eating animals is now being replaced by domestic animals. Because these animals have to be protected in *kraals* (African enclosure for animals) at night from predators, and to

Giraffe on the move in a game reserve in Uganda. Though protected by law from game hunters, they have to share the savanna with an increasing human and domestic animal population.

be relatively near water, they graze a smaller area more intensively than the game but eat a smaller range of plants. This leads to further vegetation changes.

Early explorers in Africa frequently reported on the huge herds of antelope, zebra, deer and other game roaming the savanna, but today many are being restricted to reserves and parks as a result of hunting, increased human population and changing land-use. This concentrates large numbers of game in small areas, as their former migratory routes are cut off and, under protection, their herds increase. In some places they have seriously overgrazed their natural habitat.

Even more striking is the effect of excessive numbers of elephants in the nearby savanna, where they have ripped the bark off trees which are consequently killed by fire. In East Africa, in about 30 years, several hundred acres of woodland and savanna woodland have been reduced to open grass savanna, and only a few dead tree trunks testify to the rapid change. Hippopotami have also caused erosion and destruction of grassland, and both animals are now being cropped annually to restore numbers to an equilibrium and to attempt to conserve the remaining savanna.

In his efforts to utilize his environment more fully, Man has often modified the vegetation and soils, although the extent and nature of these changes is sometimes difficult to assess. The vast savanna areas of the tropics are a classic example of this problem. Man has undoubtedly reduced the forested areas, increasing the extent of savanna both inadvertently and on purpose. He has also extensively modified savanna vegetation, even in recent historical times, and his aim now must be to conserve the present vegetation and prevent further degeneration. To ensure this, much more information and research into the environment and the growth, development and distribution of plants is needed.

When the Earth stood still

A flat disc in Babylon, Rome and Medieval Europe, a globe in Greece and Egypt – the small world pieced together by the early map makers was thought to be at the centre of the Universe.

THE OLDEST SURVIVING map is inscribed on clay and dates from the third millennium BC. It was found by archaeologists while excavating the ancient city of Gar-Sur, some 200 miles north of the site of Babylon. It shows the position of a large estate situated in a river valley – probably the Tigris – set between two ranges of hills. The directions east, north and west are clearly marked but no scale is given.

It is significant that the earliest known maps are on baked-clay tablets, a particularly durable substance. Maps wore out, were discarded or lost in flood or fire. Some were destroyed to prevent them falling into the hands of enemies; others were suppressed because they contradicted the official teachings of the Church.

Early maps reflect the social and philosophical climate of the times. Those of the earliest civilizations are simple and severely practical. Those of the Greeks showed the influence of a society where ideas were freely canvassed and developed. Those of the Romans were again limited to practical use and then, in Europe's Dark Ages, when men lived in a small world surrounded by mystery, we find maps locating Heaven and Hell, and showing fabulous beasts and monsters. It is not until the Renaissance is in sight that we again find the free-thinking mind portrayed in the cartography of the day.

Maps of clay and papyrus

The ancient civilizations needed route maps for their armies and merchants, and *cadastral* maps, plans of plots of land, for taxation purposes. In the Middle East, archaeologists have discovered a number of Babylonian maps and plans inscribed on clay tablets covering areas ranging from estates and towns to the whole of Babylonia. On one tablet, dating from the sixth century BC, is an ancient view of the Earth portraying the known world, centred on Babylon, as a disc surrounded by the legendary river, Oceanus. But the Babylonians' main contribution to the science of map making or cartography lay in their study of the movements of heavenly bodies and their method of dividing a circle into 360 degrees, the system still used today. It is probable that the astronomer-priests of Babylon knew as early as the third millennium BC that the Earth is round, for a work on astrology prepared *c.* 2870 BC for Sargon of Akkad included a long list of forecast eclipses of the moon.

Even less survives from ancient Egypt because Egyptian cartographers and surveyors invariably used papyrus. which is far less durable than clay. The oldest known papyrus map dates from *c.* 1300 BC and plots roads to a gold-mining area in the eastern desert. But there is plenty of evidence that mapping, particularly the

Ptolemy (Claudius Ptolemaus), most influential of ancient geographers. His *geocentric* theory of the Universe – the theory that the sun, moon and stars revolve around a stationary Earth – was unchallenged for over a thousand years. Little is known about his life, but his astronomical observations prove he worked between AD 127 and 145.

To be of use, maps had to be portable, and this meant that they were made of inherently perishable materials, such as the bark used by American Indians, the sealskins of the Eskimoes, the palmfibre, coconut-fibre and seashell compositions of the Marshall Islanders in the Pacific. Made of clay, the Babylonian world map, *above,* is one of the few survivors of early times. It is probably over 4000 years old.

drawing of cadastral plans, was highly developed. The Egyptians were the first to calculate areas by dividing odd-shaped parcels of land into triangles pegged out on the ground – a method called *triangulation,* still used by surveyors today. Ancient rock carvings show land being measured out with a knotted cord, prototype of the surveyor's chain.

In the East, there is evidence that maps were made in China some 2,200 years ago, but none made before the twelfth century have been found.

At the centre of the Universe

The Ancient Greeks laid the foundations of modern cartography, and their work, culminating in that of Claudius Ptolemy in the second century AD, remained the most advanced form of map making until the fifteenth century. The early Greek philosophers, like the Babylonians, at first believed that the Earth was a flat disc surrounded by water, and their maps portrayed only small areas, but by the fifth century BC they knew of the region stretching from the Atlantic Ocean to the river Indus. Their knowledge of areas to the north and south of the Mediterranean was far more limited and they were content to think of the inhabited world, *oikoumene,* as oblong in shape.

Early in the fourth century, however, Greek philosophers formulated the theory that the Earth was a sphere. They did this on religious and philosophical grounds and not for any scientific reasons. But, as often happens in the history of mankind, the truth was arrived at by the wrong route. Aristotle taught that the Earth is a stationary globe poised at the centre of the Universe. In 370 BC, Eudoxus of Cnidus tried to calculate the length of the Earth's circumference by measuring the difference in height of a star from two places. But his result was 60 per cent in excess of today's figure.

Eratosthenes (276–194 BC), who taught at Alexandria, chief seat of learning in the Empire of Alexander the Great, was the first man to measure the size of the Earth with any success. He noticed that on 21 June each year, the sun was visible in the water of a deep well at Syene, near modern Aswan, and therefore directly overhead. Assuming that Alexandria was directly north of Syene, that both lay on the same meridian, he took the distance between them. He then measured the angle of the sun at Alexandria and found it to be one-fiftieth of a circle (about 7 degrees). From this he computed the length of a meridian to be 50 times the distance between Alexandria and Syene. Although his measurements and assumptions were inaccurate, for he assumed the Earth to be a perfect sphere (in fact, it is flattened at the poles and bulges slightly at the equator), his errors cancelled each other out. The final result, according to some authorities, came to within 50 miles of today's figure. About a hundred years later, another figure for the circumference of the Earth was worked out from star observations, but it turned out to be one-quarter too small. Unfortunately it was this inaccurate figure that was used by later cartographers including Ptolemy.

As a result, in the fifteenth century Christopher Columbus mistook America for Asia – he accepted the wrong figure and believed that the Earth was much smaller than it is. Hipparchus in the mid-second century BC, undoubtedly one of the greatest Greek astronomers, developed Eratosthenes's ideas on map making. He stressed the need to fix the latitudes and longitudes of a sufficient number of places by astronomical means before attempting to compile a map, and suggested that the framework of meridians and parallels should be regular and evenly spaced.

About the turn of the first century A D, Marinus of Tyre developed a number of earlier ideas about map projections – ways of portraying the curved earth on a flat surface, showing meridians and parallels as straight lines and ignoring the convergence of meridians towards the poles. None of his writings have survived, but it was his maps that Ptolemy was asked to revise in his *Geographia*.

Ptolemy takes stock

Little is known of the life of Ptolemy, this brilliant Greek astronomer and mathematician of the second century AD. He lived and worked in Alexandria, and had access to the great library and museum there. He wrote several important works, of which the greatest are undoubtedly the *Almagest* and the *Geographia* (also called the *Cosmographia*). The *Almagest* contains his astronomical observations and theories, which were not surpassed until Newton's discoveries in the seventeenth century. The *Geographia* gives an account of the principles of map making, with descriptions of map projections, how to draw a world map, and how to divide it into smaller maps. It also contains a series of maps, but recent scholars have wondered whether they were in fact drawn by Ptolemy, or by later scholars who followed the principles and information in his writings. Ptolemy derived much of his information from the library in Alexandria, but supplemented it with information from sailors and merchants.

By modern standards Ptolemy's maps are inaccurate. His biggest source of error was his under-estimation of the size of the Earth. As a result, he thought that Europe and Asia covered from west to east about half of the northern hemisphere – 180 degrees. In reality, this great land mass covers 130 degrees. He also failed to depict India as a peninsula, greatly overestimated the size of Ceylon, and showed the Indian Ocean as an enclosed sea. But despite its shortcomings, the *Geographia* represents a monumental achievement, the peak of Greek cartographical science. It was a great misfortune to scholars in

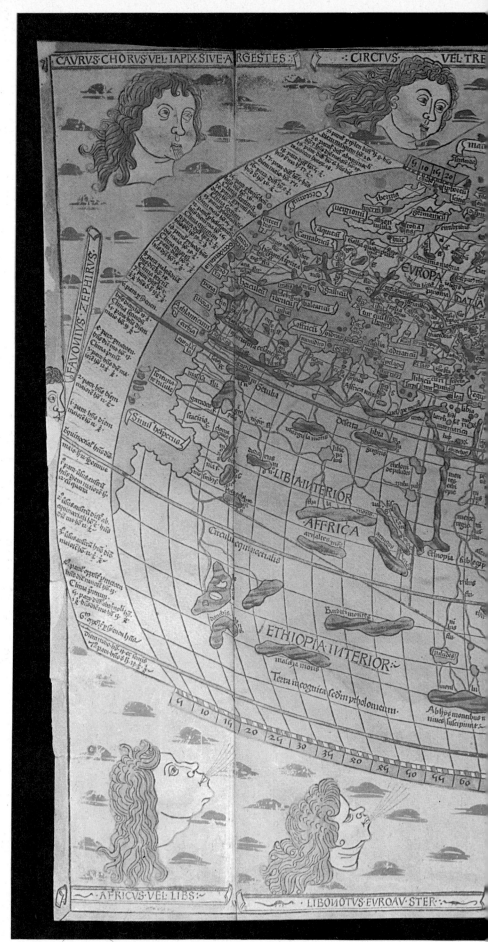

Sixteenth-century version of a second century map from Ptolemy's 'Geographia', main authority for 1200 years.

This influence was in many ways unfortunate, and held up the development of cartography in Europe for over 1000 years, since Ptolemy's map is inaccurate in many ways. Its biggest error is caused by his underestimating the size of the Earth's circumference by nearly 40 per cent – despite the fact that in the third century BC a

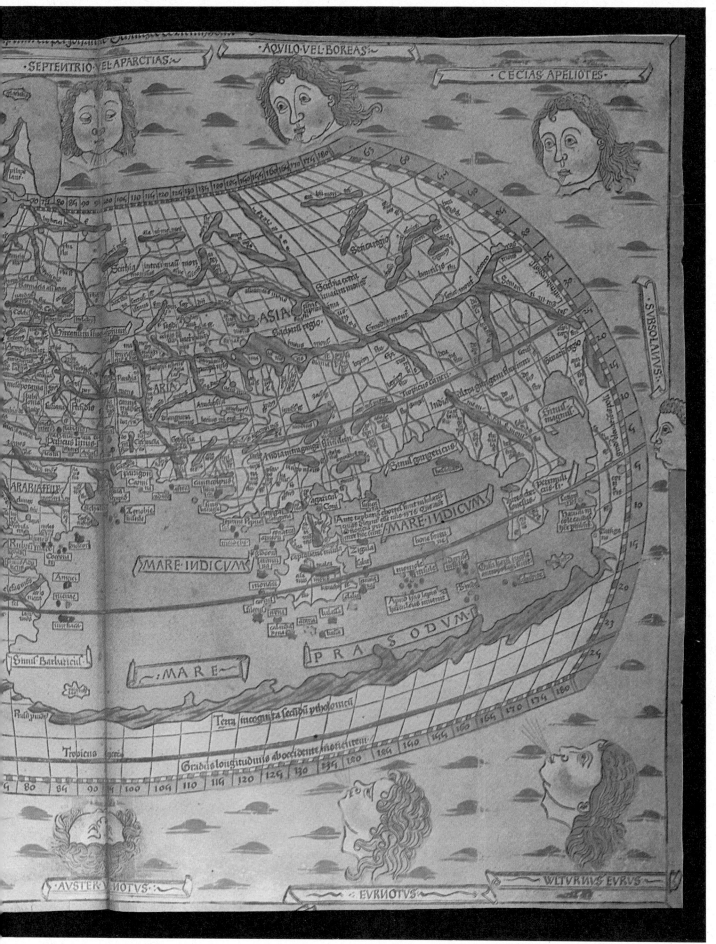

Greek astronomer had calculated the figure far more correctly. But because Ptolemy ignored his estimate, Christopher Columbus believed Asia could be reached by sailing westwards, and so discovered the West Indies when he was in fact looking for India! Ptolemy was also very wrong in his guess as to the probable shape of India, which shows as a stunted little peninsula about the same size as its neighbour Ceylon. Nevertheless, he was a very great geographer: the first to propose that the world was shaped like a sphere. He made use of meridians (great lines drawn through the poles giving the longitude) and latitudes (lines drawn parallel to the equator) by means of which any spot on the Earth could be precisely located. Ptolemy's map did not survive in its original form, but there were enough descriptions of it to enable later geographers to make detailed reconstructions. The one illustrated here was published in Munich by M. Waldseemuller in 1513.

75

Europe that, although the *Geographia* was used by Arab map makers, it disappeared in the western world until the early fifteenth century, when it was translated into Latin. The greatest part of this misfortune was the general disappearance of the concept of the Earth as a sphere. Most of the map makers who came after Ptolemy reverted to the old idea of the Earth as a floating disc.

Mapping the Roman roads

Although very few examples have survived, the Romans must have made good maps. They had highly trained *agrimensores* (land surveyors), but only a few sketches and plans remain to show their work. The Romans were not interested in Greek ideas of map projections or in fixing positions by latitude and longitude. On their world maps, which we know of from references in their literature, they also reverted to the early idea that the Earth was a disc. They probably portrayed Asia at the top of their maps, a convention which persisted into the Middle Ages.

The Romans were essentially a practical people and the most interesting relic of Roman surveying is the Peutinger Table, named after a sixteenth-century German collector who owned it. It is drawn on a roll about twenty-one feet long and one foot wide, and it records roads in the Roman Empire showing the distances from place to place. No attempt is made to show directions, but, nevertheless, it is rich in information and includes many place names. It is interesting that in the present day, simplified route maps of this sort are issued by motoring organizations.

Monsters mark the unknown

During the early part of the Middle Ages, geographical knowledge was at a standstill in the western world. Map makers often borrowed on fantasy and myth to fill the gaps on their maps. In the sixth century an Egyptian monk named Cosmas Indicopleustes denounced the idea that the Earth was a globe and resurrected the old concept of a flat disc. Christian scholars produced world maps of the Roman type, suitably modified to fit in

The map of Britain, compiled by Matthew Paris of St Albans *c.* AD 1250, is drawn around a straight-line itinerary from Dover to Newcastle.

with Christian teachings. A map drawn in 776 AD by Beatus, a Benedictine monk in Spain, took the general form of the Roman maps but depicted Paradise at the top (the far east) and greatly enlarged the Holy Land. A popular type of map during this period was called the 'T-in-O' or 'wheel' map. The 'O' represents the boundary of the Earth; the 'T' is formed by a centre line running from the river Don to the Nile, and the vertical stroke is formed by the Mediterranean. These maps varied greatly in size and detail and only a few have survived. One of them – the Hereford map – prepared towards the end of the thirteenth century, shows satyrs, griffins and monsters among a wealth of Biblical detail with Christ in majesty at the top. Land areas are greatly distorted.

But already things were changing and in the late Middle Ages, maps of a much higher quality were produced, indicating a rebirth of intellectual curiosity and

inquiry. Around 1250 an English monk at St Albans, Matthew Paris, drafted a map of Britain which is far more recognizable than the representation of Britain on the later Hereford map. Its detail suggests that new information was now available.

While Western cartography was mainly decorative and fanciful, cartographers in the Arab world had access to the writings of Ptolemy through translations in the eighth century. The most important Arabic world map was prepared by Edrisi in 1154 under the patronage of Roger II, Norman king of Sicily. Edrisi's map combines knowledge from Western and Eastern sources and is particularly notable for the information it gave about the Middle East.

On the eve of great discoveries

A major development in cartography began in the late thirteenth century when sea charts, called *portolan* charts, were produced with the aid of a new instrument, the mariner's compass. On these charts the coasts of the Black Sea, the Mediterranean, and south-western Europe were accurately recorded. Generally the maps did not show detail inland and the Earth was still treated as though it were flat. Most of the charts were drawn by Italian and Catalan draughtsmen. Related to the portolan charts were several world maps, the best known of which is the Catalan 'world map' or atlas of 1375. This atlas was important not only because it depicted coastlines accurately, but also because it greatly extended the knowledge of Asia, through information extracted from the records of thirteenth- and fourteenth-century travellers.

The Catalan atlas was the work of Abraham Cresques, a Jew living at Palma in Majorca, who was for many years cartographer and instrument maker to King Peter III of Aragon. Sometime after 1391, his son Jafuda (alias Jaime Ribes), became chart maker at Henry the Navigator's famous school or study-centre on the headland of Sagres in southern Portugal. This was an event of much significance, taking place, as it did, on the eve of the great era of discovery by the Portuguese ship-masters.

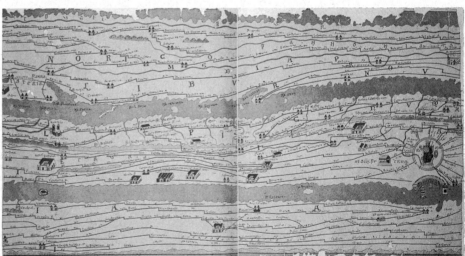

The Ptolemaic map of the British Isles, *left,* was not discovered until the fifteenth century. Ptolemy had little influence on the Roman map makers, as the Peutinger Table, *right,* shows. This parchment map was discovered originally in Upper Bavaria and is named after the German humanist who owned it. It is based on the network of military roads in the ancient Roman empire which were so important to its government and administration.

Steering by the stars

Ever since men first sailed over the horizon they have used the sun and stars to guide them back to harbour. Navigation instruments have changed but the principles remain the same.

ON 8 SEPTEMBER 1492, three small sailing ships, with the northeast trade winds filling their sails, left the Canary Islands to find the western route to Zipangu (Japan) and the East Indies. Their commander, Christopher Columbus, in his flagship, the *Santa Maria,* believed that he had a journey of about 3,000 miles ahead. He had no idea of the existence of the American continent, which barred his way to the Pacific. His estimate of the distance to Japan was derived from the writings of the Greek geographer, Ptolemy, who lived in Alexandria 1,300 years earlier. The *Santa Maria,* the *Nina* and the *Pinta* had only crude navigational instruments and a rudimentary chart. In the following March, Columbus returned to make a report to the King of Spain on the results of his voyage. How was it possible for these three tiny ships to cross the Atlantic Ocean and to find their way back without reliable navigational aids? The answer probably lies in the superb seamanship of Columbus, combined with sheer luck.

From the evening of the first day until 2 a.m. on 12 October when the *Pinta*'s look-out sighted the shore of San Salvador Island in the Bahamas, the three ships were out of sight of any land. During this period, Columbus had navigated by the method known as *dead reckoning* (an abbreviation of deduced reckoning). He set his compass bearing due west and pricked a hole in the chart each day to mark his estimated distance along the line, making what corrections he judged necessary according to the prevailing winds and currents. He estimated the speed of the ships by noting how fast waves passed their sides, helped occasionally by checking the time taken to pass floating objects. Columbus' measure of time was an *ampolleta* half-hour sand-glass. He kept two records of his progress; the one he announced to the crew gave a much smaller estimate of the distance than the other, which he kept in his private log or diary. He decided to deceive his crew, because the men believed the world to be flat and that if they sailed too far from home they would fall off the edge. But this 'false' estimate of the distance they had covered, turned out to be the more accurate.

In the 1500s navigators used a *log* to estimate the speed of their ships. The log was a piece of wood tied to a line knotted at regular intervals. A sailor tossed the wood overboard, turned the hour-glass and counted the knots as they slipped through his fingers. The number of knots paid out in an hour indicated the speed. In this way,

'knots' came to mean 'sea miles per hour'.

Dead reckoning was not the only method of fixing a position that was known at that time. Although it was seldom done, it was theoretically possible to determine both latitude and longitude. These are lines drawn on maps of the globe to locate places and positions. Lines of latitude run parallel to the equator; lines of longitude, or meridians, run from the North to the South Poles and are divided into 360°. If a navigator could fix his east-west latitude and his north-south longitude, where the two lines crossed would be his exact position.

The latitude of any place can be measured either from the angle of the Pole Star above the horizon or from the angle of the noonday sun. In the time of Columbus, navigators used two instruments to measure angles: the *astrolabe* and the *mariner's quadrant*. The mariner's quadrant, which Columbus used, was simply a quarter circle of wood, with the curved circumference marked out in degrees from 0° to 90°. Along one side were two small sighting holes in line with each other. At the apex was a brass ring, from which hung a silk cord with a lead weight at the end. The navigator sighted the Pole Star through the two holes. As soon as the star

1 The cross-staff came into use in the fifteenth century. By moving the cross piece it was possible to measure the altitude of stars.
2 The British Navy practises 'shooting the sun' with a modern sextant to find its altitude. From this the ship's position can be calculated.

came into view, he called out to his mate, who quickly read off the angle marked by the position of the cord against the scale. This was a very difficult operation on the deck of a small ship which was being tossed about by the Atlantic rollers, and the angles read were often far from accurate. Assuming that the Pole Star was visible and that the reading of the angle was correct, then the angle of the star above the horizon is practically the same as the latitude of the place at which the reading was taken.

The astrolabe, which had been developed by astronomers from an early Greek instrument, consists of a flat disc from the centre of which a sighting rule is pivoted. The disc is suspended from a brass ring, the object is sighted along an *alidade* (sight rule), and the angular measurement is read off the scale around the rim of the disc. From the sixteenth century and for the following 200 years, mariners often used a much simpler instrument than either the quadrant or the astrolabe – namely the *cross staff,* which was simply a wooden staff about three feet long with a sliding cross piece.

'Shooting the sun'

To fix the position of his ship, a navigator also has to know the longitude. The method of determining longitude depends on the fact that as the Earth rotates on its axis, the 360° of its circumference pass beneath the sun once every 24 hours. In one hour 15° of longitude, 1/24 of 360°, passes beneath the sun. For example, when it is noon at Trinidad, it is 4 p.m. at Greenwich, London, which is on the prime meridian. Trinidad must therefore be situated on longitude 60°W. It is possible to discover when it is noon at any place by taking measurements of the angle of the sun. When the sun is at its highest point, then it is noon at that place. Today, navigators use *chronometers* (extremely accurate clocks, unaffected by motion and changes in temperature), or radio time signals. But the only method known at the time of Columbus involved eclipses of the sun. If the time of an eclipse had been previously calculated at an observatory whose position was known, and if the mariner was able to observe the same eclipse and record local time (by counting the number of hour glasses from noon), then he would know the time difference between his position and that of the observatory. Multiplying the number of hours of time difference by 15° would give him his longitude in degrees. Columbus had two opportunities to make such measurements. He possessed an Almanac which gave him the time of eclipses at Salamanca in Spain and Nuremberg in Germany. But on both occasions, he missed his chance.

The first real information about early navigation comes from the Mediterranean world almost 5,000 years ago. Egyptian monuments show pictures of sailing ships which had arrived from across the Mediterranean. The eastern Mediterranean was probably one of the cradles of navigation. Sailing across the almost tideless sea, where the hundreds of islands and mountainous coastline provided landmarks, was much less terrifying to early mariners than the vast featureless expanses of the stormy North Atlantic.

Early navigational techniques depended upon knowledge of the movements of the stars, the sun and the moon in the Mediterranean skies, and on experience of the behaviour of the local winds and currents. The only aid to navigation was the *lead and line,* a piece of lead tied to the end of a long cord, which measured the depth of the sea and warned of a shelving coastline

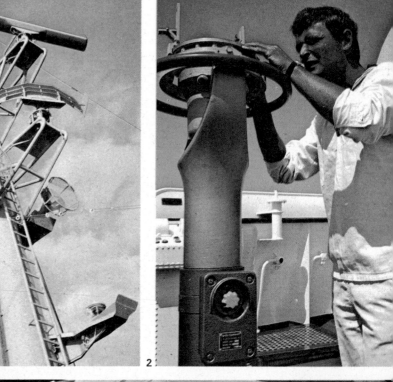

1

2

3

1 Radar aerials on the mast of a modern ship send out and receive radio waves which detect other ships and landmarks in the area.
2 A bearing is taken with a pelorus compass. This compass, which is not magnetized, is used to find the position of a landmark.
3 Aircraft use the same principles of navigation as ships at sea. Here a navigator plots his aeroplane's course on a chart.

or rocks. The end of the lead was dipped in grease so that the sand or mud on the sea bottom stuck to it. This helped to identify a ship's position to sailors who knew they would find a particular type of sand off the North African coast or mud when they neared Alexandria.

The compass was unknown as a navigational instrument until the eleventh century, although the Chinese may have understood the magnetic properties of certain stones as early as 2000 B C. But the Chinese do not appear to have used this knowledge to make a compass until the thirteenth century. There are references to the use of compasses in western Europe (1187), by Arabs in the Indian Ocean (1220) and by Norsemen (1250).

Two north poles

Although Columbus used a magnetic compass, he did not fully understand the significance of *magnetic variation* – the compass needle points not to the fixed geographical North Pole in the middle of the Arctic Ocean but to the magnetic field of the Earth which is constantly changing position. To find true north, the correct amount of variation must be added or subtracted from magnetic north. The amount varies from place to place and from time to time. On the margins of many modern maps, the magnetic variations for the sheet is given. Fortunately for Columbus, the correction required in 1492 for the region between Spain and the West Indies was only a few degrees. The early compasses were crude affairs: a magnetized needle, mounted on a pivot so that it could rotate freely and point to the magnetic north and south, was attached to a card. The captain kept a piece of lodestone to remagnetize the needle.

It was not until the late eighteenth century that improvements were made to the compass to neutralize the effect of the distortion caused by iron objects on the ship. Matthew Flinders, the great explorer of the Australian continent, invented the 'Flinder's bar', which counteracted the effects of the ship's own magnetic field. During the nineteenth century, several attempts were made to steady the compass against the roll and vibration of the ship. The experiments resulted in the adoption in 1906 of the liquid compass, which is still in use today. The liquid, usually some form of alcohol, *damps* (slows) the swinging of the card in a glass-covered bowl. In 1908 the gyrocompass, which is unaffected by the Earth's magnetic forces and always points to true north, was invented.

The problem of fixing longitude at sea was solved in the eighteenth century when John Harrison, a Yorkshire clock maker, set out to win a prize of £20,000 offered by the British Government for an accurate means of finding the longitude. In 1735 he submitted his first chronometer, weighing 72 lb, and after successful tests at sea, he

1 An azimuth compass, made about 1780, was used to sight landmarks through the two vanes. The gimbals keep it level in a moving ship.

2 This wooden-bowl type of compass dates from about 1750. In the fifteenth century the fleur-de-lis became the symbol for north.

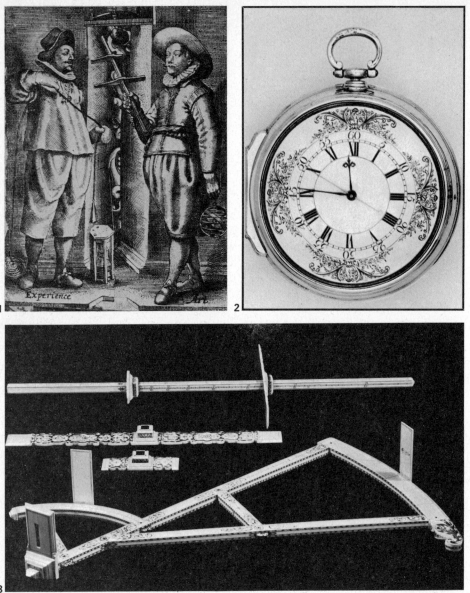

War, the navigational aids available to the sailor were in principle the same as those which had existed several hundred years earlier, although the instruments were more refined and accurate. To find longitude, the sailor had a chronometer, and to find latitude he used the sextant. Navigators had also begun to use electronic methods, which proved invaluable in cloudy or foggy conditions.

Radio beams (directional transmission), already in use before 1939, heralded a revolution in navigational techniques. Radio transmitters on land give out signals on a known frequency. Direction-finding receivers on ships pick up the signals and from them the navigators can learn their ships' courses or fix their positions. Soon radar and echo-sounders were in use, their development stimulated by the Second World War. The principles of the echo-sounders and the radar sets are similar.

In the echo-sounder, a supersonic sound wave is emitted by a transmitter directed downwards to the bed of the sea. A receiver catches the echo of the wave as it bounces from the bottom of the sea and translates the supersonic wave into a sound which can be heard by an operator. This indicates the depth of the water and ships can sail in shallow water without the danger of going aground.

Navigating by radio waves

The radar set uses very high frequency radio waves, which are transmitted in bursts of a few millionths of a second from a directional aerial. The wave travels at the speed of light, strikes an object, and is reflected back to the radar receiver on the ship. The receiver converts the echo wave into a pulse which operates a cathode-ray tube – similar to the tube of a television set. The set is calibrated so that the distance of the object to which the aerial is pointing when the signal is sent out, is known. If direction and distance are known, the position of the object in relation to the ship can be fixed, a technique often used in guiding a ship into a harbour in fog.

In the time of Columbus, the skill of the sailor in guiding his ship to its destination was an art rather than a science. The modern traveller, however, takes it for granted that the navigator knows where he is going and that he will find his way back to the exact point of departure. At any stage of the journey, the navigator can fix his position with an impressive array of electronic devices. The possibility of human error has almost been eliminated. But, in an emergency, when the navigator is thrown back on his own resources, science gives way to the ancient 'haven finding art'. The most highly trained navigator only reaches the top of his profession if he also has an instinct for seamanship – sixth sense about the ways of the sea and the changing moods of winds, tides and currents. Above all, he must know his ship and its capabilities and weaknesses. Experience at sea still counts for a great deal. And in spite of all the electronic devices aboard modern ships, their equipment still includes a magnetic compass, a chronometer and a sextant.

1 Seventeenth-century navigators: 'Experience' has a lead line and an hour-glass while 'Art' uses a cross-staff and armillary sphere.
2 In 1772 Captain James Cook took this chronometer, a duplicate of Harrison's No. 4 on his voyage to the Antarctic. It kept accurate time in the below-freezing temperatures.
3 An ivory cross-staff, with extra cross pieces, and a back-staff, measured the altitude of stars or the sun to find a ship's latitude.

was awarded £500 and encouraged to continue. Harrison's fourth prototype was ready for testing in 1761. The old man and his son William set off from Portsmouth in the company of a party of scientists and officials bound for Jamaica. Three weeks later, they were off to Madeira and, according to the chronometer, in longitude 15° 19' west of Portsmouth. The pilot, using the dead reckoning method, gave a reading of 13° 50'.

Harrison persuaded the captain to set a course based on the chronometer reading, promising that if this was correct, they would sight Porto Santo the next morning. The pilots were sceptical but let him have his way, and land was sighted just as Harrison had predicted. In other words, the chronometer had kept accurate time and, as it was set at Greenwich mean time, the difference between the chronometer and the local time gave a measure of the distance the ship had moved west of Greenwich. During the six-week voyage the chronometer lost only five seconds – well within the limit of the prize. But it

was only after many years of dispute and the eventual intervention of the king that Harrison was paid the remaining money at the age of 80.

A major improvement in angle-measuring instruments was made in 1731 when an improved type of quadrant was invented. It used the principle of double reflection to overcome the effects of the motion of the ship, and from this instrument the accurate modern sextant was developed.

As instruments improved, so maps and charts became more reliable. The greatest single step forward in map making for the navigator was the designing, in 1569, of a map projection on which all straight lines are lines of constant bearing. All map projections are in some respects inaccurate, because they attempt to show the curved surface of the Earth on a flat plane. But each projection has certain properties which are true. Mercator's projection, described by its Dutch creator as 'a true projection suitable for navigation', has been used for 400 years.

At the beginning of the Second World

Discovering Latin America

Religious zeal and the promise of gold brought the Spanish Conquistadores to Central and South America — first discovered and colonized by migrant Asiatics more than 10,000 years ago.

CHRISTOPHER COLUMBUS did not discover America – in 1492 he *re*discovered a continent which had been colonized thousands of years before by peoples from Asia. But although Columbus was not even the first European to find America, since Scandinavian seamen had already landed on the far north-eastern coasts in the eleventh century, the famous explorer was responsible for calling the indigenous inhabitants Indians.

These Indians – or less confusingly, these American Indians – were the old, long-established possessors of what, for the European, was eventually to become an exciting New World. Towards the close of the Pleistocene Ice Ages, perhaps 10,000 or 15,000 years ago, small groups of semi-nomadic hunters, probably following their game animals, had begun to drift from Asia into America across the narrow Bering Strait.

Rise of the Maya empire

These first Americans represented simple Stone Age cultures. They fished, hunted bear, bison, antelope, beaver and even an extinct type of horse, and collected fruit, nuts and shellfish. Their stone artefacts, such as spear tips, arrowheads, knives and scrapers; their cremation burials; occasionally even their footprints, have been found in caves at widely separated sites all over the continent, for some tribes had wandered for very long periods, scattering eastwards through the extensive rain forests, woodlands and scrub.

But not all the tribes continued solely as hunters and gatherers. Gradually cultivation began to supplement and often to replace the more primitive means of livelihood. For the first time, a regular food supply could be assured, harvested crops stored to offset the lean years and settled tribal groups become established within recognized territories.

The discovery and domestication of maize, or Indian corn (*Zea mays*), is an outstanding feature in the whole pattern of events, before and since. Its cultivation appears to have originated in Central America; perhaps it occurred about the same time in the Andes also, among certain groups of South American Indians. In any event, the cultivation of this indigenous cereal spread throughout the continent and the security it offered in the fundamental matter of food supply provided the opportunity for the more elaborate Amerindian cultures to develop.

Maize has been called 'the grain that built a hemisphere'. Not only was maize domesticated, but a wealth of other indigenous plants also, including such staple foods as the potato, the sweet potato (yam) and the large, edible root variously known as manioc, cassava or yuca. A plentiful

The Spanish conquest of South America remains one of the wonders of the modern world. One of its causes was the fervent desire to spread Christianity; the Roman Catholic figure of Christ in this remote part of the Andes Mountains testifies to a European presence.

food supply released leisure and energy for tribal organization, and thus the more complex Maya, Aztec and Inca empires were able to evolve.

The earliest known advanced Amerindian culture developed in Central America. In Guatemala, Yucatán and Honduras, the Maya empire emerged and flourished between 300 BC and AD 900. After a period of decline and abandonment, due perhaps to widespread epidemics, warfare or even to serious soil exhaustion, a second empire revived brilliantly on new sites about AD 1200. Its cities were beautified by massive temples to sun, moon, rain, fire and maize gods, and adorned by sculpture in plaster and stone. The Maya use of hieroglyphics and particularly of an intricate calendar, reveals their mastery of certain important astronomical and mathematical problems.

Farther north, in the cooler valleys of the central Mexican plateau, certain other Indian communities were expanding their influence by growth, conquest and absorption. Among these were the Olmecs, Zapotecs, Toltecs and at length the powerful Aztecs, who began their conquest of the Valley of Mexico in the twelfth century and extended it under Montezuma I (1440–69). Their sophisticated agricultural practices, including irrigation and the reclamation of swampland, were accompanied by the construction of imposing cities, lavishly decorated with carved stonework, sculpture and murals.

Aztec and Inca

On the island-studded lake Texcoco, the Aztecs raised their masterpiece, Tenochtitlán, now the site of Mexico City, its huge white temple-pyramids rising magnificently from the water, to be linked to the lake-shore by bridges and causeways. At the height of its prosperity, Tenochtitlán's population is estimated to have reached 300,000. More than any other Amerindian people, the Aztecs developed an elaborate religious ritual, in which priestly ceremonial and regular human sacrifice played an essential role.

In South America, the greatest of all the Indian civilizations was that of the Incas, whose empire of perhaps 16 millions

81

became one of the most extraordinary the world has ever known. As with the Aztecs in Central America, the Incas were the culmination of a long series of Indian communities scattered within the Andean basins and coastal valleys.

A people who had migrated probably from the shores of Lake Titicaca, they established their capital at Cuzco. From this sheltered basin in southern Peru the Incas systematically conquered and colonized an enormous territory nearly 3,000 miles in extent, stretching from Ecuador, through Peru and Bolivia, into central Chile and north-west Argentina. It united the Cordilleras with the coast, although it never descended far into the jungles in the east Andean slopes.

The Incas' major expansion – their imperialist phase – was in fact relatively brief, and had lasted less than a century when it crumpled unbelievably quickly in 1532 under the sudden savage blow of the Spanish conquistador Pizarro.

The tears of the sun

During its great climax, however, spanning only six generations, 380,000 square miles were ably administered, and a splendid, paved road system took couriers and officials into the four corners of the empire.

Their agriculture was the most highly developed of any Amerindian civilization, the steep flights of irrigated terraces ridging many mountain slopes to their very summits. Their cities and fortresses exhibit a superbly cut masonry whose blocks fit so neatly as to be completely watertight without the use of any mortar. Their consummate artistry in working silver, copper, bronze and, above all, gold

(the 'tears of the sun'), lights any catalogue of their achievements with an added touch of magic.

So developed the climax of the indigenous phase in Central and South America. In the case of the Incas, a passion for administrative detail and, above all, a road network branded on to a notoriously difficult landscape, combined to organize an enormous area. Neither economically nor politically in this region, has unified organization on such a scale ever been achieved in recent times.

Late fifteenth-century events in southern Europe, meanwhile, particularly in the Iberian peninsula, were about to produce one of history's great coincidences. Since the beginning of the eighth century, Moslem invaders from North Africa had gradually occupied the whole of Portugal and Spain except for the remote northern kingdoms. Slowly over the next 800 years, these small Christian states had pushed back the Moors, but these interminable wars against the infidel had become, not an episode in people's lives, but a long-established tradition. Portugal's struggle had succeeded virtually 200 years before that of Spain, for the Moors were not prised out of their stronghold in Granada until that momentous year of 1492.

Eight centuries of conflict left their mark, for the Spanish in particular had become infected with the fervour of religious crusade, while men had been kept armed and mobile. When the full impact of Columbus's voyages to America became known, the opportunities which suddenly presented themselves to Spain were quite staggering. As men sailed out of the ports of Andalusia to explore the unknown, who

can say whether the ardent wish to spread Christianity, the urge for adventure, land and personal prestige, the demand for new trade routes to the Orient or the desire for gold was uppermost in their minds? It was a question of mixed motives – 'greed, gold *and* God' pushed the Spaniards into their New World.

The Conquistadores

This second great discovery and exploration of Central and South America was indeed primarily a Spanish affair although, ironically, the continent was named after the Italian scholar and traveller Amerigo Vespucci. In 1493, the Spanish monarchs Ferdinand and Isabella lost no time in requesting Pope Alexander VI to confirm their ownership of all the lands which Columbus had discovered.

Thus it was that with one authoritative stroke, the world was divided down the middle – one half for Spain, the other for Portugal. This quite extraordinary performance depended on the acknowledgement by Roman Catholic countries that the Pope alone had the authority to allocate new territories which, at the time of their discovery, were not already in the possession of Christian rulers.

Although it proved quite impossible to interpret the Papal Bull with absolute precision, the division accepted at Tordesillas, in Spain, in 1494 ran approximately through the mouths of the Amazon. This, of course, allowed Portugal more than a mere foothold on the east coast but even so virtually nothing was done about developing Brazil for at least another 50 years. Portugal was absorbed with the enormous wealth which, by the same

As agriculture began to replace hunting as the most important means of livelihood, settled tribal groups were established. *Left*, the Inca citadel of Machu Pichu in Peru; notice the irrigated terraces, the most highly developed of any Amerindian agricultural system. The Zapotecs, an early Indian community in Mexico, built cities whose walls were carved in geometric patterns, like this example from the ancient city of Mitla, *top right*. More elaborate is the carved stonework of the Aztecs, *above right*, a later civilization which developed in the same area.

GULF OF MEXICO

CUBA

Christopher Columbus 1492-1493

South America was conquered
by the Spanish in the space of
one generation. The map shows
the routes taken by the explorers
as they crossed mountains and
seas, and plundered empires.
The Incas, whose dominion
extended for 3,000 miles (*see
inset, left*), fell in 1532, while the
ancient kingdom of the Mayas
was destroyed shortly before,
along with the Aztec civilization
of Mexico (*see inset, right*).

Vasco Nunez De Balboa 1513

Cartagena

Orinoco

Bogota

To Eldorado

Quito

Guayaquil

Mouth of
R. Amazon

Amazon

Spanish Explorers

Callao

Cuzco

Lake Titicaca

Bahia

Ferdinand Magellan 1519-1522

Potosi

Paraguay

Asuncion

Rio de Janeiro

Parana

SOUTH PACIFIC OCEAN

SOUTH ATLANTIC OCEAN

Buenos Aires

Valdivia

MEXICO

Tenochtitlan

YUCATAN

GUATEMALA

HONDURAS

ECUADOR

PERU

BRAZIL

CHILE

ARGENTINA

San Julian

Strait of Magellan

Cape Horn

Inca Empire 11th century

Inca Empire 1532

Maya culture 7th century

Expansion to c. 1520

Aztec Empire c.1440-1519

stroke, had fallen to her in the Old World – Africa, India and the Spice Islands. Spain was left to monopolize America.

The speed and skill with which Spain established its American empire astonished the rest of Europe. It is almost unbelievable, even today. When, in addition, the prodigious wealth of this New Spain became evident, its owners were the envy of the world.

The Spaniards were superb explorers. Within a single generation, they crossed mountain ranges and uncharted seas, survived storm, shipwreck and Indian attack; they toppled empires; they had to contend with jungles, fever-laden swamps – and each other. By 1513, Núñez de Balboa had crossed the narrow isthmus of Panama and waded ceremoniously into the Pacific Ocean to claim it, and all the lands around it, for Spain. Three years later the Rio de la Plata was explored, and in 1520 Ferdinand Magellan, a Portuguese navigator in the service of Spain, at last discovered the true route to the East by sailing through the straits at the tip of South America.

Pizarro plunders an empire

Reports of abundant gold in Mexico led Hernán Cortés in 1520 to the great Aztec capital Tenochtitlán, where he and his companions beheld Montezuma's lake-city, one of the most dazzling prospects ever seen by the Conquistadores, who subsequently razed it to the ground.

Attention then turned southward. Sufficient rumour had been heard of the fabulous wealth concentrated in the Inca empire to lure Francisco Pizarro into Peru. The legend of *El Dorado* – the gilded man – became both the impetus and the curse of the events which followed. With a band of fewer than 200 fellow-adventurers, mostly poor, landless and illiterate like himself, and with a noisy, bewildering array of horses, armour and cannon, all then quite unknown to the American Indian, Pizarro captured and plundered an empire. A large room completely crammed with gold ransom brought from the far corners of his domain failed to save the life of the Incas' own emperor,

A Victorian impression of the plundering of the Inca empire by Pizarro in 1532. Not even a room crammed with gold could save their emperor Atahualpa from the Spanish Conquistadores.

Atahualpa, who was treacherously killed.

The Conquistadores roamed on, establishing within the next few years cities which have remained the great urban centres of South America. Many fresh strikes of gold and silver were made, the great silver *bonanza* at Potosi (Bolivia) in 1545 for example, so that for 300 years Spain pivoted its huge American empire on the extraordinary wealth of its mines and on the Indian labour driven to extract it. That the web of organization required to convey this wealth back to Spain lasted for so long, remains one of the wonders of the modern world.

In the same period, after a slow start, the Portuguese empire developed differently. Its contrasting environment, and the absence of any densely-populated highland Indian communities, led to the early introduction of Negro slaves into Brazil from Portugal's African colonies. Sugar, cotton, cacao and other plantations were cut from the coastal forests, and a number of ports, including Bahia and Rio de Janeiro, were strung around the seaboard. While gold, diamonds and other

precious stones were later discovered inland, Brazil's economy remained primarily based on agriculture.

The great river systems – the Amazon, the Paraná and the Paraguay – pointed the way into the interior for missionary and trader, for planter, rancher and rubber-collector alike. These pioneers pushed Portugal's frontiers in America far beyond the old Tordesillas line, to the very foothills of the Andes. When in the first quarter of the nineteenth century the sweeping tide of independence engulfed the great Ibero-American empires, that of Spain splintered into separate nation states; Portugal's remained intact, first as the empire of Brazil and later, with the abolition of the monarchy in 1889, as a federal republic.

So much still unknown

The Golden Age of discovery and exploration in Central and South America was over. The indigenous phase had been replaced and extended by the European phase, for the need to find and claim new mines, new river routes, new supplies of Indian slaves, and new trading centres had urged Spaniard and Portuguese alike into the unknown. Only in the West Indies, Honduras and the Guianas had other rival European powers – particularly the Dutch, French and English – been able to stake out even a modest claim to any part of Latin America.

But thus to mark the close of the great exploratory periods is not to say that Central and South America were fully explored. In seeking to discover and develop their resources, populate their territories and settle their boundaries, the newly independent states had to grapple with the vast, isolated South American interior.

Later explorers have come not as Conquistadores, but as railway engineers, bridge builders or geologists. More recently, air routes have made their own network patterns, and regular flight paths over mountains and rain forests now leave little territory completely unseen. But, so often, this serves only to emphasize how much of the land is still unknown.

Left, Núñez de Balboa wading into the Pacific in 1513, after crossing the isthmus of Panama, to claim the ocean and all the lands around it for Spain. This might seem strange to us, but the

Spaniards of this era had authority from the Pope to claim all newly discovered lands not under a Christian ruler. The Spanish conquest of Mexico began with the overthrow of the Aztec empire

by Hernán Cortés about 1519. Excavations of the site at Monte Alban, *right,* in southern Mexico, have revealed remains of several Indian civilizations, including that of the Zapotecs.

Two sea routes to India!

In search of a sea route to India, the great shipmasters of the fifteenth and sixteenth centuries — Diaz, da Gama, Columbus, Magellan — unrolled the world map with dramatic suddenness.

A contemporary print showing Magellan's route around the world, which proved conclusively that it was round. With him is Schouten, captain of one of the ships which took part in this great though disastrous voyage. Drake and other navigators of the time are given their share of glory.

THE RENAISSANCE voyages of exploration caused an unprecedented increase in Man's knowledge of the Earth's surface, especially of the shapes of Africa, the Americas and southern Asia. In roughly two centuries – c. 1420 to 1620 – thousands of miles of hitherto uncharted coastline were surveyed by European shipmasters and the configurations of the inhabited lands, other than Australia, were mapped. Comparison of the shapes of the continents on the *Este* world map of 1466 with those on Gerhard Mercator's famous world map of 1569 gives some idea of the rapid change in Man's picture of the inhabited lands in so short a time.

The great Catalan Atlas of 1375 probably represents the best geographical knowledge available in the time of Henry the Navigator. Henry, who was a Portuguese was a Portuguese prince, has been called 'the epic figure in the first phase of Renaissance discovery'. He stimulated great interest in maritime exploration among his fellow countrymen and organized expeditions which made *systematic* coastal

surveys. Not only did he influence Portuguese navigators and the Spanish who followed their example, but he also fired the imaginations of other Europeans who set out on voyages to search the globe.

Travel was nothing new to the merchants and scholars of western Europe. A handbook for merchants completed in 1343 by Francesco Pegolotti, an agent of the great Florentine merchant house of Bardi, suggests that during the first half of the fourteenth century many merchants followed the 4,000-mile overland route to China from the Levant.

The Catalan world map of Abraham Cresques includes geographical details of China, partly derived from Marco Polo's narrative of his travels, and partly from the reports of Arab navigators and merchants who had visited Canton. Indeed there was an Arab colony well established at Canton by the middle of the eighth century A D.

The Catalan map shows the north-west coast of Africa extending southwards of Cape Bojador to a point north of Rio D'Oro

where, in 1346, the Catalan Jacome Ferrer searched for gold. It should be remembered, however, that four centuries before this expedition, Norse shipmasters had entered American waters and reached Vinland, almost certainly the North American mainland. The recently discovered 'Vinland Map' showing Greenland and part of the American coastline would tend to confirm this, if and when the question of its authenticity is settled.

One of the most remarkable features of the period between 1420 and 1620 was the generous financial support given to explorers by governments and merchant companies. This was largely due to the influence of Henry the Navigator, who in 1433 established what may be termed the first effective research centre for exploration and map making. This was his famous 'School of Sagres' which he established in 1433, in the Algarve region at the southernmost tip of Portugal, after he retired from court life. In 1443 Henry was granted a monopoly in navigation, trade and conquest on the African coast beyond

Cape Bojador; and in 1454 Alvise da Cadamosto, a Venetian trader sailing on a Portuguese vessel to the Gambia, became the first to report a sighting of the Southern Cross.

Nothing is known of the specific programmes of the many experts who worked for Henry the Navigator, but the Portuguese chronicler, Zurara, recorded that Henry was insatiable in his search for knowledge. His employees – many of them Jewish – included astronomers, cartographers, cosmographers, mathematicians, physicians and ship-designers (Cadamosto recorded that the best sailing ships afloat were the caravels of Portugal), but it is not known what became of them after Henry's death in 1460.

Chief among them was Master Jacome (formerly Jafuda Cresques) of Majorca. He and the others from Majorca joined Henry's school and enriched it with all the scientific nautical knowledge of the Catalan Jewish community which, apart from its own expertise, shared the knowledge and experience of the Italian travellers and explorers.

It was at Sagres that Henry had his hand-picked shipmasters and pilots instructed in navigation, and his charts brought up to date with each new discovery. None of the charts drafted at Sagres remain, but many Portuguese chronicles and Italian charts and maps which have survived testify to the quality of the work.

The earliest surviving map to record the Atlantic coastline of Africa as it was known to Henry the Navigator is the 1448 chart of Andrea Bianco, a Venetian cartographer who was also an experienced shipmaster. According to the 'legend' or key on the chart, it was drawn in London. In portolan style, it is criss-crossed with lines showing routes between the main parts, and shows the Atlantic coastline from England southwards to beyond Cape Bojador, the customary limit on previous portolan charts. Extending knowledge of the African coastline to Cape Roxo in Guinea, south of the Gambia river, and showing Senegal and Cape Verde, it incorporates the results of Nuno Tristao's 'African' voyage of 1446. A point of great interest on Bianco's chart is the large island lying to the southwest of Cape Verde, which some scholars now believe may represent Brazil.

A New World in the West

The charting of the Atlantic coastline of Africa by Portuguese shipmasters is recorded on several surviving maps. Among these is the chart in Grotiosus Benincasa's atlas of 1468, which extends the charted coastline a further 500 miles to Cape Mesurade in Liberia. Diego Cam extended the Portuguese charting of the African coast to southern Angola; and in 1488 Bartholomew Diaz was the first to pass Cape Agulhas, the southernmost tip of Africa, and affirm the existence of a sea route to India.

These voyages are recorded on the world map of Henricus Martellus Germanus drawn in Italy between 1489 and 1492. This map combines the old and the new – a fifteenth-century outline of the Atlantic coastline of Africa and the Mediterranean shores with a Ptolemaic version of Africa as a whole, a truncated India and two Malay peninsulas separated by the Sinus Magnus.

In the last decade of the fifteenth century, Christopher Columbus discovered most of the West Indies and Venezuela; Sebastian Cabot explored the North American east coast, and other shipmasters followed the South American coastline beyond the mouth of the Amazon. Columbus's discoveries are portrayed on the great world map of Juan de la Cosa of 1500. La Cosa was the Biscayan shipmaster who accompanied Columbus on his second voyage to the New World; and his map is the oldest still in existence to include both the Columban discoveries and Vasco da Gama's voyage to India. India is shaped in accordance with the Ptolemaic tradition, which makes it an oddly stunted little peninsula about the same size as Ceylon, but the legend on the map states that southern India was discovered by the Portuguese.

Some of the most serious problems for fifteenth-century cartographers arose from Renaissance interest in the carto-

graphic tradition of Ptolemy. Ptolemy's *Geographia* coloured geographical thinking until the end of the sixteenth century. It was one of the first works to be printed in Italy and in several ways impeded cartographical progress. But it is possible that, if Ptolemy had not underestimated the circumference of the Earth and exaggerated the west-east stretch of Eurasia – thus bringing the east coast of Asia nearer to the west coast of Europe – Columbus might never have attempted to reach Zipangu and Cathay (Japan and China) by sailing westwards as he did across the Atlantic Ocean.

Columbus was also influenced by Pierre d'Ailly's *Imago Mundi,* written early in the fifteenth century, and by his own contemporary, Paolo Toscanelli, whose studies had persuaded him that China could not be more than 5,000 nautical miles west of the Straits of Gibraltar. Columbus eventually pinned his hopes on the figure of 3,550 miles – an underestimate of some 8,000 miles! His great voyage in 1492 is undoubtedly the most dramatic and famous of the Renaissance voyages of exploration. But it was the circumnavigation of the Earth by the *Vittoria,* the only surviving ship of Ferdinand Magellan's expedition of 1519–22, which first demonstrated conclusively that the Earth had the shape of a globe.

Of course, men like Abraham and Jafuda Cresques were in no doubt that the Earth was round, although there is no evidence that the Catalan cartographers ever constructed a globe-map of the Earth. The earliest known globe, dating from 1492, is believed to be the work of Martin Behaim, a Nuremberg merchant who lived for many years in Portugal and the Azores. Educated men in western Europe had known that the world was round from at least the twelfth century.

Fixing a position at sea

From that time onwards, Christian shipmasters and pilots, under the tuition of learned Jewish astronomers and mathematicians, had begun to use navigational aids, which demanded at least a smattering of astronomy. The need for a simple manual was met before the middle of the thirteenth century by an Englishman, John Holywood, who wrote the *Sphaera Mundi* under the Latinized name of Sacrobosco. It was based on a manual by the Arab scholar, Alfraganus, and enjoyed widespread popularity until the end of the fifteenth century.

Even the *Travels of Sir John Mandeville* (now generally recognized as a work of fiction) shows that, by the fourteenth century, educated people believed in a spherical Earth. 'Mandeville' wrote of the 'roundness' of the Earth and of circumnavigating it. The *Travels* was one of the first books to be printed and it circulated widely; among the many who read it was Christopher Columbus.

In 1494, a meridian was decreed as the line of partition between the newly discovered Portuguese and Spanish territories in the western hemisphere. It was therefore important for shipmasters to be able to determine longitude – the angular distance east or west of a standard meridian. Although by Columban times a shipmaster could, with the aid of a cross-staff or an astrolabe, calculate local time with fair accuracy, he lacked a convenient method of establishing the time at an original position and so could not determine his longitude at sea with any degree of accuracy. This was a problem which beset shipmasters until the middle of the eighteenth century when the English clockmaker, John Harrison, perfected a marine chronometer which continued to record Greenwich standard time with great accuracy after weeks at sea. Only then were shipmasters able to fix the position of isolated islands to enable later sailors to find them again.

Meanwhile, Gerhard Mercator had devised a projection suitable for navigational charts. It compensated for the convergence of meridians of longitude towards the poles and enabled the rhumb lines (lines of constant compass-bearing) to be plotted as straight lines on a sheet of paper. This invention also gave a more exact idea of the lie of the continents on the surface of the Earth.

Filling in the gaps on land

Mercator's own cartographic discoveries and voyages of exploration were incorporated into his chart of the world published in 1569. By comparison with Este's map of 1466 it is highly sophisticated and strikingly accurate. India, although still drawn far too small, is correctly shaped, and the position of Ceylon is accurately fixed. North America is represented with a fair degree of exactitude; South America

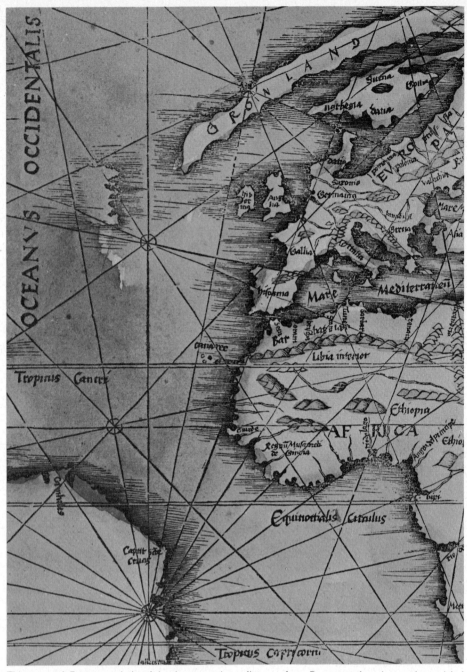

This map of Europe and the Atlantic ocean is taken from the 1513 edition of Ptolemy's *Geographia*. It shows how he underestimated the distance from Europe to America, and so misled Columbus and other explorers and map makers. The criss-cross lines mark compass points.

Bust of Christopher Columbus, who discovered the New World but died disappointed because his greatness was unrecognized in his lifetime.

Prince Henry the Navigator, whose centre for maritime research produced many great voyages of discovery and recorded them on new maps.

begins to take on its proper shape; the West Indies are shown and the whole map illustrates the great advances made in the previous 150 years.

Renaissance explorers had unrolled the outline map of the world but for the detail of the Pacific Ocean. Their knowledge of the surface features of the land masses was scant, but even so, valuable information was added to the many editions of Ptolemy's *Geographia*. During the sixteenth century a number of astronomer-mathematicians, as well as cartographers and cosmographers, showed an interest in topographic mapping, but they failed to solve the problem of indicating relief, that is, of representing accurately degrees of slope and heights above a mean sea-level. They could not map the inequalities of the surface – valleys, hills, plateaux. This advance was to come with the work of the official surveyors of the late eighteenth and nineteenth centuries.

The great South Land

A lost continent less than four hundred years ago, first colonized in the nineteenth century, Australia – *Terra Australis,* the great South Land – still has room for the explorer.

AUSTRALIA WAS KNOWN to the Malays, and possibly to the Chinese, long before European eyes first saw its shores; but the headlands most accessible from Indonesia were either desert or poor and difficult bush country fringed by mangrove. They offered little inducement to the sedentary rice-growers from the north, and the Malays were content to establish nothing but a few temporary fishing camps. Such rumours as there were of a southern continent in the East did not enter into serious geographical thinking in Europe.

However, there had survived from classical times a belief in a great *Terra Australis* or South Land, 'balancing' the inhabited northern land masses, and this played a part in seventeenth- and early eighteenth-century speculation about this last unknown quarter of the globe. Additional fuel was supplied by the thirteenth-century explorer, Marco Polo, who had brought back a report of a prosperous kingdom in the south. This was probably a reference to Sumatra, but it was widely assumed to refer to a land much farther south.

It is possible that the Portuguese had some knowledge of Australia by about 1530, for several maps were produced in northern France between 1540 and 1566 showing a large land mass about as far south of the equator as Australia. The names on these maps – which are very difficult to explain away as imaginary – suggest that there must have existed an original Portuguese version. There are other hints that north-west Australia may have been known but, whatever the truth, nothing came of it. The South-east Trades had ensured that the early circumnavigators, Ferdinand Magellan (1521), Francis Drake (1579), and Thomas Cavendish (1587) crossed the Pacific passing well to the north of Australia.

The first landfalls

The first certain European landfall was made by a Dutch ship from Indonesia, the *Duyfken,* commanded by William Jansz, who in 1606 explored the southern coast of New Guinea (already well known to the Portuguese and Spanish) and touched on the Queensland side of the Gulf of Carpentaria. Some five months later Luis Vaez de Torres sailed with part of a Spanish expedition to the New Hebrides. His route took him through the Torres Straits and he may have seen Cape York, the extreme northern tip of Australia, but this is unlikely.

About 1600 the Dutch began to build up a trading empire in the East Indies, and charted a new sea route avoiding the Portuguese bases on the coasts of East Africa, India and Ceylon. Dutch seamen struck far out from the Cape of Good Hope in the westerly wind belt before turning north for Java, and sooner or later this had to bring some ship within sight of Australia. The first landfall on the west coast was made in 1616 by Dirk Hartog, and during the next 30 years Dutch seamen acquired a

Captain Cook, *inset,* and his ship the *Endeavour* sighting Australia on the way home from New Zealand. Cook landed in April, 1770, and began to explore the fertile Pacific Coast of which the Dutch explorers of a century before had been unaware. On his first voyage, despite the dangers of the Great Barrier Reef, he charted the whole of the east coast of Australia from Point Hicks to Cape York in one brilliant, continuous voyage.

fair knowledge of the coastline from the Gulf of Carpentaria to the eastern side of the Great Australian Bight.

The climax of Dutch exploration was Abel Tasman's voyage of 1642–3. While pioneering a route in the westerly belt to South America, Tasman discovered Van Diemen's Land (now Tasmania) and New Zealand, both of which he supposed to be continental headlands. Abandoning his original objective, he doubled back to New Guinea and, in 1644, systematically explored the northern coast of Australia (then called New Holland). By this time, therefore, the outlines of the western two-thirds of the continent were known.

However, the aridity and poverty of the known coasts and the lack of any trade prospects with the Aborigines caused the Dutch East India Company to lose interest, and it was left to an English captain, James Cook who landed in April, 1770, to search out the well-watered and fertile Pacific Coast. On his first circumnavigation he charted the east coast from Point Hicks (on the New South Wales-Victoria border) to Cape York, the longest continuous primary exploration of a coastline ever carried out in a single voyage. Most of the remaining gaps in the coastal outline were filled in by George Bass and Matthew Flinders. In 1797 Bass voyaged in a whale-boat from Sydney into Bass Strait, demonstrating that Van Diemen's Land was an island, and the following year he and Flinders charted its coastline.

In 1801–3 Flinders surveyed Australia's southern coast and became the first man to circumnavigate the continent. In his book *A Voyage to Terra Australis,* Flinders first gave currency to the name *Australia,* which was officially adopted in 1824.

Beyond the Blue Mountains

The coastal exploration of Australia had been carried out in two periods, each of about 30 years, separated by a century and a quarter. But it was only in 1788, at Sydney, nearly two centuries after the *Duyfken* landfall, that the first European settlement was founded. The settlers were soon familiar with the coastal lowland, but no proper exploration of the interior took place for 25 years. This was largely due to the fact that there are hardly any rivers in the area offering easy access inland. High, rugged country backed by wide, open plateaux, lies close and parallel to the coast, but once the plateaux are gained, movement is relatively easy. Instead of a pattern of exploration and settlement up rivers, settlers breached the coastal highlands in a few places and spread out on the plateaux on a broad front. Early attempts were made to break through by following the valleys, but they were all found to end in blind canyons.

It was not until 1813 that Gregory Blaxland, William Lawson and W. C. Wentworth had trekked far enough over the Blue Mountains to see the open woodland country rolling away to the west. To do this they had to follow the ridges, not the valleys. Expansion was now rapid. Bathurst, the first inland town, was founded in 1815, and eight years later the first sheep stations were established at Canberra, 200 miles to the south. The next major achievement was the overland journey of Hamilton Hume and William Hovell in 1824. They travelled from Sydney to Port Phillip, crossing Australia's greatest river, the Murray, and opening up vast new areas for settlement. The route they took is followed fairly closely today by the main road from Sydney to Melbourne.

In the 30 years after 1813 the main geographical outlines of the south-east quadrant of Australia were made clear by the journeys of such men as James Oxley and Alan Cunningham, who worked northwards from the Bathurst entry and Hunter River to discover Liverpool Plains, the high New England plateau, and the Darling Downs behind Brisbane. The Surveyor-General, Sir Thomas Mitchell, also worked in this area, explored the Darling River, and in 1837 made a notable journey from Sydney to Portland Bay in the west of what is now Victoria, opening up a large area of good pastoral country to which he gave the encouraging name Australia Felix. The Polish immigrant Paul Strzelecki did useful work in the south-east, discovering and naming, in 1840, the highest point in Australia, Mount Kosciusko.

But the greatest name in this phase of exploration and discovery is Charles Sturt. Commissioned by the governor, Sir Ralph Darling, Sturt gave his attention to the problem of the rivers which drained westwards from the inner slopes of the great belt of Eastern Highlands. Their general set in their upper reaches is to the northwest; surely, thought Sturt, they must slope towards fertile plains, perhaps an inland lake, perhaps even a great estuary or delta on the northern coast. But he found that Australia has no Great Lakes, only salt-pans.

Sturt first attempted to follow down the Macquarie and Darling rivers. Then, in 1829–30, he took a whale-boat – in sections carried on drays – to the Murrumbidgee River and rowed down both that river and the Murray to the latter's mouth in South

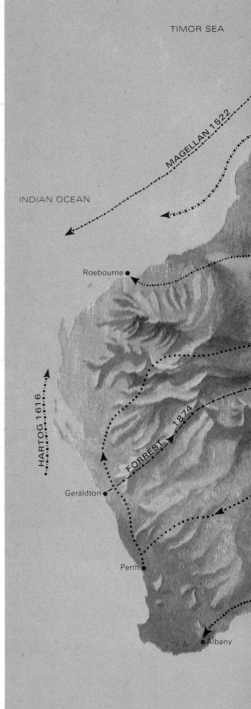

This map of Australia shows the routes of the great navigators and explorers who charted her coastline and opened up her vast and arid interior. Navigators of the Dutch East India Company explored the northern and western coastlines and the southern coast as far as the Great Australian Bight; but they eventually lost interest in the poor land they encountered, which promised nothing in the way of trade. Captain Cook charted the previously unknown eastern coast and Matthew Flinders became the first man to circumnavigate the continent and complete the outline of the land which came to be known as Australia. Exploration of the interior presented almost insurmountable problems, owing to lack of water, intense heat and hostile Aborigines; several early expeditions ended in failure or disaster. *Left,* in the blistering heat, *Ayer's Rock,* a red sandstone formation near the centre of the continent, is one of the many remarkable rock formations to be found throughout Australia.

Australia. It was found to be a wide but shallow lake with an entrance blocked by sand-bars – Australia has no Mississippi either.

In 1839–40, Edward John Eyre tried to penetrate northwards from newly founded Adelaide, but was turned back by the belt of salt-pans – Lake Torrens and Lake Eyre South – which seemed to form a desert arc blocking any advance on this line. In 1841 Eyre made a journey around the Bight to Albany in the extreme south-west. It was a heroic expedition, but it added little to knowledge of the area, since the aridity of the interior forced him to keep close to the springs near the coast.

Sturt now attempted to outflank the barrier of the salt lakes by going from Adelaide by the lower Murray and Darling and then striking north-west towards the Centre. Drought forced him to camp for six months at a reliable waterhole, unable to go forward or back in the intense heat (which averaged 101°F for weeks) until rain came. He then pushed on as far as Cooper Creek and Sturt Desert in south-west Queensland.

Death in the desert

In the north, Mitchell and Kennedy attempted to solve the problem of the rivers in southern Queensland: the Barcoo, thought to be the headwater of the Victoria river in the Northern Territory, turned out to be only part of Cooper Creek, which flows into the inland drainage basin of Lake Eyre. Kennedy himself was killed by Aborigines while trying to reach Cape

York. The major achievement here was the journey of the German explorer Ludwig Leichardt, from the Darling Downs to Port Essingron (north of Darwin) in 1844–45. Leichardt covered 3,000 miles of the new country in 15 months, a success the more astonishing in that he had previously spent very little time in Australia. But in 1848 he disappeared while attempting to cross the continent from the Darling Downs to Perth, leaving no trace but some marked trees – and much legend.

Disaster also attended the Victorian Trans-continental Expedition of Robert O'Hara Burke and William Wills, in 1861. This was the most lavishly equipped party ever sent out, and had 25 camels. It attained its goal by crossing from Melbourne to the Gulf of Carpentaria – its members heard but could not actually see the sea through the dense mangrove swamps of the Gulf. Burke, although a police officer with much more Australian experience than Leichardt, seems to have been an incompetent bushman and bad leader, and pushed his advance party to the Gulf without leaving proper instructions with his supply-line. Instructed to wait at the Barcoo river for three months, this party waited for over four – and left on the morning of the very day that the exhausted advance party returned. Burke and Wills, with one John King, decided to head for Adelaide, but after many miles had to abandon Wills. Two days later Burke died, and King, returning for Wills, found him also dead. King, the only survivor of the party who reached the Gulf, sheltered with Aborigines for three months before being found. The expedition's real contribution to Australian exploration lay not so much in its own work as in the work of the rescue parties that followed.

A prize of £10,000

At about the same time John McDouall Stuart was also attempting to cross the continent from south to north, in an effort to win £10,000 offered by the South Australian government to the first man to do so. Trained under Sturt, he made three journeys from Adelaide. On the first, he discovered the fairly good pastoral country, surrounded by semi-desert and worse, around Alice Springs and the MacDonnell Ranges, as well as Central Mount Sturt (now Stuart), which is near the geographical centre of Australia. But then he was forced to turn back. Much the same happened the following year. His third expedition in 1862, however, took him through to the sea. His discoveries gave an impetus to the pastoral occupation of northern Australia (still incomplete) and the construction in 1872 of the Overland Telegraph from Adelaide to Darwin.

The eastern third of Australia was now tolerably well known, and there had also been a good deal of exploration in the west of Western Australia. It remained to tie these two areas together by journeys across the vast and largely desert western plateaux which occupy at least half of the continent. The first success was that of A.C. Gregory, who achieved Mitchell's aim in reverse by crossing from the Victoria River to Rockhampton on the

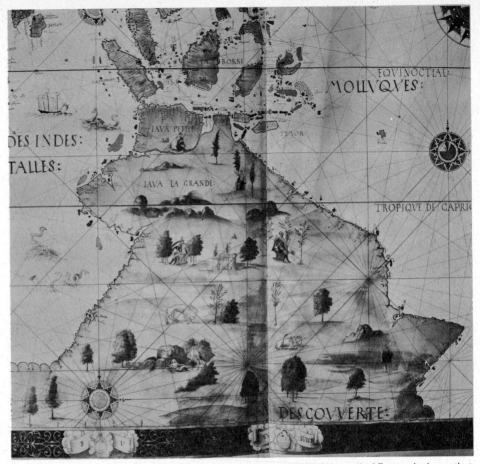

There had been much speculation about the fabled *Terra Australis*. This map was made in 1546 by order of Henry II of France. It shows that *Terra Australis* was conceived as part of Java.

Queensland coast. The methods and preparations of long-range expeditions were by now well established, and although journeys like that of P. E. Warburton from Alice Springs to Roebourne on the west coast, in 1873, faced dangers and suffered privations, there were no repetitions of the Leichardt or Burke disasters.

The most notable names in this western sphere are those of John Forrest – later Prime Minister of Western Australia and the first Australian peer – and Ernest Giles. In 1874 Forrest crossed from Geraldton, north of Perth, to Adelaide, well to the north of Eyre's coastal route, and later explored the Kimberley Ranges in the north-west. Between 1872 and 1876 Giles made four expeditions. The first two were unsuccessful attempts to cross from the Overland Telegraph Line to the Indian Ocean; the third took him across the

Nullarbor Plain to Perth on a line between those of Eyre and Forrest; while the last was from Geraldton to the Telegraph Line, on a route to the north of Forrest's.

Parts still unexplored

Giles's work virtually completed the exploration of the continent. There was still detail to be filled in by minor expeditions and the unrecorded journeys of pastoralists and prospectors – and there are probably still patches of desert never traversed by a white man. After its late start, this cartographic conquest of an entire continent in less than a century after the first European settlement was a great achievement. It is a story spiced with the mystery of Leichardt's disappearance and the tragedy of Burke and Wills, but its main results were achieved by the tough, professional craft of the Australian bushmen.

These five explorers all risked their lives to conquer the Great Australian Outback. Three of them never came back, among them Robert O'Hara Burke and William Wills, *left,* who set off on a trans-continental journey in 1861. Edmund Kennedy, *centre,* surveyed the courses of rivers in the north and was killed by Aborigines. *Right,* John Forrest and Ernest Giles explored the western plateaux and survived to tell the tale.

First stirrings of the sleeping giant

Fabulous tales of the Dark Continent swept Europe for centuries; the Cape was rounded; yet the African interior was unexplored until the time of David Livingstone and his contemporaries.

TO EUROPEAN EYES in the Middle Ages, Africa was a continent of mystery – the Dark Continent – almost totally unknown apart from its Mediterranean coast. Such knowledge that existed was based upon incomplete Greek and Roman records, for much classical knowledge, including the work of the great Greek geographer Claudius Ptolemaus, remained lost to Europe until the 1400s.

The main obstacle to exploration was the Sahara, a desert so vast and forbidding that medieval Europeans considered it impenetrable. Indeed, from early times most people believed that beyond the African coast lay a totally barren desert. This conviction did much to delay exploration of the interior until the 1800s, and was only finally dispelled by the travels of David Livingstone in central and southern Africa. Although Herodotus, the Greek historian of the fifth century BC, had reported that Phoenician sailors had sailed around the entire coastline of Africa as early as about 600 BC, most later classical geographers and Europeans of the Middle Ages believed that men could not survive the intense heat of the equator.

'Meadows of gold'

The medieval concept of Africa as a Dark Continent was, however, strictly a European idea. It is probable that the Chinese were trading in east Africa around the time of the birth of Christ, although the first known Chinese description of the region dates from 1060. To the Arabs, whose civilization kept alive and developed the classical tradition, the Sahara was not a barrier to exploration and trade, but a highway. From the seventh century AD

A caravan plodding across the Sahara. Used for centuries to carry salt, dates, wheat and ivory, onwards, Arab invaders swept across northern Africa, spreading Islam and establishing a vast empire.

Allied to military conquest and the conversion of people to Islam was the development of trade. Arab merchants and scholars followed ancient caravan routes across the Sahara and made contact with the Negro civilizations in the interior of western Africa. The ancient kingdom of Ghana, which lay to the north-west of modern Ghana, was known to the Arabs as early as the eighth century, and we owe much of our knowledge of ancient Ghana and the later medieval empires of western Africa to the writings of Arab scholars and travellers.

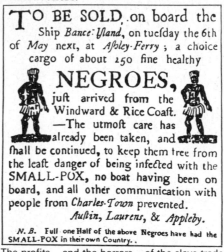

The profits – and the horrors – of the slave trade did much to stimulate European interest in Africa. Over 14 million slaves were sold in America alone. *Above*, a fresh cargo is advertised.

and invaluable in the early exploration of desert lands, the camel is still important today.

The east coast of Africa was also an important trading area to the Arabs. In the 920s, an Arab scholar, Al Masudi, travelled down the coast as far south as Mozambique. In one of his books, *Meadows of Gold and Mines of Gems,* he described the coast, its peoples and its products, and established that gold and ivory were exported as far as India and China, usually via Oman.

Slave trading, as well as traffic in gold and ivory, enriched the Arab merchants. News of the extensive slave trade carried on in Moslem Africa filtered through to the merchants of the Mediterranean in the late Middle Ages. The prospect of enormous potential wealth stimulated a revival of interest in scientific exploration.

The vast plateau

Prince Henry the Navigator, third son of John I of Portugal, conceived the idea of exploring the western coast of Africa to gain access to areas beyond the Moslem world. Henry himself never sailed on any voyages of discovery. But in 1434 he persuaded sailors (who were fearful at first that they might turn black) to travel beyond Cape Bojador in what is now Western Sahara. It was then the southernmost known point on the African coast.

By the time Henry died in 1460, his sailors had mapped the African coastline as far south as Sierra Leone. Allied to exploration was trade, and it is significant that the first African slaves were brought to Portugal in 1441. After his death others continued Henry's pioneer work. In 1487, Bartholomew Diaz, a Portuguese sea captain, rounded the Cape of Good Hope.

Forced to return by his weary crew, Diaz did not complete the rounding of southern Africa, and it was Vasco da Gama who made the triumphant journey around the Cape of Good Hope to India and back in 1497–9.

For the next 300 years, mapping of the African coastline continued, but there was very little exploration of the interior. The belief in a desert interior persisted, but physical barriers, too, hampered exploration. The continent of Africa consists largely of a vast plateau surrounded by a narrow coastal belt. Rivers plunge off the plateau in a series of waterfalls and rapids that make inland boat journeys impossible.

In quest of Prester John

The significance of the African coastline to many Europeans was that it provided stopping places on the way to India. In 1652 the Dutch East India Company sent a Dutch naval surgeon, Jan van Riebeeck, to establish a settlement at the southern tip of Africa. This settlement formed a nucleus for the later development of modern South Africa, but colonization and exploration were not van Riebeeck's objectives. His task was simply to establish a supply station for Dutch ships en route to India. European coastal settlement was not always successful. The Portuguese tried to control the eastern coastline of Africa, but they met with stiff opposition from the Arabs, and were finally expelled in 1729.

Coastal trade developed quickly in Africa, especially in the west. Unable to travel inland, European traders made contacts with African kings or merchants on the coast, and offered rewards, often trivial, for commodities from the interior.

After the discovery of the Americas, a demand for plantation slaves soon arose. Coastal war leaders raided tribes in the African interior, capturing men, women and children and selling them as slaves to European sea captains and slave traders.

To control the trade, a series of European forts were built along the west African coast. The slave trade continued well into the 1800s and modern historians estimate that more than 14 million Africans were sold in America.

Europeans did, however, visit one African kingdom in the interior at an early stage. Intrigued by twelfth-century stories of Prester John, a legendary Christian king, supposed to live in the heart of Africa, European expeditions set out to find him. Prester John was never found, but by the early 1400s the existence of the Christian kingdom of Ethiopia was established.

The Portuguese sent a large mission to Ethiopia in 1520. Twenty years later, when Ethiopia was threatened by a Moslem army, a military force under Christopher da Gama, Vasco's son, established itself there. Christopher da Gama was killed but the Christian cause triumphed. The Portuguese, welcome guests in Ethiopia, tried for the next hundred years, without success, to persuade the Ethiopian Church to accept the authority of Rome. One interesting step in the story of Africa's exploration was taken during this period when a Jesuit, Father Pedro Paez, sent to Ethiopia to convert the emperor to Roman Catholicism, discovered the source of the Blue Nile in 1618.

It was in Ethiopia that the great period of inland exploration of Africa began, when James Bruce arrived in 1770 at Gondar, then the capital of Ethiopia. Bruce, like most of the explorers that followed him, was a fascinating character. At 40 years of age, this six-foot-four-inch tall, red-haired Scot was a fine horseman and marksman who was driven by an intense curiosity about the unknown.

Bruce's book, *Travels to Discover the Source of the Blue Nile,* is a vivid and most readable account of his discoveries. It tells how he won the friendship of leading nobles and the royal family, in a country then ravaged by civil war. With their help, he fulfilled his ambition of visiting the source of the Blue Nile. During his stay in Ethiopia and his return journey down the Nile in 1772–3, Bruce did not discover anything of great geographical importance. Yet he is regarded as the first of the great European explorers in Africa, more for his attitude to travel than his actual achievements.

Disaster on the Niger

Bruce himself financed the journey, not for commercial or religious reasons, nor to win personal acclaim – in fact, on his return, many people disbelieved his accounts and even suggested that he had never been to Ethiopia. Bruce became an explorer out of a sense of adventure and a scientific desire to find out about the unknown.

Bruce's return to Britain helped to stimulate an already mounting interest in Africa, largely arising from the increasing revulsion against the slave trade. The anti-slavery movement in Britain vigorously pursued a campaign which inspired the missionary societies to send to Africa

African giants. A herd of African elephants, the world's largest land mammal, at the foot of Kilimanjaro, the continent's highest mountain at 19,340 feet above sea level.

The Victoria Falls in the dry season. The Falls were once known locally as *The Smoke that Thunders* – for when the Zambezi is in spate, a towering plume of spray can be seen from afar.

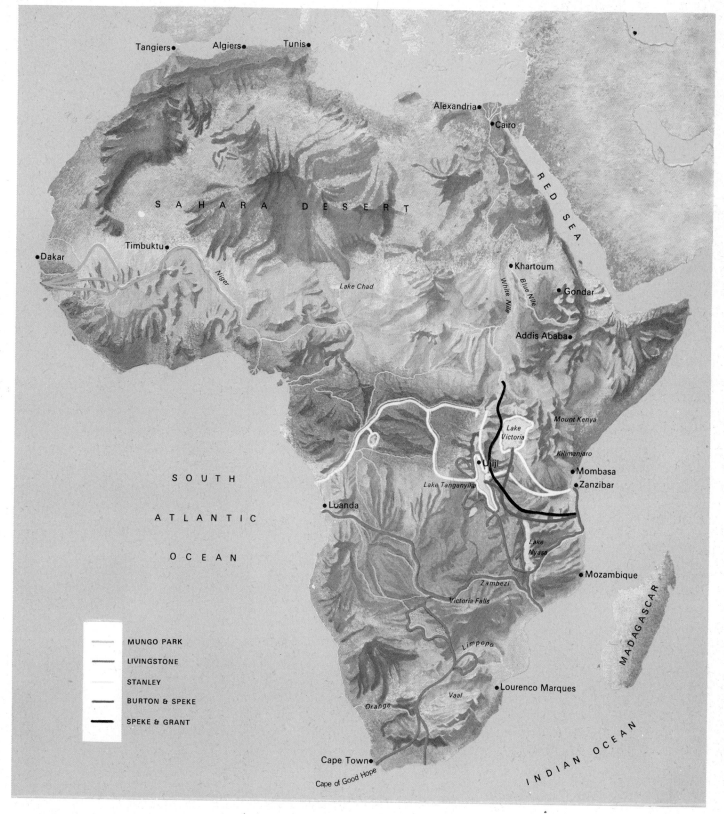

Map of Africa showing exploration routes with the following labels: Tangiers, Algiers, Tunis, Alexandria, Cairo, RED SEA, SAHARA DESERT, Dakar, Timbuktu, Niger, Lake Chad, Khartoum, White Nile, Blue Nile, Gondar, Addis Ababa, SOUTH ATLANTIC OCEAN, Mount Kenya, Lake Victoria, Kilimanjaro, Ujiji, Mombasa, Lake Tanganyika, Zanzibar, Luanda, Lake Nyasa, Mozambique, MADAGASCAR, Zambezi, Victoria Falls, Limpopo, Lourenco Marques, Vaal, Orange, Cape Town, Cape of Good Hope, INDIAN OCEAN

Legend:
MUNGO PARK
LIVINGSTONE
STANLEY
BURTON & SPEKE
SPEKE & GRANT

men dedicated to stamping out the trade.

In the late 1700s, there was also an increasing scientific interest in African exploration. In 1788, a dining club was founded called the *African Association,* a forerunner of the Royal Geographical Society. Sir Joseph Banks, a leading scientist and a member of Captain James Cook's first voyage to New Zealand, became its president. The object of the Association was to send explorers to Africa to make scientific studies. It first turned to west Africa and the river Niger.

The Association chose Mungo Park, a young Scots surgeon, to go to the upper Niger in 1795. After many hardships, which

he describes graphically in his *Travels in the Interior Districts of Africa,* Park established that the Niger flowed eastwards. He returned to Britain in 1797 but, despite the memory of his terrible experiences, he was impatient to return.

But misfortune and finally tragedy also beset his second journey (1805–6). By the time Park had reached the upper Niger, 26 of his companions had died of disease. The ten remaining members of the expedition set off with Park to sail down the Niger to the sea. Further deaths depleted the party and finally, still more than 500 miles from the sea, Park and his few remaining companions perished. The circumstances of

It was not until 300 years after Vasco da Gama had rounded the Cape (1497–8) that any real attempt was made by Europeans to explore the interior of Africa. At the end of the eighteenth century, an important era of exploration began, when the newly formed *African Association* in Britain sent Mungo Park to trace the course of the Niger. Between 1840 and 1873, David Livingstone opened up southern Africa in three great expeditions and, after his death, his friend Stanley returned to cross the continent from east to west. Meanwhile, Burton and Speke, exploring in East Africa, discovered Lake Tanganyika in 1858. In 1862 Speke returned to the area with James Grant, and together they located the northern outlet of Lake Victoria, source of the White Nile. Theirs was the last great journey of exploration carried out before the colonial era.

their death remain a mystery but it seems probable that they were attacked by hostile Africans and probably drowned in the Niger.

Park's pioneer work was followed up in the 1820s when the main geographical features of west Africa and the drainage of the Niger were established.

In eastern and central Africa, European exploration began in the 1840s. In eastern Africa, the first important explorers were two German missionaries, Johann Krapf and Johannes Rebmann, who established the truth of ancient legends about snow-capped mountains close to the equator when they discovered Kilimanjaro and Mount Kenya.

Meanwhile David Livingstone (1813–73), perhaps the most remarkable explorer of them all, began in 1841 his extraordinary career in southern and central Africa. Livingstone, yet another Scot, worked in a cotton mill from the age of ten until he was 23. His early struggles to achieve an education which culminated in his qualifying as a doctor at the age of 27 were held up as an example to Victorian schoolchildren.

Source of the White Nile

In December, 1840, he sailed for Cape Town and there began a fifteen-year stay, living part of the time on mission stations and part of the time travelling through South Africa, the Kalahari in Bechuanaland (now Botswana), Angola and the valley of the river Zambezi.

One of the most famous of his exploits was the discovery of the Victoria Falls in November, 1855. On his return to England, Livingstone's book *Missionary Travels and Researches in South Africa*, published in 1857, made an enormous impact. So, too, did his public lectures attacking the slave trade. He was admired for his humanitarianism and courage, and also for the extraordinary precision of his observations.

While Livingstone was enjoying his deserved acclaim in Britain, Richard Burton (1821–90), who is probably best remembered as a writer and translator of *The Arabian Nights,* and such Asian

This engraving shows the meeting of Stanley and Livingstone on the edge of Lake Tanganyika. Stanley had been sent out by the *New York Herald* to find Livingstone, who was feared to be dead.

erotica as *The Perfumed Garden* and *The Kama Sutra,* was sponsored by the Royal Geographical Society to explore the interior of East Africa. Burton, already famous for his daring visit to Mecca disguised as a Moslem, took with him John Hanning Speke (1827–64), a younger man with an exemplary Army record.

After many hardships, Burton and Speke found Lake Tanganyika in July, 1858. As Burton was ill, Speke travelled alone to the north and discovered Lake Victoria. He guessed correctly that it was a source of the Nile, despite Burton's view that there was insufficient evidence. Relations between Burton and Speke had deteriorated, and grew worse when Speke was given credit for the success of the expedition.

Speke returned to East Africa in 1862 with James Grant, a modest man and a far more amenable companion than Burton. They travelled inland and at last Speke discovered the northern outlet of Lake

Victoria, which he correctly considered a source of the White Nile. His feud with Burton still continued. In 1864 they were to hold a public debate concerning the source of the White Nile, but news came that Speke had accidentally shot himself.

From 1859 to 1864, Livingstone continued his pioneer work exploring the Zambezi and discovering Lake Nyasa (now Lake Malawi). His third and final expedition began when he left Britain in August, 1865 to explore the rivers of central Africa. In 1869, he reached Ujiji on Lake Tanganyika and from there explored the upper rivers of the Congo river system.

Stanley's search for Livingstone

Dogged with ill health, Livingstone's spirits were at a low ebb in 1871 when an unexpected visitor arrived at Ujiji. Henry Morton Stanley, a Welshman by birth, had been sent by the *New York Herald* to find Livingstone – about whom nothing had been heard since 1866. Greatly revived by his new companion, Livingstone set off with Stanley to explore the northern part of Lake Tanganyika, a journey described in Stanley's *How I Found Livingstone.*

Livingstone remained behind when Stanley left in March, 1872. He died about 1 May 1873, and his body was carried to the coast by his African servants, whence it was taken to Britain for burial in Westminster Abbey.

Stanley's famous journey was disparaged by many who considered him an opportunistic journalist rather than an explorer. But he went on to achieve much after the death of Livingstone. He returned to East Africa in 1874 and in less than three years crossed the continent to the Atlantic Ocean. In 1879 he joined the service of King Leopold of Belgium and returned to explore the Congo Basin.

The purpose of this expedition was political, and it marks a turning point in the history of Africa. The 'scramble for Africa' began in the 1880s, and in a few years most of Africa was parcelled up between the European powers. The colonial era had begun.

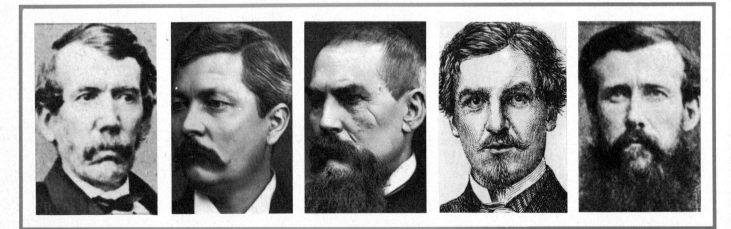

Five men who braved intense heat, disease and the unknown in Africa

Far left, the famous David Livingstone (1813–73). Born in Scotland, he worked in a cotton mill from the age of ten to 23, before qualifying as a doctor. As an explorer and missionary he contributed greatly to the knowledge of southern Africa.

Henry Morton Stanley (1841–1904), *left,* was a Welshman who ran away to New Orleans. His journey to Africa to find Livingstone was only the first of his adventures as an explorer. Apart from his discoveries in East Africa, he opened up the Congo region for the King of Belgium and established trading stations there. Richard Burton (1821–90), *centre,* was an eccentric Englishman

who, among other things, visited Mecca disguised as a Moslem. With John Speke (1827–64), *right,* he explored the interior of East Africa. Relations between the two became very strained and Speke returned to Africa with another companion, James Grant (1827–92), *far right.* The feud between Speke and Burton only ended when Speke accidentally shot himself.

The great drive to the west

The lure of the East and the hope of a northwest passage brought early ships to the coasts of North America. It was gold that finally took the American trail-blazers across the Rockies.

IN 1859, Horace Greeley, editor of the New York *Tribune,* set out for San Francisco on an overland journey which made American newspaper history. His dispatches, masterpieces of 'on-the-spot' journalism, enthralled the public. But nothing reflected the spirit of the times more vividly than his famous headline – 'Go west, young man, go west!'

In some respects, it was surprising that this should have been so, for the eastern seaboard settlements which formed the springboard of the great westward movement were themselves a rather late development – and to start with, a very limited one in relation to the early history of exploration in the continent.

Much of the initial exploration of North, as well as Central and South America, was prompted by the desire to find a westward route to the Orient. Once America had been discovered by Columbus, whatever else it proved to be, it remained a tiresome obstacle blocking the direct route to India, the Indies and China. In a vain search for a way through the great land mass, navigators probed any wide river mouth, any bay, any strait that appeared at all promising; but each time, as the land closed in upon them, they knew once again that they had failed.

Up the St Lawrence to China?

Even after Magellan had found the first answer in 1520 by sailing through the straits at the southern tip of South America, the search for an easier alternative – a northwest passage – continued.

John Cabot, a Venetian seaman sailing from Bristol, explored the Gulf of the St Lawrence and the shores of Nova Scotia in 1497 to 1498. His son Sebastian investigated hundreds of miles of the east coast in 1508 to 1509, and having passed through Hudson Strait to reach the wide entrance of Hudson Bay, was temporarily overjoyed by the conviction that he had found the Pacific.

Other famous navigators – Frobisher, Davis and Gilbert among them – were all to seek a northwest passage later in the sixteenth century, and all without success. Their names are strewn across the map of the great northern archipelago, silently signposting failure.

Meanwhile, in 1524, the Florentine brothers Verrazano had explored Delaware and Chesapeake Bays, New York Harbour entrance and the lower Hudson River area; Henry Hudson himself, however, did not explore the region carefully until much later, between 1608 and 1610, and then largely on behalf of the Dutch.

In 1535, Jacques Cartier sailed up the St Lawrence River as far as the site of Montreal, convinced for a while that he had found the way to China. He had in-

One warm May evening in 1859, the portly bespectacled figure of Horace Greeley, journalist, stood alone on the platform of the Erie Railroad Station in New York City. He was about to start on a journey across the continent by railroad, steamboat and stage coach until the trail ended at the Pacific's glorious Golden Gate in San Francisco. Greeley wanted to see a slice of mid-nineteenth-century America and he wanted his readers to see it too through the liveliness and skill of his reporting. He was following in a tradition which had been firmly established by the end of the eighteenth century when the continent was first opened up by the trail blazers and then colonized by the homesteading families, like the one below, who suffered danger and hardship in the untamed land.

deed discovered a route of immense importance, and simultaneously laid the claims of France to a large part of the New World, but he had not found the northwest passage.

Characteristically, Spain was also active in the exploration of North America, concentrating on the regions fringing the Gulf of Mexico. Ponce de León followed the Florida coast in 1513, while the subsequent expedition of Hernando de Soto between 1539 and 1543 was characterized by all the initiative and flamboyance of the Spanish *conquistadores.* De Soto had already accompanied Pizarro during the conquest of Peru and was now seeking a fortune in North America. At the head of a small band of men, he marched through the wilderness of the Deep South for more than four years, living off the land. In 1541, he discovered the lower Mississippi.

Other Spaniards, notably Francisco Coronado and Garcia Cardenas, pushed west through Texas and Arizona to gaze in awe into the gaping chasm of the Grand Canyon. Together they extended Spain's immense empire well over 500

miles into North America in a broad sweep from California to Florida, where in 1565 the small mission town of St Augustine was established as the first permanent European settlement in the whole of North America.

But the *conquistadores* failed to find what, for the Spaniards, were the real prizes of exploration – rich sources of gold and silver and the densely populated Indian civilizations which were the wonder of the Spanish empire farther south. There were in fact no North American Indian cultures ever to compare with those of the Mayas, Aztecs or Incas. Although they were very widely distributed over tundra, mountains, deserts, woodlands and prairies, there were probably fewer than one million North American Indians when the great European explorations began at the end of the fifteenth century.

Several hundred distinct Indian communities had developed, among which some, like the Sioux, the Shawnee and the Iroquois, were more powerful or influential than others. But no highly centralized, city-building societies had emerged. Once mounted on horses, which the Spaniards themselves reintroduced into America, the plains Indians particularly became highly mobile and occasionally, like the Apache and Comanche, extremely troublesome; but their numbers were always much smaller than we generally realize.

Beyond the Spanish empire's northern margin, the impressive explorations of the French drew them right into the heart of North America. Cartier's early discovery of the St Lawrence was extended by Champlain, who explored the 'river-roads' across the Canadian Shield by the Ottawa–Huron route. This, in turn, was extended still farther by the splendid seventeenth-century expeditions of La Salle, Marquette and Joliet around the Great Lakes and down the Mississippi.

The French had in fact discovered, with the help of Indian trails and portages, the key line of movement into the very heart of the continent, for only a low divide near the present site of Chicago separates the two greatest waterways in North America.

The French established a tenuous line of trading posts right down to New Orleans, for although the Spanish had already found the mouth of the Mississippi in 1543, they did not probe far upstream.

The other interested European powers were left to explore what remained open to them between the extensive French and Spanish claims. The first successful English settlement at Jamestown in Virginia was not founded until 1607; this was followed in 1620 by the arrival of the Pilgrim Fathers in Massachusetts. During the seventeenth century more colonies were established along the east coast by various groups of settlers, particularly English, Dutch and Scandinavian, until most of the Atlantic tidewater area was taken up by about 1700.

Thus, apart from eighteenth-century Russian interests in Alaska, this great wedge-shaped land mass was penetrated mainly from trans-Atlantic sources, and on the map of North America their claims were gradually sketched in: New Spain, New France, New England, New Scotland, New Netherlands, New Sweden. The old world had at last planted its feet firmly in the new.

What happened next tended to reflect not only the relative advantages of the explorers' initial footholds but also their own attitudes and abilities as colonizers. Events were to show that the most successful of the new Americans were always those who could adapt most readily from the phase of pure exploration to that of effective colonization. In this respect, the Atlantic tidewater settlements emerged pre-eminent and among these the British settlements became the major spearhead of further westward exploration and discovery; population extended across the coastal plain and followed the rivers upstream into the Appalachian ridges.

Trappers and homesteaders

Meanwhile, other factors took a hand in shaping events. War between England and France in the mid-eighteenth century resulted in a resounding French defeat both in Europe and Quebec. Virtually the whole of New France passed into British hands in 1763 and, on paper at least, the acquisition of much of Canada and the lands east of the Mississippi suddenly gave Britain the lion's share of North America.

But not for long. The colonists based along the Atlantic seaboard revolted against English rule shortly afterwards, successfully declared their independence on 4 July 1776 and found, when the dust had settled, that they had inherited a boundary along the Mississippi and a vast area beyond the Appalachians about which they knew next to nothing.

The British retained Canada, including an old, well-established, French-speaking population in the St Lawrence valley. But English and French farming and fishing clusters tended to continue as small and separate communities, while the great bulk of Canada remained a huge wilderness, given over almost entirely to the fur-trading companies – particularly the Hudson's Bay Company.

Farther south, however, the great drive to explore and take up new territory began in earnest after the Revolutionary War. In the seventeenth and eighteenth centuries, 'going west' did not mean that the new American was California-bound; but the slogan was apt all the same, for in this period the pioneer found his 'west' in Pennsylvania, in Ohio and in Kentucky. Threading a way through the ridges and plateaux of the Appalachian system, explorers found gaps and defiles which made the mountains less of a barrier than had first appeared. This realization was a landmark in the opening of the continent.

On 13 September 1759 French Quebec fell to the British, *below*. During the night General James Wolfe and his men scaled the cliffs and then took the unsuspecting town from the heights.

This exquisite drawing of an Indian village and its varied activities was made in the late sixteenth century by James White, one of the first Europeans ever to live amongst the Indians.

The Spaniards, in the process of extending their empire well into North America, were the first Europeans to see the spectacular Grand Canyon *above* when they moved west through Arizona.

ARCTIC OCEAN

Davis 1585-1587

Frobisher 1576-1578

Hudson Strait

Sebastian Cabot 1508-1509

John Cabot 1497-1498

Hudson 1610

Cartier 1535

HUDSON BAY

CANADA

GULF OF ST. LAWRENCE

Canadian Shield

St. Lawrence

Quebec

NOVA SCOTIA

Columbia

Lewis and Clark 1804-1805

Great Lakes

Champlain 1613-16

Montreal

Hudson 1609

South pass

Marquette and Joliet 1673

La Salle 1679-1682

Appalachians

Hudson

UNITED STATES

Missouri

Cardenas 1540

Coronado 1540-1542

Ohio

Jamestown

Delaware Bay

ATLANTIC OCEAN

Mississippi

Cumberland Gap

Chesapeake Bay

De Soto 1539-1543

New Orleans

St. Augustine

Verrazano 1524

MEXICO

Columbus 1492-1493

De Leon 1513

GULF OF MEXICO

PACIFIC OCEAN

Columbus 1493-1502

European exploration of North America was undertaken for various reasons by many different nations. Early attempts to find a northwest passage proved fruitless, but they furnished valuable information about the great river routes of the interior. Cartier, in his voyage up the St Lawrence, claimed a large part of the New World for France, a claim later extended by Champlain and the expeditions around the Great Lakes. The Spanish, elated by success in South America, extended their empire northward to Florida, where they founded the first European settlement at St Augustine. Other nations staked their claims, but the British settlements were to form the spearhead of future westward expansion.

Absolute figures of heights and breadth of mountain ranges often mean little in terms of their effect on human movement. Relatively low ranges can greatly discourage penetration if easy passes through them cannot be found. But if these can be discovered, it matters little how high or how rugged the mountains may be on either side.

By the end of the eighteenth century, well-worn trails following the Susquehanna, Juniata, Potomac and other valleys converged in the Forks of the Ohio River, while the Wilderness Road through the spectacular Cumberland Gap had brought settlers into the fertile Bluegrass country of Kentucky and into Tennessee.

The trail-blazers were cast in the true mould of the traditional explorer identified in this period as hunters and trappers like James Harrod, Daniel Boone and Davy Crockett. Foot-loose and mobile, the frontiersmen pushed ever farther westward as the settlers closed up behind; thus the route-finder, constantly attracted by the unknown, was continually driven into it by the sheer numbers and energy of the colonists following hard on his heels.

This speed in the claiming of land in the United States, as the homesteading family unit replaced the individual, remains the distinguishing feature of the country's development.

Gold at Sutter's Mill

Once the Appalachian watershed had been straddled, trail-blazer and settler alike found once again the great 'river-roads' which the French had followed down to the Mississippi a century or more earlier. They found rivers flowing the way they wanted to go. Above all, they found the Ohio, which carried them into the woodlands and prairies of the Middle West—a vast continental interior which future generations of Americans would develop into the richest of its kind in the world.

Meanwhile the early nineteenth-century explorers were already far ahead – at the edge of the wilderness, on and beyond the Mississippi. Some were miners and prospectors, some trappers; others were traders, Indian fighters or buffalo-hunters in the vast tract of country west of the Mississippi which the United States government had acquired from France in 1803 under the Louisiana Purchase. This area had been reclaimed from Spain by Napoleon, but in 1803 Bonaparte was too preoccupied with affairs in Europe to spare much thought for this last enormous slice of French America.

Indeed, while Napoleon knew next to nothing about what he had sold, the Americans knew little more about what they had bought. Originally intending to bargain only for New Orleans, they had come away with so much territory that the total area of the United States had been more than doubled at a single stroke.

Before many months had passed, President Thomas Jefferson had dispatched two officers, Meriwether Lewis and William Clark, to explore routes through the Louisiana Purchase territory. They followed the Missouri – that 'muddy, mis-

Above, a frontier town in Colorado, typical of many that were built during the surge westwards. Notice that the buildings are not solidly built but are mainly just façades, some even surmounted by pediments, which give an air of permanency to a very unsettled existence. More and more adventurers were pulled towards the west by the gold strikes in California. Americans realized the need for a railroad and the first was built in the 1860s with much resistance from buffaloes and Indians.

chievous river' – and worked their way to the mouth of the Columbia. The determination grew to consolidate the United States from the Atlantic to the Pacific.

Fur-trappers and prospectors soon found that the easiest of all the routes through the Rockies lay at South Pass in Wyoming, and the Oregon Trail was well established by the 1840s. Expansion westward led to the acquisition of more land from Mexico (formerly Spanish territory) and Britain – sometimes by conflict, sometimes by more peaceful means, but always by the local supremacy of the settlers themselves.

The greatest single discovery ever made in western North America was almost certainly the glint of gold in the gravels at Sutter's Mill in California in 1848 – not just because of the richness of the initial strikes, but because of the impact it made on the rest of the continent.

The location of this and other finds in the far west had an electrifying effect on westward movement, for it pulled settlers of many kinds right across to the far side of the continent, through arid, desolate country which might otherwise have put a brake on rapid expansion westward for a very considerable time.

More trails were opened; more Americans in the east became sharply aware of the extent of their country, of its wealth and variety, and of the need to lessen the isolation of western America by the construction of a trans-continental railroad. 'Men and brethren!' cried Greeley in 1859, 'let us resolve to have a railroad

to the Pacific – and to have it *soon!*' Many of them agreed with him, and the first line was completed only ten years later.

Other mineral strikes brought prospectors doubling back later in the nineteenth century, into the Rockies, into Alaska and elsewhere, often into areas which the 'forty-niners' and others had passed by in the first stampede into California. Indeed, much of the Great Plains country of both Canada and the United States, from Alberta to Texas, awaited discoveries of another sort – technological developments – before their potentials could be more fully explored.

Look to the north

More trans-continental railroads, barbed-wire fencing, the well-drill, the wind-pump, irrigation schemes, scientific breeding and selection of crops and cattle, pest control, the location of immense oil and natural gas reserves – all these, and many more, were discoveries or inventions which proved to be landmarks in the opening of America's and Canada's western plains.

Today, in terms of new resources, both nations, with their combined populations of 220 millions, are forced to look to the far north of the continent. Harsh and difficult though Canada's northland will inevitably remain, it is now the only major area of mineral wealth left in North America still to be more fully explored. Wherever the enormous costs involved appear to be justified, exploitation is likely to follow.

On foot across the frozen ocean

The Arctic Ocean has seen many famous expeditions, some ending disastrously. Early explorers had to endure incredible hardships; today scientists can travel *under* the ice cap in comfort.

EARLY EXPLORATION of the Arctic was undertaken in conditions which would horrify those who lead the well-equipped scientific expeditions of the present day. A case in point is Sir John Ross, who set off in his ship the *Victory* in 1829 to attempt to find a northwest passage from the Atlantic to the Pacific.

The *Victory* was no converted man-of-war, as its name suggests. It was one of the earliest of all paddle-steamers, bought second-hand after it had been found unsuitable for its original task on the Liverpool–Isle of Man service!

The expedition was trapped in the ice for three years. Eventually the ship was abandoned as useless and Ross and his party set out with sledges and small boats in search of help. A fourth long winter had to be spent, this time in a makeshift hut, before the party was rescued.

Not all Arctic exploration was like this. Earlier attempts to find a northwest passage achieved much in a comparatively short space of time. The earliest attempts were made by Frobisher in 1576, though he quickly became diverted into the first – and unsuccessful – Arctic gold rush. Following him came John Davis, until he too was diverted from Arctic exploration by the need to fight the Spanish Armada in 1588.

Most important of all was Henry Hudson. His contribution to Polar exploration was quite outstanding. In approximately the same amount of time as Ross spent fast in the ice two centuries later, Hudson reached 80°N off east Greenland and visited Spitsbergen (1607); attempted a northeast pas-

sage and reached Novaya Zemlya (1608); crossed the Atlantic and discovered what is now the Hudson river and the site of New York (all in 1609).

Finally he sailed northwestwards to discover the strait and bay which bear his name (1610–11). Eventually his luck ran out; his crew mutinied and Hudson and six others were cast adrift in a small boat in the Hudson Bay. They were not seen again.

This first phase of Arctic exploration, mainly – though not entirely – by British explorers, reached its culmination in 1616. In that year Bylot – one of the Hudson mutineers – and an English navigator, William Baffin, took Hudson's ship the *Discovery* as far north as 77°N. In this

The remains of Sir John Franklin and his party were found on King William Island in 1859. For three years nobody thought of looking for them.

The Viking ships of the Norwegian Eric the Red left Iceland in 982 on a voyage of discovery. The dazzling icebergs of Greenland must have been strangely attractive, for he spent three years there and on his return named the island Greenland to persuade people to go there.

tiny craft of 55 tons they discovered and explored what was later called Baffin Bay and the three channels, Jones Sound, Lancaster Sound and Smith Sound, which open off it.

At this time the immediate need for a northwest passage was small. Early exploration was distinctly commercial: the merchants who financed the voyages were less interested in the Arctic than in finding a way through to the Orient. After the defeat of the Spanish Armada, such a route became unnecessary. Interest in the northwest passage was not even revived by the establishment of the Hudson's Bay Company in 1670.

Trappers and whalers

The Company dealt primarily in beaver fur, and the beaver lived among the softwood forests of the Sub-Arctic, not on the treeless barrens of the Arctic. Not until the twentieth century were the first truly Arctic Hudson's Bay Company posts established.

For a long time, the whaling captains were the keenest Arctic travellers. Little is known about where the whales were hunted, because each captain was competing with the others, and such information was kept secret. We do not know where the whaling captains went, but we do know that there were many people engaged in whaling and that it was highly dangerous. From the port of Hull alone, 80 whaling ships were lost between 1772 and 1852.

In the seventeenth and eighteenth centuries, it was Russia that kept alive the story of Arctic exploration. In 1725 Peter the Great charged the Danish explorer, Vitus Bering, with the task of determining whether there existed a land bridge between Asia and North America.

Sailing northeastwards along the coast of Siberia, Bering and his party discovered St Lawrence Island and satisfied themselves that there was no land bridge to North America; but they made no attempt to ascertain the width of the gap which separates these continents.

Along the coast of Siberia

Another, much larger, expedition, the Great Northern Expedition, was organized by Bering in 1733–41. One of its major contributions was the exploration and mapping of the Arctic coast of Siberia, showing where a northeast passage was ultimately to be made.

In 1741 Bering led his own party in another voyage in search of North America. His ships eventually made a landfall on the Alaska coast near Mt St Elias. The party landed there for less than a day, mainly to obtain fresh water, but on the return voyage the *St Peter* was wrecked on what is now Bering Island. There, during the winter of 1741–2, Bering died.

The survivors struggled back to Siberia in the spring, together with an immense load of valuable furs. The appearance of these skins launched a 'fur rush' to the Aleutians (and subsequently to the islands off the Alaska mainland) which lasted until the end of the century.

By 1799 the fur resources were being exhausted through over-hunting and the Russian government therefore established a chartered company with monopoly powers similar to the Hudson's Bay Company. This company continued to administer and exploit the area which is now the state of Alaska until it was sold to

These white, alpine-like flowers are like many which blossom during the short summer in Alaska. The air is mild, but the ground is permanently frost-bound a few feet below the surface.

the United States of America in 1867.

Away on the eastern side of North America, the annual supply ships of the Hudson's Bay Company were mainly concerned with reaching the trading posts in the Bay itself. In the vast stretch of the northern coastline of North America between Baffin Bay and the Icy Cape reached by Captain Cook from Bering Strait in 1778, late eighteenth-century maps could show only two known points, the mouths of the Coppermine and Mackenzie Rivers.

Samuel Hearne had, in 1772, been led to the mouth of the Coppermine by Indians, whose use of native copper encouraged the Hudson's Bay Company to think that there might, after all, be something worth finding in the Barren Grounds beyond the tree line. He was disappointed; the copper, when found, was small in quantity.

At the time, the exploration of the Mackenzie produced even greater disappointment. Although the Coppermine flows across the treeless tundra, westwards the tree line extends further and further northward, until it reaches the Arctic

coast near the mouth of the Mackenzie. Where there were trees there were beaver, and this was one reason why Alexander Mackenzie was anxious to explore the area.

It was not, however, the main reason. Mackenzie was a partner in the biggest rival of the Hudson's Bay Company, the North West Company, based on Montreal. In this rivalry the North West Company was handicapped by the vast distances across which its trade canoes had to be paddled and carried from Montreal to the fur-bearing areas.

In the late eighteenth century there seemed a chance that the Montreal company could capture the advantage. From the Athabasca country of the northwest, another trader, Peter Pond, had reported that a great river flowed away to the northwest. On the Pacific, Captain Cook had also described the great gulf of Cook Inlet, apparently the estuary of a major river.

If Pond's river was the same one, and flowed into the ice-free North Pacific, then the North West Company could seize the initiative. It could avoid both the thousands of miles of weary paddling and portage from Montreal and the annual voyage through drifting ice to Hudson Bay which faced its competitors.

The River of Disappointment

On 14 July 1789, however, it was clear that this revolution would not take place. While the mob stormed the Bastille in Paris, Mackenzie stood on the Arctic Ocean at the mouth of what he called the River of Disappointment. Fortunately the river was later renamed after Mackenzie himself.

Mackenzie's discovery had coincided with the birth of the French Revolution. The aftermath of the French wars provided the impetus for a determined assault on the Arctic which began in 1818 and ended exactly a century later. The Royal Navy took a major part in this assault, partly because its energies were no longer needed in warfare.

Two expeditions were organized in 1818;

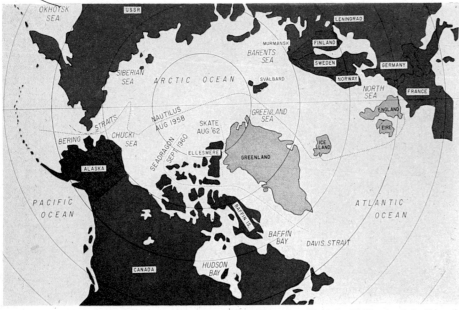

No development in Arctic travel has been more sensational than the journey under the North Pole by the American nuclear submarine

Nautilus. On 22 July 1958 she left Hawaii, passing under the North Pole at 11.15 a.m. on 3 August. Her epic voyage eventually ended at

Portland in England. Since that time, many submarines, including the newer *Skipjack, above,* have glided beneath the polar cap.

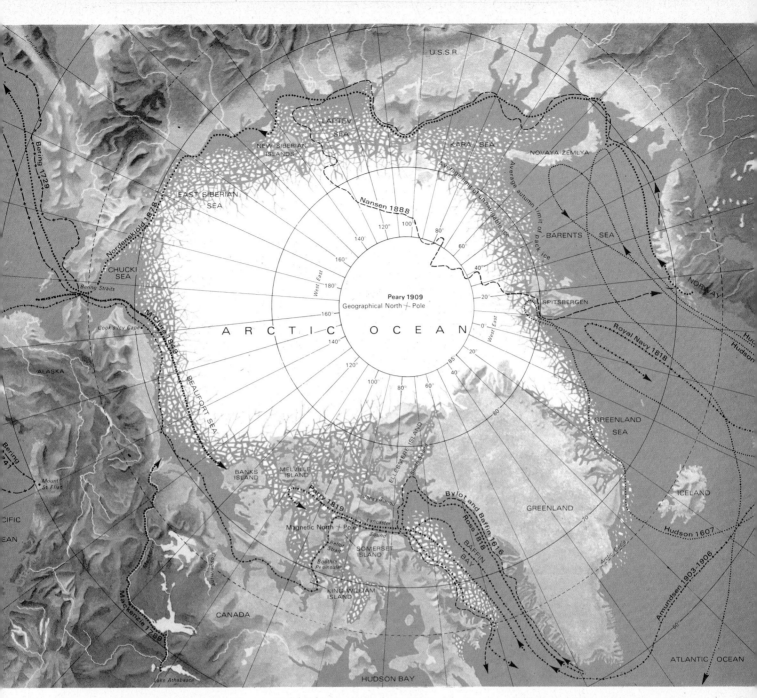

one of these sailed northwards to the Spitsbergen area, only to be turned back by the pack-ice; the second was led northwestwards by Sir John Ross, with rather better ships than the *Victory* he was to use a decade later. It was more than two centuries since Baffin's great achievement in the *Discovery*, and to the sophisticated geographers of the nineteenth century, that voyage in 1616 seemed incredible.

Ross vindicated Baffin's reputation, but he missed the opportunity of extending Baffin's work by exploring the various sounds off Baffin Bay, all of which Ross believed were merely enclosed bays. Ten years later he was to miss an even greater opportunity when the *Victory* sailed past the inconspicuous entrance of Bellot Strait, separating Somerset Island from Boothia Peninsula – an essential part of the only dependable northwest passage.

Ross's failure was Parry's opportunity. Second-in-command to Ross in 1818, Parry persuaded the Admiralty, when the expedition returned, to make him the leader of another expedition. In 1819 he returned

Since 825 BC, when the Greek Pytheas is supposed to have sailed as far as Iceland, there have been many tales about the cold land at the end of the Earth. Whalers, sealers and beaver hunters played an enormous part in exploring the area. Commercial motives also prompted early desires to find a passage from the Atlantic to the Pacific, a more convenient route to the Orient. Bering, the Danish explorer who discovered the famous straits, was sent by Peter the Great with instructions to see if a land bridge existed which would lead from Asia to North America. Later, northwest and northeast passages were found. The Arctic has now been explored, but scientific investigation is still of supreme importance.

to Baffin Bay, and triumphantly sailed along Lancaster Sound as far west as Melville Island. The ice then blocked their way, and Parry eventually returned to Britain. Nevertheless, he had pointed the main way into the Canadian Arctic archipelago. The detailed studies of Arctic life which the expedition made were also the beginnings of the scientific investigation of the Arctic.

For some time to come, however, exploration rather than science continued

to dominate the scene. A series of unsuccessful attempts were made on the northwest passage, including that in the *Victory,* and then the Admiralty made its biggest effort to solve the problem, sending the *Erebus* and *Terror* with 129 men under Sir John Franklin.

Loss of the Franklin expedition

The Franklin voyage and the search for Franklin have both been the subject of innumerable books. The ships, provisioned for four years and carefully manned, entered Lancaster Sound in the summer of 1845 and then disappeared completely. So sure was the Admiralty of the ultimate success of the expedition that little worry was felt for three years. Then there began a search for Franklin's ships on a grand scale.

During the search, the first actual northwest passage was made, although not in the way expected. McClure, in the *Investigator,* passed through Bering Strait from the Pacific (hoping to meet Franklin en route) and, sailing eastwards, was frozen in on the north side of Banks Island. His party was later rescued by another naval expedition exploring from Melville Island with sledges, and so he and his crew achieved a northwest passage round North America, though from west to east and partly on foot. Although little sign of Franklin was found by any of the searchers, the voyages and the sledge journeys contributed an immense amount to the knowledge of the geography of the Canadian Arctic.

In 1854 the first news of the whereabouts of the missing ships became known. Eskimos at Pelly Bay reported to Dr Rae of the Hudson's Bay Company that ships had been frozen in on the northwest coast of King William Island.

The final proof of what had happened was obtained by McClintock, one of the greatest of naval explorers, who in 1859 reached the area where the ships had been wrecked. He found the tragic remains of the party, which had apparently abandoned the ships and attempted to reach safety hundreds of miles away on the mainland. One group had died in the attempt to haul an extremely heavy boat mounted on a sledge.

A characteristic of the 'age of the navy' was its assumption that nineteenth-century western man represented the peak of human development and had nothing to learn from the 'savage' Eskimo.

First to reach the North Pole

Although the Eskimo survived and even flourished in the Arctic, this was not taken as a sign that his furs might be preferable to naval uniforms, that his dogs might haul sledges more efficiently than could men, or that his food might be less likely to cause scurvy than were naval rations. A vast amount of geographic and scientific knowledge in the Arctic was purchased at an equally enormous cost.

The end of the Franklin search marked the end for some time of a search for a northwest passage. Most agreed that if one existed it would be commercially useless. When a true passage was achieved, by Amundsen in the early years of the twentieth century, it came almost by accident.

After two winters spent making magnetic measurements near the Magnetic Pole, Amundsen continued westwards and eventually reached the Pacific. The first northwest passage, by Norderskiöld in 1878, had equally been something of an anticlimax.

Within the Arctic a few islands remained to be discovered north of Lancaster Sound. This task was undertaken by the Norwegians in 1898–1902, and fittingly completed by a Canadian government expedition led by Stefansson in 1913–18. By the time the American, Robert Peary, who was the first to reach the North Pole, arrived there in 1909, attention was already being concentrated on the scientific importance of the Arctic, especially as a result of the International Polar Year (1882–3).

Paradoxically, one of the last areas to be explored had also been one of the first. Eric the Red began the exploration of Greenland in 982, but his task was not

A drawing entitled 'A Wonder in the Heavens and How we Caught a Bear', from the notebooks of Willem Barrents, who set out to seek a northeast passage in 1596 and died in the attempt.

Nansen took over where Eric the Red left off. He crossed the inland ice of Greenland in 1888.

Peary reached the North Pole in 1909 and proved there was neither land nor open sea there.

completed until Nansen achieved the first crossing of the inland ice in 1888 and until the north coast was explored and mapped by the Danes in 1906–12.

In the twentieth century, the more detailed scientific investigation of the Arctic has become of great importance. Few ships attempt a northwest passage, but the northwest passage – and the North Pole – are regular routes for airlines.

In eastern Asia the Trans-Siberian railway and Aeroflot span the continent across which Bering struggled two centuries ago, and in the Canadian Arctic, where Ross was frozen in for so many winters, there are motor toboggans, helicopters and light aircraft instead of man-hauled sledges. Above all, there is radio.

What then remains to attract the explorer north? Apart from the scientific

problems, there is the attraction of the solitude and still much that is unknown and unexpected. The winter on Ellesmere Island is very long and very cold; for a third of the year the temperature may fall below −40° F. But the snow disappears from the lowlands in mid-June and does not return until late August.

In the short summer there are bumblebees and butterflies – and a little Arctic willow which hugs the ground for protection but survives thousands of miles beyond the conventional tree-line. There is a coal seam, evidence that once this Arctic area was covered with warm, wet forests.

Such discoveries not only expand our knowledge of the Arctic, but they also help to solve some of the problems of geology, of tree growth and of insect life which are important further south.

Discovery in the White South

Antarctica is a forbidding continent of blizzards and glaciers. Yet ever since a Russian admiral first sighted the mainland in 1820, it has attracted an increasing number of expeditions.

A BELIEF in the existence of a great land mass in the world's southernmost region dates back to the Greeks. But it was not until the late fifteenth century and the great Portuguese voyages inspired by Prince Henry the Navigator that the imaginary terrors of the unknown southern waters were overcome.

In 1675, a British expedition led by Antonio de la Roche was probably the first to discover the sub-Antarctic island of South Georgia, and 11 years later a Spanish ship, the *Leon,* sighted and circumnavigated the island.

In 1739 the Frenchman Bouvet de Lozier discovered Bouvet Island, and in 1772 his fellow countrymen Kerguelen, Tremarec and Marion-Dufresne discovered Kerguelen Island and the Crozet Islands, claiming them for France. These were the first recorded territorial claims in sub-Antarctic regions.

The most significant of these early voyages, however, was that of the British navigator, Captain James Cook. On his voyage round the world between 1772 and 1775, Cook circumnavigated Antarctica, crossing the Antarctic Circle for the first time and exploding for ever the myth of a southern continent stretching north into temperate zones. He took possession of South Georgia and sighted the southern South Sandwich Islands.

With club and harpoon

On his return he brought back to England not only a wealth of scientific data, but accounts of vast herds of seals on the shores of sub-Antarctic islands, of fortunes in blubber and fur waiting to be harvested by the adventurous.

British sealers started work at South Georgia in 1778, and were soon followed by Americans. The industry developed rapidly: by 1791 there were over 100 sealers working in the Southern Ocean, extracting oil from elephant seals and pelts from fur seals.

In the same year, an American, Daniel Greene, circumnavigated the world to carry fur seal pelts to the Chinese market; and in 1800 another American, Edward Fanning, took 57,000 fur seals from South Georgia in a single voyage. By the end of the 1880s the slaughter had brought the animals near to extinction in most of the sealing grounds of the Southern Ocean.

Before the end of the century, sealing had been replaced by whaling and, despite control by the International Whaling Commission, it is in danger of following the same pattern as sealing.

The year 1820 saw the discovery of the mainland of Antarctica itself. A Russian expedition, under Admiral Thaddeus Bellingshausen, sighted two areas on the coasts of Crown Princess Martha Coast

Scott and his expedition arrived at the South Pole only to find that Amundsen had got there first, *top.* On the return journey all perished. This poignant message was found by a search party.

'Had we lived I should have had a tale to tell of the hardihood, endurance and courage of my companions which would have stirred the heart of every Englishman . . .', wrote Captain Scott.

and Princess Ragnhild Coast, in Queen Maud Land.

Two days later a British expedition under Edward Bransfield discovered and charted part of the northwest coast of the Antarctic Peninsula, which they named Trinity Land. In the same year Nathaniel Palmer, captain of a United States sealer, reported the land now known as the Palmer Coast of the Antarctic Peninsula. Bransfield went on south to discover Peter I Island and Alexander Land. The first actual landing in Antarctica seems to have been made by a United States sealer, John Davis, in 1821 in Hughes Bay.

Sealing expeditions were responsible for many important discoveries. The British sealer John Biscoe, who circumnavigated Antarctica in 1830–2, discovered Enderby Land, Adelaide Island and the northern Biscoe Islands, and claimed Graham Land, part of the Antarctic Peninsula, for Great Britain.

Another British expedition, under Peter Kemp, came upon Kemp Land in Antarctica in 1833. The French, too, were active and in 1840 Captain Dumont d'Urville with two frigates, discovered and annexed Adélie Land on the Antarctic mainland, which he called after his wife.

Another circumnavigation was made by a British naval expedition commanded by Sir James Ross in 1839–43. H.M.S. *Erebus* and *Terror* were the first ships to force their way through the pack ice of the Ross Sea to discover, chart and claim some 500 miles of the coast of Victoria Land, including Ross Island, the James Ross Island group off the coast and the Ross Ice Front.

Late in the century a Norwegian whaling expedition, led by C. A. Larsen, discovered King Oscar Coast and the Foyn Coast on the Weddell Sea coast of the Antarctic Peninsula and the outlying Robertson Island, penetrating as far as 68° 10′ south.

The outline of Antarctica and the associated island groups was therefore officially known by the end of the nineteenth century, and subsequent geographical discoveries have filled in details and added inland features.

As the nineteenth century progressed, scientific work gained precedence over purely geographical aims of exploration. The years 1874–5 drew no less than four national scientific expeditions from Britain, France and Germany to high southern latitudes to observe the Transit of Venus, in December, 1874.

The century closed with a Belgian and a German expedition. In 1898–9, the *Belgica* discovered and mapped the Danco Coast area in the north of the Antarctic Peninsula. They were trapped by the pack ice and became the first exploration ship to spend a winter in the Antarctic. The German Deep Sea Expedition of 1898–9 made an oceanographical cruise to the islands of Kerguelen and Bouvet.

The voyage of the 'Discovery'

The early years of the twentieth century saw the period known as the 'heroic age' of Antarctic exploration, an era associated with the great names of Antarctic history – Scott, Shackleton, Mawson, Amundsen.

The century began with a British expedition in 1898–1900 led by C. E. Borchgrevink – the first scientific party to winter on the mainland. They examined a large stretch of the Victoria Land coast and of the Ross Ice Front, wintering at Cape Adare and carrying out investigations in the zoology, geology, meteorology and the terrestrial magnetism of the surrounding area.

Three expeditions set out for the Antarctic in 1901 from three separate countries – Great Britain, Germany and Sweden.

The British National Antarctic Expedition of 1901–4, led by Captain Robert Scott, was the first to make an extensive penetration on land in Antarctica; sledge parties examined the coast of Victoria Land and the Ross Ice Front, discovered King Edward VII Land on the eastern border of the Ross Sea, and reached 77° 59′ south and 146° east.

Perhaps most important of all, invaluable lessons were learnt and experience gained in living and travelling for long periods away from the safety of coastal bases, the techniques of depot laying and support parties, the strains and demands of a three-month sledging journey, and the proving of equipment and supplies.

The expedition included a botanist, a zoologist, a geologist, a physicist and a biologist, in addition to seven naval officers and 21 seamen. Their ship *Discovery* remained ice-bound at Hut Point, Ross

Below, left, one of Scott's well-stocked bases in Antarctica, erected during the disastrous expedition of 1910–12. Modern Antarctic travel is infinitely safer. *Right,* an American icebreaker cuts a path in the Ross Sea ice for supply ships while a Sno-cat tractor stands by to meet it.

Left, Emperor penguins stand meditatively in the snow, while towering Mount Erebus, the only live volcano in Antarctica, smokes in the background. *Right,* one of the many magnificent ice-formations to be found all over the continent, these ice-caves are on Ross Island.

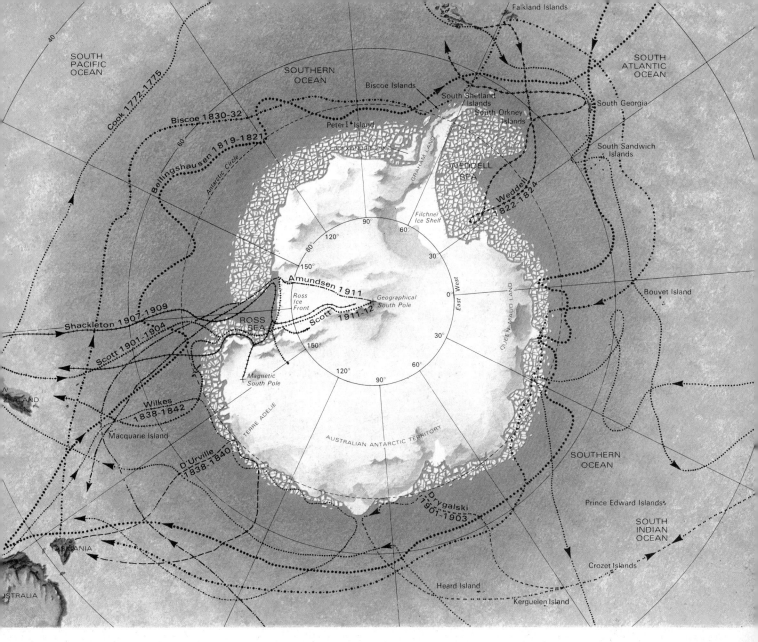

Tracks across Antarctica reveal the energetic interest taken by the explorers, whalers and seal-hunters of the world in the desolate continent of the far South. The sea passages of early travellers established the geography of

Antarctica, and gave its landscapes the names of European royalty – and even of the explorers' wives. Today, Antarctic travel is airborne, and equipped with tough motorized vehicles. The brave men who took dogs and sledges across the

snow have been replaced by well-supplied scientific researchers. But although the world's interest in Antarctica is now scientific exploitation rather than geographic discovery, the fascination of the polar continent retains its power.

Island, and was used as living quarters, while a prefabricated hut was erected on shore for use as a laboratory.

Activity was now intensified in the Antarctic Peninsula region. William S. Bruce's Scottish National Antarctic Expedition of 1902–4, in *Scotia,* carried out an oceanographical exploration of the Weddell Sea, discovering the Caird Coast. J. B. Charcot in *Français* wintered off west Graham Land, and discovered the Loubet Coast southwards from 66° 20′ south to the Adelaide Islands in 67° 46′ south.

In 1907–9 Sir Ernest Shackleton, who had been a member of Scott's *Discovery* expedition, returned to Ross Island in the *Nimrod.* He led a party to within a mere 97 miles of the South Pole, and discovered some 500 miles of mountain ranges flanking the Ross Ice Shelf.

Before the winter set in, a party under T. W. E. David penetrated as far as the South Magnetic Pole area in Victoria Land. J. B. Charcot's expedition in *Pourquoi-Pas?* discovered and charted for the first time the southern west coast of

the Antarctic Peninsula, in 1908–10.

In 1910 Scott returned to Antarctica in the *Terra Nova* to continue the scientific work of his previous expedition and to make another assault on the South Pole. Some 300 miles east of his base at Cape Evans, Ross Island, the Norwegian Roald Amundsen set up a winter base in preparation for a dash to the same goal.

Triumph and tragedy

Amundsen's party got away first in 1911, and after a superbly executed dog-sledge journey across the Ross Ice Shelf and up the Axel Heiberg Glacier in the Queen Maud Mountains – all undiscovered territory – reached the South Pole on 14 December 1911.

Scott's party, following his own earlier route and Shackleton's, reached the South Pole on 17 January 1912, just one month later, having done useful work on the biology, geology, glaciology, meteorology and geophysics of the coast of Victoria Land. Misfortune, exhaustion and illness dogged the return journey. One of the

party, Captain L. E. G. Oates, too ill to travel further, deliberately walked out into a blizzard in the hope that this sacrifice would save his friends, but storms pinned them down within 11 miles of a supply depot. It was eight months before search parties found their bodies.

Australia now appeared on the Antarctic scene, with Douglas Mawson's Australasian Antarctic Expedition of 1911–14 in *Aurora.* They discovered and explored King George V Land and Queen Mary Land, explored Adélie Land and sledged to the south Magnetic Pole area, in addition to conducting an extensive scientific programme.

In 1914–16 Ernest Shackleton returned on his ill-fated attempt to cross the continent from the Weddell Sea to the Ross Sea. His ship, *Endurance,* was caught in the pack ice and drifted for ten months in the Weddell Sea. It was finally crushed by the inexorable ice, leaving 28 men stranded on an ice floe which was drifting northwards.

Here they camped until, months later, they reached Elephant Island in the South

Shetland Islands. They rested there while Shackleton and four others sailed the whale boat *James Caird* across 800 miles of tempestuous seas to South Georgia, made the first crossing of the island and eventually rescued the Elephant Island party in August 1916.

Meanwhile a ten-man support party was marooned on Ross Island after their ship, the *Aurora,* had been driven from her moorings, and suffered severe privations while most gallantly attempting to lay depots for the expected trans-continental party, using supplies left behind by previous expeditions. Shackleton died on South Georgia in 1921.

The first flight over the Pole

Two series of expeditions began in the late 1920s with the primary objects of studying the marine biology and oceanography of Antarctic waters. The British series, Discovery Investigations, were based on the Discovery Committee's marine biological laboratory at Grytviken, in South Georgia. Between 1925 and 1939 five voyages were made for this purpose, followed by one in 1950–1.

Norwegian sealing interests in Antarctic waters gave rise to seven expeditions between 1927 and 1937, during which, in addition to marine investigations, various stretches of Queen Maud Land were discovered, though the only inland penetration was by air in the latter part of the series.

Air activities in Antarctica began with the pioneer flights of the Australian Hubert Wilkins in the Antarctic Peninsula during the 1928–9 and 1929–30 seasons, when 'Charcot Land' was proved to be an island. The 1928–9 season also saw the arrival of the first United States Antarctic Expedition, which wintered at the Bay of Whales in the Ross Ice Shelf (Amundsen's base area). Richard Byrd, besides discovering Marie Byrd Land, the Rockefeller Mountains and the Edsel Ford Ranges, made the first flight over the South Pole.

Whalemen are pictured 'cutting the blanket', as it is termed by the whalers. Strips of blubber are severed from the whale and hoisted aboard

Six years later the American Lincoln Ellsworth, at his third attempt, made the first trans-continental flight, discovering the area now known as Ellsworth Highland. Aircraft thenceforth became an accepted form of Antarctic travel, finally becoming the most important.

Permanent bases

In 1929–31, Britain, Australia and New Zealand combined in an Antarctic expedition led by Douglas Mawson. They discovered much of what became Australian Antarctic Territory – MacRobertson Land, the Banzare Coast and Princess Elizabeth Land – and made a number of air reconnaissances.

Byrd's second expedition continued the exploration of Marie Byrd Land, making extensive use of mechanical surface vehicles and he occupied, alone, a weather station 100 miles inland for seven months. The revolution which took place in the techniques of travel and communication

the whaleship *Charles W. Morgan* during a voyage in the South Pacific. One of the oldest whaleships, it is now preserved in America.

was in great measure due to Byrd's initiative.

The British Graham Land Expedition of 1934–7 to the Antarctic Peninsula, and Finn Ronne's United States expedition made ten years later to the same area, were the last of the privately organized expeditions in Antarctica; government-sponsored operations have taken their place.

The greater part of Antarctica has now been seen by man, even if only from the air. Scientific discovery, from being an incidental side-line, has become the main object of all expeditions. Nations have established permanent scientific bases which are relieved and re-supplied annually; today supplies and equipment in quantity and variety undreamt of by Scott and Shackleton are unloaded each summer on the Antarctic coast. The transformation is perfectly expressed at the United States main port of entry, McMurdo, where a nuclear power station looks down upon Scott's *Discovery* hut.

Huskies were introduced to the Antarctic from Alaska, *left.* Hitched to a sledge, they can carry men at speeds of up to 20 miles an hour for long periods of time. Their thick fur protects them from the severe cold as they sleep in the snow. *Right,* Scott's ship, the *Terra Nova,* at anchor in the Bay of Whales, is dwarfed by a huge iceberg. Soon after, Scott encountered Amundsen's party, which was to beat him to the South Pole.

Flat maps for a round world

Putting the Earth's curved surface on a flat sheet is an insoluble problem. The methods which have been devised are at best compromises. But they have enabled Man to travel the globe.

THE ONLY ACCURATE MAP of the Earth is a globe, on which countries, oceans and other features are charted on a sphere. Globes are valuable equipment for libraries and schoolrooms, but they are difficult to carry about and clumsy to use. Because of their small size they can show only the main features of the Earth. To give the detail required by such people as motorists or hikers, the globe would have to be enormous. Maps are attempts to represent the Earth's curved surface on a flat sheet of paper. It is possible to make a map of a small part of the globe without much distortion by tracing directly from it; in other words, curvature does not greatly affect the mapping of a very small part of the Earth's surface. But if the tracing paper is flattened over a large part of the globe, the paper will crumple and crease. For this reason, it is impossible to make a completely true map for any large area of the Earth.

Interruptions and projections

Many globes are covered by a paper surface, on which the Earth's features are printed. This paper consists of a series of triangles or strips called *gores* with well concealed joins. How have flat pieces of paper been fitted on a curved surface? The answer lies in the way the strips have been cut out, the skilled fingers of the globe-maker, and the careful distortion and stretching of the paper when it is wet. It is therefore possible to produce a world map which consists of the strips used to assemble the globe. Maps based on this principle are called *interrupted maps* and may be seen in some atlases. Looking rather like children's cut-outs, these maps require some imagination before the map-user can see how they represent the Earth. Oceans and continents are sometimes split into segments, and such maps are generally unsatisfactory because they do not represent the Earth's surface as a continuous whole. Interrupted maps are, however, a form of *map projection*; that is, a map-maker's attempt to show a curved surface on a flat piece of paper.

What does a map show? First and most important, a map must give the correct position of places. These are fixed on the Earth's surface by measurement of the *latitude* and *longitude*. Lines of latitude, also called *parallels,* are imaginary lines drawn parallel to the equator around the Earth. The equator is 0° latitude and the distance between the equator and the poles is divided into 90°. The latitude of any place is the number of degrees it lies north or south of the equator. Lines of longitude, or *meridians,* all pass through both poles and encircle the Earth. The angular distance

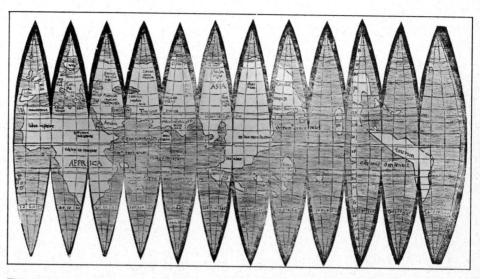

This interrupted map is believed to have been made by Martin Waldseemüller in 1509. When the segments or gores are pasted on to a globe they form a complete map of the world.

around the globe is 360°, which is measured as 180° east of Greenwich (latitude 0°), and 180° west of Greenwich. Lines of latitude and longitude intersect at right angles. Imagine a sphere with the curved parallels and meridians spaced at 10° intervals drawn on the surface. The lines then form a network called a *graticule.* The position of any place can be located on this graticule. As well as giving the accurate position of places, other valuable assets or properties of maps are that they preserve correct shapes, areas, distances and directions.

Map projections are designed to ensure that some of these properties are true. But no flat map can preserve all of them simultaneously. Hundreds of projections have been devised. In practice, comparatively few of them are used and none of them is completely satisfactory. The maps of an atlas use a variety of projections. Some have curved parallels and meridians, while others have graticules consisting of straight lines. Shapes are distorted on some maps, whereas areas are grossly inaccurate on others. On some projections, Greenland appears to be larger than South America, whereas South America is really more than eight times as big.

When map-makers are constructing map projections, they are not concerned with the details of a map. The positions of oceans, continents, cities and rivers can easily be plotted once a graticule of parallels and meridians has been arrived at. Projections are usually worked out from complicated mathematical formulae, but the simplest are *perspective projections.* To understand this group, visualize a glass sphere on which the graticule is

marked. If a light were placed at the centre of the sphere, the parallels and meridians would be projected as shadows on to a nearby flat surface. If a sheet of paper were placed touching one of the poles, at a tangent to the sphere, the shadow of the graticule on the paper would form a simple map projection. From the pole, the central point, the meridians would radiate outwards as straight lines. The parallels, however, would appear as concentric circles, which are increasingly widely spaced away from the pole. The equator would not appear on this projection, because it would be at right angles to the light at the centre of the sphere.

Distorted maps

The equator would appear if the light were moved from the centre of the sphere to the other pole. In this case, the entire hemisphere would be projected on the paper. But the diameter of the projected equator would be twice that of the diameter of the sphere. To correct this distortion, we can imagine the light source to be at infinity. The rays of light would then be parallel, and so the diameter of the equator on the projection would equal the diameter of the sphere. But in this case, the concentric circles formed by the parallels would get closer and closer together near the equator. The main feature of these three projections is that all bearings from the central point or pole are *azimuths* (true bearings). Such projections are known as *azimuthal projections.* Map-makers can use any point on the Earth's surface to develop such projections. A map showing true bearings from Johannesburg or New York, for example, can be made by using either city as the tangential point.

Using the same shadow-casting principle, similar projections can be developed by wrapping a cylinder or tube of paper around the sphere, touching the globe along a line rather than at a single point. *Cylindrical projections* are usually developed with the equator as the central line. If the shadows could somehow leave a mark when the paper cylinder was opened up, the graticule would appear on the inside. With the source of light at the centre of the globe, the parallels and meridians both project as straight lines at right angles to each other. The meridians are evenly spaced but the distance between the parallels increases enormously away from the equator, exaggerating areas to the north and south. The poles do not appear when the source of light is at the centre of the globe.

If the light source were at infinity, the parallels near the poles would be closely packed together. But a feature common to both versions of the cylindrical projection is that the parallels remain of the same length northwards and southwards. On a globe, the 80° parallel is a much smaller circle than the equator. This elongation of the parallel in the cylindrical projection causes an enormous stretching of the areas in polar regions. But this projection depicts the entire world on one sheet without interruption.

The other main type of perspective projection is the *conic projection,* also developed on the shadow-casting principle. This is drawn as if a cone of paper was placed over the globe, the top of the cone being directly above the pole, and the cone touching the globe along a parallel. Meridians project as straight lines and parallels as arcs of concentric circles. Distances are true along the parallel touching the cone. Some conic projections are developed as though the cone cuts through the globe along two parallels, giving two lines on the map where east–west distances are true.

Accurate charts

Another group of projections, called *conventional projections,* are completely unrelated to the perspective group. Conventional projections, including interrupted maps, are devised mathematically mainly for world maps. But many of the perspective projections have been so modified and adapted that their origin cannot easily be recognized. Mercator, the six-teenth-century Flemish geographer and map-maker, invented this cylindrical projection, which is still used for navigation charts. As on all cylindrical projections, the length of the parallels north and south of the equator are the same length as the equator. The 60° parallel on the projection is twice as long as it is on the globe; the 70° parallel is 15 times as long, and the 80° parallel is 33 times as long. Faced with this gross distortion, Mercator decided to distort the north–south spacing of the parallels by the same amount. At any spot on the projection, therefore, the scale along the parallels and meridians is exaggerated by an equal amount. The poles cannot be shown on this projection and the area of polar regions is greatly exaggerated, although shapes are generally preserved. Although this projection gives a very misleading impression of comparative areas, it was commonly used for maps of the British Empire. The main virtue of Mercator's projection is that any straight line on the map is a line of constant bearing.

Whenever a map-maker is commissioned to make a map, he must choose the projection that is best adapted to the purpose of the map. If a map is needed to show the distribution of population, vegetation or crops, the map-maker will not choose a Mercator projection, but one which represents areas accurately. His choice will also be affected by the area covered by the map, the shape of the area and the scale. Having chosen the projection and decided on the scale of the map, he must then fill in the details, plotting the positions of places from their latitude and longitude.

Thin lines and wide roads

The scale greatly affects the complication of the map. The finest line that can be reproduced on maps is 0·002 of an inch. On the original British Ordnance Survey maps, drawn to a scale of 1:63,360 (or one inch to a mile), this extremely fine line is the equivalent of 10 feet 6 inches on the ground. On a small scale of 1:1,000,000, the same line represents 166 feet 8 inches on the ground. A major river or road would only appear as a microscopically thin line if represented true to scale. Map-makers often represent roads on topographical maps by double lines about one-fortieth of an inch apart. On a scale of one inch to one mile, the road would therefore appear to be 153 feet wide on the map. The same width on a scale of 1:1,000,000 is nearly half a mile. For this reason cartographers usually use single lines for roads on small-scale maps. Except on the largest scales, the map-maker cannot draw such features as roads, rivers and railways accurately to scale. The problem of scale affects many other aspects of the map. On a large-scale plan, the outline of an airport can be accurately shown. On small-scale

One of the earliest known globes, this was made by the Flemish geographer, Mercator, in 1541. Globes are the only true representation of the Earth's surface, its features and distances.

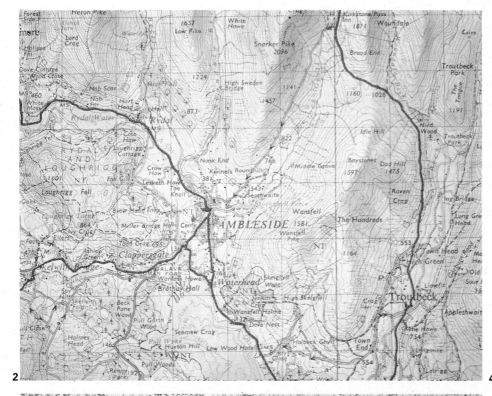

1 On maps too small to show detailed information features are indicated by the map-maker's code. The key or legend identifies the symbols.
2 This map of part of England's Lake District is on a scale of 1:63,360 or one inch to a mile. The brown contour lines, which join all points of the same height, are 50 feet apart.
3 The same part of the Lake District but this map is on a scale of 1:25,000 or two and a half inches to a mile. On this scale small features, such as footpaths and houses, can be shown.
4 Small-scale maps of the world use projections which avoid distortion of the land surface. Here atlases are checked at a printing works.

maps, the airport can only be indicated by a symbol. The amount of detail shown on a map decreases as the scale becomes smaller.

As a result of such problems, only large-scale maps and plans are genuine representations of the land as it would appear from a helicopter. Small-scale maps are essentially codified information about the land. Many maps give a table of conventional symbols, the map-maker's 'shorthand', in the map *legend* (key). The best symbols are those which can be recognized without reference to the legend. For example, a forest of fir trees can be represented by covering the area with regularly spaced green symbols that resemble fir trees.

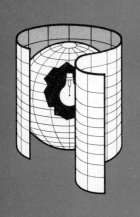

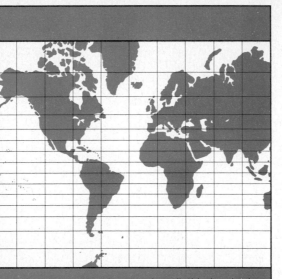

A light placed at the centre of a glass sphere would project the parallels and meridians as shadows on to a tube of paper wrapped round, producing a *cylindrical projection*.

Devised by Mercator, the cylindrical projection is still the most widely used method of map-making, though it greatly exaggerates the extent of areas in the far north and south.

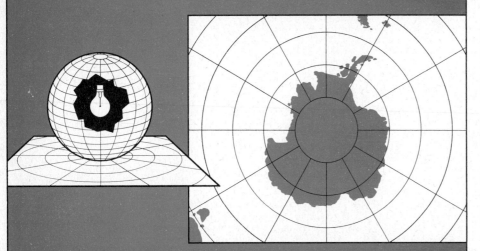

Alternatively, if a sheet of paper were placed touching one of the poles, at a tangent to the sphere, the shadow of the graticule on the paper would produce an *azimuthal projection*.

Azimuthal projection gives true bearings from the central point, and so is useful for charts. Anywhere on the Earth's surface may be chosen as the tangential point.

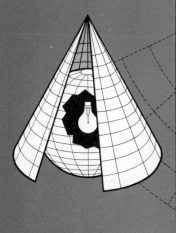

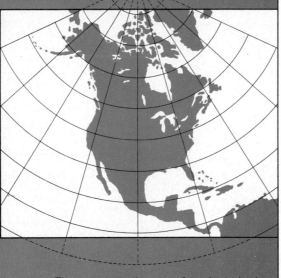

The other main type of perspective projection is the *conic projection*, in which meridians project as straight lines and parallels as arcs of concentric circles.

There are several types of conic projection in general use. Some of these are developed as if the cone cut the globe in two parallel circles.

Topographic maps contain four main types of symbols, depicting man-made features, water, vegetation and relief. Man-made or *cultural* symbols are usually shown in red or black, water in blue, vegetation in green, and relief in brown. Cultural features include cities, towns and villages. On large-scale maps, the cartographer can show the shape and size of a settlement. On small-scale maps, he uses small circles. The size of the lettering of the place names often indicates the size of a settlement on a small-scale map. Other cultural features include roads, railways, boundaries and, on large-scale maps, such features as cemeteries and mines. Rivers are depicted on small-scale maps by a single line. The cartographer does, however, distinguish between the narrow stream near the source and the broad river near the outlet to the sea, by gradually thickening the blue line from the source to the outlet.

On steep slopes

The chief method of showing relief on topographic maps is by *contours* (lines joining places of the same height). Contours are usually drawn in brown and are strongly emphasized so that they stand out clearly. The spacing between the contours varies according to the steepness of the land. On a flat plain, 50-feet contours may be spaced inches apart on a map. In precipitous mountain regions, the contours may be so closely spaced that only 100-feet contours can be shown. Combined with contours are *spot heights*, which give the precise heights of points, such as the highest points of mountains. Cartographers have devised several other methods of showing relief, including *layer-tinting*, *hachures* and *hill-shading*. Layer-tinting is a method of showing the level of the land with colours and shades of colours. Green and yellow are used for lower ground, and browns, reds, purples and finally white to show the highest areas. Hachures are lines drawn down slopes which give the impression of a three-dimensioned model. They are particularly effective in rugged mountain regions. Hill-shading also gives the impression of a model. The area is shaded as though a bright light in the northwestern corner of the map illuminates some slopes and casts shadows over the others.

Hachuring and hill-shading require considerable skill and artistry if they are to be both effective and accurate. Until the 1930s, the draughtsman was essentially an artist, who drew the map by hand. Today, cartographic techniques have been streamlined. Place names and symbols are no longer drawn by hand, but are printed, cut out and stuck into position, and plastics have replaced paper. The draughtsman is now more a technician than an artist but his skill is still needed to ensure that the final map is both accurate and clear. He correlates the findings of ground and aerial surveys, plots the positions of land features and shows detail according to the chosen scale. The final results portray a section of the world's curved surface as a flat map.

Surveyors map the Earth

Maps are pictures of the world's land surface, showing its features, resources and the way it has been developed. Modern surveying methods have made these maps detailed and very accurate.

ALTHOUGH EXPLORERS, geographers and surveyors have been drawing maps of the Earth's surface for thousands of years, only about 20 per cent has been mapped out on the small scale of one inch to a mile. But an increasing need for land and its resources has led to an enormous demand for accurate and detailed maps. In developing countries, the success of economic planning and a rise in the people's standards of living depends to a great extent on the availability of maps. These locate and show the extent of the country's natural resources, its forests, water supplies, minerals and potential farmland.

The map-maker is by no means redundant in more developed countries which have already been surveyed. In many advanced countries, maps must constantly be revised to show how the landscape is being changed. Engineers and planners need large-scale maps on which to base sites of new towns, motorways, hydro-electric schemes, reservoirs and the routes of pylons for high-tension cables.

Representing the Earth

Maps are representations on a flat plane of a part or sometimes the whole of the Earth's surface. All accurate maps are drawn to scale so that a distance measured on the map represents a distance on the ground. Developed countries have been largely mapped at scales of around one inch to one mile or, expressed as a *representative fraction*, 1:63,360 (one inch on the map equals 63,360 inches or one mile on the ground). Such maps are called *topographic maps* and include a vast amount of information. Land shapes are shown by contours; rivers and lakes are in blue; and railways and roads are classified by the use of symbols and colours. On such maps, even the smallest villages can be shown. The 1:63,360 scale was originally adopted by Britain and New Zealand, while the United States still uses a similar scale of 1:62,250, while Britain has since changed to the widely used metric scale of 1:50,000.

Surveyors use a plane table to map an area in Saudi Arabia. Known fixed points are plotted on the paper at a chosen scale and measured heights, depressions and distances drawn in.

With a trained eye and a knowledge of physical geography, a student can learn much about a region he has never visited from a topographic map. A perfectly shaped volcanic cone rising from a generally flat area, for example, is easy to identify from the circular form of the contours (lines drawn on a map to join up all points at given heights above sea level).

1 From a series of photographs, taken from the air, a map of a large area can be drawn in a fraction of the time taken by ground surveys.

2 Plotters, who draw a map of an area covered by overlapping aerial photographs, lay out a mosaic of prints of a Nigerian river.

Valley cross-sections can be drawn from contours and the gradients of streams can be calculated. Where deep valleys have been worn out by glaciers the valley cross-sections are U-shaped, with deep sides and flat bottoms, and can be identified from the contours.

An absence of surface drainage is a characteristic of many limestone uplands. Rainwater seeps through the limestone, instead of flowing in streams on the surface. The water reappears as springs at the base of the limestone. This drainage pattern can be seen on topographic maps and the area of limestone can be accurately identified. Along coastlines, cliffs indicate areas where the sea is cutting back the land; while *spits* (tongues of sand and gravel) indicate that the sea is building new land. Man's activities are also shown on topographic maps. Mining areas, farmland and forests are all shown. The positions of roads and railways indicate how the engineer has selected the best routes through valleys and round mountains. Topographic maps also help the historian to locate prehistoric sites and other historical features such as battlefields.

On smaller-scale maps far less detail can be shown. One inch on the most detailed atlas maps usually represents more than ten miles on the ground and, on most maps, it represents several hundred miles. But such maps are useful because they depict entire countries or continents, giving a broad impression of a region. Even though they contain far less detail than topographic maps, atlases must be constantly revised. Boundaries between countries change by agreement or as a result of war. New roads, railways, dams and oilfields are constructed. Names of places, countries and land features change. Place names, for example, changed throughout Africa in the 1950s and 1960s, after former colonial territories became independent. To keep atlases up to date, map-making companies need large libraries containing the latest and most detailed maps from all over the world, reports of political and economic changes from newspapers, books and periodicals and information from governments and embassies.

Plans of ownership

Large-scale maps are often called *plans*. They are drawn on scales considerably larger than those of topographic maps and cover small areas. They may show parts of cities, with each road and building accurately drawn in. Other plans show detailed parish boundaries in rural areas. In some parts of the world, including India and many African countries, the whole system of land ownership is closely linked with land surveying. Often the boundaries between farms are not marked by hedgerows and fences, and there may be no visible divisions on the surface. Concrete blocks marking the corners of a property are buried underground so that they will not be moved or dislodged. For this reason, each plot of land is mapped on a *cadastral plan,* which precisely depicts the boundaries and mathematically defines the positions of all boundary markers. When

people buy land or sell land, they must have a cadastral plan in addition to their title deeds. If a landowner wishes to divide his farm into two and sell half of it, he must first seek the permission of the government and then employ a registered surveyor. The surveyor makes the divisions, places the new boundary marks and prepares the two new cadastral plans. All the information is recorded in a government-operated Land Register. If a boundary is later disputed, government surveyors can quickly replace any missing boundary marks and settle any arguments.

To make the greatest use of maps it is necessary to know the principles of map-making. Maps are constructed from measurements of distance, horizontal and vertical angles, bearings to establish directions, and latitude and longitude to fix positions on the Earth's surface. On small-scale maps, the map-maker must allow for the curvature of the Earth and devise mathematical systems, called *map projections,* which enable him to represent the curved surface of the Earth on a flat sheet of paper. On plans which cover a small area, the amount of curvature is so slight that it can be discounted and the area mapped as though the Earth was flat.

The simplest method of mapping involves the measurement of distance. From simple geometry it is known that given the lengths of three sides of a triangle and none of the angles, only one shape of triangle can be constructed. An oblong garden, for example, consists basically

of two triangles. If the lengths of the four sides of the garden and one of the diagonals are measured, a plan of the garden can be drawn. By dividing awkwardly shaped areas, such as fields which are seldom exact squares or rectangles, into a series of triangles, it is possible to measure and map them accurately. This method, called *trilateration,* does not require any angular measurements. Easy though it sounds, this method is now used in the most sophisticated land surveys which employ electronic instruments. But how does one measure distance if one is not a surveyor? The simplest way is by walking along the distance and counting one's strides. The length of people's strides varies, but one can quickly discover the length of one's own stride by pacing an already measured distance, such as a cricket pitch. Pacing is a method often employed by explorers when preparing rough sketch maps.

The surveyor uses a variety of instruments to measure distance, including 22-yard chains and steel tapes. All distances

1 Surveyors in Ghana measure distances with a tellurometer which records the time electromagnetic waves take to travel between two points. It can be used in fog or haze.
2 With a theodolite, a telescope with horizontal and vertical plates marked in degrees, a surveyor measures angles between visible points.
3 A surveyor's level, which is used to measure heights accurately, combines a telescope with a highly sensitive spirit level.

on slopes must be corrected and reduced to the horizontal. Steel tapes expand and contract, because of changing temperatures and this must be taken into account. Until recently, the most accurate measurements of distance were made with *invar tapes.* Invar is an alloy of nickel and steel and is less affected by temperature than any other metal. Measurements with 100-foot invar tapes are extremely accurate but, over distances of several miles, the work is laborious and slow. As a result, trilateration was not a practical survey method of very large areas and some other method of finding distances was necessary.

A system called *triangulation* was, until the 1960s, the standard method of surveying throughout the world. Triangulation is based on the geometrical fact that if the three angles of a triangle and the length of one side are known, then the lengths of the other two sides can be worked out. From one accurately measured *base line,* it is possible to fix other points all over the country in chains of triangles. In Britain, three base lines were measured on the ground, one on Salisbury Plain and two in Scotland. All the other highly accurate *triangulation pillars,* those concrete monuments found usually on hilltops, were fixed by angular measurements.

Measured by angles

The most accurate instrument for measuring angles, horizontal and vertical, is the *theodolite,* which is basically a powerful telescope attached to horizontal and vertical circles. Mounted on a tripod, the theodolite is rotated horizontally by the surveyor who can take accurate measurements of the angles between visible survey points. Rotating the telescope vertically, the surveyor can read vertical angles, which he uses to compute differences in height. Another accurate telescopic instrument for measuring heights contains a highly sensitive level. *Bench-marks* cut in the sides of buildings and in rocks are points which have been precisely levelled and their height above sea level is usually recorded on large-scale plans.

Another instrument for measuring horizontal angles and bearings is the *prismatic compass.* Fitting easily into a surveyor's pocket, it is useful in quick, rough surveys. It consists of a magnetic compass and a prism mounted so that the surveyor can sight an object and read the bearing simultaneously. The prismatic compass is widely used for *compass traverses,* whereby an explorer or surveyor can measure bearings along his path. Combined with the measurements of distance, the bearings can be plotted on paper to form a rudimentary map. Detail along the path, including buildings, roads and streams, can be fixed by taking bearings from several points. Distances need not then be measured.

The prismatic compass gives magnetic

1 Colour aerial photographs, like this one of a road in England, provide an immense amount of information about an area to be developed.
2 Hong Kong Colony shows how every scrap of land is used. From such photographs vegetation can be identified and land use planned.

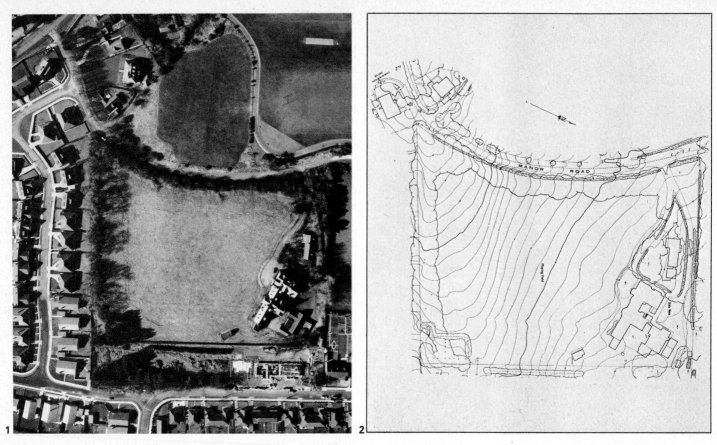

1
2

bearings, which are useful in establishing directions. But the bearings are to magnetic north and a correction, which varies from region to region and from year to year, must be made to find true north. The compass is also affected by any local iron. True bearings or *azimuths* can be measured far more accurately by theodolite. Measurements of azimuths, latitude and longitude are usually based on star observations. To find longitude, the surveyor makes star observations to find local time and compares it with the time at Greenwich which lies on 0° longitude, the prime meridian.

Once surveyors have fixed the positions and heights of a series of points in a region, they must then map all the topographic detail – hills, rivers, roads, towns – that lie between the points. Before the Second World War, this mapping was largely done by *plane table surveys*. A flat board, the table, is covered by a sheet of drawing paper. On the paper, all the known, fixed points are plotted accurately at a chosen scale. The board is then mounted on a tripod and placed at a known station or position. After the board is levelled, the surveyor uses an alidade (sighting rule) to sight other known stations and, in this way, correctly orients the board. Clamping the board firmly, he then sights other points of topographic interest, such as corners of fields and forests and houses, and draws a pencil line from his own position towards the feature. Moving to other stations, he again orients his board and sights the same details. Where three sightings to the same feature intersect in one point, its position is established. He measures heights with a *clinometer,* another sighting instrument from which he reads angles of elevation or depression or on some instruments the tangent of the

angle. In this way, a detailed map is slowly built up on the board, if the visibility is good.

Plane table surveys have been replaced to a great extent today by the mapping of detail from aerial photographs. These *vertical* photographs are taken directly downwards from the moving aircraft. Photographs are taken so that each consecutive photograph overlaps the preceding one by about 60 per cent. The aircraft fly over a particular area in a series of parallel strips and each strip overlaps the other. Each overlap can be viewed stereoscopically so that the hills and valleys appear like a three-dimensional model. Because of stereoscopy, contours can be plotted from aerial photographs.

Photogrammetry (the science of photo measurement) has greatly advanced since the Second World War, although it is still expensive for mapping small areas and there is no way of photographing through thick cloud. But a very large area which would take years to survey on foot can be photographed in a few days from the air. As in plane table surveying, there must still be a certain number of points on the ground which are fixed by ground surveys before plotting of detail can begin. These points must be clearly marked on the ground so that they can be pinpointed on the photographs. Detail can then be plotted either directly from photographs or with the use of elaborate machines, such as stereo-plotters. Recent developments, including measurements taken in the aircraft, have made it possible to extend the area on the ground between fixed points. Air photographs also provide much information about soil, vegetation, agriculture and rocks.

Ground surveying has also undergone a revolution since the 1950s, especially

1 An aerial photograph, taken from a low-flying plane, shows every detail and boundary of a new housing estate in Sussex.
2 From such photographs, accurate cadastral plans can be drawn. The details are then checked by a survey team on the ground.

through the development of two instruments which can be used in the rapid measurement of distance. The *tellurometer,* first developed in South Africa, measures distances by recording the time it takes for electromagnetic waves to travel between two intervisible points. The tellurometer can be used over distances of up to 50 miles, even in fog or haze, without any loss in accuracy. For ease of operation over long distances, tellurometers are equipped with portable telephones. The accuracy of a tellurometer is about 1:100,000, or about one inch in two miles.

Fast new surveys

Another similar instrument, the *geodimeter,* records the speed of light waves and was first developed in Sweden. The geodimeter is more effective over shorter distances than the tellurometer. Both measure distances and not angles and so the method of survey employed is trilateration, not triangulation. The triangulation of India took about 100 years to complete. The recent trilateration of Australia, using these new instruments, took less than ten years. Satellites, laser beams and computers are also being used in surveying. The surveyor's instruments and methods have changed radically from the days of pacing out distances or measuring them with chains, but about 75 per cent of the Earth's land surface still awaits topographical mapping on a scale of one inch to a mile.

Map makers orbit the Earth

Early explorers inched their way along the world's shorelines. With aerial photography and the artificial satellite, the map maker of today can take in a whole continent at a glance.

DURING THE first ten years of the space age, which began in 1957, more than 500 artificial satellites were rocketed into orbit round the Earth. One result of this remarkable achievement was to revolutionize the study of geodesy – the study of the curvature of the Earth's surface.

As a result of the wealth of new information supplied by these satellites, geodesists have come very close to solving the age-old problem of the shape of the Earth's surface at sea-level.

The first satellite specially designed to take the appropriate measurements was ANNA 1B, launched by the Americans in 1962. It was later joined by two other important geodetic satellites – GEOS A, launched in 1965, and PAGEOS, launched in 1966. These satellites provide the best known method of mapping the various ways in which the Earth's shape deviates from that of a true sphere.

The conclusion that the Earth is an imperfect sphere, slightly flattened at the poles and distended at the equator, was first deduced by Isaac Newton (who also calculated a mathematical value for the flattening) in his *Principia* of 1687. Geodetic studies based on satellite information have shown, however, that the degree of flattening in high latitudes is in fact rather less than had previously been suspected. Satellites have shown that the Earth's shape departs from the spherical in other interesting ways. The actual height of an artificial satellite circling round the Earth depends on the Earth's gravitational field, and so the pattern of a satellite's orbit reflects the shape of the Earth. Analyses of irregularities in these orbits show that it is an over-simplification to describe the Earth as 'a flattened sphere'.

One study based on satellite information has, for instance, identified four areas with excessively high gravitational pull – over Ireland; south-east of Africa; between Japan and New Guinea; and west of Peru – and this has led to the suggestion that the Earth has 'four corners'. Other flight-path information has suggested that the Earth's shape may be like a pear, a pumpkin, or a wrinkled prune. Another study

The first aerial photographs were taken from a balloon in 1858. Since then the value of such photography has been increasingly recognized, and extremely sophisticated techniques have been developed. This photograph of central London was taken at 5,280 feet on a summer afternoon.

has confirmed the fact that a section taken through the equator would be very slightly oval in shape.

If the Earth were a perfect sphere without an atmosphere (and if we ignored the small pulls of the sun and the moon), the track of an orbiting satellite would remain constant month after month. But because the Earth is not a true sphere, the orbits of satellites are distorted. The gravitational pull of the Earth varies with latitude; and, for example, the gravitational pull of its 'equatorial bulge' makes the orbit of an eastward-moving satellite drift to the west.

By carefully tracking three early satellites – Sputnik II, Explorer I and Vanguard I – American and British scientists observed that their orbits had not drifted westwards as quickly as might have been expected, if the most soundly based of the

pre-satellite values for the flattening of the Earth had been correct.

Satellite tracking

Mathematicians are now able to construct models of any shape and any pattern of gravity to represent exactly how far the Earth's shape does depart from the spherical form. World maps have also been compiled to show this and such maps reveal so-called 'mounds' and 'depressions' in the Earth's curvature. Satellite observations have provided the geodesist with more exact data concerning the size of the Earth: the average equatorial diameter is 7,926·42 miles; the polar diameter or polar axis 7,899·83 miles.

Satellite programmes make it necessary for geodesists to know the positions of tracking stations to within an accuracy of

inches. Satellites are also the instruments which enable such accurate measurements to be made. The most practicable way of determining the exact position of a satellite is by photographing it against the stellar background.

This is done simultaneously from at least two tracking stations of known position. Because at any given time the celestial positions of the stars are known, it is possible to calculate the satellite's own declination from each tracking station (the satellite's declination is the angle that it makes in the sky with the tracking station).

Conversely, provided the precise positions of a satellite and one tracking station are known, the range of another tracking station of unknown position can be determined on the same principle by measuring

the satellite's declination from each station simultaneously.

Put another way, if the positions of two fixed points are accurately known, that of the third can be calculated. The method used in these calculations is that of tri-angulation – a basic technique employed by surveyors since time immemorial.

However, satellite triangulation has at least one major advantage over triangulation on the surface of the Earth. The latter is limited by 'line of sight'; satellite tri-angulation, on the other hand, can be used to determine the distance between stations thousands of miles apart because it employs the third dimension of space.

Geodetic satellites fall into three groups: 'active', 'passive' and 'co-operative'. An active satellite (e.g. ANNA I) is one using an internal power source to send out optical or electronic signals which can be recorded on the ground. A passive satellite (e.g. PAGEOS) is one which is illuminated by the sun and can be photographed against the celestial background, but does not have its own internal power source. A co-operative satellite carries a reflector which 'co-operates' with a ground-based source of power, such as a laser beam, and which reflects the signal back to its source on the ground.

Satellites so far are being used primarily for measuring distances within the 1,000–3,000 kilometre range but techniques are making possible more precise operations to within 160–800 kilometre distances.

How aerial surveys began

Satellite photography is only an extension into space of the less spectacular aerial photography. The earliest recorded sug-gestion of aerial photography (from a balloon) appears in a French caricature drawn 128 years ago. A few years later, in 1858, the French photographer Gaspard Tournachon (alias Nadar) succeeded in taking photographs from a balloon several hundred feet up and produced a topo-graphical map showing a bird's-eye view of a village near Paris.

The value of aerial photographs (taken from balloons) in military reconnaissance was demonstrated first to the Americans in the Civil War of 1862 and later to the Russians in 1886. But in spite of early experiments, aerial photography did not play an important part in topographical surveying until piloted aircraft, capable of providing a more navigable platform for the aerial camera than the balloon, were invented a few years before the outbreak of World War I. Even then, accurate topo-graphical mapping had to wait for improved cameras.

The full value of aerial photography in military reconnaissance first became ap-parent during World War I. From then on, considerable progress was made in adap-ting photographic measuring technique to topographic mapping.

During these years, hundreds of papers were published in scientific journals set-

With the spectacular advances in space explora-tion have come new developments in aerial photography. Today pictures of the Earth's sur-face can be taken from hundreds of miles up in outer space. Three photographs from American Gemini spacecraft show, *left,* a view of India and Ceylon taken at a height of 600 miles. We are looking north, with the Bay of Bengal to the right and the Arabian Sea to the left. *Above top,* a photograph showing the 'horn' of Africa away to the south, the Gulf of Aden and, in the foreground, part of the Red Sea. *Below,* the Hadramaut Plateau, southern part of the Arabian Peninsula. Wadi Hadramaut is in the foreground with the Gulf of Aden behind it.

119

ting out the value of aerial photography in the many fields concerned with patterns on the surface of the Earth. These include agriculture, archaeology, ecology, forestry, geography, geology, hydrology and soil science as well as engineering and regional planning.

Satellites, like aeroplanes, provide navigable platforms for cameras. It was soon discovered that a camera carried by an earth satellite was capable of photographing a flight strip 3,000 miles in length every ten minutes. This meant that the entire surface of the Earth could be mapped in a few days; and topographical surveying – which once took scientific expeditions so many long and tedious months to complete – becomes comparatively simple. Any nation with the technical and financial resources to launch earth-orbiting satellites can 'map' the whole Earth, no part of which is beyond the range of cameras.

Aerial photography can reveal archaeological remains the patterns of which are not visible from ground level. It can enable naturalists to estimate the numbers of wild animals: for example, seals photographed on an ice floe can be counted accurately enough for naturalists to calculate how many need to be slaughtered in order to ensure an adequate food supply for the remainder. Aerial photographs can be used to follow the development and direction of icebergs, and to ensure that the passageways between them do not become blocked and dangerous to shipping. It was recently discovered that the scars made by meteorites colliding with the Earth many millions of years ago show up distinctly on aerial photographs as large regular circles, though from ground level their existence was never suspected. A directly practical use is the detection and forecasting of weather which may, for example, enable meteorologists to give

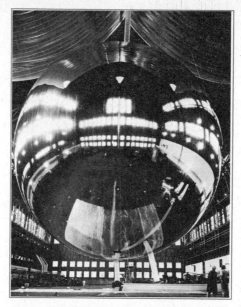

Pageos, the 1966 American satellite. Reflecting the sun's light, it is photographed from the ground against a star background enabling positions on Earth to be plotted very accurately.

Satellites – the first ten years

By the end of 1960, artificial satellites orbiting the Earth outnumbered the known natural satellites in the solar system. Only three years before, the space age began with the launching of Sputnik I by Russia on 4 October 1957: followed a month later by Sputnik II. America sent up her first satellite early in 1958, and four more in the same year. Some 148 satellites and probes were launched over the next five years – in 1965 alone, 112 new satellites went into orbit. Today, though some are disintegrating, many have long life-spans ahead of them in which to transmit information on weather and space.

advance notice of some approaching disaster, and warn the inhabitants to evacuate an area threatened by a hurricane. Such photographs are taken both from aircraft and from satellites such as Nimbus I.

The outbreak of the Second World War in 1939 gave a new impetus to the use of aerial photography in military intelligence and hundreds of men and women were trained in the techniques of photo interpretation. Improvements were also made to cameras, stereoscopes and film.

A fascinating new dimension

In the decades since the end of the Second World War, the versatility of aerial photography has been increasingly exploited. It enables surveys of underdeveloped areas to be carried out more quickly and cheaply than by ground-survey methods. Although it greatly augments ground surveying, however, it will never totally replace it. There will always be areas for mapping which are too small to justify the cost of flying an aeroplane over them. Other areas may be so obscured by vegetation as to make photography from the air impracticable. In any case, all aerial surveying needs control ground surveys to be carried out first.

Although the potential of the aerial camera was vastly increased by the successful launching of camera-carrying rockets and satellites, the method remains essentially the same, and considerations of cost will probably ensure that aerial photographs continue for at least another decade to be a more practicable tool for Earth scientists (including geographers and archaeologists) than space photography. However, the latter has added a fascinating new dimension to the studies of those who seek to understand the surface of the Earth.

The complicated instrument *above left* is called a stereo-plotter. In order to turn a photograph into a map, two aerial pictures are first taken. Inside the stereo-plotter they are combined by an optical device to form a three-dimensional image which the operator traces by means of a moving black dot on the viewing screen. Using hand controls, he then translates the image into line form on a sheet. *Above right,* a controlled photo mosaic where photographs are matched together and fitted on to a control plan. The result is an accurate photo plan of a large area.

Exploring the Earth´s hidden depths

Under the Earth lies a strange, eerie world of perpetual darkness. Scientists are now examining this realm of rock and water and the creatures who have made it their home.

FEW PLACES on the Earth's surface remain unexplored and unmapped, but underground a dark world of caverns, passages, lakes and rivers still waits to reveal its secrets to the adventurous. Caves were once considered the haunt of dragons, devils or entrances to the underworld. Now explorers have discovered huge halls of eerie beauty with fantastic rock formations in glittering white or vivid colours. Some of the more accessible caves are now lit by electricity, have flights of steps and even lifts. Conducted by guides, visitors can see the strange sights, and travel on underground rivers in safety and comfort. But *spelaeologists* (scientists who study caves) and cavers or potholers, whose hobby is cave exploration, prefer the wet, dark and often dangerous tunnels. Equipped with rope ladders, mountaineering gear and miners' helmets, they descend into deep pits, crawl through narrow fissures, paddle along streams and lakes in rubber dinghies and, wearing skin-diving suits, swim through water-filled passages. But even the best-equipped teams sometimes get trapped by suddenly rising water or stuck in narrow holes, and their adventures end in tragedy.

Life in the caves

For the biologist caves are interesting because of the unusual forms of life that have adapted to the dark conditions. Bats and moths are common and a few insects and lower forms of plant life, such as lichens, moulds and mosses are often found. In New Zealand a cave is lit by the strange blue-green light of millions of glow-worms. To the archaeologist, caves have yielded much information about prehistory. Fossilized bones of long extinct animals, such as cave bears and cave lions, and the tools, weapons, ornaments, bones and hearths of Early Man have been discovered near the entrances of caves. In many African, Australian, European and South American caves, rock paintings have been found, which were probably used in rituals associated with magic.

Some caves are man-made tunnels hewn in cliffs, others are cavities in lava flows, deep tunnels in the snouts of glaciers and caves carved in coastal cliffs by the incessant pounding of the sea. But most of the world's largest subterranean caves were formed in limestone hills and mountains by the action of water. Limestone, which is called *permeable* (water can percolate through it), is slowly dissolved by rainwater, which is weak acid because it contains some carbon dioxide from the air. Much of the rain that falls seeps into the ground and percolates slowly through the *joints* (vertical cracks) and along the *bedding planes* (generally horizontal fissures) in the limestone, gradually forming

1 A potholer, equipped with a miner's helmet, inches his way through a narrow rift in the limestone Mendip Hills in Somerset.
2 On the island of São Miguel in the Azores rainwater heated far below ground by volcanic activity bubbles out in a hot spring.

tubes and tunnels. Limestone caves were probably formed many thousands of years ago when the land surface was much higher than it is at present. At that time, the layers of limestone were completely saturated with water, which slowly circulated horizontally and downwards through the rock. The land surface was gradually worn down by erosion and, as surface rivers etched out deep valleys, the underground water level slowly fell. Air then began to enter the subterranean labyrinths, opening up a maze of formerly submerged caves. Water continued to seep into the underground chambers, and lakes, streams and waterfalls were formed within the limestone. Streams wore away the cave floors and the roofs of many chambers collapsed, sometimes opening up deep pits, called sink holes, linking the cave network to the surface.

Some of the largest known systems of caves are the Gouffre de Padirac in France, the Carlsbad Caverns, New Mexico and the Mammoth Caves, Kentucky. The entrance to the caves at Padirac is down a hole 96 feet across and over 100 feet deep. Three hundred feet underground is a chamber 280 feet high, 180 feet long and 75 feet wide. Over 20 miles of passages and rooms have been explored at the Carlsbad Caverns and many more are known to exist. The largest cave is 1,300 feet long, 650 feet wide and 285 feet high. In the Mammoth Caves 150 miles of passages, lakes, waterfalls, rivers and domes have been charted at different levels.

Oozing through cracks in the roofs of many caves are small drops of water which are highly charged with calcium carbonate. The suspended drops of water sometimes partly evaporate, leaving a tiny deposit and, in this way, a long, icicle-like formation called a *stalactite* grows slowly downward. In the same way, when drops of water fall to the floor, tiny deposits sometimes build upwards to form a *stalagmite*. When stalactites and stalagmites meet they form pillars, which often stand in clusters resembling giant organ pipes up to 80 feet high. Some stalactites grow one inch in 4,000 years, whereas in Ingleborough Cave in Yorkshire, some stalactites have lengthened by three inches in only ten years.

Where water oozes through a long crack

in the roof of a cave, a wavy band of calcium carbonate grows like a fringed curtain across the cave. Water flowing across the floor of a cave may coat the surface with a layer called a *flowstone*. Beautiful and strangely shaped formations, looking like frozen cascades, statues or animals or forming grottoes have been found in many caves. The origin of *helictites,* delicate, thread-like formations hanging in spirals and loops, awaits a satisfactory explanation. Pure calcium carbonate is white and many cave formations resemble ice and icicles, but the rainwater often contains other dissolved minerals, such as iron oxide and manganese oxide which colour the calcium carbonate blue, green or brown.

Underground water

Water which circulates underground is called *ground water*. Most ground water comes directly from the atmosphere as rain and melted snow and is called *meteoric water,* or indirectly as water which filters downwards from the beds of rivers and lakes. Some meteoric water is retained by the soil and is used by plants. But most of it sinks slowly to a level called the *zone of saturation,* where the rock is completely saturated. This zone is usually less than 100 feet down and seldom more than a few hundred below the surface. At greater depths, the rock is compacted under great pressure and is impermeable. The top of the zone of saturation, called the *water*

table, rises and falls with seasonal changes in rainfall. It is arched up under hills to a higher level than under adjacent lowlands, although it is usually closer to the surface under flat land. Where the water table is at ground level, swamps, lakes and rivers occur.

Springs are seepages or strong flows of ground water which gush from spots where the ground surface intersects the water table, often at the foot of hills or in depressions. Many oases are depressions where the water table reaches the surface. When the water table drops, wells can be drilled to the zone of saturation. Springs may occur where rainwater sinks into a layer of sandstone which is underlain by an impermeable rock. The impermeable rock is called a *ground water dam,* because it prevents any further downward percolation. Springs emerge on the surface at the junction of the sandstone *aquifer* (water-bearing layer of rock) and the underlying impermeable rock. Other sites of springs include fault lines (major fractures in the Earth's surface), or at points where an impermeable *dyke* (a vertical sheet of solidified magma or lava) blocks underground drainage.

Water from springs is generally clean because impurities and dirt are filtered out during the slow percolation of the water through porous rocks. In limestone uplands, however, the ground water drains through fissures, cracks and caves and is not filtered to the same extent. This factor

was not generally realized until the late 1800s. Pits and fissures in the limestone uplands of France were used as rubbish tips and unwanted parts of animal carcasses and other rubbish were thrown down the holes. When the ground water was polluted epidemics of cholera and typhoid often occurred in villages miles away which relied on water from the springs that flowed from the base of the limestone uplands. Scientists finally established the connection between the dumping of wastes and the epidemics by putting dyes into the limestone fissures and pits. They found that the dyes stained the waters of the springs that welled up many miles away. In 1902, a law prohibited the dumping of waste in limestone pits and cholera and typhoid were almost eliminated in the area.

Bringing water to the surface

Wells are dug to tap underground water which may lie just below the surface or hundreds of feet down. Below the water table, the ground water seeps into the wells and is lifted or pumped to the surface. To ensure a supply throughout the year, the well must extend below the *permanent water table*, the water table's lowest limit. Deep wells are generally better than shallow ones because there is less risk of pollution.

A special type of well, called an *artesian well,* gets its name from Artois, a province in France, where such wells were first struck. They occur in areas where a water-bearing layers of rock is sandwiched between layers of impermeable rock, which act as groundwater dams. The layers of

1 In the Crystal Cave in Bermuda, stalactites, formed by dripping water and coloured by minerals, hang from the ceiling.

2 The Old Faithful geyser in Yellowstone National Park, Wyoming, regularly spouts jets of hot water and steam 100 feet into the air.

1

2

rock are either tilted or folded into a large *syncline* (basin). The aquifer is exposed to the surface in a range of hills or mountains, where the rainfall is generally heavy. In this catchment area, the rainwater seeps into the aquifer and percolates slowly down the tilted rock, towards the bottom of the basin. Over a period of many years, a vast quantity of water fills the aquifer and, owing to the tilt of the rocks, it

accumulates under pressure. A well sunk through the impermeable top layer into the aquifer releases the pressure and the water may gush out in a fountain. Deep artesian wells can often be drilled in areas far from the catchment area, where the local rainfall is slight and farming depends entirely on irrigating the land with well water.

The Great Artesian Basin of Australia,

covering Queensland and parts of New South Wales and South Australia, extends over 600,000 square miles. The catchment area for the rainwater lies in the Eastern Highlands, where porous sandstones occur on the surface and where rainfall is greater. To the west, impermeable clays cover the sandstone aquifers. Artesian wells, sometimes a mile deep, ensure a water supply for the cattle and sheep. Other artesian wells occur in the Desert Basin of Western Australia and in the Murray Basin of Victoria. Without these wells little farming would be possible.

Both London and Paris are situated in the heart of artesian basins. The aquifer underlying London is the chalk which outcrops in the catchment areas of the Chilterns to the north and the North Downs to the south. The chalk is underlain by Gault clay and overlain by the equally impermeable London clay. About 100 years ago, the artesian wells in the London basin gushed forth but, today, so much of the underground store of water has been used up that the water must be pumped out. In London and in Paris, the artesian wells can no longer meet the demand of these cities and water is also obtained from surface reservoirs and rivers.

Hot mineral springs

Water from some wells and springs is warm because, under the ground, the temperature increases at a rate of approximately 1 °F. for every 65 feet. Some springs even approach boiling point. The waters of *hot* or *thermal springs* contain a great variety of minerals which may give them medicinal properties. Some of the minerals leave deposits in low domes, basins and terraces round the spring. Many health resorts have been built around hot springs, including such places as Aix-les-Bains in France, Baden in Switzerland, Hot Springs in Arkansas in the United States and Bath in England.

Many hot springs occur in regions associated with volcanic activity at the present time or in the recent geological past. In such regions, large underground pockets of formerly molten rock are slowly cooling and solidifying. Heat from these pockets warms the rainwater which seeps down towards them. Not all the water in hot springs, however, is meteoric in origin. Sometimes, hot springs contain small quantities of minerals which are not present in the local rocks and therefore could not have been dissolved by rainwater. It is now believed that a certain

1 Deep underground in the Mendip Hills a potholer climbs up a waterfall.
2 An intermittent well is not deep enough to reach the permanent water table in dry seasons, while a permanent well fills to the level of the water table. Pressure of the water table forces water up an artesian well. Springs occur where a layer of saturated rock comes to the Earth's surface and where a fault in impermeable rock acts as a ground water dam.
3 In Australia a windmill pumps underground water to the surface for herds of cattle.

amount of juvenile (new) water is liberated from the molten rock by chemical action. This new water contains the minerals which are foreign to the region. Hot springs occur in many areas, including Britain, Iceland, Japan, Morocco, New Zealand, South America, the Kamchatka peninsula of the U.S.S.R., and the United States. Hot springs also well to the surface in areas not associated with volcanic activity and the source of heat is still a matter of speculation. Some geographers suggest that the heat is caused by the friction of recent earthquakes or by radioactivity.

A special type of hot spring is the geyser, which erupts periodically, shooting a tall column of water and steam sometimes over 100 feet in the air. The name *geyser* comes

1

from an Icelandic word *geysir*, meaning gusher. Iceland, the North Island of New Zealand and the Yellowstone National Park of Wyoming, in the United States are the only places in the world that have these phenomena although some volcanic areas of Malaya, South America and Japan have boiling springs which spurt steam and water. The highest recorded eruptions of a geyser took place in New Zealand around the turn of the century, when columns of hot spray reached heights of 1,500 feet. The force and frequency of the world's geyser eruptions appear to be declining and eventually they will become boiling springs. The Old Faithful geyser in Yellowstone Park once shot a column of water and steam up to 150 feet in the air every hour; now eruptions are less frequent and seldom as high.

Bubbling geysers

The most widely accepted explanation for geyser eruptions was based, until recently, upon the supposition that ground water in the geyser tubes reached boiling point at some stage and the conversion of water into steam caused the eruption. Recent observers, however, have found that water temperatures in many geysers remain below boiling point at the moment of eruption and that the waters often contain dissolved gases. They have therefore suggested that geyser explosions are linked with the entry of gas into the geyser tubes. As the bubbles of gas rise, they heat the water and produce a violent boiling-like effect, basically similar to the miniature explosion caused when a soda-water bottle is opened and the gas bubbles upwards.

The water that circulates underground through cave systems or bubbles to the surface in clear, filtered springs is vital to the world's water supplies. Much of the water in rivers and reservoirs comes from springs, while wells are essential to Man, his animals and crops in the dry areas and deserts of the Earth.

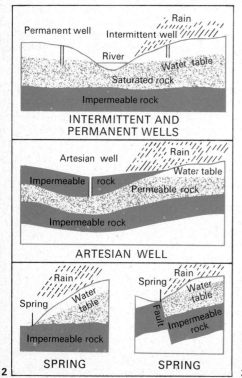

Permanent well
Intermittent well
Rain
River
Water table
Saturated rock
Impermeable rock

INTERMITTENT AND PERMANENT WELLS

Artesian well
Rain
Water table
Impermeable rock
Permeable rock
Impermeable rock

ARTESIAN WELL

Rain
Water table
Spring
Impermeable rock

Rain
Spring
Water table
Fault
Impermeable rock

SPRING   **SPRING**

2

3

The world's climates

Geographers distinguish between climates by generalizing about weather conditions experienced in various parts of the world. Equatorial forest, hot desert and ice cap are climatic extremes.

WHEN THE WEATHER is as variable as, for example, it is in Britain, it becomes difficult to relate it to climate, which by definition implies average weather conditions. There are also many problems involved in classifying climates. Many attempts have been made, each satisfactory for at least one aspect of climate. Some classifications are based on instrumental data, such as average temperature and rainfall figures, and others on Man's response to climatic conditions. But no classification satisfies all aspects of climate.

The first problem arises with the definition of the word *climate*. Average figures can conceal great variations. To take an extreme example, the mean annual temperature at Verkhoyansk in Siberia is −14·8 °C., but mean monthly temperatures vary from −46·8 °C. in January to 16·8 °C. in July. A mean temperature for a day in Britain could be, say, 16 °C., obtained from a slight variation between 14 °C. and 18 °C. on a cloudy day. But the same mean figure could also be obtained from a large variation between 6 °C. and 26 °C. on a day in autumn when clear skies at night produce marked cooling, but daytime sunshine raises the temperature considerably.

A basis for classification

Ideally, when we discuss a particular climate, we should include as many climatic categories as possible over as long a period of time as possible. These climatic categories include: temperature, precipitation, sunshine, wind, humidity, cloud amount, and subdivisions of these categories, such as maximum and minimum temperature and the number of air frosts. In this way, we can build up an increasingly clearer picture of the climatic conditions which might be experienced.

Since the days of Ancient Greece, scholars have tried to classify climates in many ways, stressing many different points. Probably the most obvious way to begin is with temperature. As we move north or south from the equatorial areas, temperatures decrease, but we cannot simply divide the world into latitudinal bands to mark temperature divisions. For example, the mean annual temperature at Bergen (Norway) is 7·9 °C., and at Okhotsk in eastern Siberia it is −4·6 °C. Yet both lie on the same latitude. Obviously factors other than latitude affect temperature.

Although we cannot make such simple divisions, we can use temperature as a means of separating areas with markedly different characteristics. For example, temperature has a considerable effect on natural vegetation and agricultural crops, and it has therefore become a popular way of subdividing climates.

Rainfall, however, is of almost equal

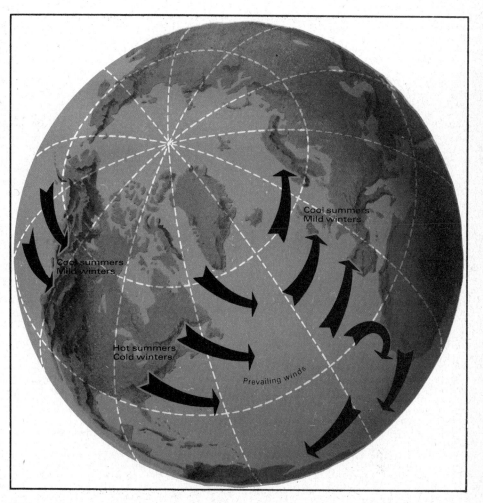

The prevailing winds, the westerlies, blow eastwards from the Atlantic on to Western Europe bringing cool air in summer and warm air in winter. Extremes of temperature are thus very rare.

importance. By combining the two elements, temperature and precipitation – rain, hail, snow, dew and frost – scientists have distinguished 11 basic climates. Attempts have been made to subdivide these further by stating the period of the dry season, if any, and the degree of dryness or cold, but these subdivisions are not really based on quantitative information.

While accepting that temperature and precipitation are the most important factors in classifying climates, we still have to give values to the boundaries separating different climates. Originally scientists based their divisions on vegetation. For this reason, tropical climates were defined as those having no monthly temperature below 18 °C., since tropical forests did not exist outside this temperature zone, while temperate areas were subdivided on the basis of their coldest months – the warmer areas having few monthly temperatures below freezing point, and the colder regions having several months with temperatures below freezing. Building up this picture, seasonal rainfall

distributions were added, and then, if the temperature and precipitation records of a particular area were known, by using the average values the type of climate normally occurring there could be identified and classified.

This system does present some problems. Average figures are used, but it will now be realized that variations occur about these mean figures, and in a particular year, a climatic boundary may be altered considerably.

Temperature zones

In Britain, 1963 was generally a cold year and the winter was so severe that parts of central England, which are normally within the warm temperate climate zone, had a mean January temperature of −3 °C., and so could be classified as having a cold temperate climate that year. Cold temperate conditions normally occur in Russia, the extreme east of Europe, and northern Scandinavia, so the magnitude of change in Britain's weather in 1963 can be appreciated.

In more normal years, the division between cold and warm temperate climates oscillates over a much smaller distance, but it never remains stationary. Thus we see that although boundaries may appear to be definite on a map, they are simply zones, with the main line representing the most frequent or mean position. Some areas, called *core areas,* will always be included within one particular region, but many areas come in the transition zones between two climatic divisions. In lowland regions, transition zones may cover a considerable area, but where the climatic boundary coincides with a large-scale physical phenomenon such as the Alps, then it will tend to be smaller and less subject to variation.

In 1918 the Russian meteorologist Vladimir P. Köppen, whilst at Hamburg, published a classification in which he defined climatic boundaries by numerical boundaries. Many of these numerical values were used because they appeared to coincide with certain significant landscape boundaries, particularly those of vegetation. Köppen's classification is based upon annual and monthly means of temperature and precipitation, and recognizes five main groups of world climate which are based on five main vegetation groups: tropical rainy climates with no cool season; dry climates; middle-latitude rainy climates with mild winters; middle-latitude rainy climates with severe winters; and polar climates with no warm season.

What is an ideal temperature?

Each of these groups can then be subdivided, depending upon the seasonal distribution of rainfall or the degree of dryness or cold. This classification is reasonably simple to follow, and in spite of its weaknesses is the method most frequently used.

A similar method, although using different criteria, has been developed by the American climatologist C.W.B. Thornthwaite. Thornthwaite did not base his classification on vegetational boundaries, but determined climatic boundaries purely on climatic data by comparing precipitation and evaporation. Although more logical, this method suffers from the inadequacy of evaporation data.

Both these methods are based on the analysis of climatic records. It is also possible to include the pressure systems involved in producing the day-to-day weather variations, so that divisions can be based on the causes of climate. This is known as a *dynamic classification.* In this method, devised by Hermann Flohn, seven zones are differentiated. Four of the zones remain within one wind belt throughout the year, and the others experience alterations of wind belts with the seasons. If there were no variations like the one in Britain in 1963, then such a genetic classification would be admirable, as it explains the climate, rather than simply describes it.

Unfortunately aberrations from the normal pattern do occur and so, once again, transition zones and core areas

This classification of climates, a simplified version of that made by the Russian meteorologist Köppen, is the one generally used today. Based on annual and monthly averages of temperature and rainfall, it recognizes five main groups of world climate based on five main vegetation groups.

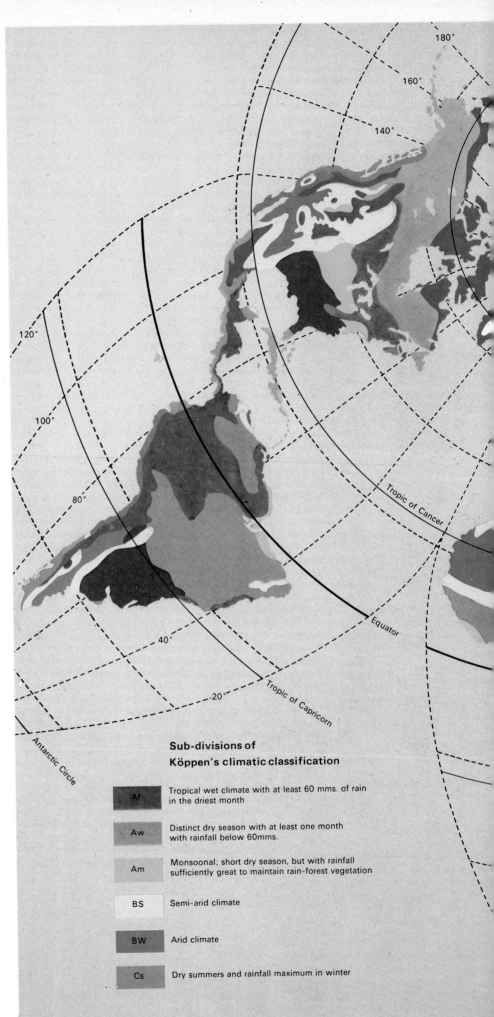

Sub-divisions of Köppen's climatic classification

Af	Tropical wet climate with at least 60 mms. of rain in the driest month
Aw	Distinct dry season with at least one month with rainfall below 60mms.
Am	Monsoonal; short dry season, but with rainfall sufficiently great to maintain rain-forest vegetation
BS	Semi-arid climate
BW	Arid climate
Cs	Dry summers and rainfall maximum in winter

Ca	Warm temperate rainy climate with hot summers—hottest month over 22°C
Cb	Warm temperate rainy climate with cool summers—hottest month under 22°C
Cc	Warm temperate rainy climate with cool short summers—less than four months over 10°C
Da	Cold-snowy forest climate with hot summers
Db	Cold-snowy forest climate with cool summers
Dc	Cold-snowy forest climate with cool short summers—less than four months over 10°C
Dd	As Dc, with average temperature of coldest month less than —38°C
ET	Tundra climate with the warmest months having a mean temperature above 0°C
EF	Permanent frost with no month having a mean temperature above freezing
H	Undifferentiated highlands

Above left, average annual rainfall is only a little over two inches in Death Valley, California, the hottest area in America. *Above right,* the world's coldest continent, Antarctica is permanently covered with snow and attacked by winds which can reach speeds of 200 mph.

appear. In addition, considerable temperature variations can exist between the northern and southern boundaries of any system, so that even though the rainfall may be produced in the same way, climatic conditions may differ.

None of these classifications really deal with the problem of how the climate feels to Man. This can be a very difficult subject, as an ideal temperature will vary considerably from one person to another. Also, the ideal temperature for a restful holiday is not necessarily ideal for work. A combination of cool temperature, strong wind and high humidity will appear more unfavourable than very low temperatures during a calm period with low humidity. Thus the climate of Montreal, with its hot summers and cold winters, appears more favourable for habitation than Punta Arenas, near stormy Cape Horn, with its cool maritime climate. Yet both have the same mean annual temperature. Temperature on its own is therefore not a good yardstick of an ideal climate.

The humidity factor

With these problems in mind, an attempt has been made to classify the climatic zones of New Zealand based on their influence on Man. To be successful in their application to Man, temperature and rainfall records have to be analysed to obtain detailed information. In addition other factors, such as sunshine, wind speed and humidity, must also be included to provide a proper balance in defining the climatic region. By detailed subdivision, the climate of an area can then be given a rating for its favourability to Man.

It is assumed that the ideal climate is sunny, warm, dry, and free from wind. But some elements, such as temperature, have more influence than, say, wind speed. To balance this, a system of weightings is used, so that the more important factors can be stressed.

In this way, New Zealand was divided into several areas on the basis of favourability. It would not have been subdivided at all in the other classifications mentioned above, although differences obviously exist. The amount of work required to calculate the ratings has prevented this

method being used elsewhere.

The above classification was based on Man's psychological response to climatic elements, but we can also consider the body's reactions – the physiological response. This has been done by W. H. Terjung in the United States. He decided on two indices: (1) a comfort index, based on temperature and humidity, and (2) a wind-effect index, based on wind speed and temperature.

The first index allows for the effect of humidity at high temperatures, when great discomfort can be felt when sweating is prevented. This index is graduated from ultra-cold, with temperatures of −40 °F. or below, to extremely hot when temperatures vary from 36 °C. at 100 per cent humidity to 39 °C. at 30 per cent humidity and values above. The wind-effect index relates the heat lost or gained by the body, which depends on the wind speed and the temperature.

By combining these two indices, a degree of comfort for an area on a monthly or seasonal basis can be obtained. This information has many uses. The choice of a site for retirement could be influenced by the nature of its climate; so could the choice and time of a holiday. Certain diseases can be intensified by climatic conditions, and such conditions could then be avoided. The application of human

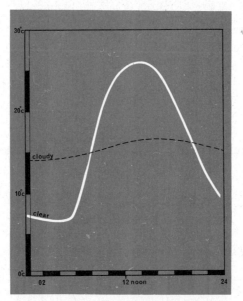

Two very different variations in temperature for a cloudy and a clear day in Britain. Both have the same average temperature, which can be very misleading as an indication of trends in weather.

response to climatic classification is still in its early stages, and is a fruitful subject for research.

No mention has yet been made of the geographical distribution of climate, but this had to wait until we knew how to show this distribution in the form of classified climates. We have to think of these climates in relation to the general circulation of the atmosphere, as this affects climatic location in many ways. For example, the temperate latitude westerlies, as their name implies, are winds which blow from west to east between latitudes 40° and 60° in both hemispheres. In western Europe, these winds are blowing on to the land from the Atlantic Ocean, which is warmer than the land in winter, and cooler in summer.

This factor tends to moderate the climate, and extremes are rare. The westerlies will normally blow from land to sea on the western side of the North Atlantic. Thus in winter, when land temperatures fall rapidly, much of this area experiences icy winds and much snow. In summer, there are no cooling sea breezes and high temperatures are reached.

Belts of high pressure

The wind belts of the Earth tend to move with the sun, so that in July, in the northern hemisphere summer, the sun will be overhead at midday on the Tropic of Cancer. This is the time when the wind belts are farthest north. Sub-tropical high-pressure systems are at their northernmost positions, producing dry Mediteranean-type summers in western Europe and western America. The southern hemisphere high-pressure systems are also in the northernmost position, with most of southern Africa (not the western Cape area, which is affected by the westerlies), northern Australia and central South America experiencing dry conditions. The area between these high-pressure belts generally receives considerable rainfall. As the sun moves south, so these belts follow, until by January the sun is overhead at the Tropic of Capricorn and the position is reversed.

The westerlies in the northern hemisphere now bring rain as far south as 30 °N.; southern Asia is dry and most of northern Africa, but most of the southern continents have their wet season. From these pressure movements, which influence rainfall and temperature, the standard climatic regions have been developed.

Climate, comfort and money

Matters of life or death for the peasant living close to the land, weather and climate still shape — and sometimes disrupt — the patterns of industry and leisure in the world's greatest cities.

THE EFFECTS of climate and weather on Man are considerable. Climate largely determines the clothes people wear, the style of their houses, the food they eat, and the plant and animal life that surrounds them. The obvious differences between the ways of life of hunters in tropical Africa and Eskimos arise largely from their climatic environment.

But climate becomes a less important factor in people's lives which are highly developed economically. A prolonged drought or an extremely severe winter can prove disastrous to an Indian peasant farmer or a nomad in the semi-arid regions of Asia. Extremes of climate disturb the lives of factory workers in the United States far less, however, because air conditioning gives them pleasant working conditions whatever the weather outside.

In 1915 a book entitled *Civilization and Climate* was published by an American geographer, Dr Ellsworth Huntington. Huntington was firmly convinced of the control which climate exerted over the actions of Man. He went so far as to state that climatic changes explained the downfall of the Inca and Roman empires. His contemporaries treated some of Huntington's views with scepticism, probably because he tried to account for practically everything in terms of climatic control.

Too hot to think?

Huntington also produced the idea of 'Cyclonic Man', on whom the rapid temperature variations associated with temperate *cyclones* (depressions) acted as a stimulus. He believed these changes prevented lethargy, which was characteristic of peoples in the humid tropics with their relatively constant high temperatures. Civilization was highest in the areas experiencing cyclonic weather, and obviously some cause-and-effect relationship existed.

Productivity of factory workers, and mental activity in students were both compared with temperature, humidity and pressure changes. He found that people were physically most active in places with an average temperature of 15·6–18·3 °C., and that their mental activity was greatest at about 3·33 °C. Although many of his ideas were dismissed, it is notable that riots in some cities in the United States tend to break out in the hot summer months.

The degree to which climate acts as a stimulus probably depends on personal temperament. Some people are happy with cooler conditions, particularly older people, who find that high temperatures quickly exhaust their capacity to work. Others may find temperatures below freezing a physical handicap, prompting them

Top, a grove of oranges brilliantly lit by night. Braziers are used to combat frost and deter thieves, but are very expensive to maintain.

Above, making an avalanche in the Caucasus: one shot from a cannon and the 'white death', the terror of mountain areas, threatens no longer.

to stay inside centrally heated buildings. However, we must not generalize and ascribe all Man's activities to climatic variations.

Extremes of climate may act as a brake on Man's progress, but at the level of our present technology this is largely an economic rather than a physical brake. For example, scientific research is conducted at the South Pole, and a permanent research station is maintained there in spite of severe weather conditions. The station gets its supplies from outside because its presence is considered sufficiently important to justify the high costs

of keeping it.

Many people live in the deserts of the Sahara and Middle East, working to produce oil because of the demand in other parts of the world. If the oil resources became exhausted, or if none had been found, then these areas would be uninhabited. It is only the economic motive that has made people work there regardless of the climate.

Climate affects Man in many less obvious ways: through its influence on agriculture, industry and transport – in short, through its bearing upon Man's economic activities. Climate has a pro-

129

Above, an oil-field in the desert is maintained at a great cost for the vast economic returns it yields. Extremes of climate are not an obstacle.

Tall poplars in Touraine, France, *top right,* act as a windbreak to protect the crops. Hedges are often grown in England to serve this purpose.

However picturesque, snow can be a serious nuisance in many countries. *Right,* a snow-plough clears the roads near Cedar Breaks in California.

found effect on agriculture, but it is certainly far less significant than it used to be. For example, wheat growing decreases in importance as we go farther northwards and westwards in Britain because the climate gets cooler and wetter. In Sweden, cereal cultivation has extended northwards in this century because of the increase in summer temperatures there. But new cereal varieties and economic factors have also contributed to the development. Crops can now be grown almost anywhere providing it is economically justifiable to do so.

Temperature, precipitation, wind speed and humidity are the most important factors controlling agriculture. Unseasonable changes may destroy an entire crop, or, at best, considerably reduce the yield. Some crops are particularly sensitive at certain times; frost at flowering time usually damages fruit crops and prevents fruit forming. Overcast, humid conditions at flowering time inhibit the movement of insects and prevent complete pollination of flowers. Some diseases and pests are especially prolific during particular weather conditions; potato blight begins when warm, humid weather continues for

a long time, and slugs are common in wet weather.

The main problem with temperature occurs when it drops below freezing point, and many crops are affected. Frosts during the growing season usually develop in low-lying sites because cold air, being denser than warm air, flows down slopes into the lowest position and then cools even more.

Shattering hailstones

If the plants are grown on the sloping hillsides, the cool air flows through them and no frost damage occurs. Small braziers can be used to warm the surrounding air, to prevent it from stagnating and becoming even colder. Obviously this technique is expensive and can only be applied to crops which produce high cash returns.

To give a crop a greater amount of warmth and sunshine, it should be planted on a south-facing slope, since north-facing slopes are in shadow for a much longer period of time.

Precipitation can fall as rain, snow or hail. Probably the most dramatic effects are produced by hailstones, which can fall in sizes as large as a grapefruit.

Although these might be rare, their effect is devastating. To combat this, scientists have conducted experiments in Kenya, Italy and Russia by sending explosive rockets into storm-clouds. The explosions shatter some of the hailstones and therefore prevent total destruction of the crops beneath. With excessive rainfall, floods may occur in valleys, and therefore levées (embankments) are necessary to protect farmland. Sheet-flooding down a hillside can remove the fertile top-soil. To combat this erosion, farmers plough along the contours.

Where rainfall is sparse and irrigation impossible, agriculturalists have developed a method of dry-farming: two years' rainfall is allowed to soak into the soil before sowing takes place. Farming in such dry areas can cause great damage. In the Great Plains of the United States, arable farming spreads westwards, because of greater-than-average rainfall in the 1920s. But this period was followed by drier conditions which prevented crops from growing. Eventually the top-soil was removed by wind action, producing the notorious Dust Bowl, and preventing farming for a considerable time.

Where winds from a certain direction prevail, a characteristic landscape appears when windbreaks are grown. An excellent example of this landscape occurs in the lower Rhône Valley of France where farmers plant hedgerows in an east–west direction to prevent the cold, strong Mistral wind from breaking down and destroying the spring crops. Similar examples occur in Britain. Here the hedge barriers are usually against the south-west to west winds in the exposed parts of the South-West and the flat country of the Fens.

Sometimes the damage from climatic conditions can be severe, as in areas subject to hurricanes. In 1965 one hurricane in the United States did $1,419,800 worth of damage.

The effects of climate and weather upon industry are perhaps not quite so marked as they are upon agriculture, but they can be important. This is particularly true for manufacturers whose sales depend on weather conditions, such as the makers of ice-creams, soft drinks, and also of waterproof clothing and umbrellas.

When winter comes

The three most important industries affected are power, transport and building. Consumption of energy in four forms – gas, electricity, coal and oil – undergoes seasonal variations in response to temperature. Most of the extra consumption in winter is for heating and lighting. For this reason, there must be a sufficient capacity of plant to produce the winter output, even though some of the capacity will not be used during summer.

The main problem arises during severe winters, such as the one Britain suffered in 1962–3, when the need for extra heating is well beyond normal winter consumption, and therefore beyond the capacity of the power industries. The question then arises: should sufficient spare capacity be maintained at a high cost to provide for occasional severe winters, or must people freeze during these conditions?

In many ways the transport industry faces a similar problem. During severe conditions railway points freeze, train and bus heating is insufficient, roads become blocked or have icy surfaces, and many areas possess little equipment to clear unusually heavy falls of snow. Some seas, such as the Baltic, freeze during severe winters, and ice-breakers have to be maintained throughout the year for use only during the winter months. In Norway, enormous snow-clearing machines remove heavy falls of snow, but such machines are expensive, and in a country such as Britain might be needed only once in ten years, or even less frequently.

Fog can also be a great hazard to air transport. It is not random in its distribution, but occurs in lowlands on cold, clear nights; on uplands as a form of very low cloud; and in many urban areas, in a particularly dense form. Ideally an airport should be sited in areas where fog incidence is low. However, other factors, such as proximity to population centres, are very important in site selection and may mean that airports have to be built on sites

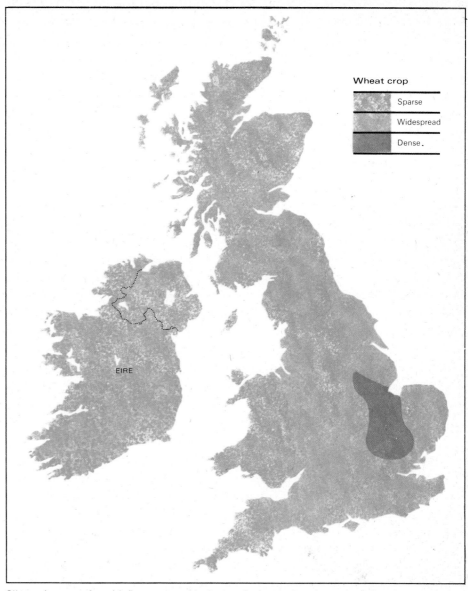

Wheat crop

- Sparse
- Widespread
- Dense.

EIRE

Climate has a profound influence on agriculture although modern farming methods have helped to neutralize its effect. Even in a small country like Britain, where variations in climate are not very great, differences in crop growing occur. For example, wheat growing generally decreases the farther north and west we go because the weather gets colder and wetter, *above*. In Sweden, as we see on the map *below*, cereal cultivation increased considerably, extending northwards, between 1918 and 1944, due to the increase in summer temperatures since the beginning of the century.

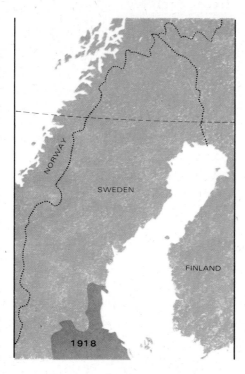

NORWAY

SWEDEN

FINLAND

1918

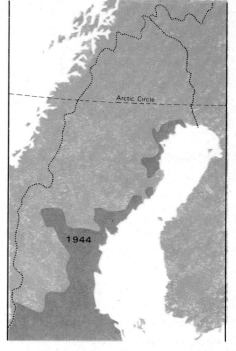

Arctic Circle

1944

with a higher fog frequency than is desirable. Flights may have to be diverted occasionally, but this is usually better than having long distances for people to travel between airport and city centre. The development of 'blind landing' systems by means of instruments should make fog less of a problem in the future.

Prolonged spells of dry weather in a climate that is not normally dry, such as that of Britain, also have a marked effect on industry. If a dry, cool spring is followed by a dry summer, then, by September, water reserves will be at a low ebb. In some cases, restrictions must be imposed on both domestic and industrial use of water. Such restrictions may reduce industrial production because of the tremendous amounts of water needed in many industries. The problem here is one of using our water resources most effectively. Sufficient rain falls to give a plentiful supply for the whole country, but much of it falls in western districts, where there are fewer people and less industry.

Sports and holidays

The weather has a great effect on building and construction. Traditionally, builders aim at completing 'ground work' during the summer and autumn, so that a reduced labour force can work under cover during the winter months. This is not a satisfactory system from any point of view, but heavy rain, strong winds and frosts in winter can prevent most forms of construction. Improved techniques are changing the situation, but during unfavourable weather conditions, building sites are still closed.

Most outdoor recreation is dependent on weather and climate. A heavy shower on a Saturday afternoon may waterlog a cricket pitch and prevent play, although for other sports, such as rugger or hockey, its effect would not be noticed. People can enjoy wonderful holidays during fine weather, but if their holiday coincides with a stormy, wet period, this can disappoint a whole year's expectations. For this reason, many people prefer to take their holidays in places where sunshine is likely throughout the whole period, rather than in areas which may be scenically more beautiful but where the climate is liable to be fickle.

Climate also has some influence on choice of work-place. This has been observed in the United States, with its many different climates, where there has been a considerable drift of population to the drier and warmer climates of the west and south.

Finally, climate and weather have an effect on economic activities within towns and cities. It has been found that temperatures are generally higher in the centre of urban areas compared with their suburbs and rural environs. This difference can amount at least to 6 or 7 °C. and is particularly well developed on calm nights when heat absorbed by the many buildings is re-radiated, and cooling of the air is therefore not so great as in the rural areas. This re-radiation of heat reduces the number and intensity of frosts in winter.

To a small degree, less fuel is required in winter to maintain adequate temperatures in buildings in central urban areas than in rural areas. Sunshine is often reduced in urban areas, firstly by tall buildings, which obscure direct sunlight, and secondly by a haze layer which frequently forms over the cities, scattering and absorbing the sunlight. When the angle of sunlight is low and weak soon after dawn or before sunset, the sunlight cannot penetrate the haze, and no effective sunshine reaches the ground. Wind can become a problem through a funnelling effect, particularly close to tall buildings, which produces strong winds at ground level. These winds can make walking difficult, and stir up dirt and litter.

Two of the most important effects produced by urban conditions are fog and atmospheric pollution, caused by smoke and industrial fumes rising into the air. Atmospheric pollution has considerable economic consequences in terms of ill-health, loss of work, cost of cleaning, and damage to crops and buildings. A conservative estimate of the cost in Britain has been put at £5 per person per year.

Smog is a mixture of fog and atmospheric pollution. In the London smog of December 1952, doctors attributed about 4,000 deaths to the prevailing atmospheric conditions; even animals at Smithfield Show appeared to be affected, particularly by the high concentration of sulphur dioxide, a colourless gas, in the air. Many metals are affected by pollution. Sulphur dioxide, when combined with water, produces a dilute solution of sulphuric acid, which can attack non-metallic objects such as leather and wool.

Dilute acids formed in the air by pollution quickly dissolve limestones and chalk, and others, such as Millstone Grit, acquire a coating of dirt.

Thus in town and countryside, in spite of scientific and technological advances, climate still exerts a considerable influence on Man's activities and environment.

The killer fog in the winter of 1962–3 covered most of Britain. *Above,* a policeman wears a 'smog mask' to protect him from the deadly mixture of fog and fumes which cost many lives.

The river on the diagram, *left,* is surrounded by low-lying land. A cross-section shows how levées (embankment) are made to prevent flooding. *Right,* cold air, heavier than warm air, flows down into valleys and hollows. Densely planted trees cause the cold air to be trapped.

The ways of the wind

The wind is a symbol of fickleness — yet the way it blows is decided by unchanging laws. The sun's heat and the shape and rotation of the Earth are the chief causes of the winds.

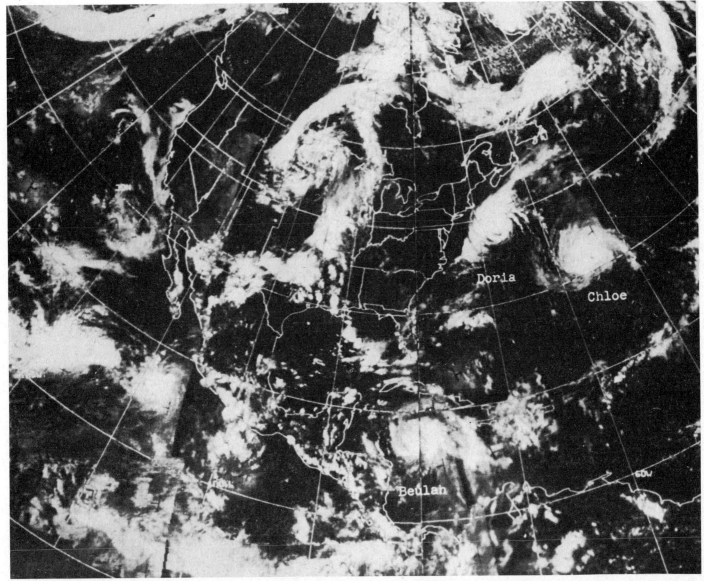

This photo-mosaic showing the position of three major hurricanes was assembled from pictures taken by an American satellite on 14 September 1967. Hurricane *Beulah* rampages over the Atlantic coast of Mexico's Yucatan Peninsula, while *Chloe* and *Doria* are further north over the ocean, east of the United States. From its position 22,300 miles above the Christmas Islands, the satellite can keep track of storms as they progress over a third of the world's surface. Ground-based meteorologists can therefore give early warning of an approaching hurricane.

FLOODING IN upon us through space, the immense energy of the burning sun does more than warm the Earth. Ocean currents and the way the winds blow, the world's weather and life itself all depend on the radiation that bombards our planet.

Only a minute part of the sun's energy output happens to strike the Earth. It arrives as waves of different lengths. Most of it is invisible, very short in wavelength, and potentially dangerous to living things. In space, these waves have no warmth: their energy is converted into heat only when they collide with another body.

As they fall on the outer envelope of air around the Earth, they deliver the equivalent of two calories a minute to each square centimetre. (A calorie is the amount of heat required to raise the temperature of one gramme of water from 14·5 °C. to 15·5 °C. Multiplied over the whole sunlit surface of the atmosphere, there is more than enough heat to warm our world.) Because it never varies, we call this energy supply the *solar constant*.

The sun and the atmosphere

Striking through the atmosphere, the radiation meets interference. Between 20 and 30 miles above the Earth's surface there is a concentration of ozone (a gas related to oxygen) which removes almost all the dangerous, very short-wave radiation. The reaction between the sun's energy and the ozone warms this zone in the upper atmosphere, which is called the *stratopause*. But most of the miles of air above our heads stay cold, for there is nothing in them to impede the path of the radiation.

Closer to the surface, clouds, dust, water vapour, even salt particles tend to obstruct the waves. Together they absorb some 17 per cent of the total solar energy before it strikes the land and sea. Some radiation, too, they reflect straight back into space. But the amount is small compared with the energy mirrored from the polished surface of the oceans. And even dry land can beam unabsorbed waves: a grassy field on a summer day in Britain reflects some 15 per cent of incoming radiation.

About half the available radiation from the sun, however, reaches the Earth's surface and is absorbed and converted into

heat. But this is not the end of the up-and-down traffic of radiation in the air about us. The sun, with its high temperature of 5,700 °C., emits primarily short-wave radiation. The Earth has a much lower mean temperature, about 15 °C., and radiates energy in the longer wavelengths invisible to our eyes. The long-wave radiation from the Earth is more easily absorbed by the atmosphere, especially by the water vapour and carbon dioxide, and thus warms the air.

If there were no clouds, then most of this heat radiated from the surface would be lost to space, but fortunately clouds and water vapour do absorb considerable amounts of heat, and are then able to re-radiate this, largely back to Earth. This is particularly apparent in late summer and autumn.

After a hot sunny day with little cloud, temperatures will be quite high, but once the sun sets, temperatures fall rapidly as much of the heat is lost to space, and ground frost may occur. If, however, an extensive cloud cover is present, then very little heat is lost and night-time temperatures will remain high.

Although the amount of radiation at the outer limit of the atmosphere is more or less constant, considerable differences are produced by the time the surface is reached. The amount of water vapour in the air varies from place to place, and is a very important factor in absorbing heat. In polar regions the radiation has to pass through a greater thickness of atmosphere, and at a lower angle. As a result, more is lost by reflection.

The nature of the surface is also important: at low angles the sea will reflect most of the light falling on it, but at high angles, most will be absorbed. Wet ground will absorb energy better than dry ground, and snow is an extremely good reflector, about 80 per cent of incoming radiation being lost. Because of these many variations the distribution of radiation is not even, but decreases towards the Pole.

Taken together, the many factors that determine how much radiation is available

The sun's rays penetrate outer space, until they strike the Earth's atmosphere and surface. When this happens, energy is absorbed, on different parts of the Earth's surfaces add up to a striking imbalance.

From the Equator to latitude 40 degrees the surface has a surplus of energy, and from latitude 40 degrees to the Pole the surface emits more energy than it absorbs from the sun. We know from many years of records that the Earth as a whole is getting neither warmer nor cooler, nor is there an increase in average temperatures at the Equator, nor a corresponding steady decrease in polar regions. From this we can safely assume that the amount of heat lost by the Earth from latitude 40 degrees to the Poles must be balanced by the transfer of heat from the areas near the tropics where there is a surplus.

Pressure gradients

It is this imbalance in heat energy which is responsible for the wind movements over the Earth. These in turn help to carry heat to the areas of the Poles where there is a deficit, preventing a steady decrease of temperature. Complications do arise from this annual pattern, as variations in the sun's altitude affect the heat budget of particular areas from season to season, but the same principles remain valid.

Let us consider how winds are formed and what controls their movement. By wind, we mean the movement of air over the Earth's surface. This takes place when a difference in air pressure exists between two points. The flow runs from high to low pressure, and the strength of the movement is proportional to the difference in pressure between the two points – the *pressure gradient*. If our Earth did not rotate, then the wind would blow directly from high to low pressure, but because of the effect of this rotation air appears to be deflected to the right in the northern hemisphere, and to the left in the southern hemisphere.

How are these pressure differences formed? Pressure at the surface is really the force maintained by the atmosphere

but much is also reflected back into space. This satellite photograph shows the Earth shining brightly while outer space is in darkness.

above that point – an area of high pressure has a greater weight of air above it than a low pressure area. This greater weight can also be due to cold dense air near the surface, or to a piling up of air at higher altitudes, because cold air is heavier than warm air. There may be a lower pressure area of warm air above the cold dense air as we rise in the atmosphere. This will initially start a movement of air towards the low pressure above the cold air. Because of the Earth's rotation the air-flow will be deflected to the right in the northern hemisphere. If the cold air lies in the north, the normal state of affairs in this hemisphere, the air will flow in a westerly direction in the upper layers of the atmosphere. In a similar situation in the southern hemisphere, the wind directions are reversed. It is this thermal gradient control which produces many of the great wind circulations of the world.

We can explain the major wind systems as a result of the unequal heating of the Earth by the sun. Ideally, we should be able to start with the known heat input from the sun, and by taking account of the astronomical and geographical features of the Earth, be able to explain the genesis and maintenance of this circulation. As yet this is not possible because of the complexities involved, but eventually we may succeed, as larger computers enable us to solve the necessary physical equations.

The pressure gradients which are produced by variations in temperature will be primarily oriented east–west, and will thus give rise to westerly or easterly winds. Yet these are supposed to be the winds which transfer the surplus heat from the tropics to polar regions. How, then, is this heat transferred?

It is done in several ways. If the winds in temperate regions blew purely from west to east, then there would be no flow of heat across them; the equatorial side would soon get hotter and the polar side

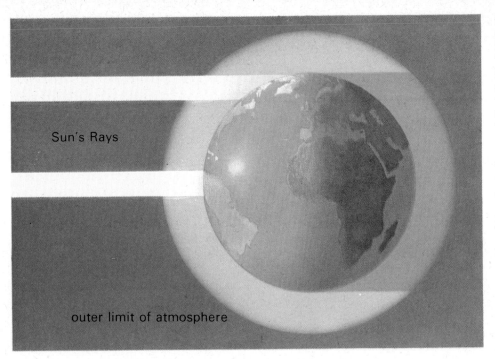

Sun's Rays

outer limit of atmosphere

In polar regions the sun's rays strike the Earth's surface at a lower angle than at the Equator and are distributed over a wide area. Less heat cooler. The temperature contrast between the two sides would then become so great that the air-flow would become unstable and begin to oscillate, thus transferring warm air northwards and cool air southwards, and allowing mixing to take place.

The prevailing winds also generate sea-currents, and these have considerable importance in effecting the transfer of heat. Some currents bring warm water polewards; the North Atlantic Drift and

is therefore available and more of what remains is lost through reflection. Polar ice and snow are particularly good reflectors of heat. the Kuro Siwo are among these. Others bear cool water equatorwards and among these are the Canaries, Benguela and Humboldt Currents. As the currents gradually merge into their new environments, they produce a better balance of heat distribution over the Earth.

If the surface of the Earth was uniform, the 'general circulation', as the major winds of the world are called, would be much less complicated. Land masses differ

in their physical properties from the oceans: they warm up much more quickly in summer and are far cooler in winter. This results in an enormous surface sea-breeze effect, in which cool, moist air sweeps into the interior of the Asian continent,, bringing the characteristic seasonal rainfall. A reversal occurs in winter with the outflow of cold dry air southwards.

Shifting wind belts

These winds travel close to the Earth's surface, and the effects of the upper atmosphere on them are considerable. It is for this reason that the heaviest rain does not fall in the Thar Desert in India, where the main low pressure centre is located; here the moist monsoonal air is too shallow to produce rain, and the dry air above prevents clouds from developing. Similar reversals of wind occur elsewhere, as for example in West Africa. In winter the northern hemisphere westerlies are at their strongest, and the high pressure system of the sub-tropics moves further south over the Sahara. On its southern limb, winds blow steadily from the northeast, extending as far as the West African coast, and giving very dry conditions from November to March. These are really the trade winds blowing over the African continent.

By April, the effect of the northward movement of the sun is to decrease the thermal gradient in the northern hemisphere. This decreases the intensity of the westerlies, and the high pressure system moves northwards towards the Mediterranean. Gradually the moist air from the Atlantic is able to move inland over West

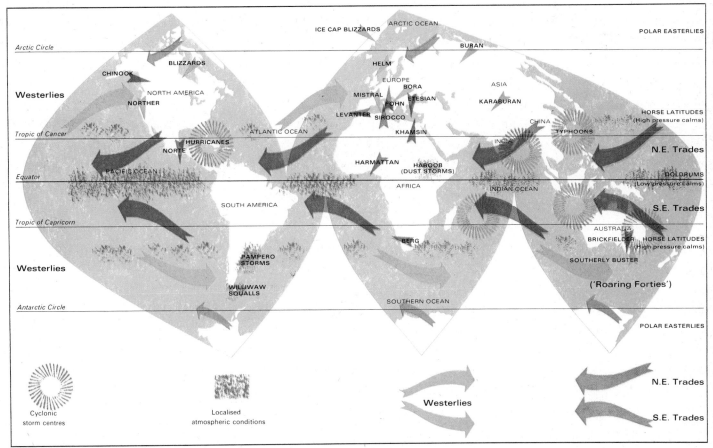

This map shows the major wind systems of the world. Movement of air over the Earth is due to the unequal heating of the Earth's surface; the

heat lost at the Poles must be balanced by the transfer of surplus heat from the Tropics. The trade winds and westerlies are mainly respon-

sible for this, but local atmospheric conditions produce secondary wind circulations which also help transfer heat from region to region.

135

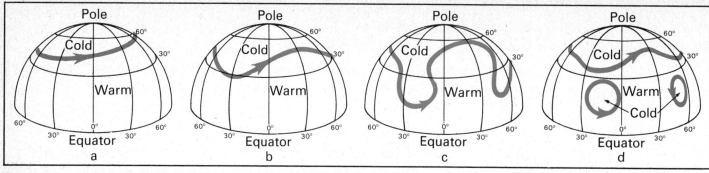

The diagrams, *above,* show how air mixes in the atmosphere. The westerly flow of air in Fig. *A* becomes unstable when the temperature difference between Pole and Equator increases and a more and more violent oscillation ensues, Figs. *B* and *C*. This produces pools of cold air near the Equator which slowly mix with the warmer air to produce a better balance of heat, Fig. *D*. Similarly, hot air moves northwards to warm the Pole.

Africa and when large clouds develop, rain ensues.

Thus the movement of the vertical position of the sun between the Tropics of Cancer and Capricorn produces a seasonal reversal of winds at the surface. These reversals were of great importance in the days of sailing ships.

Another frequently used route for sailing ships took advantage of the North Atlantic trade winds, by sailing south of Spain towards the Canary Islands and then westwards in these steady northeast to east winds. This was much easier than trying to sail across the shortest route against the westerly winds, and so it was the Caribbean which Columbus discovered first, not the nearest point to Europe on the North American mainland. The Vikings, however, appear to have travelled by a northerly route to North America, and this must have been in the easterly winds which are found on the northern side of the Atlantic depressions.

The trade winds

The trade winds blow on the equatorial margins of the sub-tropical high pressure belts, and are steady and reliable in both direction and speed. This is because the high pressure centres with which they are associated are also constant features of the circulation. To explain the constancy of the trades, we must therefore understand why the sub-tropical high pressure cells vary only slightly in their position.

Basically, two methods operate to bring about the heat transport from Equator to Pole. Between 30 degrees north and south the main feature is one of rising air at the thermal Equator, spreading northwards and southwards, carrying warm air polewards. This circulation is completed by the surface winds moving towards the Equator (the trades), but these carry less energy, and so there is a net movement polewards. These circulation cells are known as Hadley cells, after their discoverer, George Hadley, a British scientist of the eighteenth century. Polewards of 30 degrees, a different system prevails. Here the basic circulation is the westerly wind, and heat is transferred within the many disturbances or depressions which are such a frequent occurrence in these latitudes.

Even seasonal alterations only produce oscillations of about six degrees in the major high-pressure cells, which are the dividing line between these two systems of heat transfer. This suggests that their position is largely determined by the character of the Earth itself; by its size, its speed of rotation and the force of gravity. Experiments with rotating objects representing the Earth confirm the theory.

Cooled and heated in different parts, these models showed a flow (using water) with similar characteristics to movement in our atmosphere, but these change when the rate of rotation is changed. As these characteristics of the Earth remain unchanged, the position of the anticyclonic cells will vary only slightly, hence the trade winds are such a steady feature of our general wind systems.

In the sub-tropical regions where they have their source, the trades can be classed as a gentle to moderate breeze. Rainfall is relatively rare and sunshine amounts are high. As the winds progress westwards, and particularly in summer, they may be checked and piled up by low pressure areas. The Earth's spin sets the pile twisting. When warm air joins in,

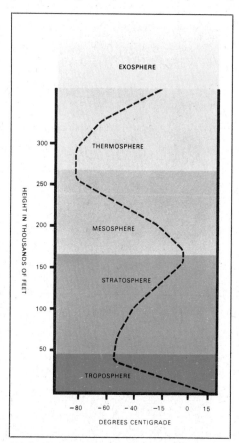

Air becomes colder in the troposphere and warmer in the belt of ozone, the heat-absorbent gas in the stratosphere. In the thermosphere, air is heated by the atomic absorption of solar energy.

the chance of hurricanes developing within the trades increases. It is only recently that the origin of hurricanes has been discovered. The importance of conditions in the upper atmosphere for their formation was unknown until radar and planes were able to penetrate the thick banks of cloud. Satellites now enable us to track these storms long before they approach land.

In spite of the damage caused by their winds, hurricanes (or typhoons in the north Pacific) play an important role in the essential transfer of heat to polar areas. Many hurricanes die out as severe storms in the westerly wind belt. Occasionally they reach as far as Britain, but only produce heavy rain and moderate winds in their decaying stage.

The movement of anticyclones

The major wind systems so far mentioned are the primary or dominant circulations. Within them, variations occur. Britain is certainly within the main westerly zone, but this does not mean that every day of the year has westerly winds. Smaller scale pressure features lie within the general westerly flow, known as *depressions* and *anticyclones*. These usually move from west to east, but bring a variety of winds with them.

Occasionally, some of these different pressure patterns may become almost stationary and produce anomalous conditions for a longer period than usual. An example of this was in the winter of 1962–3, when an anticyclone remained stationary over Scandinavia and gave bitter east winds to much of Britain. These secondary wind circulations are equally important in producing heat transfer from the 'surplus' to the 'deficit' areas.

The energy from the sun, then, is responsible for heating the Earth, but this energy is not received equally over the surface. This uneven distribution sets up wind systems which transfer heat from the 'surplus' to the 'deficit' areas and prevent a large temperature contrast. The origin of winds on our Earth, both major and minor, lies in the varying pattern of the heating over the Earth's surface.

Man has learnt much about the nature of the winds since the days of the Ancient Greeks who believed that the god Aeolus kept them in his care, locked up in a vast cavern. But even today, the names given to the world's great winds – like Mistral, Chinook, Williwaw and Brickfielder show that they retain a personality.

Rain, hail, sleet and snow

The sky is like a reservoir with a million shifting spillways. Constantly overflowing, it is constantly replenished by great rivers of rising moisture. What causes this remarkable cycle?

WITHOUT WATER, life on Earth would be impossible. The oceans contain an enormous store of water, but for non-marine life it is largely useless because of its high salt content. Man, animals and land plants need fresh water, and this is provided by rain.

We know beyond question that rain falls only from clouds, but before the use of balloons, aircraft, rockets and satellites, almost nothing was known about the processes by which clouds produce rain. Many theories were advanced through the ages, but until the nineteenth century much of the work was based on Greek ideas of fire, water, earth and air. Because many physical principles were not known, the suggestions were often totally wrong. Progress was irregular, depending on which theory was in vogue at the time.

But by the mid-nineteenth century, experimental studies in physics, particularly into the properties of heat, led to the formation of our basic ideas about water vapour in the atmosphere. Once manned flight into the atmosphere became possible, our knowledge of conditions within the clouds themselves increased, and theories of rain formation approached those at present accepted.

What is a cloud?

To discover the origin of rain, we must follow the processes whereby water vapour in the air is changed into clouds, and then how these clouds produce raindrops. Clouds form when the air temperature is cooled sufficiently for the water vapour in the air to become saturated. Air varies in its capacity to retain water vapour; when the air is warm it can hold large amounts of water vapour with no visible evidence (as over a cloudless desert). Cold

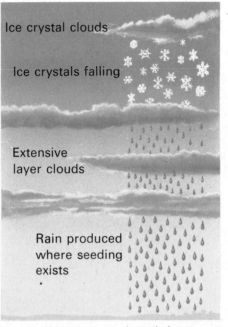

Ice-crystal clouds may end as rain in temperate zones. Once heavy enough, the crystals fall, collect cloud droplets on the way and melt to form rain when they encounter the warmer air.

air can hold only much smaller amounts, so when warm air is cooled, the amount of vapour within it does not decrease and eventually the air becomes saturated. This means that the air cannot hold any more water in the vapour state, and at this point the water is condensed into cloud droplets. This process can be seen on some nights. As the air is cooled near the ground it may reach saturation, when the moisture in the air may appear as mist and be deposited as dew, or, if the temperature is below freezing point, as frost.

For water vapour to condense, it re-

quires some sort of nucleus, and nuclei are freely available in the atmosphere in the form of dust, salt particles, chemical substances and minute particles of soil. These nuclei are microscopically small, and are usually present in sufficient numbers for water to condense on them once the air becomes saturated.

Because of the small size of the nuclei, the resulting cloud droplets are also extremely small, especially when compared with raindrops. A cloud is really a diffuse collection of these minute droplets. Even in some tropical clouds where water content is high, only one part in a million of the cloud is actually water!

The growth of these cloud droplets depends on how quickly water vapour is converted into a liquid form. Within the cloud, the droplets compete for the available water vapour, so their growth depends on the number and size of nuclei and the degree of turbulence that is to be found in the air, which will increase the number of collisions between droplets, and therefore help their growth.

Supercooled water droplets

But growth of this nature is not unlimited, and on its own is unlikely to produce rainfall. In fact these droplets are still so small that, even if they were heavy enough to fall from the cloud, they would soon be evaporated in the drier air beneath the cloud.

We know that many clouds do not give rain, so some at least must remain in this state without droplets of sufficient size being formed, but how is rain produced, especially in such large quantities as in a thunder-storm? Earlier we assumed that all the droplets within a cloud were of the same size, but this is unlikely. Some droplets will be larger because of the different sizes of the condensation nuclei, and thus will be able to fall more quickly within the cloud. Collisions with other droplets will then take place, and by this coalescence, larger and fewer drops will result.

In moist conditions over the sea, rain can be formed in about 40 minutes, assuming the cloud is thicker than 3,000 feet. Over the large land masses of continents, a time of one to two hours is required, and a much thicker cloud layer.

This process of rainfall formation is the most important in tropical latitudes, where there is a high water content in the air, and where temperatures are so high that many clouds are entirely above freezing point. But in temperate regions of the Earth, the tops of clouds are generally below freezing point, and their upper layers contain ice crystals. This fact is of vital importance in the next theory of rainfall.

Water droplets do not automatically

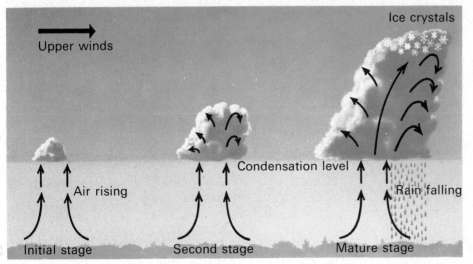

Billowing cumulus clouds tower to the high altitudes where ice crystals form. The clouds usually appear in good weather and form when rising air cools. The upper winds above the condensa-

tion level help to boost their extent. The diagram shows the three stages which lead to showers in temperate climates. Turbulent air currents within the cloud may give air travellers a rough ride.

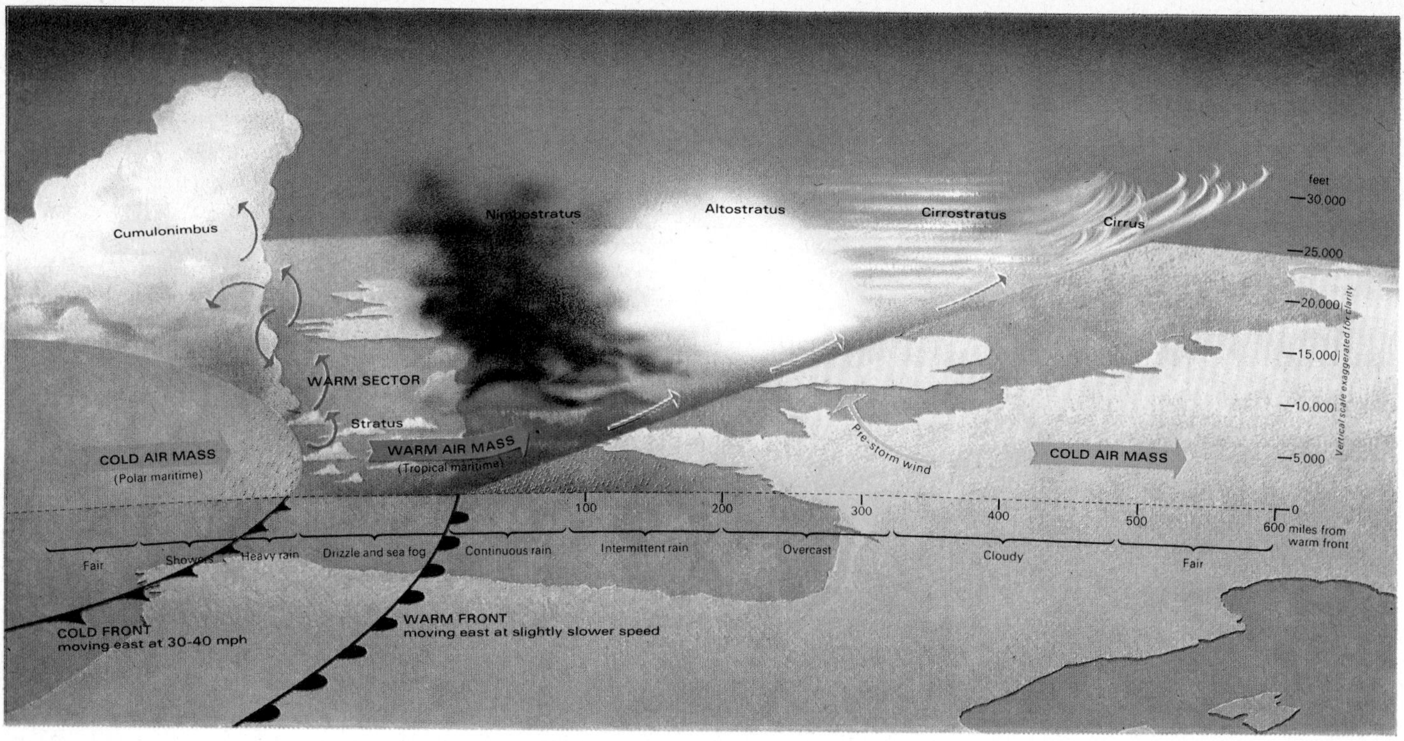
Cumulonimbus
Nimbostratus
Altostratus
Cirrostratus
Cirrus
feet
30,000
25,000
20,000
15,000
10,000
5,000
0
Vertical scale exaggerated for clarity
WARM SECTOR
Stratus
COLD AIR MASS
(Polar maritime)
WARM AIR MASS
(Tropical maritime)
Pre-storm wind
COLD AIR MASS
100
200
300
400
500
600 miles from warm front
Fair
Showers
Heavy rain
Drizzle and sea fog
Continuous rain
Intermittent rain
Overcast
Cloudy
Fair
COLD FRONT
moving east at 30-40 mph
WARM FRONT
moving east at slightly slower speed

freeze at 0°C., but can exist in the water state to temperatures as low as −40°C. They are then said to be *supercooled.* Once water freezes, however, it will not melt until it reaches a temperature above 0 °C. Thus it is quite possible for ice crystals and water droplets to co-exist within a cloud. Because of their physical properties, the crystals can extract water vapour from the cloud more easily than the droplets. The ice crystals therefore tend to grow at the expense of the droplets, and can quickly reach an appreciable size.

Rain-making

Once the crystals are of sufficient weight, air currents within the cloud are not strong enough to keep them suspended, and so the crystals begin to fall. Below the freezing level, the crystals begin to melt, and so raindrops are formed. This process with ice crystals and water droplets in co-existence has been named the Bergeron Process after its discoverer, the Swedish meteorologist T. Bergeron. At one time it was thought to be the only process, but when rain was observed to fall from tropical clouds which were entirely warmer than 0 °C., alternatives were suggested.

In Britain, the ice-phase in clouds is usual. This can be seen during showers, when the rising clouds initially have definite boundaries, but when icing takes place the upper cloud boundary develops a fuzzy appearance.

The presence of water droplets at temperatures well below freezing point shows that freezing nuclei are not as abundant as condensation nuclei. This principle has led to the process of cloud seeding for rain-making: under favourable conditions, crystals are added to clouds. These then act as freezing nuclei for the water droplets, and eventually rain may fall. Silver iodide has been found most suitable for this work, and operates at temperatures as high as −5 °C. A similar method can also be used for clearing freezing fogs.

Above, a depression is passing over Britain, bringing rain from the west. An aeroplane passing through the high, curly sheet of cirrus clouds from east to west, on through the thickening layers of cirrostratus and altostratus, soon encounters dark masses of nimbostratus, producing drizzle.

The mackerel sky that precedes a warm front is created by the high ripples of cirro-cumulus cloud, *below,* which rides as a thin sheet at between 20,000 and 40,000 feet. *Cirrus* is the Latin word for a curl of hair. Cumulus clouds, *bottom,* are named after the Latin word for pile.

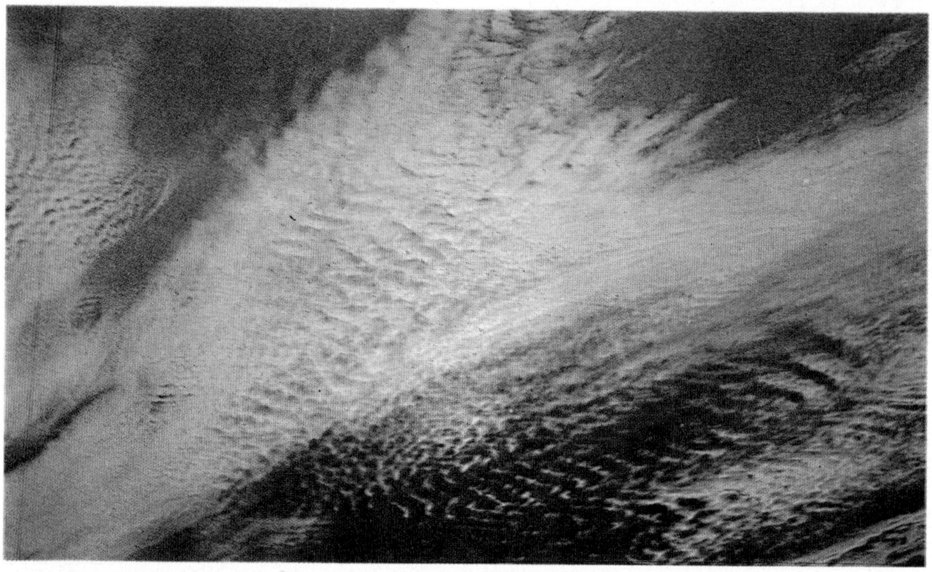

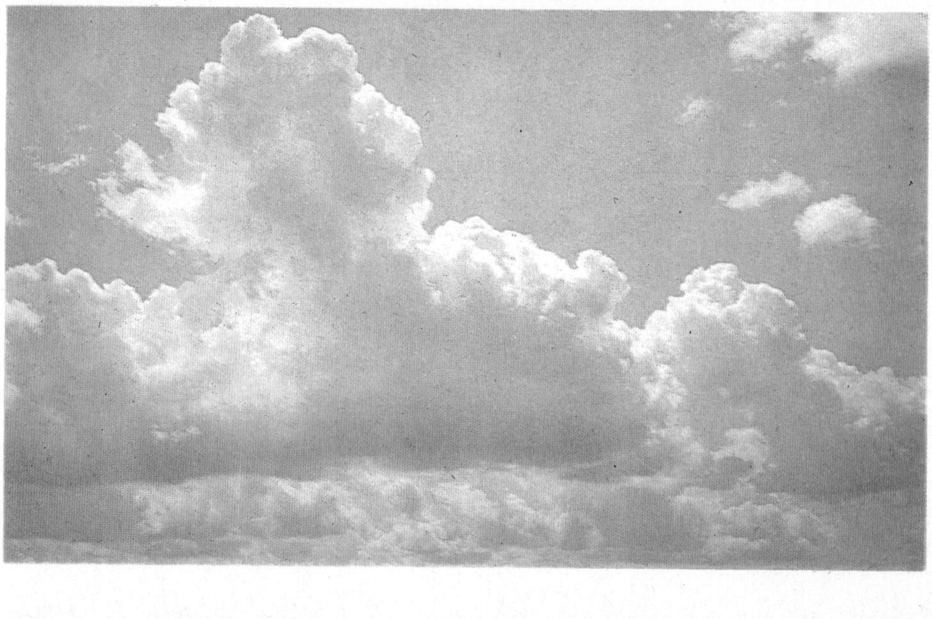

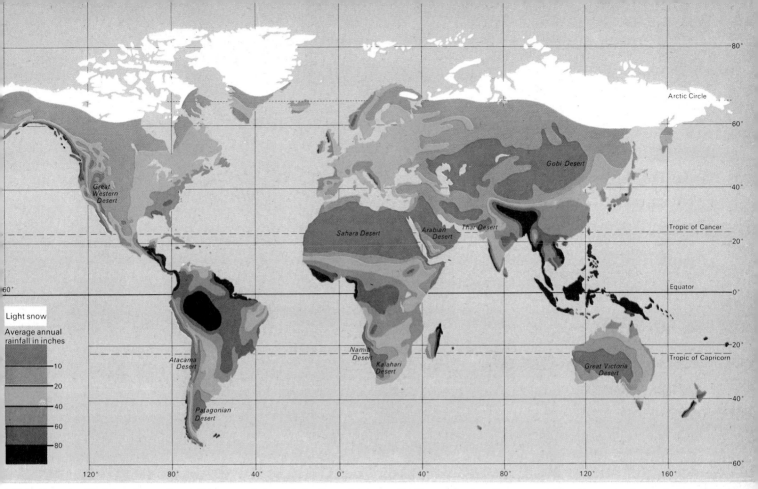

Light snow

Average annual
rainfall in inches

— 10
— 20
— 40
— 60
— 80

Great Western Desert

Atacama Desert

Patagonian Desert

Sahara Desert

Arabian Desert

Thar Desert

Namib Desert

Kalahari Desert

Gobi Desert

Great Victoria Desert

Arctic Circle

Tropic of Cancer

Equator

Tropic of Capricorn

Rain, snow and hail together make up the precipitation recorded above on the world map. Many complex factors determine the world's rainfall. Accurate reporting of climatic conditions has only relatively recently enabled scientists to understand the overall pattern.

In the atmosphere there are basically two types of cloud, the convectional cloud and the layer cloud. Convectional clouds form as rising air cools. They usually contain strong air currents, producing turbulence, and also a high water content. In temperate zones, they normally rise to the freezing level and then produce rain. Such circumstances as these are favourable for the formation of large raindrops, and most heavy showers are produced by these convectional clouds.

Layer clouds represent the slow uplift of water-bearing air over large areas, and are the monotonous grey clouds we often see before rain. In these circumstances, the updraughts are not sufficient to maintain large drops, so the layer clouds usually give prolonged light rain. The clouds must be sufficiently thick to reach well above the freezing level and avoid evaporation of the resulting drops.

From recent studies of these layer clouds, drizzle was found to fall from such clouds when they were between 1,500 feet and 10,000 feet thick. Moderate rain did not usually fall until the clouds were at least 15,000 feet, or about three miles, thick. The coalescence of raindrops was found to occur and give slight rain even in the layer clouds. Some self-seeding was also observed, the ice crystals falling on to water clouds from clouds at a higher level.

Other forms of precipitation have a similar origin to rain. Snow and hail fall when the air temperature between the cloud and the ground is too low to melt the ice crystals. Snow is generally the product of layer clouds, and hail falls from convectional clouds.

We have seen that the starting point of all forms of precipitation – rain, snow and hail – is cloud, which is formed when the cooling of air allows water vapour to condense. Now we must consider how the cloud-forming process begins. The clue to the whole process is rising air. Air gets warmer when it is being compressed: a familiar example is the way in which a bicycle pump gets warm in use as the air is compressed within it. Air gets cooler, conversely, when it is expanding. As air rises, the pressure of the atmosphere around it decreases, allowing the air to expand and grow cooler. It is because of this expansion process that balloons are only partly filled with gas before they are sent up: the higher they get the fuller the envelope of the balloon becomes, as the gas expands.

Rising air

What makes the air rise in the first place? There are several causes – mountain ranges, the heat of the sun and atmospheric depressions. When air flows over a mountain range it is forced to rise, thus cooling, and the heavier rainfall over mountains is a testimony to cloud and rain formation by rising air.

The second cause depends on the fact that warm air is less dense than cool air. As oil will float on water because it is less dense than water, so warm air will rise through cooler air, until the temperature difference between them ceases to exist. This is how convectional clouds are formed. The sun's heat on the Earth's surface warms certain areas more than their surroundings. The heated air above these areas becomes warmer and rises. It then begins cooling at a fixed rate of 1 °C. for every 100 metres that it rises. It continues to rise while it is warmer than its surroundings, and may eventually produce cloud.

The process of condensation, once it begins, releases latent heat, and this reduces the rate of cooling to about half. Once the surroundings become as warm as the rising air, then the air is no longer able to rise. If the air finally becomes cooler than its surroundings then it will begin to sink. The atmosphere can be termed stable or unstable depending whether such parcels of air are able to rise steadily or sink back to Earth. It can therefore be seen that where the air is very hot at the surface, or very cold in its upper layers, it is likely to be unstable.

Instability is likely to produce convectional clouds and local showers, but the large-scale uplift which produces layer cloud has a different origin. Large-scale uplift is associated with rising air and convergence near a depression. A depression is an area of low pressure, and even though winds are blowing towards its centre, the central pressure may still be falling because more air is being removed above than is being blown in below. This process leads to a steady uplift of air throughout the depression, and as the rising air cools, extensive layer cloud forms.

Convergence also takes place as air blows towards the centre. This also makes air rise and is a further factor in cloud formation. Much of the rainfall in western Britain occurs during the passage of these depressions. The effect of greater uplift and turbulence over the country's western mountains produces heavier and more

139

prolonged rain, giving annual average values as high as 175 inches in parts of western Scotland, the Lake District and Snowdonia.

The importance of these various factors in rainfall formation varies throughout the world. In temperate latitudes, rainfall from depressions is the most important, and in tropical areas convectional rains predominate. Here our views about rainfall formation have changed relatively recently. It was once thought that tropical rain was purely convectional in origin, and was distributed randomly. However, when climatic reporting became more widespread, these so-called random events were found to consist of several storms following similar paths, but not necessarily giving rain everywhere.

It was then realized that conditions in the upper atmosphere were equally important. Even though such storms give high amounts of annual rainfall, most of this total is produced by just a few storms. If in one particular year, there is even one storm less than average, then drought may prevail, because the total rainfall is reduced by so much. Variability is in fact a feature of tropical rainfall for this reason.

Similarly, the Indian monsoon was at one time thought to give almost continuous rain due to convection within the moist layer of air. With more detailed study, it has been found that most rain falls from storm surges within the monsoon when clouds are able to develop to greater heights.

In the northern parts of India, where the moist monsoon layer is thin, the air above is both dry and warm. Any clouds reaching this level tend to be evaporated, and because the surrounding air is warmer, the air currents within the clouds are unable to ascend further.

Where no rain falls

Even in deserts, water vapour exists in the atmosphere; in fact there is more vapour in the Saharan air than there is over Britain in winter. However, no rain falls in deserts, because the air, being warmer, has a greater capacity to hold water. More important, this air is unable to rise and cool because of the subtropical anticyclone above with its warm, subsiding air.

This condition is true of most deserts; they lie in parts of the world where the high-pressure cells are fairly stable, so at no time are conditions favourable for a general or even local uplift of air which could produce enough cloud to make rain.

It can thus be seen that for rain to fall, favourable circumstances must exist for the rain-making processes. It follows that areas with low rainfall experience these conditions for short periods only, and those with very high rainfall experience the conditions for a much longer time. The distribution of rainfall throughout the world can be understood more clearly when these points are taken into account.

The monsoon, *below,* brings torrential rainfall as cool winds move across India in summer. The floods may devastate but are welcomed as the bearers of fertility after many months of drought.

Thunder-storms move on predictable paths across a landscape, *above.* They are made up of groups of cloud cells that form and then dissipate. The movements of individual cells dictate the path.

Digging up yesterday's weather

Buried in the Earth's rocks millions of years ago are the fossilized remains of plants and animals — clues to the enormous and mysterious changes of climate which have affected the whole world.

TEMPERATE FORESTS in Antarctica, swamps in the Gobi desert, fig trees off the coast of Greenland, ice sheets in the British Isles and Australia, all sound highly improbable in the world we know. But throughout the Earth's history of about 4,550 million years the climate has changed continuously and is still changing, though so slowly that precise measurements are difficult. Alternating periods of warmth and cold, taking millions or tens of millions of years, have occurred and are still occurring. The future of our world is unknown: it may grow warmer, melting the ice caps at the Poles, raising the sea level and flooding low-lying coastlines. Or it may grow colder; the ice caps growing larger, creeping down from the north, forcing Man and the animals to crowd the cooling areas of the equator.

Clues to past climatic changes are found in such evidence as the fossilized remains of animals and plants embedded in layers of sedimentary rock in areas of the world now too hot, cold, or dry for them to have survived. This indicates that suitable conditions must have existed during their lifetimes, and by dating these fossils, a world climatic calendar can be compiled.

The relationship between fossils and climates is, however, not as simple as it sounds, because many fossils are the remains of extinct forms of life, and it is difficult to be certain what conditions were favourable to their growth. Ele-phants and rhinoceroses, for example, are now found only in tropical areas but about 1,500,000 years ago, during the Pleistocene epoch, woolly mammoths and woolly rhinoceroses lived in the Arctic. Now extinct, these two groups of animals were adapted to the cold because they were covered with thick hair.

Too cold for dinosaurs

Relics of the reptiles of the Mesozoic era, about 65 to 225 million years ago, are a much clearer clue to climate. Reptiles are cold-blooded and become sluggish in cold weather, and are helpless when the temperature drops to freezing point. The large reptiles that we know today, such as alligators and crocodiles, all inhabit tropical areas. (The reptiles of the temperate latitudes, such as some species of lizards and snakes, are small and generally hibernate in winter.) The dinosaurs and other great reptiles of the Mesozoic era could not hibernate in holes in the earth because of their great size. Unless many of these reptiles developed warm blood, which is improbable, it seems likely that such areas as Belgium, where geologists have discovered the remains of many large dinosaurs, were warm during the age of reptiles. The temperature probably remained above freezing point throughout the year.

Dinosaurs also lived during the late Jurassic and Cretaceous periods, between 65 and 195 million years ago, in Mongolia and in Alberta, Canada, and they even ventured as far north as the islands of Spitzbergen, far above the present-day Arctic Circle.

Plant fossils confirm that the temperate and cold regions of the world once had much warmer climates than they have today. On Disco Island, off the western coast of Greenland, Cretaceous rocks, between 65 and 136 million years old, contain fossils of such plants as bread-fruit trees, fig trees and ferns, all of which now grow only in warm or tropical areas. Plant fossils are particularly useful for establishing the climates of areas during most of the Cenozoic era, the last 65 million years. The plants of this era are basically similar to those which flourish today, and so the climatic conditions affecting their growth can be accurately established. From the evidence of plant fossils, geologists have suggested that the polar ice caps probably did not exist during the early millennia of the Cenozoic era.

Latitude is not the only factor that affects temperature; height above sea level is another. Mountains are progressively colder the higher one goes. Deciduous trees (trees that shed their leaves in winter) on the lower slopes give way to coniferous forests and eventually to grass meadows beyond the timber line, the upper limit for tree growth. Geologists have studied plant fossils in ancient lake beds which lie high in mountain regions

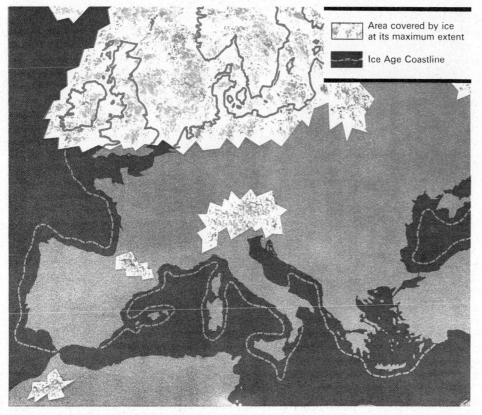

Area covered by ice at its maximum extent

Ice Age Coastline

During the Pleistocene Ice Age, which began over a million years ago, vast ice sheets and glaciers covered much of northern Europe, *left. Above,* Early Man attacks a mammoth, a woolly elephant adapted to the harsh climate. Drawings of mammoths are still found in caves in France.

where it is far too cold for such plants to grow today.

From the fossils of plants, and traces of their pollen, geologists have been able to date the epoch when the mountains which enclose the lake beds were uplifted. For example, lake beds in the Andes, lying at about 12,000 feet above sea level, contain Pliocene fossils of plants which could not have survived above 6,000 feet. Hence the mountains must have been uplifted by about 6,000 feet during the Pleistocene epoch which followed. Geologists have used similar evidence to establish that major uplift occurred during the same epoch in the Sierra Nevada in the United States, and in the Himalaya.

While fossils may sometimes mislead the student of *palaeoclimatology* (the study of past climates), the nature of the rock strata is often a good guide to climatic conditions. Layers of salt or gypsum indicate arid or desert conditions, and limestones containing corals suggest that such rocks accumulated in warm seas. Coal seams represent areas that were once tropical swamp-forest, and *glacial drift* (material carried by glaciers or ice sheets) indicates periods when the climate was cold.

From such evidence geologists have established that the climate throughout geological history has been generally warm, but from time to time periods of intense cold have occurred. The best known of such cold periods is the Pleistocene Ice Age, which began about 1,500,000 years ago. At its greatest extent, vast ice sheets and glaciers covered most of the British Isles, Scandinavia, the North German plain and the Alps, most of Canada and some parts of the northern United States, and parts of Siberia. Temperatures throughout the rest of the world were generally low during the Ice Age. The ice left clear evidence of its grinding movement. Some areas were scoured by the abrasive action of the ice, and all the soil was removed, leaving *striae* (scratches) on the surface of the rock.

Ice sheets and glaciers

In other areas, the glaciers and ice sheets deposited much material, including terminal or end moraines – piles of rock debris that mark the furthest points reached by the ice. The Pleistocene Ice Age was not a single event, but was divided into periods when the ice advanced, called *glacial stages,* and periods when the ice retreated, called *interglacial stages.* The number of glacial and interglacial stages during the Pleistocene epoch, which the geologists have identified, varies from place to place. In the Alps, they have found evidence of five glacial and four interglacial stages. In northern Germany, three terminal moraines mark the termination of three main stages of glaciation, and

in the United States, geologists have identified four or possibly five main glacial stages.

Major ice ages also occurred in earlier times, including the late Pre-Cambrian, the Lower Cambrian, and Permo-Carboniferous periods. The Permo-Carboniferous Ice Age is of special interest because ice covered vast areas that now lie in tropical latitudes. The ice was mainly confined to areas in the southern hemisphere in South America, Africa, Australia and Antarctica, the only exception in the northern hemisphere being the Indian sub-continent.

The Permo-Carboniferous Ice Age offers much support to the theory of continental drift, whereby the continents are supposed to have been united until they gradually drifted apart in the late Mesozoic era. According to this theory the continents are made up of light material floating in the denser material which lies beneath, and, like rafts in water, they are moved in relation to each other by divergent currents. Geologists have pointed out that the Permo-Carboniferous ice sheet could not have extended across the

The fossilized remains of a forest in Arizona were exposed when the shale in which they were buried was weathered away. Dating from the Triassic age, roughly 200 million years ago, these grew by streams in a subtropical climate.

The British Isles may have looked like this a million years ago during the Pleistocene Ice Age. The climate all over the world was cooler. There were ice caps in New Zealand, ice on the mountains in New South Wales, and glaciers in Tasmania. Most of the mammals we know today came into existence but were differently distributed. During the warmer periods of the Ice Age, hippopotamuses lived in the river Thames, lions and hyenas ranged over southern England.

South Atlantic and Indian Oceans to cover the now widely separated continents of the southern hemisphere and India. There is not enough water in the oceans to form such a volume of ice. Instead, some geologists have suggested that the continents were in close proximity in Permo-Carboniferous times, forming one great land mass called Gondwanaland (after the middle part of India inhabited by the Gonds), and that the South Pole was probably situated in South Africa. By the mid-Permian period, Africa was again warm enough for reptiles to live in areas which had been covered by ice.

Since the end of the Pleistocene epoch, the climate has fluctuated. Vineyards flourished about a thousand years ago in southern England and, several times, prolonged droughts in central Asia have caused the pastoral people to migrate outwards, overwhelming the civilizations which stood in their path. Geographers and historians have tried to piece together the climatic variations which have occurred in historical times.

Much of the evidence is highly conjectural and it must be remembered that reliable instruments for recording weather conditions date only from the middle of the nineteenth century. Also some of the conclusions drawn by over-enthusiastic scholars should not be taken too seriously, although variations have certainly occurred. For example, a Norse colony was established in Greenland in AD 984 when it was warm enough to grow wheat there. But the climate became colder until around 1400, the descendants of the colonizers lost touch with the outside world and the colonies died.

A cold or warm future?

One fascinating question concerning the climate of our times is whether the polar ice caps will eventually disappear, raising the level of the sea by some 100 feet and flooding all the low-lying coastal areas of the world. Alternatively, are we at present in a warm period between ice ages, which will end when ice sheets begin to creep southwards once again, depopulating the densely settled areas of the northern hemisphere and driving Europeans, Chinese and North Americans to warmer areas to the south? We know too little about our physical environment to answer either of these questions.

Many theories have been proposed to explain the changing climates of the past. The theory involving movements in the Earth's crust certainly answers many of the problems posed by the geological evidence. This movement may be the result of *continental drift* (differential movements of the continents), possibly combined with movements of the entire outer shell of the Earth in relation to the interior. Such movements have given rise to the theory of *polar wandering*, which really means the movement of the continents in relation to the poles.

The most important conclusion from this concept is that until the end of the Cretaceous period, the poles were located in the northern and southern Pacific Ocean. Ice caps did not form in the freely

143

This Protoceratops, *top left,* lived about 100 million years ago in the Gobi Desert when it was a swamp. Fossilized remains of reptiles found in the British Isles indicate that the climate about 70 to 180 million years ago was mild, and much of the land swampy plains. *Top right,* a Polacanthus lived in the Isle of Wight; *left,* a Hypsilophodon found in southern England; *above centre,* a Scleromochlus from Scotland; *above right,* a huge Cetiosaurus.

circulating ocean waters. For many years, most scientists regarded the theory as fanciful, because there was no satisfactory explanation of why the continents should drift. Recent theories concerning convection currents in the Earth's mantle – the dense rock beneath the Earth's crust – have led to a revival of the idea.

Other factors have almost certainly contributed to climatic changes. For example, an important influence on climate is the relief or topography of a region. High mountains, even on the equator, have bleak arctic conditions on their upper slopes. Some geologists have therefore suggested that there is a connection between *orogenesis* (mountain building) and glaciation. Certainly both the Permo-Carboniferous and Pleistocene ice ages were preceded by major mountain growth. The ice ages occurred several million years after the mountain building reached its greatest extent, but it has been correctly pointed out that the great Pleistocene ice sheets developed from the glaciers of ancient rather than new mountain ranges, and the Permo-Carboniferous glaciation affected mainly low-lying areas. More

serious objections include the fact that some periods of orogenesis were not followed by major ice ages, and also that if mountain building is continuing all the time somewhere on Earth – a view held by some geologists – then it may be a contributory but not a prime cause of ice ages.

The growth of mountains has certainly had many other effects on climate. Mountains block moisture-bearing winds from the sea, and deserts often occur on the leeward side of the mountains in the so-called *rain shadow* area. Also, when mountain ranges are raised up from under the sea, they are bound to affect the general circulation of ocean waters, which have a considerable effect on climate, especially on rain and snow fall, a vital factor in the growth of ice sheets.

Warm conditions do appear to be associated with periods in the Earth's history when the continents were eroded down to low *peneplains* (the lowest limit of land reduction) and shallow seas submerged large areas. The peneplains offer the minimum surface for radiation, and the continuous evaporation of the shallow seas makes the air intensely humid and

therefore capable of retaining more heat.

Some scientists have suggested that, during periods of intense volcanic activity, great clouds of volcanic dust are ejected into the upper atmosphere. The dust clouds scatter the sun's rays, reducing the amount of solar radiation which reaches the Earth's surface. But most scientists doubt whether this volcanic dust could lower temperatures to such an extent that ice ages would occur. Another theory relates to the amount of carbon dioxide in the atmosphere. Some scientists argue that a small increase of carbon dioxide, possibly as a result of volcanic activity, would raise the temperature of the atmosphere. It seems unlikely, however, that either of these factors could cause major changes in climate, although they may contribute to climatic changes, especially because volcanic activity is often associated with mountain building.

Still a mystery

Other theories relate to variations in the intensity of the sun's radiation, variations in the Earth's orbit around the sun, and fluctuations in the Earth's tilt. These and many other theories have been advanced in an attempt to explain climatic changes, but at present scientists have far too little information to assess their validity and their relative importance. The theory of 'polar wandering' as a major factor seems indisputable, but many of the other factors suggested, such as mountain growth and rainfall, may well contribute to and account for some of the more complex of these climatic variations.

Tomorrow's weather

Scientific weather forecasting began just over a hundred years ago with ground-level observations. Today, by radar and satellite, we can base predictions on conditions in the upper atmosphere.

THE 24-HOUR weather forecasts broadcast over the radio and television and published in the Press are a familiar part of our lives. To most people forecasts are of limited interest, affecting such small decisions as whether we need to take umbrellas and raincoats to work or to the seaside. Forecasts have, however, great economic and military significance. Air crews need information about cloud cover, winds in the upper atmosphere and visibility on the ground; ships' captains must have warning of gales and hurricanes; farmers need to know in advance whether to expect rain, wind or frost.

Long-range forecasts, accurate in detail for perhaps a month in advance, could one day be invaluable for planning in industry, farming and commerce. Advance information that one area faced an exceptionally cold spell of weather while another area expected drought over the following month would allow us, by preparing ahead, to avoid much of the damage which can be caused by unusual weather.

Weather maps cost a penny

How far has the science of meteorology progressed in fact? Weather forecasting became possible only after the perfection of the electric telegraph in 1844 by the American inventor Samuel Morse. The kind of weather map compiled by meteorologists today, on which forecasts are based, requires the rapid collection of information from a series of widely distributed weather stations. The centralized collection of data began in Britain and the United States in the late 1840s, and in Britain the first published weather report appeared in a newspaper on 31 August 1848. At the Great Exhibition held in London in 1851, simple weather maps showing barometric pressure and wind direction were sold for a penny each.

In 1854, the British Meteorological Office was established under its first director, Admiral Fitzroy. In 1860 the first gale warnings were issued, and in September of that year the first British daily weather report came out. In its early days the Meteorological Office had very little reliable information to work on, but, surprisingly, Fitzroy formulated a basically correct theory to explain the origin of low-pressure areas called *depressions* or *cyclones*. Fitzroy suggested that depressions, which contribute greatly to the changeability of weather in temperate regions, form where warm, generally humid air from the tropics meets cold, usually drier, air from polar regions.

Unfortunately, after his death in 1865, meteorologists generally ignored Fitzroy's theory. As a result their forecasts were not very accurate, because they had no real understanding of the causes of the weather.

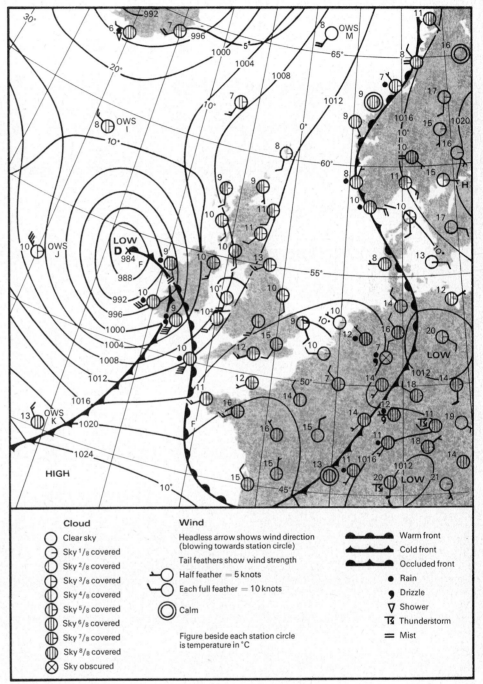

In 1911, by which time many observation stations existed both in Europe and in the Atlantic, some British meteorologists revived and developed Fitzroy's theory. But their work was not recognized by most meteorologists.

A major breakthrough in weather forecasting came during and after the First World War at Bergen, in Norway, where a group of meteorologists under Professor Vilhelm Bjerknes formulated the *polar front* or *Bergen theory* of the evolution of depressions. This theory included the idea of cold and warm fronts, now familiar features on weather charts. It suggested that a depression starts life along the polar

The map shows weather conditions over the British Isles and part of the Western European coastline on a typical Spring day. A depression is centred off the north-west coast of Ireland, together with warm, cold and occluded fronts. Thin black lines are isobars linking points of equal pressure. Thick black lines are isotherms linking points of equal temperature.

front, where westward-moving, dense, cold air-streams from the polar regions meet eastward-moving, warm and comparatively light air-streams from the subtropics.

Along the polar front, where the warm air rises above the cold air, waves develop. Some of these waves enlarge rapidly and, over a period of 12 to 24 hours, the warm

air forms a large bulge called the *warm sector*. The cold air flowing behind the bulge sets up an anticlockwise movement of air in the northern hemisphere. The warm light air in the bulge rises above the cold air along a *warm front,* while in the rear the cold dense air forces its way under the warm air along the *cold front.* Eventually the cold front overtakes the warm front and, at surface level, the cold air-stream is continuous, with the warm air trapped above it. This situation is called by meteorologists an *occlusion.*

An 'ideal' depression

Patterns of weather are associated with the passage of fronts. Considerable cloud develops ahead of the warm front, the wind veers and rain or drizzle often falls. A narrower belt of cloud forms along the cold front, and heavy rain, thunder and hail are common features of the weather. Along an occlusion, a common feature over the British Isles, rain and cloud associated with the fronts persist for some time. The Bergen theory explains an 'ideal' situation in the life cycle of a depression; in practice forecasters must allow for many variations. The introduction of the concept of fronts, however, greatly increased the quality of forecasting.

Professional weather forecasters base their interpretation of weather upon data collected over a wide area and plotted on weather or *synoptic* charts. The term *synoptic* simply means that the chart gives a synopsis or summary of weather conditions based on reports from a large number of meteorological stations. Observations are made at regular intervals at

stations on land or on ships at sea. At some stations, observations are made every hour, both day and night. Observations include descriptions of present weather and conditions since the last readings, including cloud, visibility and precipitation. Measurements are made of wind direction and speed, temperature, dew point and barometric pressure. Such measurements relate to conditions at or near ground level.

Information about the upper atmosphere is now an important part of weather forecasting. But until the Second World

War, the meteorologists' knowledge of conditions above ground level was very sketchy. The earliest observations came from manned balloons and aircraft. Free balloons were also released by meteorologists, who could estimate wind direction and speed from their upward flight. Some free balloons carried instruments which recorded pressure and temperature, but often the balloons vanished into low clouds and the instruments were never recovered.

An instrument which marked a turning-point in the meteorologists' exploration of the upper air was the *radio-sonde.* This instrument consists basically of a self-recording instrument for measuring temperature and pressure, and a radio transmitter, both attached to a free balloon. The hydrogen-filled balloon soars to great heights, while the radio transmits information to a receiver on the ground. Eventually the balloon bursts and the sonde, attached to a parachute, falls to the ground.

Information about the speed and direction of winds up to hurricane strength can be obtained by radar tracking during the ascent of the radio-sonde. Radar, which proved so valuable during the Second World War, is also useful in meteorology because it can detect falling rain in the neighbourhood. Information about the character and movement of the

The most dramatic development in the study of weather has been the launching of satellites like *Nimbus, above,* in America. Their main function is to transmit TV pictures of cloud over the Earth. *Nimbus* was originally equipped with an infra-red camera which, by detecting heat reflections, determined the temperature of cloud tops.

Most of the weather we experience in Britain comes to us across the Atlantic, so we rely on a network of weather ships like the one *below* to give us information about the advance of depressions. These data are sent to the Meteorological Office to enable experts to assess and predict rapidly changing weather phenomena.

rain can also be obtained from the radar screen.

The most recent, and certainly the most dramatic, development in the study of the upper atmosphere, has been the launching in the United States of rockets and two weather satellites named *Tiros* and *Nimbus.* These satellites can transmit to ground stations television pictures of the Earth showing cloud cover.

At observation stations, all the information is coded so that it can be understood anywhere in the world. The coded message is sent to a local centre and thence transmitted by teleprinter or radio to such national centres as the Meteorological Office at Bracknell in Berkshire, or the Weather Bureau in the United States.

There, the information is transferred to weather charts by plotters who use symbols to record the information, in much the same way that conventional signs are used on maps. Isobars (lines linking places with the same barometric pressure) are drawn, revealing anticyclones (regions of high pressure) and depressions. Fronts and occlusions are added – a rather more difficult task which requires much skill.

Now that information about the upper air is available, upper-air charts are also compiled, giving the meteorologists a view of conditions in the atmosphere. A team of forecasters, always working against time, analyse the charts, compare them with preceding charts, and make deductions as to the probable changes that will occur over the next 24 (or sometimes 12) hours. Having reached a conclusion, usually by majority vote, they then describe the probable sequence of weather that will be associated with the changes they have predicted. Finally, they arrive at a weather forecast which is issued in language which the general public can understand.

Electronic weather forecasters

So far we have discussed weather forecasting in terms of the interpretation of synoptic charts. This system, called the *synoptic method,* can never be objective in a truly scientific sense. It always requires the personal judgement of meteorologists, however skilled and experienced they may be. The scientific quantities involved in weather conditions include temperature, air density, humidity, pressure and wind velocity. With a knowledge of the known physical laws which interconnect the quantities, it should be possible to predict mathematically how they would change. The mathematics involved in such a calculation is so complicated that only an electronic computer can cope with the task.

An early attempt to compute changes in weather conditions was made by an Englishman, Lewis Fry Richardson, whose results were published in a book, *Weather Prediction by Numerical Process,* in 1922. Richardson concluded that some 64,000 mathematicians would be needed to compute a forecast in sufficient time for it to be of value. In the 1920s, this conclusion appeared to end purposeful speculation about mathematical forecasting. But the development of electronic computing machines has made the idea a practical possibility for the future.

The scientific quantities involved are interrelated by various laws that take the form of equations. One equation simply states that the pressure at any point is equal to the weight acting on it due to the column of air above it which extends to the edge of the Earth's atmosphere. Other laws are more involved, such as the laws of conservation of energy and conservation of mass (which state that there must be the same amount of energy and mass in the system at the end as at the beginning). 'Energy' in this context includes heat, radiation, and potential and kinetic energy. Mass includes the mass of air and the mass of water it contains. Another law relates wind velocity to air pressure and takes into account friction and the spinning of the Earth on its axis.

Information from meteorological stations on Earth and possibly from weather satellites in space is collected and fed into a programmed computer. The computer calculates how various

This is an antenna, 40 ft in diameter, a component of the transportable ground station used to communicate with a U.S. weather satellite. The ground station is now in Toowomba in Australia.

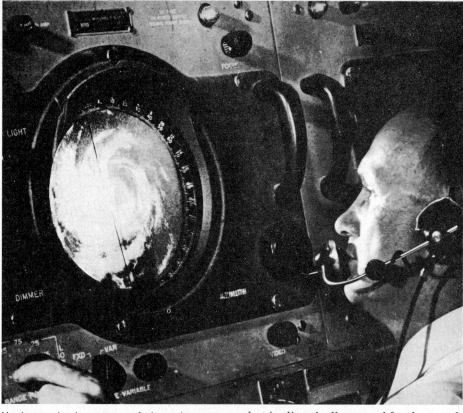

Hurricane clouds on one of the radarscopes forming a network across the Gulf of Mexico and up the Atlantic coast. Storms can be kept in view constantly so that warnings can be issued.

quantities will change in, say, 24 hours and a forecast of the weather to come may be based on the computer's prediction. Work with computers has already begun. The United States Weather Bureau has computed charts for the upper air for some years. In 1965, a large computer was installed for forecasting purposes at the British Meteorological Office.

Short range and long range

The success of this method of forecasting depends on whether sufficient account is taken of conditions outside the area under consideration. Only when a computer is built and programmed to handle meteorological data from all over the world at once will really reliable forecasts become possible. As a result, the professional meteorologists using the synoptic method will continue to be key figures in weather forecasting for years to come.

The 24-hour forecasts are often accompanied by 'further outlooks', and they can be quite accurate, particularly when the weather is settled. But long-range forecasting over such periods as 30 days has not yet proved impressive in terms of results.

The publishing of monthly forecasts dates back to 1948 in the United States and to 1963 in Britain. Many methods of long-range forecasting have been proposed. In one method used in the United States, meteorologists take daily pressure charts of the upper air over a period of time and average them to obtain a 'mean chart'. On these charts, the broad movements in the atmosphere become apparent and day-to-day complications are 'averaged out'. From the mean charts of recent air movements, meteorologists deduce how

the mean charts will develop over a long period and a weather forecast is based on their conclusions. In Britain, meteorologists search their records for a period in the past and at the same time of year which closely resembles the weather conditions of the previous month. They then make a long-range forecast based on what happened in a similar situation in the past.

In view of the controversy surrounding long-range forecasting, it is necessary in conclusion to establish precisely what long-range forecasters are trying to achieve. Their aim is to predict how the weather over a month will deviate from

A weather radome on top of the Rockefeller Centre, New York City, keeps track of weather within a 280-mile radius. It houses a 12-ft rotating radar dish which records disturbances.

what is climatically normal for the month in question. For example, a forecast for January of temperatures 'much above' average does not imply that there will be 31 mild days in succession, but simply that the mean temperature for the entire month will be 'much above' average.

Men have always been aware of the importance to our world of atmospheric changes and the vagaries of weather. As life becomes more complex, as we struggle with over-population, famine and war, prediction and even control of weather is becoming essential. With the advance of science, new knowledge regarding the nature of the atmosphere becomes available and its effect upon the weather of the world is gauged. Forecasts spanning two or three days can now be made with accuracy. Techniques in long-range forecasting will continue to be explored with the help of computers until this problem, with all its vital implications for the future, is solved.

Our daily bread

For thousands of years, cereals have been mankind's basic food. But improved farming methods and new seed strains, which increase yields, are vital if the world's growing millions are to be fed.

MOST OF THE FOOD eaten by Man consists of cereals. Cereals, or grains, are varieties of edible grasses which grow in a wide range of climatic conditions. More than two-thirds of the world's cultivated land produces cereals which supply Man with starch necessary for maintaining his body heat and energy.

The main varieties of cereals are wheat, rice and rye, which are grown mainly for human consumption, and barley, corn (maize), oats, sorghum and millet, which are used mainly as animal foodstuffs. In the more affluent countries, which have surpluses of food, cereals form less than 30 per cent of the diet; grains are fed to animals to convert them into animal products, such as meat and milk, to provide a more balanced and varied range of foods. In the poorer developing countries, where food supplies are generally inadequate, cereals are the only substantial source of food and they form about 70 per cent of the daily calorie intake.

The cultivation of wheat and barley, probably the first plants grown by Man, originated in the Middle East about 8,000 years ago and provided, for the first time, a surplus of food which could be easily stored. This led to the establishment of settled communities and the development

of cultural activities. From the early centres of Mesopotamia and Egypt the cultivation of cereals as a staple food spread to all regions of the world.

Many changes have occurred since cereal cultivation first began but until the present century these have been slow. Innovations and improvements in farming practice were localized and particular to cultural groups, and the spread of knowledge was very slow. Generally, however, a natural balance existed between the production of cereals and the growth of population, between supply and demand. But since the end of the Second World War the rapidly increasing population, particularly in the developing countries, has outpaced production. However, progress in the agricultural sciences has increased food production and, since 1955, world production of cereals has increased

at a rate equivalent to the growth of population, an annual growth rate of 2·3 per cent. With increasing affluence in the economically advanced countries, the amount of cereals consumed per person is steadily decreasing which should mean that there is extra food available for the hungry. But the massive increases in cereal production achieved in Europe and North America and the modest gains made in Africa are cancelled out by the relative losses elsewhere. In South East Asia and Latin America traditional and out-dated farming methods are unable to keep pace with the growing population and, in spite of increasing production, the food available for each person is decreasing. A broader application of science in agriculture would increase production in these poorer countries.

The annual production of all cereals

1 Wheat, native to the Middle East, is the highest yielding grain crop in the temperate areas, and produces over a quarter of the world's cereal.
2 Rice is the major source of food for more than half the people of the world. New strains are being developed to increase yields.
3 Barley, although still used for bread-making, is grown mainly as an animal feed and for the malting and distilling industries.
4 Oats, cut and drying in stooks in a field, will be used for breakfast foods, such as porridge, animal feed and the straw for litter.

since the end of the Second World War has risen from 450 million tons to nearly 720 million tons. About one-third of the increase is due to an expansion in the acreage planted and harvested. Since 1948, the total area given to cereals has increased from 1,500 million acres to 1,700 million acres. During the same period the cereal acreages in Europe and North America have fallen by 3·5 and 20 per cent respectively, while acreages have risen markedly in Latin America, the Near East, the Far East and in Africa.

The greater part of the increased cereal production has come generally from increased yields but the most spectacular increases have been in the economically advanced countries. Here research and capital are available to ensure the most suitable farming methods. In Britain, for example, the same acreage of wheat is producing more than ever before and yields have risen from about 20 cwt. per acre to 32 cwt. per acre over the last 50 years. In India during the same period, wheat yields have risen from 5 cwt. per acre to 7 cwt. per acre. In Europe generally intensive farming methods produce average yields of 30 cwt. per acre, while in the major wheat areas, such as North America, extensive farming over huge areas produces yields of about 11 cwt. per acre.

One of the major reasons for these higher yields is the introduction of new varieties of seeds. By cross-fertilizing existing plants, new hybrid seeds are produced which bear heavier yields, are more resistant to disease, or are better suited to a particular climate or soil.

Besides new varieties of seed, chemical fertilizers, insecticides and fungicides have brought impressive advances in the quality and quantity of harvests. Farmyard manure has been replaced by artificial fertilizers, lime, nitrates and phosphates which are applied in carefully balanced quantities. Mechanization has helped to increase the area cultivated. Tractors and their attachments for ploughing, hoeing, seeding and harvesting provide the power formerly supplied by manual labour or animals, and the huge combine harvester compresses the many separate processes of reaping, threshing and baling straw into one unit.

In spite of these advances, the weather is still the primary dictator of cereal production, causing considerable variations in yields and success of the harvest. However, grains are easy to store, transport and distribute and most countries try to establish a surplus in their granaries so that the harvest of good years makes up for the bad years. Once the grain has been threshed from the stalk and husks and then cleaned – or in the case of rice, polished – kept cool and free from pests, it can be stored for a considerable time without loss of quality.

The trade in cereals between the surplus producers, North America, Australia and Argentina, and the deficit areas, chiefly the European countries and Japan, has established an important world grain market, although grains seldom play a large part in the export trade of an individual country. The exceptions are Burma, Cambodia and Thailand which are heavily dependent on the export of rice. Rice provides nearly two-thirds of Burma's total foreign earnings, and forms nearly half of the value of Cambodia's and Thailand's exports.

To ensure the efficiency of the international grain markets, price ranges for all cereals are fixed by agreement. An international agreement for wheat, the

3

5

1 Huge kettles at a brewery in Milwaukee, Wisconsin, brew a light, foaming beer from malt, which is usually made from barley.
2 In Indonesia, the steep hillsides are terraced to provide level fields for growing rice under a few inches of water.
3 In affluent countries which have a surplus of grain, cereals are ground into meals, enriched with vitamins and fed to livestock.
4 Part of the rice harvest is carried to the threshing yards in Anatolia, Turkey.
5 Millet, which grows in climates too dry for rice, is sorted and stacked in India. It is used for bread flour, as fodder for livestock, and the seeds are fed to poultry.

most important cereal in commerce, was reached by the Cereals Group within the Kennedy Round of Trade Negotiations in June, 1967. Such agreements mean that individual countries must make internal adjustments to ensure that their cereal production meets the needs of home consumption and world trade, and protect their own farmers from unequal competition. Governments, therefore, set tariffs, introduce guaranteed prices or subsidies to equate their farmers' costs with world prices, or control the acreage of a particular crop to avoid over-production. The actual amounts of cereals entering world markets are relatively small –

only 20 per cent of the total wheat production and 4 per cent of the total rice production.

The purpose of trade in cereals is to feed both human beings and animals. Rice is the staple food of the Asian peoples, and wheat and some rye are the bread grains of the cooler temperate latitudes. The nutritional values are similar for all cereals; the whole grain contains starch (carbohydrates), protein, fats, minerals and vitamins but is deficient in vitamin A and calcium. It is understandable, therefore, that diets which consist mainly of cereals are unbalanced and cause diseases, such as beri-beri and pellagra. Such deficiencies are aggravated by the fact that when cereals are prepared for human consumption, most of the nutritional content, which is in the outer layers of

the grain, the bran and endosperm, is removed. It is now increasingly common for essential nutrients and vitamins to be replaced artificially in such cereal products as white bread and breakfast cereals. In fact, breakfast cereals were developed as health foods in America during the second half of the nineteenth century, based on the benefits of the whole grains as opposed to milled white flour.

The processing of cereals for food and for industrial purposes is rapidly expanding in the industrialized nations. The common industrial products, which include alcohol, syrups, pastes, dextrose, edible oils and starch, rely on the needs and the surplus cereal production of the economically advanced nations.

Wheat is native to the Middle East, and two varieties of wild wheat, emmer wheat and einkorn, from which the modern hybrids have been developed, are still to be found there.

Wheat grows best in temperate regions between latitudes 30 degrees and 60 degrees with an annual rainfall of between 15 and 35 inches. It is the highest yielding grain crop in temperate areas, occupies 30 per cent of the world total grain area and produces 27 per cent of the total grain. It is grown under a wide range of weather conditions, aided by research into hybrid varieties resistant to more extreme conditions. Wheats are divided into three main types, based on their suitability for bread-making. Hard wheats, produced as surplus, provide a good bread flour, rich in gluten, and can only be grown in areas with a hot, fairly dry summer. It is the principal wheat type of the United States, Canada and Argentina. Most Australian wheat is known as semi-hard wheat, while the third type, soft wheat, is grown mainly in Western Europe. Soft wheat is used mainly for cake flour and biscuits. The only other important wheat is durum wheat, a very hard wheat grown in the Mediterranean region which is particularly suitable for making macaroni, spaghetti and other pastas.

Rice, like wheat, has been established as a cultivated cereal for more than 5,000 years and is now the major source of food for more than half the population of the world. It is the principal cereal of the tropical monsoon lands and the warmer, humid parts of the temperate zones. It is quite different in its requirements from all other grains. The seeds must be sown in a clayey soil under a few inches of water and the plants grow up through the water. As a rule, the seeds are sown in nurseries and then the young plants are transplanted by hand, again under water. As the plant ripens, the fields are allowed to dry gradually. Rice, therefore, needs a great deal of water and flat land so that the water does not run off.

The best lands for rice are coastal plains, river deltas and flood plains. In more hilly country, *paddy* (rice) fields are made by terracing. To grow well, rice requires an annual rainfall of between 60 and 80 inches, or irrigation, as in the drier parts of Burma and the Indus Valley. The present world production of rice is about 110 million tons, which is 66 per cent above the figure for the immediate post Second World War period.

Improving rice yields

Substantial increases in rice production since 1954 are due to an increase in acreage and an increase in yields from an average of 7·6 cwt. per acre to 9·6 cwt. per acre. As with wheat, improved yields stem from a combination of improved strains of rice and the use of fertilizers. The highest yields are found in the sub-tropical and temperate zones where the *japonica* variety, which responds well to fertilizers, is grown, as in Australia (where yields are as high as 37 cwt. per acre), Japan, Italy, Spain and the United States. Rice is grown mainly for human food and only a very small proportion is fed to animals or used industrially. In some countries, rice is used to make alcoholic beverages; 4 per cent of Japan's rice harvest is used for making *saké* (rice wine).

Indian corn, more commonly known as maize, is native to the American continent. It was brought to the eastern hemisphere by explorers in the sixteenth century. It is now the grain most used for animal feed in the temperate regions of the world, but in many tropical areas it is used as human food. Total world production is nearly 200 million tons a year and has increased markedly during recent years because of the recently developed high-yielding hybrid corn. The United

Sorghum is harvested near Ansham in China. It can tolerate drought and is an alternative to maize in the hot, dry regions.

States produces more than half the world's output and has increased its production by 46 per cent since 1950.

Oats, barley and rye, cereals of the temperate latitudes, are able to grow in colder conditions than wheat. Barley is grown primarily as an animal food and for malting and distilling by the beer and spirits industries. It is believed that it was an important human food in early civilizations and in some countries is still added to rye flour to make bread. The U.S.S.R. is the major producer and accounts for nearly a quarter of the total annual production of 90 million tons.

Oats is now a less important crop since the drastic reduction in the numbers of farm horses. It is well suited to cool, wet climates and is mainly used as an animal feed. Since 1950 oats production has remained fairly constant although the

At Kano in Nigeria, a wife prepares ground maize flour for bread-making. Maize is an important subsistence crop in Africa.

Maize is grown mainly for human food. The kernel contains protein, oil, starch and sugar; the stalk is made into paper and wallboard.

acreage has been reduced by nearly half. World production is about 45 million tons a year, of which about one-third is produced by the United States.

Rye is a cereal noted for its hardiness, and in eastern Europe and the U.S.S.R., where conditions are too severe for wheat, it is still a principal bread grain. Elsewhere it is used as an animal feed and a small proportion is used by distillers for whisky and gin. World production has been falling since 1950 and is at present about 35 million tons, of which nearly half is grown in the U.S.S.R.

Sorghum is a recently-developed animal feed crop which is thought to be native to tropical Africa. Its tolerance of dry conditions makes it an ideal alternative to maize. Sorghum grain is used for beer-making in Africa, and in China the stalks are made into paper.

Millets are grown in the drier parts of India and Africa where the climate is unsuitable for rice. It is used as bread flour, as fodder for livestock, and the ripe seeds are fed to poultry and cage birds. Both sorghum and millets have the advantage that during drought the plants are able to remain dormant and then resume growth when moisture is again available.

As in the past, cereals will play a major role in feeding mankind in the future. To feed the world's population in 2000 AD cereal production must be doubled. If the progress that has been achieved by the wealthy nations can be equalled by the developing countries, this target can be met. Ideally, cereals should become less important in the world's diet and if the present trends of the economically advanced countries continue to spread, greater proportions of grains will be used for animal feeds and for industrial purposes. But the main purpose of cereals will be to provide the daily bread or bowl of rice for the world. In this role, a failure of cereal cultivation to meet the future demands for increase may be a factor threatening world peace. A hungry world is never likely to be a peaceful one.

Crops and livestock

All farmers face the hazards of climate, pests and fluctuating prices. But by keeping livestock and growing crops by rotation to feed them, they maintain soil fertility and spread the risks.

IN AN AGE when specialization is increasing in many aspects of life, some farming methods seem to be inefficient and old fashioned. When a number of different enterprises are undertaken on one farm they are termed *mixed farming*. These farms are normally family farms and although complete specialization may be found, it is unusual. Mixed farming can be associated with pigs, poultry, or cattle fattening but is most widespread where dairy is one of the farming activities.

Mixed farming is particularly characteristic of northwest Europe. The agricultural revolution marks its origin as a commercial force. Previously, most livestock had to be slaughtered when grass growth ceased in the autumn and only a very small number were kept through the winter for breeding purposes. This resulted in alternate meat gluts and shortages, and made the breeding of good quality animals impossible. The stumbling block was lack of winter feed.

During the eighteenth century, new machinery, seeds and improved animal strains were introduced and *crop rotation* (different crops continually grown on one piece of land in a specific order) was pioneered. By using a rotation, the farmer was able not only to plant all his land each year, and so avoid the wasteful *fallowing* system (ploughed land is left uncultivated for at least a year), but also to maintain and improve soil fertility. The rotation consisted basically of grain, root, grain, and grass crops and has since been widely adopted in many countries. Now the rotation is frequently much more complicated and may last for 12 or more years. The inclusion of roots in the rotation provided a winter feed for the animals and it became increasingly possible to keep them throughout the year.

Complex modern farming

From its early beginnings in the late eighteenth century, mixed farming has become increasingly complex. The repeal of the Corn Laws in Britain in 1846 led to an influx of cheaper imported grain and later the effect of cheaper grain from the New World was felt in northwest Europe. To meet this challenge, the emphasis of farming gradually moved from cereal-growing for human consumption to the provision of animal feedstuffs and livestock farming, and has remained so to the present day.

Being a commercial enterprise, mixed farming is influenced not only by soil and climate but also by market prices. For example, in Britain's eastern East Anglia, sugar beets have been replaced by the more profitable growing of peas, beans and soft fruit for the frozen-food industry. Choice of crops is also influenced by the

1 A Danish farmer ploughs in stubble in winter to prepare the ground for the next crop to feed his dairy cattle and pigs.

2 Mixed farms in Ontario are surrounded by pasture, crop-growing fields and barns for livestock, machinery and fodder storage.

government. By varying its price supports, hill farm subsidies and other financial aids to farmers, a government can influence the type and proportion of crops grown.

What are the advantages and snags of mixed farming? The advantages are, firstly, the variety of crops grown in rotation maintains the fertility of the soil. The principal crops grown in Western Europe are: barley, oats, beets, turnips, swedes, mangolds, kale, clover and temporary grasses; and in the Americas alfalfa and maize are included. Secondly, the rotation provides animal feedstuffs that are often cheaper than those purchased off the farm. Thirdly, having more than one enterprise means that risks are spread so that

disease, crop failure and climatic hazards do not normally hit so severely as on a specialist farm. Finally, a mixed farm enables the farm work load to be spread more evenly throughout the year and very little extra seasonal labour is needed.

The snags lie partly in the dangers of over-diversification so that the farmer gets none of the advantages of scale or specialization. In such a case the farmer cannot afford to buy all the necessary specialist equipment and machinery. Also, if too wide a range of activity is undertaken it is impossible to have adequate detailed knowledge of all the activities. In an age of broiler houses, grain farms, and the more exacting marketing quality and packaging demands, to survive commercially a mixed farmer must not cast his net too wide.

Mixed farming began in England and the neighbouring parts of Western Europe where the climate was suitable both for grass and crops and lacked the extremes of temperature and rainfall which occur in some parts of the world. From this area this type of farming has spread to many other parts including Australia, New Zealand and the Americas. In the United States corn belt and its northern fringes, mixed farming is widely practised. Although in some localities the emphasis is on grain for sale, in many parts (eastern Nebraska, Iowa and Illinois) the grain is used for fattening cattle and pigs. On the northern margins where the corn and hay belts merge and close to the large urban areas of Chicago and southern Michigan, fodder crops are grown mainly for dairy cattle, while in parts of southern Michigan the farmers also grow fruit and vegetables to meet the increasing urban demand.

Size of farm, type of stock, crops and many other features of mixed farms vary enormously in such countries as New Zealand, Denmark and Ulster. However, certain similarities are apparent, whether we compare England, Jutland or Ohio – the farms tend to be small to medium sized, relative to their national yardsticks; almost nowhere are there really large units. The key to this lies in the fact that mixed farms are predominantly family farms and in the majority of cases are either owned by, or are in the process of being bought by, the family. Dairy cattle need milking twice a day, seven days a week, which means considerable work and affects farm size; although the actual work has been made somewhat lighter by electric milking equipment and modern milking parlours. In some places, especially the United States, the seven-day week

1 Followed by flocks of seagulls, a farmer in Kent ploughs up pasture. By rotating his crops and grass he maintains the soil fertility and grows feed for his livestock.
2 The cheese market at Alkmaar in the Netherlands where the traditional round cheeses, made from milk from Holland's many dairy farms, are sold for distribution and for export.
3 Early summer grass is cut and stacked on a mixed farm at Ridley in Kent to provide fodder for dairy cows when grass growth ceases during the winter months.

has made it difficult for the dairy farmer to recruit labour so that he has to rely largely on family labour, together with whatever machinery he can purchase or, as in the case of Denmark, the Netherlands and some other parts, own co-operatively. Generally, there are seldom more than a couple of farm hands on mixed farms. Because of this difficulty of getting labour, and its cost, farmers try to mechanize as far as is possible, and invest in tractors, seed drills, harvesters and silage makers, apart from the equipment for milking and other livestock enterprises.

Formerly, farmers kept cattle for milk, meat and hides. Now, in the agriculturally advanced countries, such a practice is uncommon. The development of selective breeding over the past 200 years, the establishment of pedigree herds and new cross-breeds for either meat or milk, has resulted in specialization of animals. While all animals will ultimately provide hides, they are just an extra saleable product. The development of tuberculin-tested cattle strains leading to the establishment of attested herds, and in many countries, rigorous national or state government controls over quality and cleanliness of milk cattle, milk and the hygiene

as butter, cheese, cream and canned and dried milk. Specialization has affected this aspect of farming, too. Gone, in the main, are the days when the farmer made his own cheese and butter and when he sold them from door to door in the villages and small towns along with milk. Now, regional creameries, butter and cheese factories handle the milk, frequently collecting it direct from the farms in their areas and then distributing the processed products to markets themselves. One of the deciding factors of fresh milk production is access to markets. In England, the urban milk farms where feed was brought in and the animals provided fresh milk for the town are gone. Only occasional street names remain as a reminder of their existence.

Fresh milk production

The advent of fast railway transport, and later refrigeration and road transport, has enabled fresh milk production to move further afield away from the immediate environs of the large city to areas where grass growing conditions and land prices are more favourable. Because of the distance involved in some countries, each large town and city has tended to encourage the growth of fresh milk production within a few hundred miles of it, particularly in Canada, the United States and Australia. In some cases dairying and mixed farming has taken over from one-crop farming in these areas in response to the growth of the city and the economic demand for milk. In the United States the main fresh milk producing area lies in the zone from the southern Great Lakes belt to the Atlantic seaboard encompassing Chicago, Detroit, Toledo, Pittsburgh, Boston, New York and Washington.

In contrast butter and cheese, once manufactured, can be more easily stored and transported without loss of quality. In the western part of America's dairyland (Wisconsin, Minnesota and central and southern Michigan) where distances are greater from the main urban markets, the emphasis is upon butter and cheese production and processed milk (dried and

of milking parlours and collection, has encouraged specialization within mixed farming.

The breed of cattle kept varies according to local custom and market demands. Very rich, creamy milk is provided by the Jersey and Guernsey cow not only in the Channel Islands but in many other areas where the strain has been introduced. If, however, a larger bulk of good quality milk is required, then the Friesian cow is very popular. These three breeds, in various crosses, compose a large part of the world's dairy herds. As so much bloodstock has been sent overseas from Western Europe, especially the United Kingdom, over the past two centuries to start new, or improve existing, herds the traveller would find much familiar in the agricultural scene in countries like Australia, Argentina and America. The skilled observer, however, would notice that crosses have been developed to suit particular conditions – Charollais and Brahman cattle crosses have been introduced into Florida in order to provide strains of beef and dairy cattle able to withstand the climatic conditions and, at the same time, yield good quality products.

The milk from the dairy farm has a number of processed end products, such

4 In clean, light and well-ventilated modern cowsheds, like this one in Germany, cows can be fed controlled amounts of fodder, and milk yields maintained during the winter.

5 A Spanish dairy farmer and his donkey still deliver milk daily in large churns.

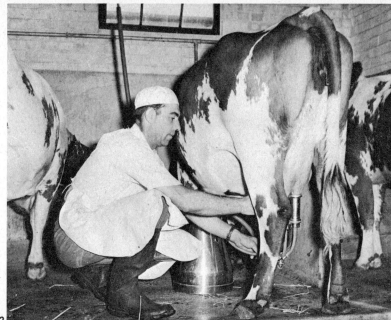

1 A Dutch boy milks by hand a Friesian cow, which yields large quantities of good quality milk, in the fields near the Zuider Zee.

tinned). In North Island, New Zealand, the very fertile volcanic soils and the year-round grass growing season are almost ideal for dairying, but the local population of only two and a half million and the distance from the world's major markets has meant that large-scale fresh milk production is out of the question. So New Zealand has concentrated upon butter and cheese, which it exports in very large quantities.

Today the farmer seldom sells his produce direct; in the main the vast bulk is handled by central creameries and factories. Here again, the size of a farm affects its economy; a farmer who can offer a larger guaranteed supply of milk will have more frequent collections and probably a better price per gallon, as the factory creamery will have lower transport costs per gallon than the farmer with only a small amount to sell. Today, with improved transportation methods and bulk carriage in glass-lined tankers and refrigeration, it is not distance in terms of miles that is important in deciding the economic feasibility of a particular type of farming, but the cost of transport. On the larger farms the once familiar sight of milk churns on the collection bench by the road side is being replaced by the glass-lined container which is collected periodically by the creamery company.

Houses for livestock

Mixed farming requires a greater variety of farm buildings than specialized farms. Sheds are needed for equipment, various types of housing for livestock, and barns and silos for storing fodder. The number and size of buildings varies with the farm size and also with the climate. In North Island, New Zealand, for example, the growing season is year round, so there is less need for storing winter feed and the animals can graze in the fields throughout the year. In Denmark, the Netherlands and northern America the animals have

2 In modern milking parlours cows are milked by electrically driven machines. Milk flows through transparent pipes into churns.

to be stall-fed for three to six months and this means larger cow sheds as well as more extensive barns for the fodder storage. There is increasing conviction in some quarters that feeding cattle out in the fields is an inefficient use of acreage. A more efficient way, it is argued, would be to use most of the land to grow high-yielding fodder crops and keep the cattle in a much more restricted area with feed troughs, barns, sheds and exercise areas. This would eliminate feed wastage and enable the cattle to be fed controlled amounts of food. This idea has been introduced into some of the cattle and pig fattening farms in the United States but is being increasingly applied to dairying; already supplemental feeding throughout a great part of the year is quite widespread.

What is the future of mixed farming? Is lack of complete specialization outdated? Will the typical mixed farm of much of northwest Europe be replaced by factory farming? The answers to the last two questions would seem to be in the negative. Whatever the moral issues of factory farming and however efficient it may be for chickens, pigs and barley beef,

3 An insulated tanker regularly collects milk from an English dairy farm where it has been stored in refrigerated tanks.

it seems unlikely to be easily adaptable to dairying or other branches of mixed farming.

The specialization necessary with factory farming is not without its dangers and risks (of disease for example), nor can the highly specialized factory farm adjust so easily to market changes as the mixed farm. However, the time when a farmer could sell a little grain, fodder roots, milk, meat, fruit and eggs has gone; casting the net so wide is inefficient in the modern, commercially agricultural world. However, by concentrating on a limited range, and using specialized buildings and equipment where appropriate, the mixed farmer will be able to compete with the other types of farming. The fodder-growing English dairy farmer, the Danish counterpart who grows crops to feed his dairy cattle and pigs, and many others are likely to be able to remain in active existence for decades. The farms will tend to get larger as the smaller ones are forced out by economic circumstances, but the 'typical' mixed farm of northwest Europe will remain a feature of the landscape.

Arable farming

Many hazards face the specialist farmer but with careful fallowing systems, chemical fertilizers and modern machinery, this type of farming produces huge quantities of grain for a hungry world.

ARABLE FARMING is the cultivation of crops, either for sale or for use on the farm. This alone, however, does not provide a complete definition. Farming systems without livestock are relatively rare and the growing of crops is usually complemented by the keeping of livestock for meat or milk. The term arable farming, therefore, must not be taken to exclude livestock entirely, though they are essentially of secondary importance to the production of crops in the farm economy.

Nevertheless, the role of livestock as suppliers of manure has been of the greatest significance in the development of arable farming. Settled cultivation becomes possible only when means are available to make good the soil depletion that all arable cropping entails. Until the discoveries of the agricultural chemists in the nineteenth century, this was achieved by natural organic manures. Fertility depended almost entirely upon the quantity of materials available and every effort was made to expand the supply. Human wastes and household rubbish were saved; reeds, vine prunings and small branches were rotted down; the droppings of sheep and poultry were carefully collected and sold. In marshy districts, rich swamp mud was spread on the fields; near the coasts seaweeds and shelly sands were used. But the most important source of fertilizer was the dung of farmyard animals.

Throughout Europe in the Middle Ages and in many parts of the world at the present day a variety of factors has tended to restrict the livestock population and to limit supplies of animal manure. Rural poverty, linked with the small size of peasant farms has operated in a vicious circle. A poor peasant can afford only a small herd, often of small animals such as donkeys or mules. Thus the cultivation and manuring of his land is inadequate. Yields are low and, because yields are low, the peasant remains poor. The shortage of winter feed for animals was even more important and, in Europe, until the introduction of maize, potatoes, root crops and clovers, the wintering of large numbers of animals was impossible.

Fertilizing and fallowing

In these circumstances, it was inevitable that natural grasslands should play a significant role in the provision of winter fodder and each settlement maintained a part of its land for hay. In southern Europe, where the climate does not favour grass, meadows were confined to the vicinity of watercourses and were minutely sub-divided in order that each farmer should have his share. In the summer, and at least for part of the winter, pasture was provided by clearings which extended around the villages. In western Europe, the clearings were dominated by heath and coarse grasses, reeds and scrub vegetation. In addition to grazing, the clearings supplied stable litter, were burned to yield fertilizing wood ash and their upper layers, rich in humus, were often lifted bodily and strewn on arable fields. All these devices, however, failed to restore to the full the supply of soil nutrients depleted by cropping. As a result, arable farming

This Canadian farmer, who flies his own aeroplane, is able to run his 2,700-acre wheat farm almost single-handed, except for help at sowing and harvest times, by using modern machinery.

had, as an essential feature, the periodic resting or *fallowing* of land which was impossible to fertilize because of the shortage of manure.

Land lying fallow is untilled, but the fallow period is not merely a negative interlude; it is intended to have a positive, recuperative function. The soil regains a cover of grass and weeds which, if ploughed in, makes a valuable addition to fertility. In drier areas, as in the Mediterranean lands, fallow may be ploughed to reduce soil moisture losses, a practice comparable with the dry-farming techniques of the sub-humid states in the United States. Historically, two basic systems of fallowing may be distinguished: *biennial* fallowing, under which one half of the crop land was rested each year, and *triennial* fallowing which set aside one third of the arable area each year. The former was the system characteristic of southern Europe, the latter of northern and western Europe. The origins of the two systems have long been disputed but their survival and persistence must be viewed in terms of physical or economic necessity.

At the beginning of the Christian era, Roman agronomists suggested a crop rotation which offered an apparent escape from the rigidity of the biennial rotation. Their remedy was to include a *leguminous* (pulse) crop in the place of fallow and to

157

1 Wheat is poured into a huge modern tractor-drawn planting machine on an arable farm in Canada. With such equipment, as much as 100 acres can be sown in a day.

take, whenever possible, a *catch crop* of roots or lupins after the wheat had been harvested. The practice appears to have been developed on the better soils; on poorer land, because of the small amount of animal manure available, it was scarcely a practicable proposition. Thus, although the direction of future developments was indicated, little progress was made for the next 1,500 years. To bring about a funda-

mental change, the cultivated plants which could take the place of the fallow year had to have certain clearly defined characteristics. They had, for example, to be adaptable to a wide range of soil and weather conditions. They had not only to increase the fertility of the soil but also to contribute to the peasants' food supply. It was this latter feature that stood in the way of improvement. The simple cereal-

3 On the arable farms of the Canadian Prairies, wheat can be continuously grown by careful fallowing, which conserves the moisture and the fertility of the soil.

2 Shaded from the hot sun by an umbrella, an Australian farmer cuts and threshes his wheat with a combine harvester on the dry plains of the Winnera District of Victoria.

legume sequence proposed by several ancient writers, though excellent from the point of view of the land, did not add appreciably to the output of grain and it was with grain output that the farmer was most concerned.

The opening up of the New World revealed a wealth of new plant species, two of which, maize and the potato, were destined to have a profound effect on

European agriculture and on the agriculture of those areas into which European colonists subsequently penetrated. Together with the leguminous fodders and root crops, their introduction led to a two- or three-fold increase in yields and to the reduction or elimination of fallow. By the end of the eighteenth century in western Europe, the practice of bare fallowing had virtually disappeared and, in the second half of the nineteenth century, the development of chemical fertilizers helped to bring millions of acres into productive agricultural use. Without artificial manures, it seems likely that the expansion of arable farming would have been confined largely to the better soils; their increasing application has made possible continuous cultivation on soils of even low fertility. A further point of great significance is that the widespread availability of chemical fertilizers has, to a considerable extent, enabled arable farming to dissociate itself from livestock rearing, thus reversing the trends of the early agricultural revolution.

Old methods on new lands

The commercial grain farming of the United States, South Africa, Australia or the U.S.S.R. frequently depends upon *dry farming* techniques that demand the use of fallowing to preserve moisture. Large areas of crop land are involved and here the limiting factor is water deficiency rather than a lack of mineral nutrients in the soil. Ploughing and harrowing allows water to enter the soil and, by controlling the growth of weeds, prevents the loss of moisture through *transpiration* (loss of water vapour through plant leaves) and retains water for the next crop. In China and the Middle East the principles of dry farming have been known and applied for many centuries but their modern practice began in the United States during the 1860s, gradually spreading with the agricultural development of the Great Plains and the Prairie Provinces of Canada. That development was part of a new phase of expansion and settlement based on the commercial cultivation of wheat. It involved many hardships and imposed severe problems of adjustment but eventually succeeded in establishing a highly specialized type of arable farming with clearly defined and distinctive characteristics.

The evolution of specialized wheat farming depended greatly on the improvement of transport and communications. The steamship linked the potential wheatlands of North America and the Southern Hemisphere with the food-deficit areas of Europe. The steam train and the railway opened up the Great Plains, the Argentine Pampas and the interior plains of Australia: areas that were virtually uninhabited in the pre-railway era. Mechanization and methods of large-scale production offered marked advantages and enabled large tracts of thinly peopled territory to produce vast quantities of grain for export.

The wheat plant does not find its most favourable conditions in the sub-humid or semi-arid lands with their scanty, unreliable rainfall and their susceptibility to erosion. But wheat has a greater ability to tolerate such conditions than do the majority of the cultivated crops and it is this ability, and an ability to withstand transport over long distances, that account for its present pattern of distribution. Especially in the drier sectors of the great wheat-growing areas, cultivation takes on the character of *monoculture* (one crop), based either on continuous cropping with wheat or on a simple wheat/fallow/wheat rotation. This is largely because it is difficult to find ancillary crops which would tolerate the climate and might be used to build up balanced rotations of the type still found in western Europe. The dangers of specialization have been clearly shown by every period of rainfall below normal and it is not surprising that there has been a trend towards a more diversified system of farming. This is most marked in areas where the climate is sufficiently humid to favour a wider range of crops or where irrigation can be introduced to support forage crops and livestock.

The farmer in western Europe rarely has all his eggs in one basket; his risks are spread over a range of crops and farm enterprises. So, in the event of a long-term depression of prices he can adjust his production accordingly. The specialist wheat farmer producing for export is much more vulnerable to economic fluctuation. Price levels are governed by factors beyond his control; if he tries to offset falling prices by increasing production he may simply aggravate his problems. Not until 1949 was it possible to impose some measure of control on the world wheat trade. This was achieved by implementing the International Wheat Agreement which lays down production quotas for the

1 An Australian farmer watches his combine harvester pour grain into a lorry. The building of railways opened up the plains of Australia for commercial wheat growing for export.

2 Mobile spray irrigation equipment, on the plains of South Alberta, Canada, waters dry wheat stubble to increase the growth and yield of the next crop to be sown.

wheat-growing countries, tries to match production to the estimated future demand and fixes approximate price levels. Even then, the wheat producer may suffer from great irregularities of income because of drought, hail, frost, plant diseases and insect pests.

The use of mechanical power and machinery has been a distinctive feature of the large commercial wheat farm. Men have always been few in relation to the amount of land to be cultivated and the machine offers an enormous increase in the productivity of labour. The tractor makes the farmer more mobile, enabling him to cover a larger acreage in a given time or a given acreage in a shorter time. Mechanization improves the timeliness of farm operations and, together with the selective breeding and improvement of new varieties of wheat, has helped to extend production and maintain yields.

In all types of farming, the yearly rhythm of work must be adjusted to the seasonal cycle of crops and, in the case of the grain farmer, there are very sharp seasonal variations in employment. One third of the work to be done is during the

A ship is loaded with grain from elevators at Duluth in Minnesota. Wheat can be transported over long distances and stored almost indefinitely without deterioration.

relatively short harvest, another half is taken up at sowing time; for the remainder of the year wheat production requires very little work. One of the consequences of this seasonal routine was the employment of large numbers of temporary workers during the harvest periods. At one time in the United States, a quarter of a million migrant workers might follow the wheat crop as it ripened, moving northwards from the winter-wheat states of Oklahoma and Texas to the spring-wheat areas of the Prairie Provinces of Canada.

Today, the migrant labourer has given place to the combine harvester and survives only in a few states where the process of mechanization is incomplete.

Elevators are a familiar sight in the prairie towns of the Canadian wheat belt. Grain from surrounding farms is stored in them for transport by rail to mills and ports.

The nomadism of machine has replaced the nomadism of men and it is now the combine that travels slowly north following the path of the ripening wheat.

A further consequence of the seasonal cycle of wheat cultivation in the United States is the emergence of a large group of part-time farmers or town farmers. These fall into two classes: the so-called *suitcase farmers* who live outside the farming area and come into it only at sowing and harvest time; and the *sidewalk farmers* who live in the towns of the area, frequently combining another occupation or profession with farming.

Pattern for the future

Nowhere is the importance of the cultural factor more clearly illustrated than in the story of the specialized wheat areas. Vast tracts of level land suited to extensive farming remained undeveloped until technical progress, exemplified by the railway and steamship, the elaboration of well-sinking techniques and the invention of barbed wire, permitted their massive agricultural occupation. Yet arable farming has often led to the systematic plundering of soil resources; the fundamental weaknesses of the 'all or nothing' farm pointed the need for change, and further modifications seem inevitable. The most significant trend may well be the growing diversification of land use, aimed at providing basic food products for the farm family and at broadening the whole structure of farm production.

Types of farming are rarely permanent in form or static in their location. They represent stages, sometimes prolonged, in a dynamic process of adjustment between farming communities and their environment. The highly specialized arable farms of the great wheat belts, whether in the United States or elsewhere, are no exception and the evolutionary processes that brought them into being have not yet come to an end. The current course of evolution is tending to soften the contrasts between the specialized grain economies and the mixed farming systems. The pattern of large farms and heavy mechanization will remain but the proper combination of crop and livestock enterprises could bring a new-found stability to the granaries of the world.

Fruits of the Earth

Vital to a balanced diet, fruit is now a major part of commercial farming. The problems of production, storage and transport are being overcome to meet the growing demands of the world's markets.

1

2

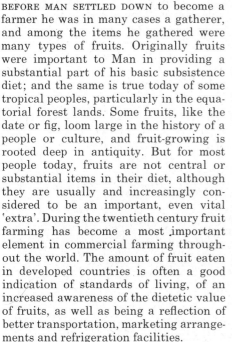

3

BEFORE MAN SETTLED DOWN to become a farmer he was in many cases a gatherer, and among the items he gathered were many types of fruits. Originally fruits were important to Man in providing a substantial part of his basic subsistence diet; and the same is true today of some tropical peoples, particularly in the equatorial forest lands. Some fruits, like the date or fig, loom large in the history of a people or culture, and fruit-growing is rooted deep in antiquity. But for most people today, fruits are not central or substantial items in their diet, although they are usually and increasingly considered to be an important, even vital 'extra'. During the twentieth century fruit farming has become a most important element in commercial farming throughout the world. The amount of fruit eaten in developed countries is often a good indication of standards of living, of an increased awareness of the dietetic value of fruits, as well as being a reflection of better transportation, marketing arrangements and refrigeration facilities.

Leaving aside all the 'soft' fruits, the main fruit crops of the world may be considered to be of three main types – *tropical, citrus* and *deciduous* fruits. Of the tropical fruits the most important are probably the banana, pineapple and date, although there are many other 'exotic' fruits – like the avocado pear, mango, guava, breadfruit and pawpaw (papaya) – which may be important in the country where they grow but which have as yet made few inroads into world trade. They are, however, becoming increasingly familiar in the fruit markets.

The banana – a term best used to cover a wide range of banana/plantain varieties

1 Stems, or bunches, of bananas are loaded on to a train in Mexico for transport to the coast. Ships with refrigerated holds will carry them to the markets of the United States and Europe.
2 Machines grade apples, which are then carefully wrapped and packed in a factory in Kent. Apples

– is a particularly interesting tropical fruit because of its very ancient origins, probably in southern Asia, the way it had spread throughout the tropics by the sixteenth century, and because it is still a major part of the diet of many tropical peoples today, such as in Brazil, East Africa and the Ganges delta. It is a very heavy producer, yielding up to 300 *stems* or bunches per acre annually and giving about ten times the weight of potatoes per acre. In world trade the chief banana-producing areas are in Central America, the West Indies, the Canaries and the

are a hardy fruit, with good food value and have excellent keeping qualities.
3 Huge piles of oranges on sale at the orange market near the Jaffa Gate in Jerusalem. Widely grown in sub-tropical and Mediterranean lands, this fruit is a rich source of vitamin C.

former French-administered parts of equatorial Africa, notably in the Cameroons. All these areas possess ideal conditions for banana growth: plenty of virgin land, good rainfall, high temperatures, high humidities, numerous coastal locations with access to ports, and nearness to the major markets of the Americas and Europe.

The commercial cultivation of the banana requires a great deal of hard work and care in harvesting, although this is now becoming more mechanized. Other problems of cultivation include the particular susceptibility of the crop to strong winds – the hurricanes of the West Indies have been most destructive – and plant diseases, notably the Panama disease, which have restricted cultivation in many of the older areas of the Caribbean. But perhaps the most difficult problem of all has been in the handling, shipping and marketing of a fruit that is perishable and destined chiefly for the distant markets.

Partly because of these difficulties, bananas are commonly grown commercially under the plantation system of agriculture (see pp 181–184). Large and highly capitalized units can more effectively organize the complicated sequence of production, handling, shipping and overseas marketing of the produce. And a large company, like the United Fruit Company of America, is able to set up plantations in several widely separated localities, not only to assure a constant supply of fruit but also to reduce the risks of hurricanes or disease completely destroying a crop. In each area there is a port at which refrigerated ships, able to keep the temperature of the holds constant at 14 °C., can be loaded for export.

The pineapple is the other tropical fruit which has become familiar in the markets of America and Europe and is now gaining ground rapidly in many countries of the world. It is in some ways a more difficult crop than the banana because, unlike the banana, it should be picked ripe and so needs to be cultivated in areas that are provided with good transport and marketing facilities; for these reasons the pineapple is commonly grown under the plantation or estate system of agriculture. The leading producer is Hawaii, which accounts for rather over half the total world trade in pineapples. Production, cultivation, harvesting and marketing are all highly organized and often by mechanical processes. Much of the crop is now canned before export, and plantings are usually staggered to produce a steady flow of pineapples from the field to the factory. The other major producing areas are in the Caribbean (with easy access to American markets) and Manila, in the Philippines.

The useful date palm

The date, for long the main crop of the Arab world and the oldest known cultivated fruit tree, is an oasis crop of the tropical deserts. It is a remarkable crop for, like the coconut, the date palm provides a great many useful items apart from the fruit: animal food, fibre, wood sap and leaves. California and Arizona are notable producers in the United States, but the world's major producer and exporter is Iraq in the Middle East.

The main citrus fruits today are oranges, lemons, limes and grapefruit. Their commercial importance is enormous and increasing for three reasons: the thick, oily, leathery skins protect the pulpy interiors to give good storage and shipping qualities; they are available all the year round from some part of the world; they are popular in developed industrial countries because of their now well-known

1 Ripe apples are picked in the orchards of Victoria, Australia. Many different varieties suit different climates and a wide range of uses – for dessert, cooking and cider-making.
2 Dates, an oasis crop of the tropical deserts and the oldest known cultivated fruit tree, dry on the sand near Tozeur Oasis in Tunisia.
3 Lunch-time during the orange harvest in the groves of Sicily. Temperature is a major factor in citrus-fruit growing; there is little or no growth in temperatures under 15 °C.
4 Pineapples, a tropical fruit now familiar in the markets of America and Europe, are usually grown on plantations. They should be picked ripe but tough skins protect the soft flesh.
5 Cherries are gathered in the orchards near Avignon in France, one of the world's leading cherry-growing countries.

dietetic value. In this sense fruit growers have done excellent promotional and marketing work.

Although the ancestral home of the citrus fruit is probably the warm, humid lands of Asia, it is nowadays especially characteristic of sub-tropical or Mediterranean lands. Temperature is probably the most important single factor in citrus growing, for little or no growth takes place while temperatures are below 15 °C. The control of temperatures, therefore, is a critical problem in growing these fruits, and many devices, such as the artificial heating or circulation of air, are employed to try to reduce the hazards of a sudden cold snap in an orchard. In Florida and California crude oil is burned in the citrus groves; and wind machines which mix the cold lower and warm upper air are common in California. Experiments are also in hand to utilize the heat derived from condensation while spraying fine jets of water into the air. Many citrus groves are located on the leeward shores of stretches of water, such as lakes, to take full advantage of the locally modifying effects of large water surfaces: in the Central Lake District of Florida, for instance, citrus groves lie along the southern and eastern shores.

As with most citrus fruits, the term 'orange' covers a number of different varieties, ranging from the sour (Seville) orange, introduced by the Arabs into the Mediterranean in the eleventh century and now important in the marmalade industry, to the sweet, large Jaffa orange. Although the orange is grown widely and used as a food in many parts of the tropics and sub-tropics, the major commercial producing areas include the United States, which grows about one-third of the world's commercial crop. California, with its Mediterranean-type climate and large amounts of capital for irrigation, temperature controls and efficient estate management, is able to market oranges all the year round by growing different varieties in different parts of the state. Florida, which needs relatively little irrigation, is especially noted for the manufacture of canned and frozen orange juice. The other major commercial producing areas are the Mediterranean – Spain, Italy, Israel, Egypt and North Africa. Production here is commonly on a smallholding basis, although large plantations do exist. Europe is easily the major import region for oranges in world trade. Oranges are also grown commercially in the Orient, especially Japan; in South Africa (which

exports a large amount) and Australia (which consumes most of its own production); and to a lesser extent in Latin America.

The other citrus fruits have a similar world pattern of distribution, but the lemon and lime are perhaps less widespread than the orange, because these two fruits are particularly susceptible to damage by frost. Lemons are grown particularly in California, Italy and Spain, and limes are produced commercially in southern Florida and in Mexico, which grows about half the world's commercial crop. The United States dominates the world production of grapefruit, the major producing areas being Florida and Texas. The United States and Israel are the major exporters; Canada and Europe the main importers.

Hardy apples

The deciduous fruits – apples, pears, peaches, plums, cherries and figs – are not exclusively temperate crops, for several varieties of all these fruits are to be found widely in tropical countries. But most of the deciduous fruits now entering world trade are grown in middle latitudes. Apples are produced in quantities greater than the total production of all other deciduous

6 A stem of green bananas hangs down from a banana plant, which grows from 10 to 25 feet high. Inside the *bracts* (modified leaves) at the end of the stem are rows of small flowers from which the tiny fruit develops.

7 Oranges are harvested on the huge, commercial groves of Florida where 80 per cent of the citrus crop is processed into frozen juice concentrate, canned juice and segments.

all fruit farming involves a good deal of risk. Late frosts during growth or strong damaging winds just before harvesting can ruin a farmer, especially if he is solely dependent upon his fruit for his livelihood and if he experiences a run of bad years. Plant diseases and pests, too, can have disastrous effects upon his income and prosperity. A good deal of a farmer's time is taken up with trying to ensure the best possible conditions for growth and protecting his trees against physical or biological attacks.

Pruning, spraying, fertilizing, weeding, and the maintenance of access roads and machines are all crucial operations on the farm and must be carried out thoroughly, with great care and at the right time. Spring frosts have to be countered, where possible, with artificial heating or by wind machines. Then the harvesting of fruit has to be well organized and timed to meet the needs and capacity of the sorting and packing sheds and market demands. The price the farmer will get for his fruit will depend upon so many factors lying as yet outside his control: the volume and pattern of production in the country as a whole, labour costs, competition from imported fruit, transport and marketing costs, as well as the demand for his fruit varieties.

Disastrous seasons

How can a farmer be protected against the natural and economic hazards that confront him? To some extent, the risks have to be built into the structure of fruit farming. In California, for instance, it is expected that a crop is likely to fail one year in seven; and this means that disasters such as that of the 1957–8 season, when no less than six cold waves destroyed over one quarter of Florida's citrus crop, can be absorbed without real damage or distress. A good deal, too, can be done by developing new crop varieties, with shorter growing seasons or with more resistance to frost, heavy rains or wind, pests and diseases; by developing higher yielding varieties; and by producing strains with better storage qualities. Research into the waxing or 'painting' of fruit to improve their durability is well under way, and new ways of mechanizing many of the processes of cultivation, harvesting and packing are continually appearing. On the marketing side there is a need for rationalization, for more government protection against foreign competition in the home market and, perhaps, for guaranteed price policies.

Progress is now rapid in most of these fields and fruit farming is expected to become increasingly productive and widespread as demand rises because of the now widely known and accepted importance of fruit in a balanced diet. In only a few places are traditional attitudes preventing a speedy increase in consumption: in Puerto Rico, for instance, fruits are commonly believed to be poisonous or at least highly indigestible. With continued research into the problems of fruit production, processing, transportation and storage, fruit farming is likely to be able to meet the challenge to increase production it will undoubtedly have to face.

1 Pear trees are pruned in an orchard in Kent. This is just one of the many operations a fruit farmer must carry out with skill and care at the right time to ensure good crops.

2 Fruit growers are always at the mercy of the weather. A farmer in Kent took advantage of a still night to spray his pear trees by floodlight after days of bad weather.

fruits put together. They are a hardy fruit, with good food value and excellent keeping qualities. The many different varieties are suited to different environments and cover a wide range of uses – for dessert, cooking and cider manufacture. Western Europe is especially important for the commercial production of apples, one country at least – France – specializing in the cultivation of cider apples; but the United States, at present, produces more apples than any other country. In terms of exports, however, Western Europe comes first, followed by Australia and Canada.

Pears are very similar to apples in their world distribution, but peaches are much more delicate and so are restricted in their cultivation to areas where conditions are well protected and mild, for instance around the sides of lakes. The United States is the leading producer of peaches,

but the major source of peaches in Europe is Italy. Plums are produced throughout the middle latitudes of the world, but the major commercial areas are in the United States – especially in the Californian area where sun drying is common – Yugoslavia, Germany and the United Kingdom. Cherries are of importance only in Europe and the United States. Figs, which have been grown in the Mediterranean basin since prehistoric times, are now limited mainly to the dry subtropics. At least one third of the total annual crop moves in world trade. The major producers are Italy and Algeria, and the chief exporting countries are Turkey, Greece and Algeria.

The fruit industry faces a number of problems, limitations and opportunities. So dependent is the growing of fruit, even the hardy apple, upon weather, that

Out to grass

The herding of domestic animals is an inefficient use of land, but on the world's rugged hills and dry plains, which are unsuitable for agriculture, it converts sparse vegetation into food for Man.

THE BASIC NEED behind all agriculture is to make available the riches of the soil for human consumption. This need can be met by both plants and animals. Plants provide the mineral nutrients contained in the soil and, with the help of energy from the sun, use the carbon dioxide in the atmosphere. The farmer selects only those plants which he can use easily. The ability to choose carefully is highly developed among even the most primitive peoples who harvest wild seeds, fruits and nuts. Animals, too, feed on plants which, in their original form, may be useless or unattractive to Man. Grass, for example, is converted by cattle or sheep into milk and meat; so the hunting and rearing of animals is an additional way of using plant food.

The collecting of food and the hunting of animals both mark an important stage in the building of a complex involving Man, the soil and the biological environment. It is essentially a *passive* phase and illustrates very clearly the significance of the balance between Man and his environment. Everything depends upon the skill he shows in observing, in choosing, in exploiting and in sparing what have been termed his *biological auxillaries*. If he succeeds in establishing a stable and harmonious relationship with them, he will at least survive; if he over-exploits, kills or gathers unwisely, then he will starve. This passive phase provides only a moderate amount of food and supports only a very low density of population. Many square miles of territory are needed to keep starvation at bay and the life of people involved can be precarious in the extreme.

But advance towards greater security and the accumulation of wealth is possible in at least two directions: first, by intro-

ducing storage techniques to conserve surplus food; second, by reducing the number of plant or animal species utilized. The latter involves a closer liaison between human societies and their biological resources and provides a basis for progress towards cultivation and stock-rearing. It presages the end of the passive phase, heralds a revolution in the social and economic organization of mankind and ushers in the *food-producing* era.

The factors that have led particular people to begin cereal agriculture or to domesticate livestock are still unknown and much of the evidence is lacking. It is only possible to speculate on motives. In

In the rugged Highlands of Scotland, pastoral farmers graze herds of hardy sheep for wool and meat. It is the only type of farming possible on the cold, sparsely vegetated slopes.

the case of livestock, it seems likely that the animals concerned were already pre-adapted to dependence; they could be tamed without losing their ability to reproduce. Even so, to achieve control Man himself had to evolve an effective system of organization. He had to protect his animals from beasts of prey and from thieves, and he may have had to provide food for them in times of scarcity. The details and the degree of domestication differ widely; the factors at work are evidently complex and vary from one human group to another. Difficult as it is to generalize, there remains one issue of quite fundamental significance; once the nucleus of a herd had been established then, however indifferent the knowledge and practice of animal husbandry, the process of human *selection* became automatic.

Most systems of agriculture combine livestock with arable crops. The two products complement each other and, notably in Western Europe, their association laid the foundation of scientific agriculture with livestock playing an important role in the maintenance of fertility of the soil by providing manure. But the production of food from animals themselves is a

Sheep are grazed on the hills of Montana where the rainfall is low and the grass thin. Once a year they are rounded up, loaded on to railway trucks and sent to the markets.

relatively expensive method and, where land and climate permit, the cultivation of suitable crops brings higher rewards than livestock breeding. A hectare under grain can produce 10 million food calories, a hectare under grass producing milk yields only 1·7 million calories. A cow utilizes for its growth about 6 per cent of the dry matter it consumes; the remainder is either excreted or used up in body processes. Only three-quarters of the critical 6 per cent is available for direct human consumption. In consequence, *pastoral farming* tends to become the dominant activity only where arable cropping is limited in proportion to the area over which domesticated herds can be grazed.

Grazing the rugged hills

Generally, rugged landscape and its associated climatic and soil conditions limit the cultivation of the high uplands of western Britain and Ireland. In these areas farming is characteristically pastoral and centres on the rearing of sheep or cattle on the natural upland vegetation. Steep slopes have always made ploughing difficult or impossible, and this is increased today by the fact that fields once accessible to the horse-drawn plough can no longer be reached by the modern tractor and its implements. In mountain areas extreme altitude and ruggedness may make the land useless for agriculture.

The pastoral agriculture of the hills was formerly self-sufficient, based on *transhumance* (cattle, goats and sheep were wintered on lowland farms and were moved in the summer to the high upland grazings). The summer pastures produced mainly *store* (growing) cattle and some dairy products. The enclosure of vast areas, and the depopulation of the Highlands in the eighteenth and nineteenth centuries led to the transformation of the

rural economy and to a steep decline in cattle numbers. In Scotland, many of the Highland glens were emptied of people and leased to graziers who put sheep to pasture on the lands of abandoned homesteads. It is in this period that modern hill sheep farming finds its immediate origin.

The agricultural landscape has two main features: the valleys with their farmsteads, small enclosed arable fields and sheltered winter grazings; the high, open hill land of natural grass and heather, often unfenced and in some areas grazed in common. It is upon the balancing of these valley and hill elements that the success of farming depends. The plants that survive on the hills start their growth late in spring and grow grudgingly at the best of times. But the factor limiting livestock numbers remains the provision of winter feed. The success of all measures to improve the output from the pastoral hills depends on the production of winter fodder from the enclosed grassland and arable fields of the valleys.

The dominant enterprise in British hill farming is the maintenance of permanent flocks of hardy mountain sheep, able to find food and shelter at all times of the year and to produce lambs and wool. Farms are generally large, in many cases extending to well over 1,000 hectares, of which some 95 per cent may be under rough grazings and permanent grass. The hill grazings produce large numbers of sheep which are kept and reared on the hills, as well as lambs and ewes which are moved down to lowland farms either for fattening or for future breeding. In addition to sheep, there are quite large pastoral farms based exclusively on cattle-rearing. The number of these farms is limited because of the generally poor quality of upland grazings and because cattle require large quantities of supplementary feeding stuffs in winter. Apart from this limitation, it is difficult to combine sheep and cattle on the same grazing land and to establish a level of stocking at which they are balanced, acting as complements to each other and

not competing to their mutual disadvantage.

Pastoral hill farming in Britain is an extensive, highly specialized branch of livestock-rearing, set apart by its location in bleak highlands on land which could otherwise hardly be used for agriculture. Throughout the world the term 'pastoral farming' embraces a range and variety of environmental circumstances, but it is related geographically to areas difficult for the cultivator.

One of the best-known areas of commercial pastoralism is the Great Plains of the United States where, in the last third of the nineteenth century, a range cattle industry was introduced on a vast scale.

The death of the buffalo

This was the home of millions of the North American bison or buffalo, which browsed over the grassland and desert shrub of this semi-arid, treeless region. The whole existence of the Plains Indians, their economy, law, religion and folklore, centred on the buffalo. Almost every part of the animal was used. Its meat was dried, its hide made into tents and clothing, its horns were shaped into spoons and ladles, its hooves boiled into glue. Four years between 1868 and 1872 were enough to upset this primitive yet highly sophisticated way of life and bring dramatic changes to the Great Plains. The westward extension of the railroads, the hunters with their repeating rifles and the advance of white settlement meant disaster for the buffalo. They were slaughtered wholesale and, with their Indian hunters, gave way to the rancher and his cattle.

Enormous ranches grew up and cattle were bought, branded and turned out to graze much as the buffalo had done. Early each summer the cattle were rounded up, calves were branded to settle the question

1 Expert sheep-shearers at Beaufort, Victoria, use electric shearers to remove the fleece in one piece. Australian sheep provide over a quarter of the world's wool supply.

2 In Argentina, pastoral farming on the pampas was made possible by the building of an extensive railway network. Here cattle have been rounded up and are branded to establish ownership.

of ownership and, in the autumn, the animals intended for eastern American markets were separated from the herd. The cowboys who performed the work had to be highly skilled horsemen, and in the pioneer era they had also to defend the interests of their employer against his rivals and enemies. The cattlemen were enormously successful, until they overstocked the range and, by trying to graze too intensively, lost a majority of their animals through starvation in the severe winters of 1886 and 1887. Then followed a period of prolonged adjustment lasting some 40 years when, from 1890 till 1930, the rancher retreated before the homesteader and crop farmer in all but the most difficult and arid sections of the Plains.

The history of this period is, however, one of great tragedy and disillusion. Many thousands of farmers who tried to settle as cultivators in the West failed disastrously and were forced to abandon their land. Their farms were too small,

1 These colourful *gauchos* (cowboys) of Argentina tend the huge herds of cattle on the ranches of the pampas. The leather guards protect the men and horses from thorns.

2 Sheep, kept and reared on rough grazing or permanent grass of large Welsh hill farms, are sold for meat or breeding under the critical eyes of farmers at a market.

3 Cattle from the Argentine pampas are brought to the Buenos Aires market. After they are sold, they go to the slaughter-houses and the meat is refrigerated for export.

The American Plains, once the home of millions of bison, now support a range cattle industry on a vast scale. In the autumn the cattle are herded into ranch corrals for sorting.

their cultivation methods and their cropping systems unsuited to a land where rainfall was irregular and insufficient. A long series of humid years encouraged wheat farmers to expand their acreage in the 1920s; a long series of droughts in the 1930s drove tens of thousands off the land. In the spring wheat area 60 per cent of the crop was abandoned between 1934 and 1936.

Many areas since that date have seen the re-establishment of cattle-rearing, encouraged by scientific range management, by improved breeding, and supported by the high meat consumption of the American people. The High Plains are now the home of the ranch livestock industry and, though conditions vary greatly throughout the area, the basic problems of water supply, grazing and marketing are broadly the same.

Opening up the plains

In the western interior of the High Plains, ranchers often keep both cattle and sheep, the latter grazing on shorter grass in the more arid parts. In northern Colorado and eastern Montana, the sheep ranchers move their flocks in spring and summer to the meadows of the high mountains, bringing them down again to winter in the protected valleys. Goats, too, are found on the Texas range where the shrub vegetation is too poor for cattle or sheep. Here the Angora goat is raised for its fleece, and the increasing popularity of *mohair* as a clothing fibre seems to hold promise for this sector of the pastoral industry.

The commercial development of pastoral farming has depended greatly on the availability of effective means of transport for, by their nature and history, the pastoral regions lie far from their market. In the opening up of the North American frontier, the westward extension of the rail network played a crucial part and many cities in the United States owed their existence to the railway. In South America,

the building of an extensive railway network, centred on Buenos Aires and the Plate estuary, was a vital element in the pastoral exploitation of the Argentine *pampas* (grasslands). Here, as in Australia and New Zealand, the markets were overseas and were built up notably during the latter half of the nineteenth century by sea transport and the growth of merchant shipping.

The *Merino* sheep was introduced into Australia at the end of the eighteenth century and extensive sheep farming to produce wool was successfully established by the 1820s. New Zealand followed suit and later introduced new breeds designed for meat as well as wool. A new era began with the introduction of refrigeration and, in 1882, the first shipment of frozen meat and dairy produce gave further impetus throughout the country to the development of pastoral farming.

Argentina's pastoral farms support a huge meat industry which processes, tins, refrigerates and chills meat products. Here sides of chilled beef are inspected before shipment.

New technology, improvements in equipment and transport methods are part of the scientific, mechanical and commercial revolution that has brought into being many of the pastoral farming regions of today. They are the product of an age of expansion into areas where land was plentiful but people were few. The land itself has been developed by persistent adaptation and at the cost of many setbacks.

Beyond the many areas of commercial farming there are still vast tracts of the Old World where herbivorous animals represent the only efficient means of livelihood. Such areas of more primitive culture stretch from the Arctic tundra of Europe and Asia across the high desert steppes to the tall grasslands of the tropical savannas. The climate of the far north gives Man little opportunity for farming. Only a few animals can survive on the sparse natural vegetation, notably the reindeer, and reindeer nomadism is to be found in different forms from Lapland to the Bering Strait.

In Kenya, the Masai tribe are representative of an eastern African people, formerly nomadic and more widespread, who live by and for their cattle. They practise a form of dairy ranching, but the aim and ambition of every member of the tribe is to own large numbers of livestock. The more cattle he owns, the more power and prestige he can command. These people, like other primitive pastoralists have clung of necessity to a traditional way of life. Now that opportunities for change have come, they still tend to resist the pressures of civilization. These pressures are insistent, however, and they affect primitive pastoralists throughout the world. To meet them, modern methods of land utilization and animal husbandry have to be adopted. Many will have to give up their nomadism and settle down to modern ranching, on land which is owned either individually or co-operatively. The effort demanded is immense; money, technical knowledge and the ability to communicate it are needed. The process may be long, but it has already begun.

Fresh fruit, vegetables and flowers

Every day a harvest of crops, intensively grown in the open and under glass, is rushed from market gardens to local shops and to central markets for distribution to dinner tables all over the world.

1 Neat, carefully tended rows of daffodils and tulips bloom in early spring on a Danish market garden. They are grown for sale to local shops and for wholesale distribution.

2 Strawberries, which thrive in a cool, moist climate, are picked and packed into punnets in Denmark. The straw round the plants keeps the fruit clean and free from pests.

WALK DOWN any high street and into a greengrocer's shop. Most of the goods on display will be the produce of local market gardeners, but some will have travelled a greater distance and may well have been imported from other countries.

In general, *market gardening* involves the intensive production of vegetables, soft fruit and flowers for direct sale to the general public. This, of course, covers a wide range of possibilities. In America large-scale horticulture which specializes in one or two crops only and which usually lies at some distance from the city markets is known as *truck farming* – a term probably derived originally from the French *troquer* (to barter or exchange) but now firmly associated with marketing by motor-truck. The term market gardening is reserved for the smaller, more mixed horticultural production which lies close to the city markets. In most countries the distinction between these two types of market gardening is not made, but there are a number of general characteristics which distinguish it from other types of farming.

Market gardening is usually far more localized than other forms of agriculture. It takes up barely 3 per cent of the total area under crops and grass in England and Wales and appears in strength only in a limited number of localities. In the United States, where agriculture generally is more extensive, it occupies less than 1 per cent of the farmed land. Market-garden crops require far greater amounts of labour and often more capital than other farm crops: much hand-work is involved in planting, tending and reaping, and

capital investment can be high, particularly where crops are grown under glass. The necessity for early production is another important feature of the industry. Market prices in the early part of a crop season can be unusually high but generally fall to a more normal level quite quickly. With some crops, a few days' advantage can make the difference between a modest and a highly successful year's trading.

Fresh vegetables

Until relatively recently, nearness to market was a very important factor in deciding the location of market gardening. Speed of delivery and the difficulties of moving bulky and sometimes highly perishable goods ensured that, where possible, horticulture clustered near the fringes of the major urban areas. London, for example, was supplied from areas on its immediate fringe, such as those in northwest Kent, in western Middlesex and in the Lea Valley north of Waltham Cross. New York received its vegetables, fruit and flowers from Long Island and from adjacent parts of New Jersey, while Paris obtained the bulk of its supplies from within the Paris Basin. However, as the speed of transport increased, refrigeration and forced ventilation developed and transport costs, relative to the total costs of producing market-garden crops, fell, so the importance of this factor declined. In

consequence, the comparative advantages of soil, landscape and climate have been enhanced. Southwest England and the Channel Islands can now exploit their agricultural 'earliness' by producing out-door spring flowers, such as daffodils and anemones, for the London market when only the costlier glasshouse blooms are available from local sources. California, Florida and southern Texas can not only market vegetables in New York and in the other major cities of northwestern United States, well before local growers, but can also supply produce, like citrus fruits, which the local market gardeners of the northeast can grow only under glass. Similarly, the growers of Brittany, and particularly those of southern France and Algeria, can ship to the Paris market at great advantage.

There has naturally been a see-saw effect. The market-gardening areas distant from the major cities have gained markedly in importance over the last 50 or 60 years. Market-based gardening has declined, though not as rapidly as might be expected because over the same period the urban areas themselves have been expanding rapidly and the purchasing power of their residents has been rising. The urban-fringe areas of market gardening have contracted but have also become more concentrated, particularly in regions which possess some inherent natural advantage of soil, climate or landscape.

1 Daffodils being picked near Swanley in Kent, where flowers and vegetables are grown in the open and under glass for wholesale distribution at the New Covent Garden Market in London.
2 In the State of Oregon, horticulture thrives on the fertile soil and in an ideal climate. On a bulb farm, hybrid lilies are pollinated to produce new strains.
3 Conventional farms, as well as market gardens, grow vegetables for human consumption. In Kent, a field of cabbages is cut, packed and loaded for speedy transport to the markets.

There is really no such person as a typical market gardener. He may be a man who has a holding of less than an acre, particularly if he produces crops under glass. He may grow vegetables in the open, in which case he would have a larger holding, but not as large as would be usual for a dairy or grain farm. He might be a specialist fruit grower with a holding ranging from something slightly larger again up to what are, in California and South Africa, among the largest crop farms in the world. Or he might even be a conventional cropland farmer with several hundred acres, growing vegetables for human consumption as part of his normal crop rotation. At a purely financial level he might, in Britain, be spending £50 per acre each year producing outdoor vegetables, or close to £20,000 per acre on growing tomatoes in a heated glasshouse. Again the degree to which he specializes in market-garden produce might vary. In Britain, two-thirds of the fruit grown is supplied by specialist fruit farmers, about half the choicer vegetables are produced by specialist market gardeners, but only about one-fifth of the coarse vegetables are grown by specialists. In the United States and other countries similar differences occur.

The market gardens themselves also differ very widely within the fairly compact horticultural regions, and between regions the contrasts are even greater, since regional specialization in a limited number of crops is a characteristic of the industry. There is often no simple and obvious reason why certain areas develop substantial amounts of market gardening or why, within these areas, specialization in a particular crop occurs.

Some general principles are, however, evident. Because earliness is an important factor, areas of moderate rainfall, with long growing seasons and freely drained soils, will be preferred. Sunshine early in the year and at the ripening stage will be an advantage, and at a more local scale, shelter from high winds and freedom from late frosts will help to determine the detailed sites for market-garden cultivation.

In the United States, which stretches from 25°N to 49°N, ranges in altitude from plains little above sea level to peaks of over 14,000 feet, has a variety of soils and all rainfall conditions between a few

the consumers of the urbanized areas of Europe. In Britain it is the eastern and southern parts of England which have become the most important market-gardening areas. Here the climatic and landscape conditions are best suited to market-garden crops, but they do not always explain why particular parts of the region have been favoured. In some areas it seems likely that the demand for hand labour has encouraged the expansion of market gardening, and sometimes it seems that distance to market has been important, especially where bulky, low-value crops like cabbages are required. But widespread mechanization and the location of canning or freezing plants in the market-garden areas have recently mitigated these effects. Often the origins of particular types of market-gardening are buried in the history of cropping practices of an area. The region around Sandy, in Bedfordshire, for example, has a history of market gardening which goes back to the seventeenth century.

It is clear that the market gardening of no country is typical of the whole, but that of England and Wales serves as an example of temperate horticulture. Open-air market gardening in England and Wales may be thought of as falling under three headings: vegetables, flowers and bulbs, and fruit. Vegetables are by far the most important of the three. They take well over half the acreage devoted to outdoor horticulture and provide a little under half the output, judged by value. While some vegetables are grown in most parts of the country, the bulk of the production is concentrated in mid-Bedfordshire, the Fenlands and East Anglia, the Vale of Evesham, Kent, southwest Lancashire, south Yorkshire and on the eastern and

1 A busy stall at the market in Mainz in Germany sells locally grown vegetables. Market gardeners must adjust their produce to comply with changing public tastes.
2 Scarlet runner beans are picked by hand in Kent. Commercial vegetable growing needs constant work, which cannot be done by machinery, to plant, tend and harvest the crops.

inches and 100 inches per annum, many potential market-gardening sites are available. Physical conditions and a competitive market have led to the development of four major areas of early crop production: southern Florida, the Gulf coast, the valley of the Rio Grande, and central and southern California. Here the hardier vegetables are planted in the autumn and are marketed early in the winter. Other crops are put into the ground during the coldest weather and are ready for the markets in the early spring. On the Atlantic coast there is a succession of harvest dates, beginning in the south in Florida and gradually getting later northwards until the areas close to the urban markets, such as those in New Jersey and New England, are in production. As the later areas are able to market their goods at a lower price, since their transport costs are lower, the earlier and more distant areas fade from the scene until early in the following season.

In Europe a similar system operates. Market gardeners in Algeria, Italy, Spain and Mediterranean France are the first to get their goods to the market. It is only later that the produce of northern France, Germany, Holland and Britain reaches

western fringes of London. But production is concentrated within these areas and is highly diversified. For example, most of the Brussels sprouts are produced in two highly localized areas in mid-Bedfordshire and the Vale of Evesham, while cabbages and savoys are grown more widely, but are most evident around the Wash, in southwest Lancashire and on the fringes of London and the cities of Midland England. Peas picked green for market are grown principally in Essex, north Kent, the Vale of Evesham and south Yorkshire; peas harvested dry are produced mainly in the Fenlands, Lincolnshire and southeast Yorkshire, while peas harvested green for canning or quick-freezing are produced principally in the Fenlands, southeast Lancashire and East Anglia.

Specialized areas

The same holds true for the choicer vegetables. Asparagus, confined to very sandy soils, is found only in the Vale of Evesham and upon the Brecklands of East Anglia. About half the rhubarb production of England and Wales is derived from a small triangular area in Yorkshire defined by the towns of Dewsbury, Leeds and Wakefield. Lettuce, a highly perishable crop which has to be delivered fresh to market, is much more widespread and is found mainly in the districts adjacent to the cities, the most prominent being around London and in Lancashire.

Outdoor flowers and bulbs take far smaller acreages; they occupy only about 4 per cent of the area devoted to horticulture but, because of their high value, their economic importance is much greater. Since London has the largest market in the country for fresh flowers it is not surprising that areas with access to the metropolis are predominant.

Bulbs and bulb flowers are far more concentrated than the other types. The silty districts of the Fenlands are the outstanding producers, with Cornwall as the

only minor producing region worth mentioning. Daffodils and tulips are the principal bulbs grown. About half the acreage provides flowers for direct marketing, the remainder produces bulbs for sale, some for immediate public sale but some to florists who in turn grow flowers for sale.

Fruit growing, like vegetable growing, is an important occupier of land. Something like two-fifths of the horticultural acreage is taken up by fruit trees and bushes, which produce about the same proportion of total outdoor horticultural output by value. The orchards providing top fruit are concentrated in Kent, and in the western counties of England. Small fruits, such as gooseberries, strawberries and blackcurrants, are found in much the same areas.

Market gardening also takes place under glass. The acreage taken is small, but the value of the output is very high. Although the environment of a glass house is controlled and the soil is sterilized, local physical conditions play a large part in locating glasshouses. Temperature, wind, light intensity and atmosphere pollution are of considerable importance. They have a direct bearing upon 'earliness' and upon heating and cleaning costs. The south of England, and particularly those parts of the southeast close to the London conurbation, have become important for glasshouse production. Northeast of London, for example, where pollution from the conurbation has reduced effective sunshine, recent shifts in location have been made away from the area.

Glasshouses, particularly where heated, allow cropping throughout the year. By far the most prominent summer crop is tomatoes, though in recent years tomatoes and other vegetables have been losing ground to mushrooms and to nonvegetable crops. The most important winter crop is lettuce, although in winter, flowers and foliage plants take more glasshouse space than vegetables.

The traditional method of supplying market-garden produce to the consumer is through the markets. These range from the simple roadside stalls of the small-town market-day to the highly complex

regional and national markets, like Covent Garden in London. Most of the large markets, where produce from a wide area is collected, passes through the hands of dealers and is then redistributed to the consumers through the retail outlets, are now grossly overstrained and congested. Covent Garden, which grew up as a local market and only later came to serve consumers on a national scale, is no exception. Its trade continues to grow and a completely new market has been planned.

Changing public tastes

There are indications that the large wholesale markets may not continue to expand indefinitely. Direct contract selling, in which large consumers like supermarket chains or canning and dry-freezing firms buy under contract from market gardeners or groups of market gardeners, is already well established. There are advantages on both sides: the supermarkets and big firms need a guaranteed supply of good-quality produce at a fairly steady price, the market gardeners need sure markets, and although they might not make large profits, a reasonable income agreed in advance and spread over a longer period is ensured. Both gain by avoiding the costs and congestion of the existing markets.

Apart from the natural hazards of climate, perhaps the biggest problem of the future for market gardeners is the fickleness of public tastes. In Britain, the consumption of fresh fruit and vegetables is falling and an increasing amount is imported. Greengrocers' shops now contain a range of produce – such as melons, peppers and sweet potatoes – which might have surprised the shoppers of 30 years ago. On the other hand the consumption of canned and bottled fruit in Britain has nearly doubled since the Second World War. The biggest changes in market gardening at present are a result of the increasing affluence and changing tastes of urban dwellers of temperate latitudes.

1 A market garden in Malta, which specializes in growing carnations and geraniums, packs and dispatches its valuable blooms by air transport to London for distribution.

2 In England, vegetables take well over half the acreage devoted to outdoor horticulture. These women, with their children, are picking a field of green peas in Kent.

Food from the seas

Every year the highly organized commercial fishing industry supplies millions of tons of fish to the world's markets. But the oceans are still a vast, largely untapped store of potential food.

THE HARVEST of the sea depends upon a crop that is never sown, a crop of minute plants and animals called *plankton* which varies in quantity from place to place and from season to season. The plankton is most plentiful where there are many nutrients in the upper, sunlit layers of the water; these nutrients are the remains of organisms which lived in the sea or the salts brought into the ocean by the rivers. On the plankton pastures feed fish of all sizes, even the giant mammals of the ocean, the blue whales which may weigh 100 tons and be up to 100 feet in length. Some fish, of course, are predators and hunt the smaller fish for food but together they form a chain of food supply into which Man can break at any level. In the past he has normally been a hunter but there are signs that he may begin to farm not only the fish, as already happens in Japan, but also the plankton pastures themselves.

The main fishing grounds, however, are not necessarily where there is the most plankton and the most fish because, until comparatively recently, most of the world's fishing took place near land where the water is sufficiently shallow to catch both the bottom-feeding fish (the *demersal* types) and the fish which feed near the surface (the *pelagic* types), by lines and hooks and by nets. Fishing also requires good harbours within easy reach of the grounds and, of course, a population which is used to eating fish as part of its diet either through choice or religious prescription. In practice this has meant that the main fishing grounds have been located on the shallow waters of the continental shelves, where the water is less than 600 feet deep, and with fairly dense populations on the near-by coasts. Here conditions are also favourable for a plentiful supply of plankton. The continental shelves are, however, by no means continuous round the land masses; sometimes they are relatively wide, as off Northwest Europe or off eastern Asia, but they may be very narrow or completely absent.

1 Modern commercial fishing is an expensive and highly organized operation. Ships, like this stern trawler in the North Atlantic, use electronic navigation equipment to guide them to and from the fishing grounds, and echo-sounding devices to locate the shoals of fish.
2 Fishermen anxiously watch small icebergs slide past the ship as powerful winches haul a full net of fish aboard a stern trawler.
3 Oysters, dredged from the sea-bottom of the shallow water off South Island, New Zealand, are harvested with a steel trawl-net.

Off the west coast of South America, for instance, the bottom plunges steeply to great depths and there would be no chance of finding fish in quantity if water did not well up from the depths and bring to the surface the nutrients on which the plankton thrive. Elsewhere plankton and large numbers of fish are found where cold and warm waters mix, particularly on the shallow banks off the coasts of Newfoundland where the great cod fishery attracted the fishermen of Europe to the American coast before Columbus sailed to the West Indies in 1492.

At present, the main fishing grounds still lie relatively close to large centres of population whose needs can be served by efficient transport systems by sea and by land. Judged on the basis of the number of fish caught, the main fishing grounds are off the coasts of Asia, seas from which about half the world's annual catch of fish is taken. The coastal waters around Europe account for about a third of the annual total while the fisheries of North

America produce about one-eighth.

In the Asian fisheries the majority of fish are caught by simple methods and are consumed locally. The most intensive and most highly commercialized fishing takes place from shore bases on the northwest coast of Europe from which vessels make voyages ranging from a few hours to several months. Such fishing began as the population of the North Sea coastlands increased, in creeks and estuaries where traps were set to catch the fish as the tide receded.

Cod and herring

Later the fish in the inshore waters were caught with hooks and nets but, by the Middle Ages, fishing vessels were ranging far to the north, to the banks round the Shetland Islands, Faroe and Iceland while others crossed the Atlantic to Newfoundland. Two kinds of fish have dominated the fisheries of Northwest Europe, the cod and the herring, and on them the fortunes of nations have hung in the balance.

The cod is a demersal fish which feeds on smaller fish and may grow to more than three feet long. Fish of the cod family, such as hake and haddock, are often called *round* fish to distinguish them from the *flat* fish such as plaice and halibut which are also demersal types. Demersal fish were originally caught by long lines, each with many baited hooks, suspended either from a large fishing boat or from many small vessels. Now most of the demersal fish are caught by trawl-nets which are dragged through the water just above the sea-floor; the fish are then gutted

1 Standing on stilts to reach deeper water, a fisherman on the southern coast of Ceylon, catches sardines for the local markets.

2 Gutted and split herring are *kippered,* or smoked, over smouldering oak chips in Denmark. Herring intended for distant markets must be cured as it quickly putrefies.

3 Trawlers came to the aid of this Norwegian ring-net seiner when it caught nearly 1,000 tons of herring, more than three times its loading capacity, in its net. While the fish were being loaded on to the ships, the net broke and swarms of herring escaped. But the total catch amounted to nearly 500 tons.

4 The catch is unloaded at the fish market at Aberdeen in Scotland, where it will be sold for local processing or packed in ice for transport.

5 Cleaned, gutted cod, from the fishing grounds of the northeast Atlantic, dry on racks in the Arctic winds at a Norwegian fishing port.

and packed with ice in the fish rooms for the journey back to port. Rapid transport by rail or road ensures that the fish reach the shops in good condition. But the great cod commercial fishery began under far more difficult conditions when it was necessary to dry the gutted fish on stony beaches in the heat of the sun in Newfoundland, Iceland or the Shetland Islands or pack it in salt before sending it to the great fish-consuming countries of the Mediterranean.

In contrast, the herring, and its relations the sprat and the pilchard, or the mackerel and the salmon, are pelagic fish. They swim in shoals near the surface and although some of the larger fish, such as the tuna are caught by line, most fish of the pelagic type are caught in nets. The freely swimming shoals of herring were traditionally caught in drift-nets, which hang like huge curtains from floats on the surface, in the North Sea and the Atlantic coasts of Europe. The fish were caught in vast quantities in the nets and brought to the nearest port for gutting before curing. Curing the herring is necessary if it is to be transported to distant markets because its high fat content means that it putrefies quickly; curing was originally a secret of the Dutch who built up an important trade based on the quality of their 'cure' in the Middle Ages. It consists of pickling the fish in barrels of brine although the flesh of the herring can also, it was discovered, be preserved by smoking, or *kippering*, the split fish over smouldering oak chips. Whether cured or kippered the herring became an important item in

trade and Scotland's fishing ports, in particular, suffered severely when their European customers began to fish for herring after the First World War.

Expensive and dangerous

Compared with the sailing trawlers, drifters and long liners, modern fishing vessels are complicated and expensive. The elaborate nets require powerful winches for the haul. They are also very expensive; a purse-seine net, which is used increasingly for herring fishing, may gather in so many fish that it breaks even when made of the latest man-made fibres; the skipper of a purse-seiner must also be constantly on his guard in case the weight of the fish in the net drags the vessel under. He, like the trawl skipper, finds his way to the fishing grounds by elaborate electronic navigation gear; he finds the fish by echo-sounding devices which indicate the schools of fish and may drive them into the net by noise or by releasing chemicals in the water. The largest trawlers and purse-seiners are owned by companies who employ the skipper and the fishermen – they operate from large ports such as Hull and Aberdeen, Ijmuiden or Stavanger.

Yet much of the fishing in the northeast Atlantic is by smaller vessels up to 75 feet long in which the skipper and crew are shareholders in the boat. Norwegians, Dutch, Danes, Scots, Faroese and Icelanders with seine-net boats converge on the fishing grounds in all weathers and at all times of the year, to search for

the harvest of cod, hake, halibut and herring. Winter storms, especially in northern latitudes, may lead to icing up of the vessels and to disaster but the losses of fishing boats are much less than they were even 100 years ago, when the number was increased by the losses of whaling ships in the Arctic and Antarctic

Whaling began originally from shore stations and spread to the waters of the Arctic, the Tropics and the Antarctic where large numbers of whales were taken by harpoons thrown from oared boats. The open boats have now been replaced by whale catchers driven by powerful engines and equipped with explosive harpoon guns. More recently sound waves have been transmitted through the water to drive the whales until they become exhausted. Radar fitted on the whale catchers then guides them back to the factory ship where the whales are hauled aboard by giant winches. There the blubber is stripped away and rendered down in boilers while the meat and other organs are processed into fertilizers, meat and bone-meal, and oil for lubricants and products such as margarine and soap. After the Second World War the number of factory ships and catchers increased as Norwegians, British, Russians and Japanese flocked towards the southern ocean. The number of whales has been greatly reduced and, in spite of international agreements on the quantity to be taken each year, scientists are worried that the whale population will be exterminated.

Whether caught in the North Sea, on the Icelandic grounds or in the Denmark

1 Fish are gutted and filleted in a large, modern factory in Greenland. Research is discovering and developing many new methods of keeping fish in prime condition for the consumer.
2 Armed with long knives, the crew of a Russian factory ship in the Arctic, wait as a huge whale, harpooned from small catcher ships, is hauled up the ramp for processing.

Strait, fish is normally sold in Britain by auction at the fish markets of the main ports although some fish is sold on a fixed price agreement. Some of the fish bought at the quayside goes for local processing where it is filleted either by hand or by machine; it may be canned, smoked or cured in brine. Some, especially when landings are very heavy, goes for tinned pet food and the surplus is rendered at local factories into fish meal for fertilizers. The higher quality fish for the table is taken by fast train or lorry, packed in ice to ensure that it is fresh when it reaches the consumer. Much research goes on to discover ways of keeping the fish in prime condition from the moment it is hauled aboard the fishing boat. With the development of frozen foods, many new methods have been discovered and applied to fish marketing, such as frozen fillets, while *Klondyking* or the quick-freezing technique permits long voyages in the holds of refrigerated ships.

This is, of course, not common practice over the whole of the world – in some countries fishing is still on a small scale and the catches are sold at local markets on the coasts, but under the guidance of the Food and Agricultural Organization not only are fish being more intensively taken but more care is being taken to ensure hygiene and quality control.

The by-products of fishing are fish-meal which may be used for animal feeding or for fertilizer. Recently a flour has been made from fresh fish-meal which can be used for baking bread or for thickening soups, but the best-known by-product is fish-oil, especially oil from the liver of

cod, which has excellent medicinal properties. Research increasingly shows that vitamins and amino-acids may be derived from fish products.

Some fish have become known as high-quality fish fit for the tables of restaurants; the main fish of this type is the salmon caught in rivers and along the coasts, especially on the Pacific coast of North America. Much of this salmon is canned and reaches the table in processed condition, whereas the salmon from the coasts of Europe is sold fresh or lightly smoked. Many shellfish, such as crabs, lobsters, oysters, prawns, shrimps and 'scampi' are all high-quality sea-foods and are sold to hotels and restaurants rather than for home consumption. These shellfish are far less mobile than the freely swimming pelagic and demersal types and they are much more difficult to transport in a fresh condition – lobsters are sometimes kept in storage ponds of sea-water until

they can be sent to market.

For fishing, shellfishing and whaling there are certain limits of exploitation. Beyond these limits the fish stocks will become depleted since the rate of reproduction of the species is too slow to keep up with the numbers caught. To conserve fish stocks in the breeding grounds and to keep certain fishing grounds for their own use, many countries impose a limit within which vessels of certain size and of foreign nationalities may not fish. Such waters are patrolled by Fishery Protection cruisers and offenders may be fined and have their gear and catch confiscated. Over-fishing may be counteracted by international agreement to limit the mesh of the nets, or to fix a close season for breeding or to establish a quota at the beginning of the fishing season so that all the fishing vessels cease fishing when the quota has been reached. The quota system is only effective if all the parties observe the rules which means, in effect, a degree of international co-operation which is not readily achieved. Over-fishing results in too few fish for the effort and expense of the catching operation so that the catches must be kept to a level which the fish stocks can sustain.

Farming the sea

Over-fishing, however, applies to only some of the areas where fish stocks are known to be plentiful. Fishing vessels are now being built with a much greater range and endurance, sometimes with processing units aboard or on a factory ship. With such ships it is possible for the advanced fishing nations to exploit distant grounds, such as the waters off South America which hitherto have been scarcely fished. But the answer to the problems of conservation of fish stocks must be to apply to the sea the techniques of farming, which means sowing and cultivation as well as harvesting.

Fish farming has long been important in China and Japan especially in inland waters where the necessary fertilizer can be added to the water. In the sea there are obvious difficulties unless shellfish, which are relatively immobile, are cultivated; oyster farming is an age-old practice in the tidal creeks and lagoons of southeast England and France. More recently experiments have been conducted to establish fish farming in some of the sea lochs of western Scotland, particularly for the breeding of plaice.

There is no doubt that fish farming on the edge of the sea is possible, but whether it will be the solution to the problem of the continuing supply of food from the sea is another matter. It may be that the answer lies not in the farming of fish but the collection of the plankton crop itself. The main problem then will be to persuade the consumer that plankton is as palatable as smoked salmon or a well-grilled kipper. For the foreseeable future technical improvements in fish finding, catching, preserving, processing and distribution will be the keynote of this industry which must play an increasingly important part in the provision of food supplies for the world's expanding population.

Wealth beneath the waves

A farm under the sea, a fabulous source of minerals, a vast supply of oil and natural gas; the ocean is a source of untold wealth which will one day be essential for mankind's survival.

BY THE YEAR 2000, there will be more than 142 people for every square mile of the Earth's land surface, according to the latest predictions. There will, in fact, be more than three times as many people in the world as there were in 1930. This rapid – and still accelerating – growth of population, so graphically termed the population explosion, presents an equally growing host of problems. The most basic of these problems is that of food supplies.

Economists warn us that, at a not too distant point in the future, some areas of the Earth will face a serious food shortage. It is difficult to predict when this will happen, because much has yet to be done to improve the international distribution of food, and to make the best possible use of available supplies. But it is also clear that the total quantity of food produced must be greatly increased. At present about one-third of the land surface of the Earth is cultivated, and it produces most of our food requirements. It can certainly produce more as methods are improved. The rest comes from the oceans and seas, which, though they cover more than 70 per cent of the Earth's surface, supply only a small fraction of what we eat. Despite the rapid growth of the world's fishing industry in recent years, the oceans and seas remain the greatest, though relatively untapped, source of food left on Earth. In fact, the oceans have many potentialities, which so far have been under-exploited.

Underdeveloped industry

A basic requirement in our diet is protein, which the body needs to repair damaged tissues and to build new ones. Generally foods derived from animals are the main source of proteins, although such vegetable foods as soya beans and groundnuts also have a high protein content. Large numbers of people in the world already suffer from a shortage of proteins in their diet.

In most developed countries, people obtain proteins from such foods as meat, milk and eggs, but in Japan, the world's leading fishing nation, the chief source of animal protein comes from fish. Fish flesh also contains fats, minerals and vitamins, and is therefore an excellent food. In addition, fish meal is used to feed animals and as a fertilizer, thus making an indirect but valuable contribution to the world's food supply.

Despite the example of Japan, the world's fishing industry has not yet been developed to the same extent as its agriculture. Although oyster beds are cultivated, and in some places fish are bred in inland lakes, most fishermen are still hunters, who search the sea for their catch. Some oceanographers believe that

Above, a glittering shower of fish hauled from the sea and draped over the boat – yet another big catch for Japan's fishing fleets. *Below,* a school of tunny fish thrashes the water wildly after being forced to the surface by the bottom-net. The big ones are worth as much as £50 each.

it may be possible one day to 'farm' the sea and greatly increase the fish harvest, especially in coastal waters. Many techniques have been proposed, but most of them are not very practical.

For example, we know that fish thrive in areas where sub-surface water, rich in chemicals needed for marine life, wells to the surface. Scientists have suggested that these conditions could be artificially brought about by underwater nuclear reactors. This is not an economic proposition at present because of the tremendous waste of energy involved The development of *aquaculture* (farming of the sea) is further hampered by a lack of knowledge. We know far too little about the behaviour of fish and the nature of plankton – the basic food for marine life – and the effects on both of changes in the temperature and the salinity of seawater.

The oceans certainly contain an enormous variety and quantity of life. There are some 25,000 species of fish, and only relatively few species are caught for commercial purposes. In 1957, a Soviet ship sailing from Ceylon to the Gulf of Aden came across a vast mass of dead fish floating over an area of thousands of square miles. The fish were probably killed by an oxygen deficiency in sub-surface water that had welled up to the surface. But the main point here is that it was estimated that the total weight of these dead fish was about the same as that of the world's commercial catch in a year. It is notable that, despite natural disasters of this kind, the oceans are constantly renewing their life.

By how much, then, could the world's harvest of fish be increased? This we do not yet know. The Food and Agriculture Organization of the United Nations estimates that we could double the world's production without danger of overfishing. Some oceanographers regard this as a conservative estimate. Most commercial fishing takes place in the relatively shallow waters that border the continents. At present, deep-sea fishing is far less important as a source of food, although tunny fishing is often carried out in deep waters. A further point is that most fishing is done in only four areas, all in the northern hemisphere: the traditional fishing grounds of the north-east Atlantic, including the North Sea; the north-west Atlantic; the north-west Pacific; and the west-central Pacific.

Only one ton a year

The southern hemisphere contains a much greater area of water but, apart from the coastal waters of Peru, comparatively little is developed as fishing grounds. The reason is that the southern oceans are too distant from the densely populated continents of the northern hemisphere, where the greatest demand for fish lies. Fishermen who venture from the northern hemisphere into southern waters are also faced with the problem of getting their catch home before it is spoiled.

The world's production of fish has increased enormously in the past few years. The 1964 catch of 52,000,000 metric tons was double that of 1953. (One metric ton is the equivalent of 1,000,000 grammes.) We have noted that some underdeveloped parts of the world are already short of high-protein foods, but it is worth adding that the great expansion of the fishing industry has taken place in the developed countries. The main reason lies in the progress in fishing techniques in the more technologically advanced countries. Experts estimate that one Icelandic fisherman nets 100 tons of fish a year, whereas a fisherman in the tropics catches only about one ton. Some ten countries take more than six-tenths of the world's total catch.

New fishing techniques developed by technologically advanced countries include the use of echo-sounders, which can locate shoals of fish as well as measure the depth of ocean waters. Aircraft pilots radio to fishing vessels reports on fish near

Salt is essential for our survival and has many industrial uses too. Men have extracted salt from the sea for hundreds of years — each gallon of seawater contains about a quarter of a pound. *Top,* dried salt ready for collection; these salt pans are over 400 years old. *Above,* the British gas rig *Sea Quest,* stationed in the North Sea, drills far down into the sea-bed to extract natural gas, yet another valuable commodity hidden in the secret depths of the ocean.

the surface, whose presence and quantity can readily be detected from the air. Even television cameras are used to help fishermen guide their trawl nets accurately under the water. So-called factory ships have been built which can stay at sea for several months. Their catch is not spoiled because the fish is processed on board almost as soon as it is caught.

Experiments continue, including those to attract fish with underwater lights and suck them aboard by pumps. Improved methods and intensive fishing do, however,

lead to the danger of overfishing in certain areas, particularly when great numbers of immature fish are caught. Evidence of overfishing occurs when each year the fish netted are smaller and therefore younger than in previous years. Overfishing can only be prevented by international co-operation.

Apart from fish, the ocean contains other forms of life, including crustaceans, molluscs and mammals, which can all be caught and used as food. One factor of importance in any discussion of the ocean's

method is to boil the seawater. The steam, which is salt-free, is then collected and condensed.

Another method, using far less power, is to freeze the water. Sea ice is always far less salty than seawater. There is also an electrical method of filtering salts from water. The discovery of a cheap method may one day become essential when the potential fresh-water supply on land is almost entirely utilized.

Salt water can turn fertile lands into barren deserts, but salt itself is essential to human and animal life. It has many other uses, especially in the food-processing and chemical industries. A gallon of seawater contains about a quarter of a pound of salt, and men have extracted salt from the sea for hundreds of years. The simplest and oldest method is to catch seawater in shallow basins at the time of the high spring tides. The water trapped in the basins gradually evaporates and impurities settle to the bottom. The remaining water contains a higher concentration of salt. This more saline water is then transferred to a second basin, where evaporation continues until only the salt remains.

Minerals in the sea

Seawater contains other substances apart from salt, but the problem involved in recovering these substances is again one of economics. For example, among the many elements in seawater is gold, but it is present in such minute quantities that it is not worth extracting. More important than gold are potassium chloride, magnesium chloride, magnesium sulphate and bromine, all of which are recoverable. This was demonstrated during the Second World War, when the prices of these substances rose so high that their extraction from seawater became economically justified. Metals can also be extracted, and metallic magnesium was the first to be recovered on an economic basis. For full-scale development of these resources, however, we must probably await a time when land supplies are nearly exhausted.

A further source of minerals from the ocean lies in the manganese 'nodules' which are scattered over large areas of the ocean floor. The origin of these nodules, which are usually about the size of a potato, is unknown, but if collected in quantity they could be very valuable, because in addition to manganese they contain cobalt, iron, nickel and copper. Nodules were first discovered in the last century. We now know that the richest areas are in the Pacific. They are also found in the Atlantic, but it appears that these Atlantic nodules contain more iron and less of the other minerals than those in the Pacific. As many of the nodules are found in deep waters it will be difficult to bring them to the surface, but scientists have proposed a suction pump which would work like a marine vacuum cleaner on the ocean floor.

Other deep-sea deposits are far less attractive. Globigerina ooze covers about half of the ocean bed, and contains a very high concentration of calcium carbonate, which is used in cement. It seems unlikely,

Blubber from a fin whale 64 feet long is hacked off at a whaling station in Iceland, *top.* The various species of giant whales are now almost extinct in the northern hemisphere, due to the ferocity with which they have been hunted. *Above,* peasants return in a seaweed boat with a full cargo at Aveiro in Portugal. Seaweed is eaten here and in some Mediterranean countries. It is also an important source of iodine and is gathered in many lands on a commercial basis.

food potential is the question of personal taste. Sea cucumbers, sea urchins, octopuses, squids and even certain seaweeds are eaten as delicacies in some parts of the world. Other people view them with distaste. And what of plankton, the minute animal and plant life which forms the 'pasture' of the sea? Scientists believe that one day it will be possible to convert it into food, and certainly it would be valuable as a fertilizer.

Water, as well as food, is a basic necessity of human life. The oceans and seas contain vast quantities of water, but it is far too salty to drink or to irrigate land. The fresh water we use comes from rain, and is in fact seawater which has been naturally distilled. Artificial desalination is an expensive process, and is completely uneconomic if fresh water is available. But in some places, such as on ships, on isolated islands, or in oil towns on the edge of a desert, like those in Kuwait, water may be very scarce, and desalination is essential, despite the cost. This is accomplished in several ways. The simplest

Left, an ingenious craft for under-water research, the American 'Flip' boat. This floating laboratory is towed to its research station in a horizontal position. On arrival, its bows rise until it is vertical. *Top right,* a desalination plant in Kuwait. Desalination is very costly, but in the desert fresh water is very scarce and the process is justified. *Above right,* the hydro-electric plant in the estuary of the river Rance in Brittany, inaugurated by General de Gaulle in 1966. Engineers had dreamed for years of harnessing the tides to create electricity.

however, that underwater mining for oozes will become a practical proposition.

A much publicized activity now taking place at sea is the drilling of wells for natural gas and petroleum. Scientists estimate that about one-third of the world's remaining petroleum resources lie under the continental shelf that surrounds the continents. As engineers improve drilling techniques and solve problems caused by corrosion and the movement of seawater, so the extraction will increase.

Radioactive waste

Like rivers and lakes, the sea is a traditional dumping ground for unwanted materials ranging from cars to sewage. A new problem of waste disposal has arisen since the development of atomic power. Nuclear power plants now produce large quantities of radioactive waste and, faced with the prospect that the volume of waste is likely to increase, scientists have been exploring ways of disposing of it. At first the ocean seemed an obvious place, and already wastes with a very low radioactivity are pumped into the sea. The more dangerous highly radioactive wastes have so far been stored on land. But it has been suggested that this dangerous material might be sealed in special containers and dropped into the deepest part of the sea, the oceanic trenches. There, seven miles under water, it was supposed it would be safe.

Until recently, scientists thought that the lowest parts of the trenches were devoid of life and the water in them was still. But creatures have now been seen at the bottom of the trenches, and these creatures need oxygen for survival. If the water was completely still, all the oxygen in it would have been used up long ago, and would not have been replaced. But this is not the case. The waters in the ocean depths do move, although the movement is certainly slow by comparison with that of surface water. What would happen when the seawater ate through the walls of the containers and released radioactive substances into the water? The length of time it would take to rise to the surface is not known, but the possibility exists that it might poison marine life at the surface, marine life that is caught and eaten by Man.

We must remember, too, that, although we speak of the oceans and seas as separate bodies of water, they are all in fact interconnected. Poison released in one part of the ocean can be carried almost anywhere by the constant movements of the water. Another factor of importance is that seawater naturally contains only a minute amount of radioactive substances, far less than exist in the rocks of the continents. So even a small increase in radioactivity might endanger marine life that is not accustomed to it.

For years, engineers have considered the possibility of harnessing the tidal movements of the sea to create hydro-electric power. The United States government sponsored a project in the 1930s at Passamaquoddy, Maine, on the Bay of Fundy, where the highest known tides occur. But the project was eventually abandoned because it was too costly.

An enormous potential

In 1966, General de Gaulle inaugurated a hydro-electric plant in the estuary of the river Rance in Brittany, the first time tides have been used to produce electricity. Such projects are generally expensive, however, and in time may well not withstand competition from the successful development of atomic power plants.

The world's oceans and seas have an enormous potential, particularly as a source of food, fresh water and minerals. But it is clear that oceanographers have yet to find the answers to many questions. Until our knowledge is far more advanced, there remains a danger that we may overexploit and damage in a serious way this great natural resource. The encouraging sign is that the present study of the oceans is being undertaken on an international basis by scientists who recognize that co-operation is essential in the future development of our global waters. As our understanding grows, our management of this vast treasurehouse will ensure a better life for us on land.

Tropical plantations

Long associated with slavery and exploitation, plantations are now labour-saving, scientific and efficient, and bring prosperity by producing large harvests for home consumption and export.

SLAVERY, COLONIAL EXPLOITATION, poverty and oppression in the American 'Deep South', and overcrowded, insanitary labour lines in the rubber estates of South East Asia are some of the pictures popularly conjured up by the term 'plantation agriculture'. But probably nowhere in the world are any of these pictures still true. Plantation agriculture is perhaps best thought of quite simply as the opposite of peasant agriculture; it represents a system introduced by Europeans into the tropical and sub-tropical lands and refers to the large-scale, capitalized and often highly centralized cultivation in plantations or estates of 'cash crops' (crops produced for sale) for export.

Bananas, cocoa, coconuts, coffee, oil-palm products, rubber, sugar-cane, tea, sisal and cotton are crops especially characteristic of true plantation agriculture in the tropics, but they cannot strictly be called plantation crops because all of them are also grown on peasant smallholdings. Historically the production of cash crops for export on a large scale has been most closely associated with the plantation in the tropics. But in West Africa the great cocoa industry has been built up almost entirely by native smallholders. The same is true of cotton in Uganda, and, in Malaya, smallholders are responsible for about two-thirds of the rubber production. The distinction between plantation and peasant agriculture is often very difficult to measure precisely and varies from country to country and from crop to crop. In Malaya, for example, a rubber small-holding is defined simply by size, 100 acres or more constituting a plantation; anything smaller is a smallholding. In the

On the moist, tropical island of Martinique, nearly 80 per cent of the cultivable land is used to grow sugar-cane. Here the cane is cut by workers using long, sharp knives.

Green, mature tea-leaves are picked by hand on a tea plantation in southwest India. The leaves are taken to factories, crushed, dried and cut. After grading, they are packed for sale.

United States, the term plantation refers officially to 'any large farm several hundreds or thousands of acres'. But many of these 'plantations' in America were long ago – after the Civil War – divided up into small tracts or 'farms' of 20 to 40 acres each.

Plantation agriculture may have originated in the late fifteenth century on the islands in the Gulf of Guinea, although there is no certainty about this. Some authorities place the first plantations in the Middle East, in Indonesia or in South America. But it is known that the Portuguese introduced the system into north-east Brazil and that it subsequently reached the West Indies and the North American mainland. Here plantation agriculture acquired much of its evil reputation. It was in the Americas that plantations of sugar-cane, tobacco and cotton were introduced; these crops required abundant cheap labour which, when white 'slave'

labour ran out, had to be supplied through the Atlantic slave trade with Africa and Europe.

The plantation system also reached out into the East Indies, Africa and other parts of Latin America, yet the form in which it spread throughout the world varied enormously. Whereas in some areas plantations depended upon imported labour – as in Malaya, where Indians were introduced to work the rubber plantations – in other areas the labour supply was entirely local. In colonial Java, government plantations were established and the *Culture System* introduced whereby native communities were compelled to employ one-fifth of their cultivable area for the production of export crops, especially coffee, sugar and indigo (a plant from which blue dye is obtained).

Although it began in what are strictly tropical regions, the plantation system of agriculture is now to be found widely scattered within the belt roughly delimited by the 35° parallels of latitude. In the Americas it is found in the southern United States, West Indies, Central America and in patches around the coasts of South America; in Africa plantation agriculture occurs along the coasts of East and southeast Africa as well as in West Africa, Malagasy and Zaire. Meanwhile in Asia plantations can be found in parts of southern and northeastern India, in Ceylon, Malaysia and Indonesia as well as northeastern Australia. Yet although plantation agriculture is so widespread in the tropics, its present importance must

Anyone visiting a plantation is perhaps most immediately struck by the sense of order and by the way in which capital is being directed at increasing efficiency at all stages, including the industrial processing stage of production. A typical oil-palm plantation in Zaire or West Malaysia, for example, has row upon row of trees stretching monotonously over the country-side; there are many access roads, labour settlements and, perhaps, a large central processing factory and packing plant. Mechanization is evident at many stages, although some processes are less adaptable than others: for instance, the tapping of rubber in a plantation still employs many skilled workers, whereas the spraying of the trees is likely to be done mechanically. Plantation agriculture seems to be an ideal field for the application of mechanization to agriculture, especially as supplies of cheap labour dry up and the international migration of people to work on plantations becomes less likely.

Research successes and failures

Scientific research into the cultivation of crops most associated with the plantation system has, for commercial reasons, been particularly active. A great deal of research has gone into the major cash crops in world trade – sugar, cocoa and cotton in particular. Higher yielding strains, pest-resistant varieties, knowledge about fertilizers and their role in increasing productivity: many developments such as these have come out of research. But not all the more 'scientific' methods have been successful. One of the most notorious failures concerned the weeding of ground between rows in rubber and tea plantations. This practice, it was found, accelerated soil erosion, loss of soil moisture and

1 A tapper on a rubber plantation in Malaya cuts a groove in the bark of a tree. Latex, a milky fluid, drips into a cup and is collected.
2 Coffee beans are sorted in Haiti where, in the eighteenth century, Negro slaves were brought from Africa to work on the plantations.

not be exaggerated. This whole alien system, introduced into regions suitable for the production of tropical commodities needed by industrial countries, occupies in total a very small area compared with other types of agriculture in the tropics; plantation agriculture accounts for less than one-third of tropical cash crops.

Plantation agriculture has traditionally been financed by European, or at least Western, countries. The managerial and technical staff, too, is typically imported from outside, and sometimes much of the labour is not local, having been brought in either forcibly or under contract. Although this foreign element is still present in some plantation areas, capital now frequently comes from large international companies, or even from local government corporations, as in Uganda through the Agricultural Enterprises Limited, a subsidiary of the Uganda Development Corporation. In these latter cases the capital may be provided by shares raised by public or private subscriptions within the country.

1 Latex from a rubber plantation in Malaya is processed to produce these sheets of crude, brown rubber. Here they are being graded, before being baled for shipment.

2 In Honduras, the seeds and white fluffy fibres are picked from the open cotton bolls. A by-product of cotton plantations is cotton-seed cake, which is used for feeding animals.

3 Wrapped bunches of bananas are loaded on to a ship at St Lucia in the West Indies. The bananas are picked while unripe and exported to Britain, the United States and Europe.

soil deterioration. It was eventually abandoned in favour of planting some kind of leguminous (pulse family) cover crop between the trees or bushes.

Many plantations produce crops which are not only grown and exported for consumption in the industrial nations, but which now also form the basis for local and ancillary industries of a great range and variety. Sugar-cane in the West Indies, for instance, may go straight to a local factory for manufacture into raw sugar; but molasses and rum are two of the many other products made from the raw material. By-products of other plantation crops include cotton-seed cake for animal fodder and coconut coir fibre or copra.

As many of the crops are grown for consumption in temperate, industrialized countries, the distribution and marketing of plantation products is a most complicated business. Moreover, the marketing of tropical crops frequently involves enormous distances, so that crops must be of sufficiently high value to bear the heavy transport costs. For this reason, plantations are often located along coasts or rivers, have good rail or road connections

and may own long-distance transport systems. The United Fruit Company of America, for instance, maintains its own line of refrigerated ships for the transport of bananas from its Central American plantations to the United States. In most cases marketing is organized by government or centralized marketing boards which may attempt to protect producers against the fluctuations in world demand and prices by laying down guaranteed internal market prices for the producers. There are several international agreements, such as the International Coffee Agreement, which attempt to avoid the ever-present dangers of over-production.

It is difficult to generalize about the way of life of plantation workers. In Malaya an Indian rubber tapper usually lives in a labour line – a long hut divided into separate one-family dwellings, often with a common veranda and with communal sanitation and drinking/washing facilities. These lines are placed in groups, located centrally in the plantation so that the labourers can easily and quickly reach all parts of the estate. Modern requirements as far as conditions of living are

concerned normally guarantee the tapper a level of living and economic and social security somewhat above the local standards. On the same estate there will be paid technicians, foremen and a manager, all with rather different ways of life and conditions of living. Some of the workers will be tractor or bulldozer drivers; some may be employed in a latex factory or in a further processing plant of some kind.

In a large plantation the settlement may well approach town proportions, with schools, hospitals, stores and places of entertainment. In a few cases these settlements are very large indeed, with populations of over 70,000, as in the Firestone rubber plantations of Liberia. Some plantations, as in parts of Mississippi, Brazil and the Sudan, draw in labour daily from surrounding settlements lying outside the plantation boundaries.

There is a good deal of disagreement about the advantages and disadvantages of plantation agriculture. Much of the prejudice against the system arises from its association with colonial control and the exploitation of low-latitude countries and peoples; it is therefore politically

183

Cacao tree seedlings are carefully tended on a plantation nursery in Nigeria. The mature trees grow up to 30 feet high and produce pods which contain the seeds or cocoa beans.

unacceptable to many newly independent governments today. It is clear, too, that the racial or colour problem in many parts of the tropics – in Malaya, Ceylon, Mauritius, Natal, Jamaica, Costa Rica and the Southern United States, for example – dates back very often to the plantation system of agriculture. Dense populations and serious overcrowding, too, appear to have been created in the former plantation islands, notably in Jamaica, Barbados and Mauritius. Physically there have been several ill-effects. Forests have been cleared, as on the islands of São Tomé, Ceylon and Java; and soil erosion and soil deterioration have often resulted from the demands made upon the soil by monoculture (cultivation of one crop). Monoculture has frequently encouraged

the ravages of pests and crop diseases, resulting in the virtual destruction of coffee in Ceylon, cocoa in Ecuador, cotton in parts of the United States and bananas in Central America; and several plantation areas provided what proved to be ideal conditions for the serious and rapid growth of human diseases like malaria and yellow fever.

From an economic point of view, too, many difficulties or hazards have been associated with plantation agriculture. Overhead costs are high and rises in wages and salaries have in modern times contributed to a weakening in the competitive position of plantations. Furthermore, plantations are always likely to suffer heavily from deteriorating market conditions, especially where alternative

Workers on the rubber plantation near Singapore in Malaya live with their families in these long huts on the plantation. Large settlements have schools, hospitals and stores.

sources of supply (like sugar beet for sugar and synthetics for rubber) upset demands. In this sense plantation agriculture can never provide security for the worker.

On the other hand there are strong arguments in support of plantation agriculture. Apart from the economies of scale enjoyed by the very large plantation, much of the final production and processing can be carried out in what has been called a combined agricultural/industrial enterprise. High returns on money invested can be expected and the prosperity resulting from successful plantation agriculture within a country is difficult to ignore. In Malaya, for instance, rubber plantations have certainly helped successive governments to make Malaya one of the healthiest, most developed countries in the tropics, and the relatively high standard of living in Hawaii has also been caused partly by the sugar and pineapple plantations.

Hope for the future

Plantations, moreover, can assume more readily the risks of large-scale cash-crop production, and can act as experimental stations, apply research findings and produce more uniform, high quality products. An example of what can be done in increasing production in this way is to be found in the West African oil-palm research plantations at Pobe in Dahomey. Here a short-trunked, high yielding palm has been developed to facilitate harvesting, so that what was formerly a time consuming, dangerous and costly operation can now be carried out swiftly and cheaply from a moving trolley. Advanced techniques of farming, too, such as mechanized ploughing along the contours of hills, can help to reduce some of the ill-effects of plantation agriculture, notably soil erosion. Many authorities support plantation agriculture because it refers especially to tree crops. Where soils are of medium or low fertility, as they are widely believed to be in the tropics – and not ideally suited to continuous cropping with shallow-rooting field crops – the cultivation of deep-rooting perennials, such as trees, is a satisfactory way of using the land for agriculture.

The poor reputation plantation agriculture has acquired over the years is preventing its more widespread and rapid acceptance in low-latitude countries today. Viewed as an instrument created by and for colonial exploitation, the plantation has already in places been taxed out of existence or actually confiscated. The plantation system of agriculture, however, has a great deal to contribute to modern scientific, efficient farming in tropical countries. Its economic advantages may eventually make the system more acceptable in developing countries generally. This is particularly likely in those crops, such as tea, where the economic advantages of the plantation are most obvious. Indeed some adaptation of the plantation system is likely to prove in the long run to be the most logical vehicle for modern, scientific, labour saving and, above all, efficient and highly productive agriculture in the tropics.

Primitive farming

Throughout the world, millions of farmers produce only enough food for their families. Although amongst the most primitive, their methods are the background to advanced technological agriculture.

1 Bananas are widely grown by the subsistence farmers of the tropics, brought home here by a cheerful girl in Malawi. Cultivated bananas probably spread from monsoon Asia.

2 Maize, probably a native of the savannas of South America, is pounded into flour by the women of a Zambian subsistence farmer's family, using a tree-trunk trough.

WHEN ANYONE grows potatoes, native to the high Andean plateaux, in his garden or allotment, for his own use and not for sale to others, he is practising a form of *subsistence farming*. And, when he hoes the potato rows to encourage greater root and tuber development he is copying methods of cultivation evolved by the root-crop cultivators of the tropics. The subsistence farmers, therefore, although many are among the most primitive of contemporary farmers, have made a basic contribution to advanced technological agriculture.

Subsistence farming is the cultivation of plants or the keeping of animals to feed the farmer and his family. It is normally practised in environments not very suitable for animals which, therefore, play a very minor role in the economy. Technically, subsistence farming can, and does, occur in many parts of the world, if only to an extremely small extent in more advanced societies, but it survives as the major economy of peoples mainly in the tropical and monsoon lands. In tropical lands, the constant need to clear land and create new fields means that there is over the years a constant movement from old to new fields, a movement which has been termed *shifting agriculture*. In the major rice-growing areas of monsoon Asia, agriculture is anchored to a particular locality by the need to maintain the irrigation schemes and, frequently, the hillside terraces on which it is mainly dependent.

Tropical lands, where a combination of great heat and abundant rainfall supports a luxuriant growth of forest, give an impression of an environment in which some crops can grow so freely that farming is extremely easy. Such an impression is far from the truth. The heat and rainfall encourage an indiscriminate growth of plants and makes the maintenance of cleared fields difficult. Heavy rain *leaches* (washes) plant nutrients from the soils and creates the *latosols* of the tropics to which oxides of aluminium and iron near the surface give a distinctive reddish tinge. The fall of leaves and other organic material from the thick forests provides the humus of the thin surface layer of the soils and a delicate balance between forest and soil is maintained. When this balance is disturbed, by the clearing of forest for agriculture, fertility is quickly lost. The importance of this thin top layer of soil has led some writers to refer to the 'fragility' of tropical soils.

Dangerous pests

Not all tropical soils, however, are fragile latosols. Flooding rivers can maintain the fertility of flood plains by depositing silt; in some localities relatively new volcanic deposits remain fertile; in limestone areas, a high lime content can counteract the damaging effects of leaching. Great heat and heavy rains not only affect the soils and vegetation, but also create conditions in which pests dangerous to cultivated plants and to the farmers themselves flourish. A long list of dangerous diseases, such as malaria, fevers, cholera and dysentery, cause high death rates and greatly reduce the strength and effectiveness of many who remain active.

The activities of the subsistence farmer are closely related to his environment. During the periods of lesser rains, or 'dry seasons', clearings are made in the forest by such methods as felling trees by ringing and by burning the scrub and grass. These methods of clearing have been given the term 'cut and burn' or 'slash and burn'.

3 Bullocks wait patiently in a flooded rice field in India to pull a primitive wooden plough. Rice needs a warm, moist climate and grows best on flood plains and river deltas.

The ash from the fires gives some fertility in areas where the absence of large animals denies manure to the land, but it has been argued that the disturbance of the ecological balance by fire does more harm than good. Certainly the fertility of fields in such clearances is of limited duration. In West Africa the land in the forest belt can be tilled for two periods of five to six years, with a two to three year fallow interval. It may then be abandoned for some 20 years and the forest re-establishes itself. The absence of means to maintain fertility compels the farmers to clear new tracts of forest, perhaps some distance from their village. When the distance between the new fields and village becomes too great, a new village must be built. The term *shifting agriculture* has been applied to the practices of many of these tropical farmers.

Hoes and digging sticks

The fields are cleared and the top-soil lightly turned by a digging stick and hoe, the latter being largely confined to the Old World. Ploughs are rarely used in these areas because of the lack of draught animals, and shifting agriculture is characterized by the almost exclusive use of human labour. Careful use of the hoe is particularly suitable for the turning of the fragile top-soil whereas deeper turning by a plough would quickly destroy the soil structure. Women can use digging sticks and hoes, leaving the men free for forest clearance, for hunting and for other activities. For this reason shifting agriculture is sometimes classified as *semi-agriculture,* leaving the term *full agriculture* for agriculture requiring male labour for such tasks as terracing hillsides and constructing irrigation schemes. Hoes are not only used for clearing fields but also to form small mounds to encourage the root development of the principal crops.

Root crops divide tropical agriculture from the agriculture of the temperate zones where the emphasis is on domesticated grasses such as wheat and maize. The main crops are grown for the food value of either their tubers, as in the case of yams, or for their enlarged lower stems and roots, in the case of manioc. In both cases the main source of food is the starch stored by the plants to help their survival during the periods of lesser rains. Yams, of which there are over 100 different varieties varying greatly in size, have the broadest distribution in the tropics but are most typical of Africa and parts of South East Asia and Oceania. They are much less important in the tropics of America where manioc is the main root crop. Many yams and the cultivated type of manioc are poisonous, but the poison can be extracted by washing and pressing. It is thought that some poisonous types may have been cultivated because their poison protected them from pests, ensuring a better growth and a greater harvest. The potato, native to the Andes from their northern limit to the south of Chile, is a special case in the tropics of root-crop agriculture at high altitudes.

The distribution of cultivated root crops has been much influenced by the carrying of plants by Man. Manioc, now grown to some extent in Africa, may have been originally carried to Africa from the Amazon valley by early Portuguese navigators. Taro is an interesting case of the spread, or diffusion, of a root crop. This plant is a native of monsoon lands, possibly India, and has been spread to the islands of Oceania. It is small and lily-like and will not store well. Constant cropping in areas with a pronounced dry season demands the use of irrigation, and thus the spread of the plant into the tropics has meant the spread of irrigation farming.

Subsistence farming in the tropics does

1 The whole family helps to tend the rice fields in India, weeding and thinning the plants. Rice is the principal crop grown by the subsistence farmer to feed his family.

2 Potatoes, native to the Andes, are harvested in Bolivia. They provide a basis for farming on the high plateaux which are too cold for any other available crop.

not depend exclusively upon root crops. Bananas are widely grown. Wild forms of banana are found both in monsoon Asia and in tropical Africa, but the African types lack the side shoots which are used for planting. The cultivated banana has probably been spread from monsoon Asia. Cereal crops, developed from cultivated grasses and native to grasslands are, in some cases, being incorporated into root-crop agriculture. Rice, with its liking for heat and moisture, is the most obvious example. Maize, probably native to the savannas of South America and accustomed, to a lesser degree, to the same conditions, is grown in areas of more moderate rainfall. Wheat, native to the dry grasslands of the eastern Mediterranean border lands, cannot tolerate the combined heat and moisture and stays out of the wet tropics. Domestic animals are not widely kept. The chicken has spread through the tropics from its Asiatic home. So has the pig, but there is the possibility of some independent domestication of the pig in West Africa. Animal keeping only comes truly into its own in the drier margins of the tropical lands.

Mention has been made of the spread of plants and animals from the monsoon lands into tropical agriculture, sometimes involving changes in agricultural methods, as in the spread of the taro-irrigation farming. In monsoon Asia, particularly in South China and Japan, there are survivals of a subsistence farming differing in its physical bases and its methods from that of the tropics. Rice, the principal crop, does best on low-lying water-retentive alluvial lands such as are found in the flood plains and deltas of rivers, and in certain coastal areas. Under these conditions, seasonal floods help to renew fertility and the farmer need not change his fields. In these areas subsistence farming need not be shifting agriculture.

In monsoon lands, the dry season is more pronounced than it is in the wet tropical lands. Crop raising throughout the year is dependent upon the development of irrigation schemes, which tend to

3 Traditional subsistence farming is yielding to technological change but in many parts of the world, such as the Andes, wheat is still separated from chaff by animals' hoofs.

4 Many types of manioc, grown for their starchy roots, are poisonous. These Venezuelan girls have grated the roots and are squeezing the pulp to remove the poison juices.

5 The shifting cultivators of Guinea burn and cut scrub and grass to make new fields for crops. After a few years, the soil loses its fertility and a new clearing must be made.

put agriculture on a permanent basis. The work on the irrigation schemes is men's work and the employment of both men and women gives *full agriculture*. The pronounced dry season is also cooler than the periods of lesser rains in the tropics and a wide range of vegetables and even wheat in the dry winter season can be grown, giving a wider range and more diverse basis to agriculture. Further variety is given by the cultivation of trees and shrubs, such as tea and mulberries, on the balks between the rice fields.

Within this variety, rice is the principal crop. A distinctive feature of its cultivation is the growing of seeds and the keeping of the young plants during the first month of their growth in nursery plots. This concentration of the young plants reflects the scarcity of suitable land and, by allowing time for the harvest of winter crops and the preparation of the fields for the main rice crop, gives to this agriculture in parts of Japan and China an intensity of care and effort which almost merits the term horticulture, rather than agriculture, an impression further strengthened by the intense sub-division of the available land.

Even where supplemented by terracing, suitable agricultural land is so scarce that there is little room for animal husbandry. Of the larger animals only the water buffalo, the draught animal used with the plough and providing another contrast with tropical agriculture, is kept. Otherwise animals are limited to chickens and pigs, which find most of their food around the homes of their owners. It has been suggested that usable land is so scarce that the keeping of the larger domestic animals has been eliminated for economic reasons, but the environment itself does not favour pastoral farming.

The forms of traditional subsistence farming which have been described are yielding to change in the modern world. King, an American agriculturalist who travelled through Japan and China early in this century, told his readers that in studying the rice farmers of these lands they are, 'considering practices of a virile race of 500 million people with unimpaired inheritance moving with momentum acquired through 4,000 years'. Even such a massive, self-perpetuating momentum has, however, been halted by social change in China. Small land holdings are being amalgamated and machinery introduced. In Japan social change has taken a different course but here, too, modern technology is relieving the burden of traditional farming methods. Small powered ploughs suitable for small fields are now being used, transforming traditional agriculture and increasing food production.

Improved crops and methods

Change is affecting also the simpler economic life of the shifting agriculturalists of the tropical lands. In West Africa, cocoa production is largely in the hands of native producers who have made a *cash crop* (crop produced for sale) a major element in their economy. Perhaps a more general influence has been the development of plantation farming by Europeans, attracting subsistence farmers by the wages offered and bringing money increasingly into the economy of subsistence-farming communities. Change also affects directly the older farming pattern. It has been argued that a major need in tropical lands is a more assured and plentiful supply of food.

Modern technological change must come slowly in these lands and the disastrous effects of applying the machinery and agriculture of the temperate latitudes to the fragile soils of the tropics, which resulted in erosion, should have been learnt from earlier failures. Changes in crops may provide a solution, and in this context the extension of the cultivation of rice, the cereal suited to tropical climatic conditions, offers possibilities for the future.

The shifting agriculturalist, despite the apparent simplicity of his economy, has made notable contributions to human development. Indeed, many believe that root-crop cultivation is the oldest form of farming and that the later cereal agriculture is derived from contact with it. Other attainments have followed. In West Africa, the Yoruba people have proved to be skilled metal workers and wood and ivory carvers. They have also, in the past, evolved an elaborate and flexible political structure but at present, in Africa, such peoples are going through the extremely difficult transition from tribal to national organization.

In the Americas, the Mayan civilizations of Central America were based on shifting agriculture, and the Inca civilization of the Andes on root-crop farming. The latter is a special case where potato cultivation provided an agricultural basis for life on the high Andean plateaux above the limit imposed by altitude on other available crops.

In 1537, a Spanish expedition up the Magdalena valley made contact with Andean potato growers and the potato was probably introduced to Spain as early as 1570. It made little progress in Europe until introduced by Raleigh on his estates near Cork, from where it spread among the peasant subsistence farmers in Ireland. Its remarkable development, both as a subsistence and a cash crop, in Europe from the late eighteenth century went on concurrently with the industrial development of the continent so that today a factory worker with an allotment may supplement his earnings by a form of subsistence agriculture, or at least horticulture, based on a crop and the methods of tropical subsistence farmers.

1 In Nigeria a hoe is used to prepare the ground for crops. Although ploughs, drawn by draught animals or tractors, are becoming more common, they can damage the fragile soil structure.

2 Motor-driven ploughs, suitable for small fields, are increasing food production in Japan and easing the burden of traditional methods of the subsistence farmer.

Crops for industry

Vegetable oils, which are manufactured into a huge variety of products, and tobacco, are grown all over the world to meet the increasing demands of factories for supplies of raw materials.

1

MOST OF the world's agricultural land is used to grow food for human and animal consumption, but a large amount is occupied by a wide range of crops that are processed and transformed into many of the products that contribute to our high standard of living. These are called *industrial crops* and include the vegetable-oil plants and trees, and tobacco. This branch of agriculture has a direct link with industry and forms an interdependent relationship between two sections of the economy. Many of these vegetable raw materials are now providing the bases for manufacturing industries in the developing countries, while in the developed countries new discoveries and uses keep up the demands for these materials, despite the development of substitutes for their more traditional end products.

Fats and oils form an indispensable part of our diets, but they also have growing uses in industry and medicine. Until this century, nearly all fats and oils used by millions of people in temperate latitudes for edible – and some industrial – purposes were obtained from animals, especially from cows, pigs and whales. With the great population growth of this century and increasing discoveries of new uses for oils and fats, the demand now far exceeds the supplies from these traditional sources. Advances in chemistry have made it possible for the fatty oils stored in the seed, fruit and stems of certain trees and plants to be used for both edible and industrial purposes, and it is mainly from these sources that growing demand has been satisfied. Scientists found that by varying the proportion of hydrogen in these substances it was possible to raise or lower their melting points (a process called *hydrogenation*) to create solid fats from liquid oils.

World-wide oils

During this century such advances in chemistry have made possible a high degree of interchangeability among edible and industrial oils and fats obtained from plants and animals. Each oil has its individual characteristics and is better for some purposes than others, but there is a relative ease of substitution that makes for keen competition in the fats and oils market which helps to keep prices low and fairly steady. These developments have also meant that, not only are the sources of oils and fats of a varied character, but their distribution spans all the climatic zones; from whales in cold climates to the coconut palm of the equatorial coastlands. The supply of such fats and oils is therefore now world-wide and there is particular competition between the animal fats of the temperate zone and the cheaper vegetable oils of the tropics, exemplified in margarine

	Margarine	Lard substitute	Salad oils	Cooking oils	Soap	Sardine oils	Confectionery	Glycerin	Cosmetics & Perfumes	Medical and Pharmaceutical	Paints and Varnishes	Lubricants	Linoleum	Textile & Leather processing	Illuminants
Groundnut	■		■	■	■		■							■	
Cottonseed	■	■	■	■	■		■								
Soya Bean	■		■	■	■						■		■		
Coconut	■	■			■		■	■	■						
Rapeseed			■	■								■			
Olive			■	■	■				■	■					
Sunflower	■		■	■	■										
Palm	■	■			■									■	■
Palm Kernel	■	■			■		■								
Linseed					■						■		■		
Sesame	■		■	■	■										
Castor									■	■	■	■		■	
Tung											■		■		

2

1 Buyers for the cigarette manufacturers follow the auctioneer along the bales of cured tobacco leaves at an auction in Salisbury, Rhodesia.

2 This table shows the principal uses of the major vegetable oils and how they can be interchanged for many manufactured products.

and cooking fat competing with butter and lard.

Hundreds of different species of trees and plants contain fatty oils and at least 40 of them have been used commercially for oil production. However, nearly all the international trade derives from eight vegetable sources: the groundnut, coconut, palm, palm kernel, soya bean, cottonseed, linseed (from flax), and sunflower. Olives, rapeseed, sesame, tung and castor are among others of importance but most of their oil is used locally and does not figure largely in world trade.

The main use of vegetable oils is for food, and far more is used locally than ever enters into international trade. Fats have a high nutritional value, they are easily digested and provide fuel and energy for the body. Some oils are consumed exactly as produced, others are first refined or their characteristics changed. In temperate latitudes much of the fat is eaten in solid form (butter and margarine) but in the warmer climes liquid oil is widely used in the preparation and cooking of food.

Butter and lard are manufactured from animal fats and no large increase in the numbers of cattle and pigs has been possible because they have specialized requirements. They need a great deal of labour and because animal fat is the product of two-stage agriculture, it is more costly than margarine and cooking fat. With vegetable oils there is minimum waste and greater yield. In a year an acre of groundnuts (peanuts) gives 260 lb of vegetable fat; an acre of plantation oil palms gives 2,000–3,000 lb of vegetable fat, but a cow yields only 50 lb of butter-fat per acre per annum. It has been the rapid increase in the production of vegetable fats that in the main has met the greatly increased demand for edible and industrial fats since 1945.

Another major use of vegetable oils is in the production of soap. In recent years soap manufacture in the developed countries has been declining with the increasing production of synthetic detergents, but this decline is being offset by increased soap manufacture in the developing countries. The principal vegetable oils used in Britain for soap are coconut, palm and palm kernel; in the United States it is coconut. Both countries blend these with even larger quantities of animal tallow and grease. Some oils and fats are used in detergent manufacture but here the principal raw materials are chemicals, many derived from by-products of oil refining. Detergents compete successfully with soap for household and industrial uses, but toilet-soap production holds its own. Various vegetable oils also satisfy a host of other industrial uses, such as in the manufacture of printing inks, of dressings and softeners in leather manufacture and *fluxes* (substances to promote fusion) in the tin and steel plate industries. The quick-drying oils, such as linseed, tung and soya, are used for the production of paints and varnishes.

Staple food in the tropics

Groundnuts provide one of the world's most important sources of vegetable oil. They are grown widely in tropical and sub-tropical regions where moderate rainfall and abundant sunshine give high yields. The crop does best in light sandy soils, the nuts or pods forming in the surface soil. India, China, West Africa and the United States are the four major producing areas, but of these only West Africa is a major exporter. The nut is a staple food in many tropical regions and is grown for the domestic market, being eaten whole or crushed to produce oil. About 20 per cent of world production enters world trade, of which about 80 per cent is imported by Western Europe, three-fifths of world exports come from Nigeria and Senegal where domestic consumption of the crop is small. Here cultivation of the crop absorbs much labour, but some mechanization, such as ploughing between the rows to lift the plants and turn the nuts to the surface, is now more common. The nuts are left on the surface

to dry before being collected for cleaning, grading and bagging.

Soya beans are now the largest single source of edible vegetable oil, accounting for nearly a quarter of all edible oil supplies. Native to China, cultivation has spread throughout the world – partly as a result of the Second World War when supplies from the Far East were cut off. The United States greatly increased its production during the war and is now the foremost world producer, responsible for two-thirds of world production, and 90 per cent of world exports. China, Brazil, U.S.S.R. and Indonesia are the next most important producers. The soya bean is a most versatile crop; the quick-drying oil was originally used as an industrial raw material but in more recent years it has gained favour as an edible oil and high protein food and now is used in scores of food products from margarine to breakfast cereals. There is also a growing range of industrial uses both as an oil and a fibre, for example, the manufacture of insecticides, printing inks, floor coverings and containers. The oil content of the bean is not high (up to 20 per cent) but the residue

Malaysia. Most producers export some copra or oil; the leading exporters are the Philippines and Ceylon.

The oil palm, from which palm oil and palm kernel oil are extracted, is grown principally in the African tropics, especially in West Africa. This palm is the most efficient producer of vegetable oil in the world: in some well-cared-for plantations yields of up to two tons per acre have been recorded. Palm oil is obtained from the pulp of the palm nut, and palm kernel oil from the kernel. To get the maximum return palm fruit is pressed as soon as it is gathered and this can be done by the peasant producers, but the kernels need heavy crushing machinery and much of this extraction is done in the importing countries. These oils are used by the margarine, cooking fat and soap industries and palm oil is used as a flux in the tinning of sheet steel. All the West African countries from Sierra Leone to Angola grow the oil palm; smaller numbers are grown (mainly in plantations) in parts of South East Asia and Central America. Nigeria

is by far the largest exporter, with Zaire, and Sierra Leone in West Africa being next in importance.

Cottonseed is a by-product of cotton. The plant is grown for its lint throughout tropical and sub-tropical latitudes and in comparison the value of the seed is low. It has a small oil content but the residue after crushing provides a valuable animal feed. Only a small proportion of cotton-seed and cottonseed oil enters international trade (the United States is the leading exporter); domestic markets claim a great deal but throughout the world much is wasted.

Many of the nuts, beans and seeds also provide valuable meal or oil cake after the oil has been extracted. These residues are valuable as concentrated feeding stuffs for milch cows and for fattening stock. The oil content is small but the protein content is very rich. The most important oil cakes are derived from cottonseed, soya bean, groundnut and linseed. In the past nearly all crushing plant was established in the chief importing countries of northern

from the bean is made into an oil-rich cattle cake, particularly in the United States and West Europe.

Among the tree crops the oil palm and coconut palm are outstanding sources of vegetable oils. These trees are found in the wetter parts of the tropics, close to the Equator and generally in coastal or near-coastal locations. The coconut palm particularly is found on islands and sea shores; the oil-palm belt extends further inland, in places for over 200 miles in West Africa. Coconut oil is pressed from the dried flesh (copra) of the coconut. Copra has a high oil content (60–68 per cent) and the oil is put to many uses, especially the manufacture of margarine, cooking fat, confectionery, toilet products and perfumes. There are some carefully cultivated high-yielding coconut-palm plantations, but most production is by small-holders who rely on their few palms as a major source of subsistence as well as of income. But much of this oil is of indifferent quality, commands a lower price and is mainly used for inedible purposes. The most important producers are the Philippines, Indonesia, Ceylon, India and

1 To separate the seeds from flax, farmers and their wives in Turkey thresh the straw. The seeds yield linseed oil which is used for quick-drying paints and varnishes.
2 The dried flesh of coconuts contains a high proportion of useful oil. The palms, which grow particularly on islands and sea shores, line the sandy coast of Kerala in India.
3 The United States is a major grower of soya beans, the largest single source of edible oil.

The residue from the crushed beans is made into an oil-rich cattle cake.
4 Rhodesia is one of the leading growers of Virginia type tobacco. In this cigarette factory machines feed a fixed amount of shredded leaf into paper tubes and cuts them to length.
5 Gambian growers pound oil palm nuts to obtain a thick, yellowish oil from the pulp surrounding the kernel. The oil is used for the manufacture of margarine, cooking fat and soap.

1 Oil-palm nuts grow in clusters of about 200 at the base of the palm. Well-tended plantations yield up to two tons of oil per acre.
2 Huge pyramids of groundnuts, which can be stored for long periods without deterioration, await transport at a railhead in Nigeria.
3 A Bulgarian woman sits in the shade, threading green tobacco leaves on a string for curing, a process which will take about two months.

Europe (at such ports as Liverpool, Hull, Rotterdam and Hamburg). In recent years more of the producing countries have been establishing their own crushing industries and are exporting both oil and cake, thus providing employment and cheaper supplies of oil and cake for their own markets.

A very large proportion of vegetable-oil crops is produced by smallholders and it is possible that up to a third of world exports still comes from wild or semi-wild plants and trees. The high yields obtained from oil and coconut palms grown carefully in plantations hint at the vast potential of the equatorial and tropical areas for vegetable-oil production. The increasing population and changing economic conditions will continue to stimulate the production of, and the discovery of new uses for, vegetable fats and oils. Their importance in world economy and world trade is likely to increase in the future.

Tobacco is obtained from the dried leaves of the tobacco plant and is used by mankind the world over. Its chief use is for smoking, but it is also chewed, taken as snuff and is the principal source of the alkaloid nicotine. The plant grows in a variety of soils and climates thanks to the work of the plant breeders and the world-wide demand for the leaf. Environmental differences, especially those of soils, affect the quality and character of the tobacco, and differences in taste relate certain markets to particular areas.

Tobacco is mainly a tropical and sub-tropical crop but if protected from frost is also grown successfully in temperate lands. It is grown in nearly 70 countries in the world but 60 per cent of exports come from four countries – the United States, Rhodesia, Turkey and Greece. The first

two countries account for most of the Virginia type tobacco entering world trade, whereas Turkey and Greece, smaller exporters, are noted for the smaller-leaved aromatic tobacco generally called 'Turkish' although they, too, now grow some Virginia type tobaccos. Cuba and certain West and East Indian islands grow stronger tobacco used particularly in cigar manufacture.

The method of curing (drying) as well as the character of the leaf affects its flavour. The three main methods of curing are by air, fire and flue. Curing causes the wilting and yellowing of the leaf, and the desired chemical changes are regulated by the method and speed of the curing. In Turkey and the Mediterranean countries some sun curing is carried out, but usually air curing takes place in well-ventilated buildings. The process may take up to two months. For fire curing wood fires are lit in the barns in which the leaves are hanging, giving them a characteristic aroma. This may also take up to two months. The bulk of tobacco entering world trade is flue cured which takes four

to six days; the warmth from a furnace is conducted round the barn in metal pipes.

The cultivation of tobacco requires much labour (estimated at nearly 500 man-hours per acre) and this is one reason why actual areas under tobacco on most farms are small, but the return is large. Where tobacco is grown for sale, often the labour of the whole family is used in such tasks as seed-bed and field preparation, transplanting, cultivating, topping (disbudding to prevent seed formation), removing suckers or lateral shoots and harvesting. The leaves are cut at intervals as they ripen; five or six cuttings may be required. Mechanization makes slow headway, for many operations still need manual labour. Tobacco not only makes great demands on the soil, but to do well must grow on weeded ground. On sloping ground this leads to soil erosion and gullying, and considerable parts of the rolling tobacco-growing areas of Tennessee and North Carolina now show such erosion.

National tastes in tobacco

The world tobacco industry is highly specialized and conservative. It is not easy to change habits and style of smoking and the markets in the developed world rely on specific areas and particular tobaccos to meet their national tastes, and they expect reliable grades and standard-quality leaf. For this reason the peasant production in the majority of tropical countries is consumed domestically and does not enter world markets. Tobacco may be aged two or three years before being manufactured into cigarettes, cigars and pipe tobaccos and practically every country has its own industry, frequently operating as a government monopoly.

The vegetable-oil crops and tobacco demonstrate the growing part invention and technology now play in enlarging the food and resource base provided by agricultural products. The differences between these products are also illuminating; the economic geography of oils and fats is dominated by the far-reaching effects of substitutability; that of tobacco by the varied and yet almost traditional pattern of demand that sustains world-wide production with relatively little competition.

Natural fibres

Plants and animals provide the fibres for clothing, household and industrial textiles. In spite of competition from man-made fibres, they still play a major role in agriculture and world trade.

CLOTHES ARE ONE of the necessities of life for most of the world's population, and over the centuries a wide range of plants and animal fibres have been used to meet this need. These natural fibres are now having to withstand heavy competition from man-made fibres – fibres made either from other vegetable matter or from a number of chemicals.

In everyday life, fibres are used to supply a huge variety of goods – not only clothing, but also carpets, curtains, upholstery materials, sheets, blankets, sacking, cord, string and so on. According to the end-product, fibres can be divided into clothing, household and industrial groups. Most fibres have more than one end-use, dictated by the characteristics of each one.

Hundreds of species of plants and many types of animals can provide useful fibre, but less than 20 of them are responsible for over 90 per cent of the world's natural fibre production. The four principal sources, which account for about three-quarters of the total, are: *seed fibres,* such as cotton and kapok, where the fibres form inside seed pods; *bast fibres,* such as jute, flax and hemp, which are obtained from the inner bark of plants; *leaf fibres,* such as sisal and abaca, which are found in the pulpy tissue of leaves and leaf-stems; and *wool* and *hair* from animals such as sheep, goats and camels.

The need for labour

Although they occupy only between 5 and 10 per cent of all agricultural land, natural fibres hold an important place in world agriculture because of the amount of labour involved in their intensive cultivation. In the United States, for example, cotton growing demands three times the amount of labour needed for wheat, while the wheat acreage is three times greater than that of cotton.

World trade in natural fibres is high; they account for about a quarter of all agricultural produce exported, and a far higher proportion of fibre produce is exported compared with the other main primary products. Nearly 40 per cent of world production of cotton and wool and 45 per cent of hard fibre (jute, hemp, sisal) are exported for manufacture. Nearly every country in the world produces fibre of one kind or another, but the majority entering world trade comes from the United States, U.S.S.R., Mexico, Egypt and Brazil which provide 65 per cent of world exports of cotton; over 80 per cent of raw wool comes from Australia, New Zealand, South Africa and Argentina. Tanzania and Brazil export 60 per cent of the world's sisal, and 80 per cent of world jute exports come from Pakistan. Competition from man-made fibres and price fluctuations can have severe repercussions

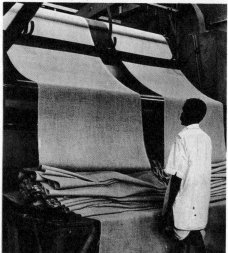

1 The layers of short, stiff fibres round coconuts, called coir, are made into ropes, doormats and brushes. Women in south India use special hammers to separate coir from the nuts.
2 At a mill in Bradford, England, which takes a fifth of the world's wool exports, wool is gathered for spinning after it has been cleaned and carded to straighten the fibres.
3 The Indian spinning and weaving mills near Calcutta process more than half the jute grown. It is processed into coarse, cheap cloth for sacking, and linoleum and carpet backing.

upon the economies of those countries which rely heavily upon such exports.

Cotton is the world's most important textile fibre. It is now grown by more than half the countries in the world and total production is over three times as great as its nearest rival, jute. This predominance owes much to the favourable characteristics of the fibre: it does not perish and can be stored and marketed when convenient; it is strong, durable and is easily spun and woven by mass-production methods. The various types of cotton grown make this fibre suitable for a considerable range of clothing and industrial uses; it has earned the reputation of being the great all-purpose fibre.

Cotton may be put into four classes, mainly according to the length of the fibres: Sea Island and Egyptian types are silky, fine yet strong fibres of extra long staple (1⅜ to 1¾ in.); Upland Long Staple (1⅛ to 1⅜ in.); Upland Short Staple, forming much of the United States crop (¾ to 1⅛ in.); Asian or short staple cotton (⅜ to ¾ in.). Generally the longer the staple the

more demanding the crop and the more difficult to grow. Most of the world's cotton is grown in the Northern Hemisphere in tropical to sub-tropical latitudes. The plant needs a growing season of about 180 days (less for the shorter staples) with hot, sunny weather and at least 20 in. of rainfall (or irrigation equivalent) with a dry ripening and harvesting period. Too much rain during the summer builds up foliage at the expense of lint and favours certain diseases and pests. Rich and well-drained soils are necessary and best yields come from light loams with a high lime content.

The finest cottons of long staple are grown mainly in Egypt, Peru and Sudan; the very finest Sea Island varieties are produced in small quantities in the West Indies. Coarse and short staple cottons, used in carpet manufacture, comprise part of the crops of Turkey, India, Pakistan and Burma.

Nearly one-third of the world's cotton is grown in the United States, mostly in the 'Cotton Belt' of the South. Great changes have occurred since the 1920s; whereas the Mississippi bottom lands remain important, the chief cotton-growing areas have now moved from east of the Mississippi to Texas in the west. Among reasons underlying these changes were the ravages of the boll weevil, the loss of soil fertility, and the possibility of more economic cotton-growing in large flat fields, favourable to mechanization, on virgin soil in Texas. The main cotton areas are now on the Red and Black Prairies of Texas and Oklahoma and in the Mississippi valley, and some cotton is also grown under irrigation in California and Arizona. The traditional image of one man, one mule cotton cultivation has also changed. Mechanization now plays a large part, from preparing the ground and drilling the seed to mechanical pickers which harvest the bolls. A mechanical picker can replace about 40 men and has almost halved the cost of picking. The proportion of the American crop picked by machinery is now about a half and it increases each year.

In Egypt cotton growing is carefully controlled by the farmer. In the desert climate the crop is watered by irrigation, great care has been taken over seed selection and breeding and the dense population ensures plentiful labour. The cotton is cultivated intensively, mainly on small-holdings in the Nile Delta. Egyptian cottons are of very high quality, extra long in staple, of fine silky appearance, yet very strong. They are in demand for special uses, such as the manufacture of typewriter ribbons, the inner linings of rubber tyres, book-bindings, and high-quality shirtings. The whole economy of Egypt is geared to the cotton crop which accounts for 70 per cent of the total value of her exports. China is the second largest producer of cotton and her crop, plus small imports, supplies her own large textile industry. The quality of the cotton is medium to poor and it is mostly grown on tiny holdings in the great river valleys of the Yangtze, Hwang Ho and the Szechwan Basin.

Russian cotton

The U.S.S.R. is striving to produce enough cotton for its own needs by expanding the acreage. Most of the crop is grown under irrigation in the hot, dry parts of the Turkmen and Uzbek Republics, east of the Caspian Sea and between it and the Black Sea. Other cotton is grown in the south Ukraine but the climate is less suitable and the quality is poorer.

In India cotton is grown widely but the main concentration is on black fertile soils east of Bombay on the Deccan plateau. Farming methods are primitive, yields are very low and the quality of the cotton is poor. Better, irrigated cotton is produced in the Punjab and lower Indus Valley in Pakistan. Here, by using fertilizers and rotating the crops, larger yields of higher-quality cotton are obtained.

Jute, the world's second most important fibre, is obtained by *retting* (softening) in water and stripping by hand the inner bark of the jute plant. The fibre is coarse and cheap and is mainly used in the manufacture of bags, sacks, wrappings and cordage. Jute cloth is used for furniture webbing, for backing linoleum and carpets and for upholstery. A virtual monopoly of world jute production is held by India and Pakistan who produce 90 per cent of the world's supply. The jute-growing area is located in the Ganges-Brahmaputra delta

where great heat and humidity and the monsoonal rains give ideal conditions for the plant. The availability of a large cheap labour force is another important factor, for much labour is required. The plant grows very quickly: from seed planted in April stalks 10–12 ft high are ready for cutting at the end of August. Cutting is done by hand and bundles of stalks are soaked in water for two to four weeks. This retting weakens the outer tissues and the fibre can be freed from the stalk; it is then washed, dried and bleached on bamboo frames.

The Indian spinning and weaving mills, centred on Calcutta, process more than half the jute grown, followed by Pakistan, the United Kingdom and Western Germany. The United States is the major importer of jute goods but weaves practically no cloth. The increasing use of paper bags and sacks and bulk movement

1 Cotton, the most useful textile fibre, is grown in over half the countries of the world. This Guatemalan woman is weaving a cotton shawl.
2 Kapok, a cotton-like fibre which forms inside the seed pods of the kapok tree, is used for filling cushions, mattresses and life-jackets.
3 The sword-like leaves of sisal plants, the source of long fibres used for cord, webbing and sacking, are harvested in Tanzania.
4 Unimproved native breeds of sheep provide wiry, coarse wool. In Turkey it is hand-woven into carpets of traditional design.
5 A girl in Bangkok, Thailand, unreels the long fine, golden silk thread from a silkworm's cocoon and winds it into skeins.

1

3
4

of goods now restrict the expansion of the jute industry, but production has almost doubled since 1948.

Flax is cultivated in temperate lands either for its seed (linseed) or for its fibre. The crop matures in three and a half to four months; much of the harvesting, retting and baling is done by hand and a plentiful, cheap labour supply is necessary. The main producers are the U.S.S.R. and East European countries. The fibre is manufactured into fine linen and has many industrial uses including household linens, cords and twines.

Among the general group of hemp fibres, *sisal* is the most important. It is a strong hard fibre and used for rope, cord and sack manufacture. Sixty per cent of the world's sisal comes from plantations in Tanzania and Kenya and it is also produced in Brazil and Mexico.

Wool is the thick coat of the domesticated sheep. It grows in tufts of up to a dozen fibres and the fleece of a full-grown merino sheep may comprise over 120 million fibres. Merino sheep are the world's foremost wool sheep and are reared best in warm, dry regions. Their sole value lies in their thick heavy fleece as their meat is tough and stringy. These sheep, originally natives of Spain but now reared mainly in the Southern Hemisphere, provide 40 per cent of the world's wool, nearly all of it being used in the clothing industry.

The wool industry

The main merino flocks are in Australia, South Africa and the Argentine. The bulk of the remaining wool is termed *crossbred* but is obtained from both pure breeds as well as crossbreeds. Most of these sheep are English breeds or crosses of them that do well under rainy conditions. Their wool is intermediate between the fineness of the merino and the coarser carpet type. Many of these animals are reared for a dual market – wool and mutton. The largest flocks are in New Zealand, the Argentine and Uruguay, Australia and U.S.S.R. Carpet wool obtained from unimproved native breeds of sheep, often living in arid or mountainous areas, is coarse and wiry and of little use for clothing. It is produced in India, Pakistan, North Africa and the Middle East.

Wool is the major commodity of the Southern Hemisphere countries; they produce about 70 per cent of world supply and account for 80 per cent of world exports. This is understandable, for Australia, New Zealand, the Argentine, South Africa and Uruguay are sparsely peopled and contain large areas which are too dry for agriculture but where sheep can thrive. These animals need the minimum of care and are thus well suited to countries that are lightly populated. (Here are one and a half per cent of the world's population but 40 per cent of the world's sheep.) In addition wool does not deteriorate and is sufficiently valuable to stand the cost of lengthy transport. For these reasons it has proved an ideal export for these more remote Southern Hemisphere lands.

In Australia the principal sheep grazing area lies in a crescent west of the moun-

tainous rim of the southeast of the continent and stretches inland to the desert fringes where no more than 10 in. of rain falls in a year. These conditions are also repeated in the southwest of the continent where there is a second sheep-specializing area. Wool exports make up 35 per cent of Australia's export trade.

The pastures of New Zealand are wetter and favour dual-purpose sheep for both wool and mutton. In the Argentine, the cooler, more arid Patagonia is the home of merino sheep (brought here by Scottish and Welsh settlers) whereas dual-purpose sheep giving crossbred wool are mainly in the moister areas nearer Buenos Aires and in Uruguay.

Britain, the largest importer of wool, takes a fifth of world exports, and is closely followed by Japan. The other major importers are France, the United States, Italy, West Germany and Belgium; together these manufacturing countries import 88 per cent of all wool entering world trade.

Textile manufacture also makes use of other animal hair, some coarse, some fine. Coarse hairs are mainly common goat hair and horse hair. Among the finer hairs are *mohair* and *silk*. Mohair is the long, silky and strong fibres of the angora goat and is widely used in the upholstery trade. The United States, Turkey and South Africa are the world's principal producers; most

exports come from South Africa, and Britain provides the largest market. Silk is a luxury fibre that has now lost ground because of competition from man-made fibres, especially nylon. It is a fine filament produced by the silkworm, reared commercially in Japan, China and Korea on the leaves of the white mulberry tree. World production is small relative to the other major fibres and is used mainly for high-quality textiles.

Man-made fibres, which include nylon, orlon and terylene, are competing with natural fibres and account for 35 per cent of world production; in 1958 they accounted for only 19 per cent. They can be produced in factories in variety, quality and quantity tailored to the taste and volume of the market – a considerable advantage over natural fibres which take many months to grow. Cotton, the world's major fibre, while slowly increasing production, has been steadily losing markets to man-made fibres but wool, a higher-quality product, has been holding its own. Fashion can have a definite effect on this competition; in 1967 mini-skirts and the associated tights reduced the demand for cotton while increasing it for nylon. A great deal of blending of natural and synthetic fibre is taking place, marrying the best of both materials, so that the long-term prospects of natural fibres are by no means gloomy.

1 Flax, which is made into linens, cords and twines, is *retted* (soaked in water) in Co. Down, Northern Ireland, to loosen the fibres from the woody parts of the stalks.

2 At a mill in Montevideo, Uruguay, cotton is twisted into yarns for weaving. Cotton is strong, durable, stores well and can easily be processed by mass-production methods.

Timber!

For centuries the world's forests have provided materials for housing and fuel. Now technology is finding an ever-increasing range of by-products that have earned timber the name of 'green gold'.

TIMBER IS a word which has different meanings to different people. To the practical lumber-jack of the Canadian big-woods, it is the cry that echoes through the forest as a giant tree crashes to the ground. To the economist it is a study in the statistics of area and volume. For the landowner, it has an aesthetic as well as a financial meaning, while for the chemist, timber is a formula in which the chief constituents are cellulose and lignin.

One of the world's principal resources, timber covers about a quarter of the Earth's land surface, a much greater area than is cultivated. Formerly, the forest area was much more extensive but about a third of the originally wooded land has been destroyed or cleared for cultivation. Timber is a renewable resource, although the trees which produce it grow at different speeds according to their type and the climatic conditions. Towards the limits of the areas, growth is slower and its physical appearance differs, so that the annual rings in the tree trunks are closer. Timber has always had a variety of uses for the people who live and move in the forested areas, and the demand for it is increasing beyond these regions.

The families of timber-producing trees have long been distinguished by botanists. The basic division is into *hardwoods*, consisting principally of broad-leaved or deciduous trees which shed their leaves annually, and *softwoods*, chiefly cone-bearing or coniferous trees, which remain for the most part evergreen. There are three main forest zones. In the northern latitudes and mountainous areas, coniferous trees dominate. They consist chiefly of spruces (the Christmas-tree type) on moister soils, and pines on the drier soils. These cold or cool temperate forests are most extensive in the U.S.S.R. and in

Canada, but are limited in the southern hemisphere, where land areas in the higher latitudes are much more restricted. Other types of coniferous trees, such as the larches of the Old World and the tamarack of the New World, shed their needles in winter.

The lands of the Mediterranean have small amounts of highly distinctive conifers – cypresses and cedars among them. Cedarwood has been coveted since Old Testament times and was used by Solomon to build his temple. In California, a New World 'Mediterranean land', grows the most magnificent of all trees – the redwoods. They include the celebrated *Sequoia sempervirens,* the largest and oldest of all living things, which grows up to 300 feet high. The annual rings of Sequoia trees can be counted through thousands of years. The forest cover of the Pacific seaboard of Canada, though lacking these Californian giants, also contains immense timber trees. The valuable

1 A huge mahogany tree is felled with axes in the forests of Ghana. This heavy, dense hardwood, which can be easily carved, stained and glued, is used for furniture and veneers.

2 The equatorial hardwood forests have a thick jungle undergrowth, making the timber difficult and expensive to harvest. In Ghana, roads are cleared for the transport of logs.

Douglas firs are up to 250 feet tall, with trunks 12 feet thick. High altitudes reproduce in some respects the vegetation of high latitudes, so that mountain ranges such as the Himalayas also have their distinctive coniferous species.

The timber trees of temperate latitudes, principally hardwoods, are most extensive in western and central Europe, in the eastern United States and in China. Among those favoured for their timber are the oak, beech, maple, elm and chestnut. Of the three main forest types, the temperate hardwoods are least extensive; they occupy only about 15 per cent of the world's timber-covered area. This is partly because Man's assault upon them has been most intensive and partly because they take longer to renew themselves than the softwood timbers such as the pine and spruce. Under the most favourable conditions, the pine renews itself in about 60 years: the spruce, in less. Hardwoods such as oak or beech take the better part of a century or more.

Bamboo of the north

The one important hardwood associated with the softwood forests is the birch. It serves a variety of purposes in daily life in the cold temperate woodland areas and, for this reason, has been nicknamed the bamboo of the north. It grows quickly and has shared the general revaluation of all timber.

By far the most extensive timber stands are found in tropical and sub-tropical latitudes. Almost half of the world's woodlands consist of evergreen or deciduous hardwoods – ebonies, mahoganies, teaks and similar types, which have heavy, dense timbers. Hardwoods tend to occur as relatively uniform forests in the tropical grassland areas, but as mixed stands in equatorial areas. The equatorial hardwood forests also have a dense jungle of undergrowth and are frequently difficult and expensive to harvest.

By contrast, the softwood forests of higher latitudes have a much more uniform character – the communities of spruce woods and of pine woods are not generally mixed, but stand apart from each other. Both the temperate deciduous woodlands and the softwoods of higher latitudes have a far more open character than the forests of the equatorial hardwoods. It is easy to move between their trees and, therefore, easier to remove logs after felling. The cold temperate softwoods occur mostly in areas where the landscape was modified by the continental ice sheet of the last Ice Age. It is richly veined with rivers, streams and lakes which provide natural waterways for floating the timber to the sawmills. The tropical forests are less generously provided with a natural system of communications – and in any case, the weight and size of tropical hardwoods makes them more difficult to transport than the lighter softwoods.

Climate also plays a role in the harvesting of the high-latitude softwood timbers. Northern Russia, Canada and the Scandinavian countries have prolonged winters, with relatively abundant snow. Although low temperatures close the network of waterways, softwood timber can be easily moved by horse- or tractor-drawn sleighs over the snow-covered ground. The seasonal division of labour between winter lumber-jacking and summer logging still characterizes high-latitude timber-producing lands, but year-round lorry transport is changing this pattern. The formerly casual logging migrations with their associated felling operations are planned today with all the care of military manoeuvres.

Timber has been and remains a more critical constituent of life in higher latitudes than in lower latitudes. It provides material for housing, and fuel for heat, and is consequently fundamental for protection in cooler and colder climates. Demand for timber reaches a maximum in the lands of the temperate hardwoods. These are areas of large population concentrations, of affluent societies where the timber resources have been heavily exploited. Among them, the countries of western Europe and the northeastern part of the United States are the principal consumers. Western Europe draws its timber supplies principally from Scandinavia and Russia; the northeastern United States principally from Canada and the southeastern states. There is also a flow of timber from the tropics to these

areas, though it is more limited in volume and employed for a more restricted range of purposes than that of the coniferous imports.

Western Europe has long looked to the Baltic and Scandinavian lands as a source of timber supply. Deals have been shipped from Norway and Sweden to the cities of Britain, the Low Countries and France for the better part of a thousand years. Some buildings, such as Windsor Castle, Holyrood Palace and the older Cambridge

colleges used Norway pine for their construction. London relied heavily upon south Norwegian and west Swedish timbers for its reconstruction following the Great Fire of 1666. The timbers of the Baltic and Scandinavian lands supplied wood for shipbuilding and for naval needs. In former times vessels might have hulls of oak, but they had hearts of spruce and pine. They were made watertight with pitch, tar and resin which – until alternative methods of supply were realized from

1 In the cool, temperate-latitude forests, the evergreen coniferous trees stand apart and are easy to remove after felling.
2 Modern machinery in a sawmill in South Africa cuts logs into boards and trims off the bark before the timber is seasoned.
3 Softwood boards from Scandinavia, which has supplied timber to Western Europe for over 1,000 years, are unloaded at Poole in Dorset.

methods. The world of printing began to depend upon timber instead of rag and straw, so that the paper, newsprint, wrapping and packaging industries turned to softwood as their principal raw material. Today, large-scale production of sulphate and sulphite pulp from wood takes precedence over sawmilling in most of the timber-producing areas. And while merchants list more than a thousand different kinds of paper in their catalogues, chemists identify an ever-growing range of by-products from contemporary timber processing.

Diversity in timber production has been greatly extended through the wallboard industry, while prefabrication of the components of the building industries introduces new economies into manufacturing. It is already several generations since manufacturers employed the techniques of gluing together thin layers of wood to produce cheap plywoods. The art of laminating hardwood (such as birch) and softwood (such as pine or spruce) has been supplemented by laminating timber with other materials, such as plastics and rubber. Plywood factories also look to a variety of timbers in tropical as well as in high-latitude lands. The extent to which any timber-using industry can turn to tropical supplies greatly adds to the

2 In Sweden, the system of streams, rivers and lakes provides natural waterways for floating the cut and trimmed softwood logs from the forest to the sawmills for processing.

1 Thin boards of softwood, which are seasoned in the open air or in kilns, are stacked at a sawmill in the United States, one of the world's leading timber producers.

coal tar and the Trinidad pitch lake – also derived from the coniferous woodlands. Until a century ago, Britain looked first to the woodlands of Finland and Sweden for its 'naval stores'; while the United States, having exhausted its New England supplies, turned its attention to the so-called Southern pines of the Carolinas, of Florida and Texas.

The Industrial Revolution increased the demand for softwood timbers in both western Europe and northeastern America. The rapidly growing urban areas needed constructional timbers, floorboards, window frames, doors, fences; the spread of railways called for sleepers (originally they were of softwoods, later of tropical hardwoods); mining increased the demand for pitprops; the invention of the telegraph and telephone called for poles to support wires. The introduction of larger steel-plated ships and of steam for their propulsion precipitated a decline in freight rates, while steam saws reduced milling costs. As a result, the range of areas from which timber could be harvested was correspondingly extended.

It was not long before experiments showed that softwood timber could be converted into other products which were in short supply. In the 1870s spruce was already being made into pulp for the manufacture of paper – at first, by mechanical methods, subsequently by chemical

potential of production.

The age of plastics provides substitutes for timber in many fields, yet demand for timber continues to grow and the maintenance and improvement of supplies are critical. Assessment of timber resources has proceeded relatively slowly. Their accurate survey has been eased by aerial photography, but detailed and regular sampling of timber stands is a necessary complement. Surveys of the precise volume of their timber and its speed of renewal have been made of relatively few areas outside Scandinavia (including Finland) and North America. There is no fear of exhaustion of forests as such – Canada and Russia alone have thousands of square miles of untouched softwoods. The problem is that most wooded land lies beyond the commercial limit of exploitation.

The art of silviculture

Two aims are vital for those who plan timber policy – first, to conserve forests which lie within the commercial areas of production; secondly, to increase the yield of timber in the more favourable located areas of supply. *Silviculture* (the cultivation of trees) is rapidly becoming an art to rival agriculture. Not surprisingly, areas where the pressure on supplies is most intense, such as Scandinavia and North America, have become specialists in timber cropping. Seed collection, widespread planting, thinning, draining, disease prevention, fire protection, restraints upon forest grazing, are characteristics of forest management in such areas. The creation of a silvicultural

légende in progressive forest communities serves two purposes. First, it transforms attitudes to the timber harvest, by explaining its associated rotations and long-term returns, and by encouraging an interest in experiment. Secondly, the experiences gained in this manner can be transferred from one area to another; the lessons of the countries advanced in forest management can be profitably passed on to the underdeveloped lands – especially of Latin America, Africa and South East Asia.

Since timber is a bulky product and the operations surrounding it need a great deal of labour, mechanization has eased a variety of operations. The axe remains inviolate, but power-driven saws are the hallmark of all progressive lumbering areas. Power logging (with tractor and cable), power trimming and barking, and mechanical hoisting have all reduced labour outlay and increased speed of operations. If capital is available, such mechanization can also be passed on to developing lands. Saving in the consumption of timber also calls for greater care in processing and for improved seasoning which increases its durability. Timber used for constructional purposes is improved through artificial seasoning and various methods of chemical impregnation. Much timber has been wasted and continues to be wasted; it has been said that out of four trees felled, the equivalent of less than one reaches the consumer as finished products. The amount of waste varies greatly from one operation to another. In veneer manufacture it may exceed 90

per cent, and even in pulp milling it may be more than 60 per cent.

Experts of the Food and Agricultural Organization of the United Nations have estimated that there are 15 million square miles of forest. It is a measure of underdevelopment in the mid-twentieth century that most of the timber cut from them is still used for primary purposes; about two-thirds of the hardwood and nearly a third of the softwood that is felled are used as fuel. Only a modest amount of timber is converted into manufactured goods, though timber for construction accounts for a third of the total cut.

Food from trees

Timber is a multi-purpose commodity and has a great range of uses at each stage of the manufacturing process. Technology extends these alternative uses continuously. The days when bread was made from the powdered phloem of the birch tree in the coniferous forests of Scandinavia and Russia have passed. They are replaced by an age which is capable of converting wood sugar into animal fodder, so that forests even have a potential contribution to make to an underfed world.

Half a century ago Sir James Fraser chose as the title for his epic anthropological study, *The Golden Bough*. It is small wonder that, in earlier times, many peoples attributed magic properties to timber and to the forests. From sub-Arctic Finn to equatorial African, gods of the forest have held their sway; from Ygdrasil, the mighty ash of the Scandinavian sagas to the totem poles of the Pacific coast Indians, timber has had a place in mythology. In the twentieth century, the tangible wealth of timber has earned for it the title of green gold. If magic properties are no longer ascribed to it, many features of its technological conversion come near to the miraculous.

1 In Newfoundland, felled logs are hauled over the snow-covered ground in winter and floated down the streams after the spring thaw.
2 Thousands of logs, enclosed in a boom, are towed by a tug along the Newfoundland coast to the pulp and paper mills.
3 Softwood is the principal raw material of the paper and packaging industries. At a mill, paper is cut into flat sheets.

1

2

3

In the shade of tropical forests

Dark wildernesses teeming with plant and animal life. Vast, barely penetrable storehouses rich in rubber, drugs and valuable timber — these are the great tropical forests of the world.

UNDER THE GREEN FOLIAGE UMBRELLA of tall trees, no wind moves the hot stifling air. Only where a tree has fallen can the sun pierce the constant twilight. From the thin undergrowth to the vaulted canopy a hundred feet or more overhead, the oppressive air is noisy with countless forms of unseen wild life. This is tropical forest: dense and luxuriant, it covers the great lowlands of the Amazon and Congo basins and large parts of southeastern Asia. A huge variety of plants grow quickly in these hot, wet regions; in a few square miles, several hundred different species of trees may be found. Only on river banks, along the forest boundaries, and in clearings, is the undergrowth well developed. Of all the vegetation zones on Earth, these dense forests have proved to be among the most difficult for Man to conquer. As a result, large areas still remain a challenge in a hungry world, and the tropical forests remain one of the least developed parts of the world.

Wild life in the trees

The animal life of dense tropical forests is generally less varied than the plant life. The largest group of creatures, including apes, birds, monkeys, lizards, snakes and tree frogs, live high up in the *canopy* (the upper surface of the forest formed by the crowns of the trees) where food is abundant. Gorillas and chimpanzees live in African forests, and orang-utang and gibbons in the forests of southeastern Asia. Birds, such as the macaws and humming birds of South America, the paradise birds of New Guinea, and parrots, add splashes of colour to their green world. Much of the animal life is difficult to find.

Some creatures never leave the canopy and touch the forest floor, while many other animals are nocturnal. On the gloomy forest floor, animal life is less abundant, because food supplies are often scarce. The rivers form a distinctive environment with such characteristic creatures as the crocodile and the hippopotamus. Animals on the edge of the forest are more abundant, and several, including the elephant and varieties of antelope, often penetrate deep into the forest. Apart from the elephants of southeastern Asia, however, few animals of the tropical forest are useful to Man.

Insects are the most varied form of life. Many carry diseases, such as malaria, yellow fever and sleeping sickness. The prevalence of various diseases has made the forests a hostile environment to Man. Many journeys of exploration in the nine-teenth century ended in disaster, when the members of the expedition succumbed to tropical diseases. The local peoples of these regions also suffer from epidemics, which take their toll of life. Many of the indigenous diseases have now been controlled and some areas, such as the coast of West Africa, are no longer 'the white man's grave'. Because of medical advances, the expectation of life of the local people has lengthened considerably, but constant vigilance is still necessary.

Geographers have suggested that the high incidence of disease, which generally lowers the vitality of the local people, making physical effort difficult, explains why many of the indigenous peoples of the tropical forests are backward. The Ituri forest pygmies of the Congo basin still live by hunting animals and collecting berries

The tangled stems and aerial roots of a banyan tree, a species of fig, grow like a thicket on the moist forested slopes of St Lucia, the most attractive island of the West Indies.

and fruits in the most remote parts of the forests. Living in a similar way are the Indians of the dense *selva* (equatorial forest) of the Amazon basin. Their hostile environment largely determines the peoples' economy and way of life. How long they can survive the penetration of the forest by more advanced civilizations is a matter of conjecture. Such peoples find it difficult to adapt and fit into the rapidly evolving political and economic patterns of the newly developing countries in these areas.

Tropical forests flourish in those parts of the *tropics* (the area between 23° 30′ N. and 23° 30′ S.), where the climatic and soil conditions allow extensive tree growth. In South America, tropical forest covers large sections of the Amazon and Orinoco lowlands and the foothills surrounding the basin, flanking the slopes of the plateaux in Brazil, Bolivia, Venezuela and Paraguay. It also occurs to the north, in the Caribbean and Gulf of Mexico region. It spreads over a less extensive area in Africa, in the Congo basin and on much of the West African coastlands. In south-eastern Asia, forest distribution is more sporadic and its character is rather different, but it covers wide areas in both the southeastern Asian peninsula and the islands of Malaysia, Indonesia and the Philippines. Similar rain forests occur in two areas outside the tropical latitudes: in the hill country of northeastern India, Pakistan and northern Burma; and on the

coastal plain of southern Queensland, Australia.

Two main types of tropical forest can be distinguished: the *selvas* or *equatorial forest,* found where the rainfall is distributed fairly evenly throughout the year; and the *monsoon forests,* which have a marked dry season. The temperatures are always well above the minimum required for plant growth, and the boundary of the tropical forests conforms generally with the 68 °F. isotherm for the coldest month. In addition, the rainfall must be heavy and well distributed throughout the year, often ranging between 80 and 160 inches.

Heavy rain and good soil

The equatorial forests grow in regions where there is no month without rain. In some places, rain falls every afternoon and at night on every day of the year. The monsoon forest covers areas where the overall rainfall is so heavy that there is always sufficient ground water to sustain the growth of large trees during the dry season. A further requirement for the development of such forests is that the soil must be deep and well drained. While many of the soils of wet tropical areas have been *leached* (rainwater has washed the minerals in the soil down to the lower layers) the heavy leaf fall from the luxuriant vegetation provides a constant source of humus. In hot, moist conditions, rapid bacterial decomposition takes place.

Such are the conditions of soil and climate that the tallest trees grow to great heights, often more than 100 feet. Their exceptional height is largely the result of the perpetual struggle of most plants to reach the light. The tallest trees rise above

the general level of the forest as *emergents*. Below the occasional emergents, shorter trees form a canopy over all other species. The trees reaching the canopy generally have long, straight trunks and spread out at the highest level. In many parts of the forest, this canopy layer is almost complete. Below the canopy other trees, which are smaller and slender, have a conical form similar in appearance to the coniferous trees of northern latitudes. When the canopy is broken, these smaller trees are more highly developed.

At the dim, sunless lower levels there is little ground vegetation. Herbaceous plants thrive in places where sunlight reaches the forest floor. Elsewhere, *saprophytes,* plants that contain little or no chlorophyll, obtain their nutriment from dead organic matter. One of the most impressive features of the plant life of tropical forests is the widespread growth of creepers and lianes (or lianas). The lianes hang from branches, twine around the trees, often binding the trunks together as they spread throughout the forest. Sometimes a tree will remain standing after it has been cut because it is held in position by the lianes. These woody climbers may reach a foot in diameter and their clearance is another hindrance to the economic exploitation of tropical forests.

At higher levels, where there is more sunlight, many trees support parasitic shrubs or bushes known as *epiphytes.*

In the dense tropical forest of Antigua, the trees are tangled with lianes and creepers. Parasitic shrubs, called *epiphytes,* grow on the branches and trunks of the trees.

A heavy annual rainfall and high temperatures ensure the rapid growth of hundreds of species of trees, flowering plants and ferns in the luxuriant forests of Hawaii.

forest with many intervening trees. The more important trees include ebony, mahogany, the oil palm, rosewood, cedar, rubber and teak. In many places, large tracts of what was once tropical forest have been cleared.

In the clearings, plantations have been established where the trees can be easily managed, scientific techniques applied, and the products readily extracted. In 1900, the world's supply of rubber came from the *Hevea braziliensis* or rubber tree. The rubber was collected from trees in their natural habitat. The plant is indigenous to the Amazon basin, and the Brazilian government strictly prohibited the export of seeds or shoots. But in 1876, some seeds were smuggled out to Kew in London, and these later formed the basis of rubber plantations in the Malayan peninsula, then the Dutch East Indies. Today about three-quarters of the world's rubber comes from plantations; the rest comes from synthetic rubber processes. Similarly, the bulk of the world's palm oil now comes from plantations along the West African coast whereas, until recently, Africans gathered it from wild trees.

The most useful of the hardwoods found in tropical forests is mahogany. Mahogany has been cut in many areas near water and the trees floated downstream for export or

1 In Trinidad the clouds hang low over the rain forest during the regular wet season, which lasts from May to January.
2 On the banks of the muddy Amazon river, the forest crowds down to the water's edge, thick with undergrowth. Below the few tall emergent trees, the others struggle upwards towards the light under a canopy of foliage.

These plants cling to the trunks, branches, and even grow on the leaves of trees. *Stranglers* are plants which start as epiphytes but send long roots down to the ground. They often coil around a tree and eventually kill it. The strangling fig encases a tree and continues to live and grow after the tree has died.

The vegetation of monsoon forests is generally not so luxuriant as in equatorial forests. Trees tend to be more widely spaced. During the dry season, many of the trees shed their leaves, although some evergreens retain their foliage. But leaf-shedding does not give the forests the lifeless appearance of temperate deciduous forests in winter, partly because many plants flower in the dry season.

Evergreen forests

Most of the trees found in tropical forests are evergreens, although they do in fact shed their leaves. They remain green overall, because leaf-shedding is not conditioned by any seasonal rhythm but is a continuous process, moisture and temperature conditions being sufficient for growth at all times. The shed leaves provide an abundant and never-ending supply of humus on the ground. The trunks of the tallest trees are straight and the dominant species are hardwoods. Many of the trees are of economic importance, but the species generally do not grow in stands, but are widely scattered throughout the

for processing. The remote and isolated forest interiors have, as yet, been largely untouched. The main sources of supply lie in the coastlands of British Honduras and the Dominican Republic, around the shores of the Caribbean Sea, in the forests of West Africa, and in southeastern Asia and the Philippines. The most easily worked of all tropical trees is cedar, and it ranks second to mahogany in production. Teak is an important export of Thailand, Burma and Indonesia. It is resistant to fire and to white ants, and does not corrode as easily as some other hardwoods.

Other valuable commodities collected in tropical forests include chicle, balata, several drugs and tannin. Chicle, the basis

The trees of the evergreen forest in Tanzania are festooned with lichens. The treetops are alive with feeding mammals such as mice and squirrels, and brilliantly coloured birds.

of chewing gum, comes from the Zapote tree, which grows in the forests of Belize (British Honduras) and Mexico. Balata, used in the making of cables and the outside covering of golf balls, comes largely from the rain forests of South America, and Brazil nuts are found in the same area. Drugs, such as camphor and quinine, also grow wild, but the importance of gathering has declined since the introduction of plantations and synthetic products. The bark and leaves of mangrove trees, found in the swamps of

tropical forests, yield valuable tannin, used in tanning leather. Tannin also comes from the Quebracho tree and from a number of other roots and plants.

How much of the tropical forest of the present time represents the *climax vegetation* of the area, that is, the most flourishing type of natural vegetation which could develop under the prevailing soil and climatic conditions? For thousands of years, many of the peoples of the tropical forests have practised a system of agriculture called *shifting cultivation*. Under this system, a patch of forest was cleared, a temporary settlement established, and the land continuously cultivated for subsistence crops until the fertility of the soil was impaired. Then the clearing and settlement was abandoned and the settlers moved to a new clearing, beginning the cycle all over again. Land was normally cleared by burning, which even in a moist climate can destroy large areas of natural vegetation. Such cultivation is clearly suited to a very low density of population and a low level of economic life. Recently, shifting agriculture has been largely abandoned, but large areas must have been affected by this constant forest clearance.

When a clearing has been abandoned, a secondary growth rapidly reasserts itself. Where the period of cultivation has been short, the secondary vegetation resembles the original, and something approaching a climatic climax may be achieved. But where the land has been stripped of its protective forest cover for a longer period, the lack of humus makes the soil completely inorganic, and the climatic climax vegetation may never return. Cultivators have affected large areas of West African forests, and it is likely that little of the original forest cover remains. In South America, the inroads have probably been far less great and the forest is largely of the climatic climax type.

Valuable agricultural land

Perhaps the most dramatic of all the vegetation types, tropical forests offer a great challenge to Man. They contain many valuable products unobtainable elsewhere, and today their future lies in the balance. In more accessible areas, and those with a dense and rapidly growing population, vast inroads have already been made into the traditional and natural landscape. The rice lands of southeastern Asia, the most abundant granary of the world, have replaced vast areas of forest, and plantations, particularly in Asia, now cover large areas. But the process still has far to go. Only one-sixth of the total land area of Malaysia is cultivated and large stretches of forest still separate densely settled valleys and plains.

UNESCO has begun an extensive programme of research and investigation into the problems and possibilities of the moist tropical regions. Agricultural research stations are now operating in most of the developing countries of this region. In countries where the population is at present confined to only a small part of the country's surface area, the natural forests have a tremendous potential for a more economic use of the land they cover.

A porter hacks his way through the tangled rain forest of Brazil. Here there are no distinct seasons; leaves fall, flowers bloom and fruit ripens all the year round.

Pygmies still live by hunting animals with bows and arrows or nets in remote parts of the Congo rain forests. Their diet is supplemented by nuts, roots, berries, ants and mushrooms.

The world's mineral wealth

For thousands of years, Man has tapped the vast supplies of minerals stored in the Earth's crust. It is on this successful exploitation that civilization and technological progress depend.

CIVILIZATION DEPENDS for its survival on the provision of a wide range of minerals drawn from the great storehouse of the Earth. Were the supply of these to cease, there would no longer be the metals, fuels, fertilizers, chemicals and building materials needed for our present way of life. Progress in utilizing this mineral wealth largely determines the rising standard of living, a relationship acknowledged by the terms 'Stone Age', 'Bronze Age' and 'Iron Age' to denote the main stages of technological advance.

Every natural element exists in the Earth's crust, but in widely varying quantities. Oxygen forms just under half and silicon a further quarter, while the familiar metals aluminium (8 per cent) and iron (5 per cent) rank third and fourth. However, apart from these, the only commonly used metals to be found among the 20 most abundant elements are manganese (0·1 per cent) and chromium (0·02 per cent). All the other useful metals – copper, gold, lead, tin and zinc, to name a few – are present only in traces. For example, the crust contains only 0·007 per cent of copper and 0·0000005 per cent of gold.

Fortunately the useful metals are not distributed evenly throughout the Earth's crust but each occurs here and there in unusual quantities. Where the rocks forming a portion of the crust contain a sufficiently high proportion of a particular metal, it is commercially possible to mine it and extract the metal content. Such metal-rich rocks are the ore-deposits.

Metal in molten rock

From time to time molten rock from the deeper parts of the Earth has been emplaced within the crust and has sometimes brought with it vast quantities of metallic elements. As a mass of molten rock cools, the metals it contains can be concentrated by two processes. In some cases, as the temperature drops, a portion rich in ore separates and, being denser, sinks to accumulate near the base. Such *segregation ore-deposits* are rare but, because of their large size, are of great value; the deposits of nickel at Sudbury, Ontario, and of chromium in Rhodesia were formed in this way. More frequently such a portion does not form but, as the mass of molten rock cools and solidifies, the valuable metals are retained in the portion which remains liquid. The last one or two per cent to remain molten contain a very high proportion of the tin, lead, copper or other metals. On further cooling the ore-rich *mineralizing solutions* may either deposit their metals within the once-molten mass or may escape and form ore-deposits in the surrounding rocks. Deposits which have been formed in this way include the lead-zinc ores of Broken Hill, Australia, and, on a smaller scale, the tin and copper veins of Cornwall.

Sedimentary ore-deposits were formed on the surface of the Earth in the same way as beds of rock such as limestone. Chemical and biological processes are very efficient in extracting from water metals present only in traces and, where conditions proved favourable in the past, have built up vast deposits, largely of iron and manganese ores, such as those mined in Lorraine and the Crimea.

A third group of ore-deposits owes its origin to a combination of sub-surface and surface processes of concentration. The ore minerals were first formed within the crust, either as segregations or by mineralizing solutions. Subsequently they were exposed at the surface and broken up by the weather. If the ore was chemically stable, its particles, being denser, tended to remain behind while wind erosion, rain-wash or stream action removed the lighter constituents. Such deposits are called *residual* if they have remained at or near their original position, *eluvial* if they

1 Aluminium, the world's most abundant metal, is obtained from bauxite. At this factory near a bauxite mine in Hungary, the silvery, light-weight metal is made into tubes.
2 Workers return to the surface after a shift underground at an iron-ore mine in Israel. Iron is the most widely used of all metals.
3 Cassiterite, the main tin ore, is dredged from a mine in Nigeria. The ore is separated from the gravel in sluice boxes.

have been concentrated by rain-wash and gravity, and *alluvial* or *placers* if they have been formed by streams. It was the rich gold-bearing placers of California which caused the 1849 gold-rush.

Chemically unstable ore-deposits can also be concentrated when they are broken up by the weather. Many such deposits react with the air to form sulphuric acid. The acid attacks the ore, converts the metals it contains to sulphates and removes the soluble sulphates downwards in solution. The solutions react with the unaltered ore below, and the metals they contain are precipitated. By this means, as the upper part of the deposit is eroded away, its metal content is not lost but is carried downwards to produce the phenomenon known as *secondary enrichment*.

Modern 'Iron Age'

Iron, the backbone of modern industry, is the most widely used and indispensable of all metals. To supply the world's annual needs of some 300 million tons of metal, twice that tonnage of ore has to be mined – the volume produced in five days equals that of Egypt's Great Pyramid. The largest producers are the U.S.S.R., the United States and France, and substantial contributions come from Sweden, Venezuela, Britain, Canada and West Germany. The metal is extracted from four minerals: magnetite, the richest, forms the famous segregation deposits of Kiruna and Gellivare in northern Sweden and is also abundant in the Ural Mountains. The commonest ore is haematite; formed by mineralizing solutions it is sedimentary in origin. Limonite and siderite are also sedimentary, the former is the principal ore worked in Lorraine, while the latter is mined in eastern England.

Several million tons of aluminium are produced each year, largely for use in aeroplanes, vehicles and ships and in the electric industry. Over 40 million tons of bauxite, the only important ore, are extracted annually, the major suppliers being the southern Caribbean countries, the United States, the U.S.S.R. and France. Bauxite is a residual ore formed where rocks rich in aluminium are weathered in a moist, hot climate. Under such conditions the rock-forming minerals are broken up and their products *leached* (washed down by rain). Only aluminium oxide and ferric oxide (found in bauxite as an impurity) are insoluble and remain after all the other constituents are removed. In Guyana, Surinam and Jamaica bauxite is still forming; in France, the United States and northern Russia the mines work bauxite formed many millions of years ago when the climate was warmer.

Copper is a metal greatly in demand for the electrical and chemical industries. Its alloy with zinc, brass, has many uses, while large quantities are used in coins. Several million tons are mined each year, the largest producers being the United States, the U.S.S.R., Chile, Zambia, Canada, and Zaire. While deposits of iron and aluminium ore must contain more than 25 per cent of their metals to be valuable, copper ores containing as little as 1 per cent copper can be worked at a profit if

1

the deposit is big enough to pay for highly mechanized working. Although almost 400 different copper ores are known (the largest number for any metal), the majority are of minor importance. Chalcopyrite is the most important and was characteristically formed by mineralizing solutions. Ores produced by secondary enrichment include the basic copper carbonates, malachite (a spectacular green mineral used in jewellery) and azurite. Native (uncombined) copper occurs naturally, the best known locality being in northern Michigan where the biggest 'nugget' of copper found weighed over 400 tons.

The most obvious uses of lead are in bullets, plumbing and building. Most of the production, however, is used in car batteries, cable coverings, anti-knock petrol, paint, solder and type metal. Lead is produced in similar quantities to copper, the chief deposits being in the U.S.S.R., Australia, the United States, Mexico and Canada. Typically they are formed by mineralizing solutions and consist almost entirely of the grey, cubic mineral galena which generally contains a small proportion of silver as a welcome 'impurity' and is the source of much of the world's silver supply. Britain's former richness in lead was one of the reasons why the Romans (who used it for lining aqueducts and plumbing their baths) incorporated England and Wales in their empire.

Although few people see or handle the metal, several million tons of manganese are produced annually. It is used in the smelting of iron, the production of manganese steels, and its ores, sedimentary in

origin, are raw materials for the chemical industry and the manufacture of dry batteries. About half the world's output comes from the Ukrainian and Caucasian fields of the U.S.S.R. – other important suppliers include India, Brazil, South Africa and Ghana.

Although tin is a much more familiar metal than manganese, its annual production is only about a quarter of a million tons. Its principal uses are in the manufacture of tin-plate, in alloys, solders, bearing metals and in the chemical industry. The only important ore, cassiterite, has been formed by mineralizing solutions derived from some granitic rocks. Cornwall and Spain were formerly important tin suppliers but today the bulk of the world's supply comes from Malaysia, Indonesia, China and Thailand.

Not all minerals are mined for the metals they contain. A few are worked for the extraction of a non-metallic element, such as sulphur, while others are used directly in industry.

The value of asbestos lies in its properties – resistance to fire, fibrous texture, flexibility, chemical inertness and insulating powers for both heat and electricity. Its uses are many and varied – roofing material, building boards, fireproof cloth, brake and clutch linings for cars, firemen's ropes and acid-resistant filters. World production, about two million tons per annum, comes largely from eastern Canada, the U.S.S.R., southern Africa and Japan.

Half a million tons of graphite are mined each year, largely in Korea, the U.S.S.R.,

1 A huge, open-cast copper mine at Chingola in Zambia. The metal is widely used by the chemical and electrical industries.
2 A prospector uses a geiger-counter to test a rock face for radioactive metals.
3 Rock salt, which was formed as sedimentary rock when isolated arms of the sea evaporated, is found in many countries of the world. This deposit is in southwest Africa.
4 Red-hot strips of steel, an alloy of iron and small amounts of other minerals, are rolled out at a works in Newcastle, New South Wales.
5 Copper, which has been in use since the Stone Age, can be easily hammered and shaped. These utensils are on sale at a Turkish market.

Austria and Mexico. The mineral is used extensively in crucibles, lubricants and 'lead' pencils.

Gypsum and the related mineral anhydrite are used for the manufacture of plaster, as a filler for paper and cotton and as raw materials in the chemical industry. The minerals were formed as residues laid down when ancient seas became dry. The United States, Britain, Canada, France and the U.S.S.R. supply much of the 40 million tons mined annually.

Mica is flexible, transparent, fire-resistant, an excellent electrical insulator and can be split into very thin sheets; it is used mainly in the electrical industry. Large crystals occur in very coarse-grained varieties of granite and these are extensively worked in India, Madagascar, eastern Siberia, Brazil and the United States. Annual production is about 150,000 tons.

Phosphates are very extensively used as

Millions of tons of phosphate, which is widely used as a fertilizer, are produced from this mine in Florida. The mineral is separated from the host material and loaded for transport.

fertilizers; part of the demand is met by basic slag from blast furnaces but most of the remainder is obtained from the mineral apatite which occurs as magmatic segregations and in veins of unusual composition. About 80 million tons are produced yearly, mainly by the United States, Morocco, the U.S.S.R. and Tunisia.

Rock salt, one of the most important raw materials of the chemical industry, is used for the manufacture of caustic soda, washing soda, sodium sulphate and chlorine, and is widely employed throughout industry and in the home. In origin it is a sedimentary rock formed when isolated arms of the sea, replenished with salt water during storms and high tides, were evaporated to dryness. Over 100 million tons are worked annually, the United States being the largest producer while China, the U.S.S.R. and Britain are other major sources.

The chief uses of sulphur lie in the chemical industry and in rubber manufacture. In volcanic regions crystals of sulphur, deposited by escaping gases, frequently occur and once provided the only source of supply. Now most of the annual production of ten million tons comes from sedimentary deposits around the Gulf of Mexico. Much of the sulphur used by the chemical industry is derived, not from the element itself, but from sulphur dioxide produced by the roasting of iron pyrites; anhydrite is also used as a source of sulphur-bearing compounds.

The search for ore began as soon as metals came to supplant stone as the most desirable raw material. It led the Ancient Egyptians to the Sudan, it brought the Phoenicians to the shores of Cornwall and it encouraged medieval Europe to explore and colonize the world. At first success depended on chance, but with

The search for ores is now a highly developed science. A favourable site for bauxite has been found in Australia and test holes are drilled to establish the presence of the ore.

growing experience, prospecting developed first into an art and later into a science.

Geology has been applied to the search for ore for many years. Many ores are associated only with certain types of rock, while some rocks, such as limestone, readily react with mineralizing solutions and are therefore especially favourable sites for the deposition of ore. A study of geological maps, on which the distribution of the different rock types is shown, can point to where the best chances of finding ore lie. Stresses originating within the Earth have compressed the rocks of the crust into folds and have broken and displaced them along great cracks known as faults. Faults provide natural channels for mineralizing solutions, and folds influence the concentration of ore. An understanding of the complex pattern of faults and folds is therefore very useful in finding ore-deposits. A geological study of a sequence of bedded rocks can determine the changing climatic conditions of the past and provide clues to the likelihood of the existence of sedimentary ores, whereas an investigation into the development of a landscape is an essential preliminary to any search for residual, eluvial and alluvial deposits.

In search of ores

Geophysical methods of prospecting use the differences in physical properties which distinguish ore bodies from normal rocks; these, though very small, can be detected on the very sensitive instruments developed for this purpose. Most ores are denser than normal rocks and show their presence by a slight increase in the force of gravity on the overlying surface. Some ores, in particular magnetite – the lodestone of the Ancients – are magnetic and disturb compass needles. Shock waves and electric currents are transmitted differently through ore bodies and normal rocks, and the ores of the radioactive metals can be detected through their activity.

Geochemical methods of prospecting search for unusual concentrations of metals in soils and plants. Over great areas the bed-rock – and any ore it might contain – is obscured by soil. Soils are largely composed of disintegrated and decomposed rock and those formed from an ore body contain greater concentrations of the ore metals than soils formed from normal rock. Plants growing on metal-rich soils also contain unusually high amounts of metal and point to the probable existence of a nearby ore body.

After an ore-deposit has been found, it is explored, sampled and evaluated by boreholes. The size, form and metal content are estimated and considered in conjunction with a number of other factors – the price obtainable for the ore, the ease of transport from the site, the distance to potential markets, the likelihood of recruiting local labour and the political stability of the area. If the project seems unlikely to prosper the deposit will remain untouched. If, however, enough factors are favourable, the costly operation of mining will begin to supply an increasingly industrialized world with raw materials.

Black diamonds

Millions of years ago, vast amounts of coal were formed in the Earth's crust. This store of power has long been a source of fuel and now provides the raw material for many major industries.

1

2

FOR OVER 200 YEARS, coal has been Man's major source of power and the basis of industrial civilization. It sustained the Industrial Revolution, fed the Age of Steam and today, when there is a tendency to regard it as an outdated fuel, world production continues to rise. Over 3,000 years ago, coal was used for funeral pyres in South Wales; it is referred to in the Bible; it is mentioned by the ancient Greeks, and cinders from coal fires have been found in Roman buildings in England. Throughout the Middle Ages it was burned locally in England as a substitute for firewood and by 1200 ships were carrying coal from Newcastle to London. But it was not until the sixteenth century, when wood became scarce and expensive, that coal mining increased and by 1770 British output exceeded six million tons. By 1894 world output had risen to 600 million tons, had reached 1,400 million tons 50 years later and today amounts to 2,800 million tons – slightly less than a ton for each of the world's population.

Energy from the sun

Coal is a 'fossil fuel' composed of the remains of plants which lived millions of years ago. As they grew, the plants absorbed energy from the sun to build their tissues. When these tissues, now coal, are burned, the energy that first reached the Earth as sunshine millions of years ago is released.

The first requirement for the formation of coal is luxuriant vegetation. Normally when plants die and fall to the ground they are entirely decomposed by bacteria and fungi. The plants that formed coal seams grew quickly in temperate and subtropical climates where decomposition was slow and greatly hindered by submergence in stagnant water. The dead and partly decomposed vegetation accumulated until subsidence brought the area below sea level, burying the vegetation

1 Deep underground in a Nottinghamshire coal mine, a powerful machine cuts and loads coal from the side and roof of a seam.

under muds and sands. Swamps and low-lying coastal areas, therefore, provided particularly suitable conditions for coal formation. During millions of years of burial, often beneath thousands of feet of rock, the plant remains were altered by the pressure of the rocks and by the rise in temperature in the depths of the Earth's crust. They lost most of their resemblance to woody material and became the black substance familiar today.

The earliest stage in the formation of the coal is peat, still burned as a fuel in many countries of the world. This forms wherever plants grow in swampy conditions and is an accumulation of partly

In spite of safety measures, many accidents still occur in coal mines. An explosion of methane gas at this Yugoslavian mine killed 115 miners.

2 Plants that grew in swamps and on lowlands and were later submerged to form coal are often found as fossils, such as these ferns, in coal.

decomposed plant material – the plants it contains can be identified quite easily by botanists. Some biochemical breakdown of the vegetable matter takes place and is caused by peculiar types of bacteria which extract the oxygen they need, not from the water in which they live (because this, being stagnant, does not contain any) but from the plant material they 'feed' on. These bacteria produce the gas methane – the gas which causes the flickering 'will-o'-the-wisp' seen over peat bogs.

When peat is buried under other rocks and compressed, a number of further changes take place. The vegetable material becomes less easily recognizable, water is squeezed out, more methane and other gases are produced by bacterial action and are lost, the material loses its porous, fibrous nature and becomes much more

of plant material can be seen. Anthracite occurs in quantity in Pennsylvania, where 50 million tons a year are mined; about $4\frac{1}{2}$ million tons are produced annually in South Wales.

The discovery of coal seams depends on identifying sequences of sedimentary rock formed in conditions favourable for the accumulation of vegetable matter. Such rocks show evidence of accumulation at or near sea level, including features such as fossil ripple marks (resembling the ripples seen on sandy beaches) and systems of polygonal cracks (similar to those seen where mudflats dry up). The fossils they contain should be a mixture of marine and freshwater forms. Once likely rock sequences have been identified, their outcrops can be mapped and test boreholes sunk. By investigation of the geological structure of wide areas it is possible to predict the occurrence of potentially coal-bearing rocks beneath younger strata and these predictions can again be tested by

1 Shafts to underground coal mines are fitted with winding gear to lift coal and miners from the workings to the surface.
2 At a modern mine in Britain, coal is separated from impurities, graded and loaded for transport by streamlined machinery.
3 At the world's largest open-cast coal mine, at Fushun in China, the thickest known deposits of coal lie close to the surface.

compact. As a result of these changes peat is converted to *lignite* or brown coal. Deposits of this material are usually found in relatively young rocks and are extensively worked in East Germany, the U.S.S.R., West Germany, China and Hungary. Lignite crumbles rapidly on exposure to the air and when burnt only gives about half as much heat as good quality coal. Total production amounts to approximately 700 million tons per year.

Plant material which has been buried deeper in the Earth for many millions of years undergoes further consolidation, during which it loses more water and gases and is converted into bituminous coal – the coal used in Britain. The fragments of vegetable matter cannot easily be seen with the naked eye and the coal consists of a series of bands of different appearance and composition representing variations in the original vegetable matter. Bituminous coal does not break up significantly when exposed to the weather and can therefore be stored in vast heaps. The production of bituminous coal is approximately 2,000 million tons per year. The main producers are the United States, the U.S.S.R., China and Britain, while important contributions are made by West Germany, Poland, France, Japan, India and South Africa.

If bituminous coal is subjected not only to deep burial, but also to heat from nearby volcanic rocks (for example, the feeding pipes of volcanoes) or to folding caused by disturbances in the Earth's crust, it rapidly loses most of its remaining moisture and gaseous constituents and is converted into anthracite. This is a hard, compact, rock-like material which has a glassy lustre and shows little banding. No traces

drilling a series of boreholes.

The coal burned by prehistoric Man and by the Romans came from outcrops or was 'sea coal' collected from the sea shore. About 800 years ago, however, coal was mined in *bell-pits*. A shaft was sunk to a shallow coal seam and the coal worked in all directions from the shaft. Sufficient overlying rock was removed to prevent collapse and a bell-shaped cavity was made. When the base of the pit exceeded a certain area and the roof was liable to collapse, the pit was abandoned. Large numbers of these 'bell-pits' were sunk in British coalfields wherever flat-lying coal seams occur near the surface; their positions are unmapped and they are now a hazard to mining and building.

In the typical modern coal mines, the coal-bearing strata are reached by two or more shafts, one at least with winding gear to raise the coal and waste rock and to provide access for the miners. The other shaft, or shafts, provide ventilation and can be used as emergency exits. From the bottom of the shafts, a system of 'main roads' is cut through the coal. In some pits a grid of narrow roads is cut parallel and at right angles to the main roads, dividing areas of the coal seam into squares. The coal is removed from the edges of the squares, leaving pillars to support the roof. This form of mining – the *pillar and stall system* – is used where the

1 A charge of explosive is put into a hole drilled in an underground coal face and detonated by electricity to break up the coal.
2 Pit ponies, first introduced into coal mines in the eighteenth century, are still used to pull trucks of pit props in a Yorkshire mine.

seams have been broken by earth disturbances into relatively small areas or where subsidence of the surface above must be avoided. If subsidence is permissible, the pillars are removed in succession and the roof allowed to sink.

In the mines worked on the *long-wall system*, the entire coal seam, apart from that around the foot of the shaft and beside the main roads, is removed in one operation; long coal faces are steadily and evenly advanced and the waste material produced with the coal is stacked where the coal has been mined to give partial support to the roof. Along each face where the miners are working the roof is held up by pit props. These are removed as the face moves forward and the roof over the worked-out zone allowed to sink.

Gradual mechanization of coal mining has been in progress for many years but has only recently become rapid. The earliest machines, which replaced human labour, were horse gins to raise coal up the shafts and steam pumps to prevent flooding. The first practicable steam engine was designed in 1712 for pumping water from mines and was later used for raising material up the shafts, although in the early nineteenth century women were still carrying coal in baskets up ladders to the surface and hand windlasses and horse gins persisted until the 1840s. At first all transport of coal from the faces to the shafts was by human effort; women and

A massive power shovel strips away earth and rock to uncover a coal seam 90 feet below the surface in the United States.

Peat, the earliest stage in the formation of coal, is used as a fuel. Here a loader transfers dried turfs on to trucks in Ireland.

children were employed to haul coal on sledges or in small wheeled trucks. When pit ponies were introduced, about 1763, they were too high to work except along the main roads. Steam-driven rope haulage of trucks was introduced in 1812 and was common by 1840, though boys were still employed as draught animals on the subsidiary roads. Electricity now powers the winding gear in the shafts, and small electric locomotives move the coal and waste rock underground.

Cutting out the coal

The coal which powered the Industrial Revolution was blasted by black powder and extracted by hand pick and crowbar. Towards the end of the nineteenth century the first coal cutter, which worked like a circular saw and was driven by compressed air, was introduced. Later this was replaced by electric coal cutters, and in 1902 conveyors for transporting coal from the coal face to nearby trucks were in use. More recent introductions include machines which remove several inches of coal from the bottom of the seam, allowing the remaining coal to break up more easily when blasted, and continuous mining machines which remove the whole of the seam at the rate of several tons per minute. The use of such machines, however, is restricted to parts of the coal seam which are relatively flat-lying and in which long faces can be worked.

Roof falls were the original hazard of coal mining in bell-pits and, despite many centuries of progress, they are still the chief cause of colliery accidents. In shallow mines the only gas encountered was carbon dioxide, called 'black damp' by the miners; it caused little danger for, though it suffocates, it is easily detected as it extinguishes naked lights. When explosives were introduced into the mines, poisonous carbon monoxide or 'after damp' was produced. This gas is difficult to detect and only improved ventilation could prevent disasters.

As mines grew deeper, a new hazard, methane or 'fire damp', was encountered. This gas, which forms explosive mixtures with air, is produced in the formation of coal. At first certain miners acted as 'firemen' and, dressed in wet sacks for protection, crawled along the workings carrying a lighted candle on a long pole to explode any methane present. This method of dealing with methane was extremely hazardous and caused many deaths; these led Sir Humphry Davy to invent in 1816 his famous lamp which could be used with safety in a methane-charged atmosphere and also indicated the presence of the gas. The Davy lamp was used for many years until supplanted by electric lights. Further hazards in coal mining lie in the risk of workings breaking into old flooded mines or into waterlogged deposits of sand and gravel lying above the solid rock. In areas which contain many old uncharted workings, they can be avoided by not coming within 200 or 300 feet of the surface where such mines are likely to occur. Adequate geological knowledge, based on the sinking of trial boreholes, can greatly reduce the risks of leaving the solid rock and breaking into superficial deposits.

Great quantities of coal are used as a fuel in the production of electric power, in industrial processes and in the home; until the introduction of diesel traction, the railways were also large customers. Much coal is used as an industrial raw material, principally for the production of coke – coal gas and a large number of other substances being obtained at the same time. Coke is an important industrial commodity used as a source of carbon – used mainly in the smelting of iron and other ores, in the production of industrial gases and as a smokeless fuel.

About 40 million tons of coal are converted to coke in Britain every year. Each ton yields about $14\frac{1}{2}$ cwt of coke and 11,000 cu. ft of gas (not all of this is available for sale or use as almost half of it is required to heat the ovens in which the coal is roasted), as well as about $7\frac{1}{2}$ gallons of tar, three gallons of crude benzol and 25 lb of ammonium sulphate. These by-products are used widely in a whole range of industries and form the raw material for plastics, synthetic fabrics, fertilizers, insecticides, disinfectants, preservatives, dyes, synthetic rubber, paint colorants and solvents, drugs, explosives, perfumes and many other products. A large part of the world's chemical industry, both industrial and pharmaceutical, is based on coal and whatever the future may hold for coal as a fuel, it will certainly always be required as a raw material by these industries.

In some of the most developed parts of the world, coal production has reached a peak and is now tending to decline as other and more sophisticated fuels take its place. Elsewhere, however, production is still increasing. It would appear probable that world coal production will reach a maximum in the foreseeable future for, as the most accessible and profitable seams are worked out, costs rise and coal becomes less competitive with other fuels – oil, natural gas and radioactive metals.

Coal in the future

The coal resources of the world have been estimated at 5 million million tons of coal (including anthracite) and perhaps 2 million million tons of lignite. At the present rate of production these reserves would be sufficient for 2,500 years. In view of the progressive development of newer fuels – in particular atomic energy – the coal reserves are more than sufficient for the foreseeable future. Even if oil reserves were to be exhausted tomorrow and mankind forced to depend solely on coal (from which petrol can be made at a price), the reserves of coal would last for 1,000 years. Although the future of the coal industry in some countries, including Britain, is perhaps somewhat bleak in the short term, there is at least the certainty that the world industry is not going to fail through lack of the coal to mine.

'Gushers' and gas

All over the world the search goes on for oil and natural gas, trapped in domes of rock deep in the Earth. Formed millions of years ago, these fuels are now the raw materials for many huge industries.

THE AGE OF PETROLEUM began just before the First World War and since then has shaped our lives both in peace and war. Petroleum is the fuel that now provides the energy to turn most of the wheels of industry, transport and agriculture, and oils and greases them so that they run smoothly.

The petroleum found in the Earth is an extremely complex mixture of hundreds of different *hydrocarbons* – compounds of carbon and hydrogen – accompanied by small amounts of more complex substances of nitrogen, oxygen and sulphur. Among the hydrocarbons, members of the paraffin group predominate and range from gases such as methane to liquids including hexane, heptane and octane (constituents of petrol), and solids such as paraffin wax.

How was petroleum formed? It contains nothing from which its origins are easily recognized, it shows no stages of development and, once formed, does not seem to develop further. Indirect evidence, however, leads to the conclusion that petroleum forms from organic matter, both animal and vegetable, which accumulates with muddy sediment in stagnant parts of the sea. Highly specialized bacteria can extract the oxygen they need from the organic debris and in so doing convert it

into fatty and waxy substances. These, when buried by the accumulation of more sediments, are subjected to a rise in pressure and temperature and are converted into petroleum, while the surrounding mud becomes the rock known as *shale*.

How long it takes for petroleum to form is unknown but the period required is certainly less than ten million years – a short period on the geological time-scale and much less than the 200 million or more years required to form coal. Sediments which will eventually be a source of petroleum are known to be accumulating at present in various parts of the world, such as in the deep stagnant parts of the Black Sea.

Crude petroleum is, therefore, formed in fine-grained, muddy rocks. It is not

allowed to remain there, for water can force the petroleum out of the shales into the spaces between the particles of coarser grained rocks, such as sandstone, or into fissures. The pressure which converted the mud into shale squeezes much of the petroleum out of the rocks in which it formed.

When petroleum has left the fine-grained rocks it is still subject to the action of water. As it is less dense it tends to rise until it reaches a barrier, and moves along it to the highest point, where it accumulates. This movement, or migration, of petroleum often results in its being discovered far from the rocks in which it formed and in concentrations of oil from a great volume of source rocks. Such concentrations occur where the rocks have been forced up into the form of a dome by pressures originating in the Earth's crust; petroleum trapped beneath a bed of clay or some other stratum through which it cannot pass, rises into the crest of the dome where it is trapped.

The oldest method of finding petroleum is based on signs or 'shows' at the surface produced by the leakage of petroleum from deposits underground. The most volatile constituents escape most easily and can be set on fire by natural causes, such as lightning. Such 'eternal fires' have been known for thousands of years in the Caucasus and in Iraq. The rising oil and gas frequently carry mud with them and build up conical mounds – mud volcanoes. Springs of oil and natural bitumen, left as a residue when all the volatile constituents have escaped, are also found. The best-known occurrence is the Pitch Lake of Trinidad. Surface shows indicate that

1 A huge toothed bit, which bores through hard rock to an underground oil pool, is fitted to the end of the long pipes of a drilling rig at Lake Maracaibo in Venezuela.
2 In New Guinea, a jungle clearing marks the successful end of a search for petroleum.
3 Springs of oil and bitumen, the residue of petroleum when the volatile constituents have escaped, form Pitch Lake in Trinidad.

petroleum exists at a slight depth, but there is no guarantee that most of the original deposit has not already been lost.

Such shows sufficed for the discovery of the first oil-fields. In 1912 geology was applied to the search for deeper-lying deposits, as a geological study of an area can identify the best localities for sinking trial wells. Since 1920 geological methods have been supplemented by those based on geophysics, especially in parts of the world where the surface geology does not reflect the structures found in more deeply buried rocks. Such investigations rely on the detection of differences in the physical properties of different rock types. The speed of shock waves through different types of rock varies, and from an analysis of the speed of such waves, caused by artificial explosions, underground structures may be deduced. The use of such scientific techniques has greatly increased the chances of discovering petroleum and, in particular, they have made possible the discovery of deposits at great depths.

A typical oil deposit is built up of three layers. A zone where the pores of the rock are filled with natural gas lies above a zone where the rocks are saturated with oil containing dissolved gas, and beneath the oil is water. In some fields the gas exerts considerable pressure and when a well reaches the oil the gas forces it to the surface as a 'gusher'. Eventually, as the gas pressure is used up, the oil is no longer forced to the surface and the well has to be pumped. It is important to preserve the supply of gas so that it can keep the well flowing naturally. By carefully controlling the rate of production and by using the accompanying gas to the best advantage, over 80 per cent of the petroleum in the reservoir rock can be extracted.

Oil for the ancients

Bitumen, the earliest form of petroleum used by Man was employed in the Middle East for caulking ships, waterproofing floors and as a mortar for bricks, more than 5,000 years ago. In medieval Europe oil seepages were used only for medicine and it was not until the discovery of bitumen in the New World that any wider interest was taken in petroleum products. By the mid-nineteenth century, the drilling of wells for water and brine was commonplace and at least 15 of the wells sunk for brine in the United States between 1840 and 1860 produced petroleum. When samples were investigated chemically it was found that petroleum would provide illuminating gas, lamp oil, lubricants and paraffin wax.

In Pennsylvania, on 27 August 1859, Edwin L. Drake, a retired railway guard, hit oil at a depth of $69\frac{1}{2}$ ft near Titusville and produced petroleum commercially for the first time. By 1874 $1\frac{1}{2}$ million tons of petroleum were produced per year from Pennsylvania alone. In 1873 production started at Baku in southern Russia, and 28 years later Russia, with a production of $11\frac{3}{4}$ million tons a year, had overtaken the United States as the largest oil producer. World production now exceeds 1,600 million tons per year, the main producers being the United States, the U.S.S.R.,

Venezuela, Arabia, Kuwait, Iran and Libya. Britain's oil wealth from the North Sea is valued at £800 billion.

In the forms of 'bottled gas', petrol, diesel oil and fuel oil, petroleum is mainly used as a convenient source of energy. It also provides lubricants, waxes and asphalt and is the raw material for a wide range of industrial and chemical products, including anti-freeze, insecticides, paint solvents, artificial fabrics, celluloid, synthetic rubber, plastics, detergents and explosives.

Since its beginning, just over a century ago, the petroleum industry has always appeared to be within a decade or two of exhausting its known recoverable

1 A refinery at Jeddah in Saudi Arabia where the crude petroleum is changed into fuels and a wide range of useful by-products.
2 Waste gas flares off pipes at the Dahra oil field in Libya. In some fields gas under pressure forces the oil to the surface in a gusher.
3 Many oil derricks stand in the shallow Lake Maracaibo, Venezuela, one of the world's largest petroleum-producing areas.

reserves. In 1938, for example, the proved reserves were sufficient for only 16 years' supply, at the then relatively low rate of production. Improvements in techniques of discovering and exploiting petroleum deposits and the spread of the intensive search for oil over remote parts of the world have, in recent years, improved the position so that, instead of a petroleum famine developing in 1954, the present known recoverable reserves of approximately 50,000 million tons would maintain the present rate of consumption until the year 2000. It cannot be expected, however, that in the future the rate of discovery of new petroleum deposits will continue to be greater than the rate at which they are used up. Accordingly, if the present upward trend in production continues, a shortage will develop in the twenty-first century. Such a shortage could well be postponed if the development of other sources of energy were spectacularly advanced or if developments in the electrical industry (such as lighter and more efficient batteries) were to allow the electric motor to take over the present duties of the internal combustion engine.

Oil-shales and tar sands

Sooner or later, however, it will be necessary for the world to turn for the source of its hydrocarbon fuels from liquid petroleum to *oil-shales* and *tar sands*. When oil-shales are roasted their organic material breaks up and yields oil. There are vast reserves of such rocks – in the United States alone deposits are estimated to contain at least 70,000 million tons of oil, equivalent to 45 years' supply at the present world rate of consumption. Tar sands consist of sand grains cemented by bitumen and are the residue of oil deposits from which the volatile constituents have escaped. When suitably treated they can be made to yield oil and it is estimated that from the known deposits in Canada alone, more oil could be obtained than the world's known reserves of liquid petroleum. At present, oil obtained from oil-

4 In the North Sea a mobile platform taps natural gas from a huge field nearly two miles below the surface of the water.

5 An oil rig in the Persian Gulf. The raft-like drilling platform, housing the crew, stands on legs which rest on the sea bed.

shales and tar sands is more expensive than that obtained from petroleum, but when supplies of the latter run out it will be possible to obtain oil for many years – at a price.

The world's known reserves of hydrocarbon fuels have recently been substantially augmented by the discoveries of natural gas-fields in many parts of the world. Gas and petroleum have much in common: they have the same origin and are found together. The distinction between fields worked for oil and fields worked for gas lies solely in the different proportions in which the gaseous and liquid hydrocarbons occur.

Natural gas consists largely of the gases methane, ethane, propane and butane and the vapours of the liquids pentane, hexane, heptane and octane. Impurities, including carbon dioxide, nitrogen, sulphuretted hydrogen and helium, occur in varying proportions; in parts of Texas, for example, they are so abundant that the gas cannot ignite. Some impurities, in particular sulphuretted hydrogen, are a nuisance and must be removed; others, such as helium, are valuable by-products.

1 Pipelines are one of the main ways of carrying oil overland. These stretch 95 miles from wells at Agha Juri to the refineries at Abadan.
2 Geophysicists in search of oil in the Libyan desert measure shock-waves from small explosions to identify underground rock structures.

The natural gas industry was developed largely in the United States and that country remains the world's chief producer. The first natural gas wells pre-dated those sunk for petroleum. In 1821, a well was drilled near a 'burning spring' (a natural gas seepage which had caught fire) at Fredonia in New York State and struck gas at 27 ft; in 1854 a 1,200-ft well was sunk at Erie, Pennsylvania. The first company to exploit natural gas was organized in the United States in 1858 and 12 years later natural gas was supplied to Bloomfield, New York State, through a pipeline several miles long made of hollowed-out pine logs. In 1873 a two-inch iron pipe, five miles long, supplied natural gas to the town of Titusville in Pennsylvania. From these early beginnings, development of the natural gas resources of the United States has continued and now supplies the country with five times as much energy as does electricity.

Apart from its use as a fuel, natural gas is an important raw material for the chemical industry and is used in the production of ammonia, alcohols, synthetic rubber, solvents, synthetic fibres and detergents. World production in 1956 was 11 million million cubic feet per annum and had risen by 1966 to 26 million million cu. ft. Deposits of gas are found in many countries of the world, and large producers include the U.S.S.R., Venezuela, Canada, Romania, Mexico, Holland, Libya and Algeria where huge fields lie under the Sahara desert.

The possibilities of gas or oil occurring beneath the North Sea have interested geologists for many years. The geological history favoured the formation of petroleum and gas, and suitable structures for their accumulation were believed to exist. Exploration around its coast, begun in the 1930s, proved the existence of small oil and gas fields, but it was not until 1959 that a well being drilled near Graningen in Holland struck gas in enormous quantities. Further holes proved the size of the find and this field alone has reserves of over twice the world's annual consumption. The gas is trapped in a dome about 20 miles long and 15 miles wide at a depth of almost two miles below the surface of the sea; it is the largest single gas-field in the world.

Fuel for the future

Following this Dutch discovery, a geophysical survey of the whole of the North Sea basin was made and a number of structures favourable for the storage of gas discovered. Drilling platforms, which can operate in water up to 300 ft deep, were erected over the most favourable prospects, and trial holes drilled. The first major strike was in 1965, 42 miles off the mouth of the River Humber; the first gas was brought to the British shore in March 1967 and fed into the national gas grid. Later three more gas-fields were discovered to the northeast of Norfolk, and gas was first brought ashore through underwater pipes in August 1968.

The discovery of considerable quantities of gas under the sea reinvigorated exploration in Britain. This was crowned with success when a well drilled in eastern Yorkshire struck substantial quantities of gas. Gas has also been discovered in the Norwegian part of the North Sea, about 150 miles southwest of Stavanger and 230 miles to the east of the Scottish coast.

At the present rate of consumption the world's reserves of petroleum and natural gas, in their dual role of fuels and raw materials for the chemical and manufacturing industries, will be sufficient for the foreseeable future.

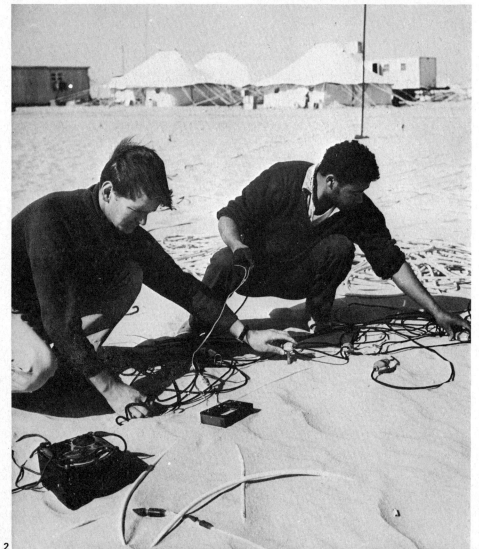

Sharing out the living world

Wherever Man moves in, plants and animals are forced to adapt, move out, or die. The struggle also goes on between animals and vegetation but over all climate is the deciding factor.

THERE ARE few places on Earth where plant and animal life has not been affected by the activities of Man. Even at the most primitive level of human culture, we can trace his impact on nature. In New Zealand, it has been shown that the destruction of natural vegetation by pre-Maori Stone Age settlers a thousand years ago led to the erosion of soils from the lower slopes of the mountains of South Island. Areas which were once forested are now either completely bare of vegetation or will support only poor grassland.

In the United States thousands of farming families fled Texas and Oklahoma in the 1930s, when bad farming methods created a 'dust bowl' where once there had been good farmland and pasture. But Man's role has sometimes been more constructive. The draining of the British fenlands around the Humber and the Wash during the seventeenth century by Dutch engineers made arable farming possible in an area which had been a wasteland of infertile and treacherous marshes.

Man the predator

The activities of hunters throughout the ages has greatly affected the distribution of various species of animals. Sometimes a particular species is completely eliminated from a large area, and other species, taking advantage of the disappearance of their natural enemies, have multiplied and spread into areas where they were previously unknown. Men killed the last wolves in Britain during the eighteenth century, and in France in the early 1900s. Wild boars have almost disappeared from Western Europe during the last few hun-

dred years, surviving today mainly in Eastern and Central Europe. Since the Second World War, wealthy Arabian sheikhs have systematically hunted the Arabian oryx in cars. This beautiful animal is now rarely seen, even in the remote corners of the 'Empty Quarter' (Rub al Khali) of south-western Arabia. Amongst sea creatures, the whale is now extinct in large areas of the Arctic seas around Greenland, northern Canada and

Europe, and its existence is threatened by the unregulated activities of whaling fleets in the Antarctic.

Today the use of chemical fertilizers and insecticides, and the pollution of the atmosphere and the waters of rivers and lakes, resulting from the uncontrolled dispersion of industrial waste, are causing major changes in the geography of living things. The geographical study of plants, animals, fish, insects, and even micro-

Men at work changing the map: *right,* slow and expensive reclamation goes on year after year at Zuiderzee in Holland, pushing back the sea and extending the land area. Urban development all over the world is altering the landscape. *Below left,* in 1923 Hendon Station, a suburb of London, was surrounded by open fields. Now, *below right,* concrete and bricks submerge the countryside.

organisms which cause human and animal disease, is called *biogeography*. This study is sometimes divided into two main areas: *phytogeography* (plant geography) and *zoogeography* (animal geography). As with all other branches of geography, the biogeographer draws upon the specialist knowledge of other scientists – in this case, botanists and zoologists. The task of the biogeographer is firstly to describe the patterns of distribution of plants and animals, and then to attempt to explain the significance of these patterns, especially studying their relationship to the physical and human environment. The role of Man is clearly an essential factor in determining the distribution of plants and animals on the surface of the Earth.

The term *natural vegetation* is often used to describe the characteristic plant cover of any area. But this term presupposes that the plants of any given area have developed undisturbed by human intervention, following a process of natural evolution. But any cover of natural vegetation also depends very much upon climatic conditions. There is abundant evidence that the climates of the past have undergone profound changes and may still be changing. We know, for example, that coal is derived from enormous tree ferns which grew in tropical conditions along the shores of shallow seas. But coal is now mined in temperate or even Arctic conditions. There have also been significant climatic changes since the end of the last Ice Age.

Apart from the role of Man, climate is clearly the predominant influence in determining the pattern of natural vegetation. The amount of rainfall and its distribution from season to season, the average monthly temperature, frost, the strength and direction of winds, the intensity of sunlight all have great influence.

Developing plant life

The nature of the soil in which plants grow is also greatly affected by climate. The first step in soil formation is the breaking-up of the original rock surface by weathering. This is partly a physical and partly a chemical process. To form a soil, the inorganic material derived from the rock is mixed with *humus,* organic material derived from the decay of plant and animal remains. The extent and character of soil formation depends partly on the nature of the underlying rock and also on the climate.

On a naturally well-drained surface, which has been left undisturbed by Man, by any natural upheaval (such as a volcanic eruption), or by any major climatic change for many centuries, a cover of vegetation will gradually develop. The first community of plant species which establishes itself will probably be replaced after a time by a new community in which different species predominate. A process of natural selection over a long period of time will finally produce a stable community of plants, which will persist indefinitely, providing that there is no major change in conditions. Biogeographers use the term *climatic climax vegetation* to describe the stable community of plants which is the end result of this process. It consists of those plants which are best adapted to the particular soil and climate of that area.

In studying the evolution of patterns of natural vegetation and soils, we are dealing with slow natural processes and, in the brief span of our lifetime, it is not easy to observe the whole cycle. Occasionally nature provides a laboratory example by rubbing out the natural vegetation and soil over a large area and starting the whole process again from scratch. Such a cycle began in 1883, when the volcano of Krakatoa erupted, completely destroying the surface of a small island in the Java Sea. The original cover of tropical rain forest was completely wiped out, and all that was left was a bare heap of volcanic rubble on which no plants grew.

Stable plant communities

Within a few months, a *pioneer community* of plants had established itself – a greenish algal slime, which could grow on a surface without soil. Within a few years a simple soil structure developed by the mixing of the humus from the decaying algae and the minerals in the volcanic rubble. Soon grasses appeared and, by 1900, a *savanna* type of vegetation covered Krakatoa. By 1916 a third stage was evident – shrubs and trees had become established. Today Krakatoa has got back its original natural vegetation – the climatic climax community of tropical forest. The earlier stages of algae, savanna and shrubs were therefore not the stable community. The climatic climax vegetation is likely to remain unchanged for many centuries on Krakatoa unless Man intervenes, the climate changes or the volcano erupts once again.

The process from bare rock to tropical forest took only 70 to 80 years because all around Krakatoa were other islands where the volcanic eruption had not destroyed the natural vegetation. As a result, there were nearby sources of seeds, which were carried by winds and birds to re-stock the stricken island. This would not have been the case when large, newly uplifted land masses were bare of soil or plants, and so the first development of a cover of natural vegetation would undoubtedly have been much slower.

The close relationship between climate, soil and natural vegetation has led geographers to base their classification of natural regions on these criteria. The relationship between these factors is highly complex and the intervention of Man further complicates the matter. Any attempt to define broad natural regions, therefore, is bound to oversimplify the facts.

From the map of natural vegetation it is clear that many of the regions run in broad belts from east to west across the land surface. If the continents consisted of level plains, uninterrupted by high mountain ranges, then there would be few exceptions to this pattern. But mountain ranges, such as the Rockies of North America and the Andes of South America, extend for thousands of miles from north to south. They have a great effect on the climate and natural vegetation, both on the mountain slopes and in neighbouring

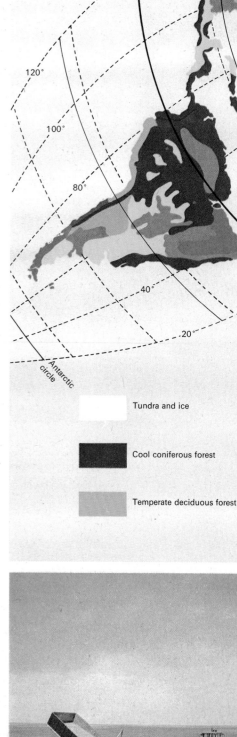

120°

100°

80°

40°

20°

Antarctic circle

Tundra and ice

Cool coniferous forest

Temperate deciduous forest

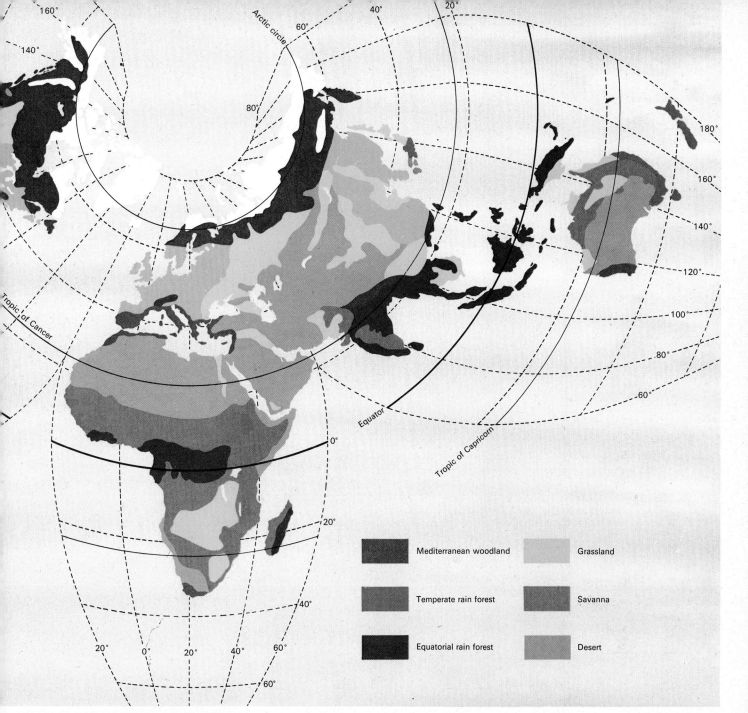

Mediterranean woodland

Temperate rain forest

Equatorial rain forest

Grassland

Savanna

Desert

Above, this map of the world's main groups of natural vegetation shows that many regions run in broad belts from east to west across the land surface. Mountain ranges interrupt this pattern and have a profound effect on climate and plant life. *Below left,* seed mixed with fertilizer is sown by giant machines on the great wheatlands of Alberta in Canada. The herds of bison which roamed these prairies before settlement are now preserved in a few parks. *Below right,* a llama grazes near Lake Titicaca in Peru, a region too high and therefore too cold for any trees to grow.

areas. The belt of barren treeless *tundra* along the northern coasts of Canada and Alaska extends southwards along the high plateaux of the Rocky Mountain system. Further, the higher one goes up a mountain, the colder it gets. If the average temperature at the foot of a mountain is 60 °F. in July, then it will be below freezing point on the summit of a 10,000-foot high mountain. Trees will not normally grow where the average temperature is below 43 °F. for the year and, as a result, the higher slopes of a mountain will be tree-

less. As a result a separate classification, mountain vegetation, is often used to describe such areas.

South of the northern tundra region is a belt of coniferous forest, extending across the Canadian Shield and most of the Eurasian land mass north of latitude 60°N., approximately the latitude of Helsinki and Leningrad. This belt is often known by the Russian word *taiga.* In much of this region, the forest remains in its natural state, but in the more accessible areas, such as Finland and Russia, forestry workers have systematically cut and replaced the trees, and clearings have been made for farms and houses.

Eastern Canada, the United States and Western Europe in mid-temperate latitudes come within a belt of broad-leaved *deciduous* trees, such as oak, ash and elm, which shed their leaves in winter. Man has cut down a large part of the natural forest in this belt, so much so that the term 'natural vegetation' has little meaning.

Between latitudes 30°N. and 40°N., there are areas of Mediterranean scrub vegeta-

winds from the oceans. These regions get insufficient moisture for tree growth, but many types of grasses grow there. Man uses these areas for cultivating cereals, which are domestic grasses, and for grazing sheep and cattle on the wild, natural grass.

The pattern of natural vegetation, described for the northern hemisphere, is repeated with various modifications south of the equator in southern Africa, South America and Australasia. We have already seen how these broad classifications do not always hold true for particular localities and, increasingly in recent years, biogeographers have concentrated their research on small regions, covering perhaps only a few square miles, rather than on the attempt to define natural regions on a world-wide scale.

Distribution of disease

Medical geography is a comparatively new branch of biogeography. It attempts to understand the environmental factors which cause disease in human beings and animals, and in particular to prepare maps which show the distribution of diseases. An early example of this technique occurred in the middle of the nineteenth century in London. Dr John Snow, a general practitioner in the Soho district of London, attempted to discover the causes of cholera, a disease which reached epidemic proportions in many European cities at periodic intervals. During the 1832 epidemic, Dr Snow became convinced that the disease was caused by bad drinking water. He finally proved his theory in 1854, during another epidemic. He marked on a large-scale street map the exact position of the houses of the 500 victims. He also marked the positions of the pumps from which the drinking water was obtained. He found that the houses affected by cholera were clustered around a pump in Broad Street (now Broadwick Street). He removed the handle of the pump and the outbreak almost immediately ceased to spread. Dr Snow, whose portrait appears on an inn sign near where the pump once stood, was a pioneer of medical geography.

Since his day, studies have been greatly advanced and disease atlases have appeared in recent years in a number of countries. In the early 1950s, an atlas of diseases was produced for the United States and, in 1963, one for Britain was published by the Royal Geographical Society under the editorship of Dr Melvyn Howe. This fruitful co-operation between medical scientists and geographers is a new and growing branch of biogeography.

Vegetation and climate still determine the environment of many communities throughout the world. In temperate areas, farmers may clear the forests and substantially alter their environment, but in doing so, they may run the risk of losing the soil cover as well, which can be washed away by water on exposed slopes or blown away by wind, once the retaining vegetation is removed by agriculture. But in some regions of the world, such as the tundra of the cold northern latitudes, and the hot tropical deserts and tropical forests, the environment still largely dictates the way of life of the people.

Top, only coniferous trees and short grass can grow on the high mountains of Olympic National Park, Washington. Above the clear timberline, lack of soil and low temperatures limit plant growth. An optimistic fisherman, *above,* waits by the detergent-covered river Trent in England. The pollution of rivers and lakes by industrial waste is causing major changes in plant and fish life.

tion. This type of vegetation is adapted to the climate in the Mediterranean areas of Europe and of southern California, where there is a long, hot and dry summer and the moderate rainfall occurs during the milder winter. Characteristic plants are broad-leaved evergreens, including the olive, and fragrant bushes, such as rosemary and lavender.

The Mediterranean type shades imperceptibly into desert on its southern margins. A vast area of North Africa and Southwest Asia receives less than five inches of rain a year. Such plants as coarse grasses, tamarisks, cacti, palms and acacia trees will grow in favoured spots. But large tracts are virtually empty of any form of plant life. The desert merges southwards into a region of grassland – the savanna region. The amount of rain, which practically all falls in summer, increases to the south. The main vegetation is grassland, but shrubs and trees are found, especially near watercourses.

On the southern side of the savanna lies the equatorial rain forest or *selva* as it is called in the Amazon basin. Such forests are characterized by luxuriant vegetation including many varieties of tall, evergreen hardwoods, such as teak and ebony, other trees such as the wild rubber tree, and a dense surface cover of undergrowth. The hot, steamy conditions resemble those in an enormous greenhouse.

The temperate grasslands of the interior of North America and Eurasia are another great vegetation region. Called *steppelands* in Russia and *prairies* in North America, these grasslands lie in the heart of the continents, far from the rain-bearing

Man lays waste the Earth

Man makes his own deserts. Erosion of the soil and the spoliation of once fertile land are seldom completely Acts of God. What is being done to conserve the scarce resources available to us?

IF THE SOIL which covers the Earth were stripped away, the land areas of our planet would be as lifeless and barren as a lunar landscape. The thin and delicate layer of soil is seldom more than a few feet deep and in places only a few inches, but most life on land depends on it. Plants send down roots into the soil to obtain water and foods. Human and animal life depend on the plants which grow wild or are cultivated in the soil.

Soil usually develops over a very long period from the underlying rock by a process of weathering. As the rocks crumble, a loose mantle begins to form providing support for living organisms. Earthworms and microscopically small creatures penetrate and modify the soil, and plants begin to develop. The roots of grasses, herbaceous plants and trees bind the soil particles together. When the plants die or the trees shed their leaves, bacteria decompose the dead material which rots into organic substances.

Protected by plants

In regions of strong winds and heavy rainstorms, the plants shelter and protect the soil. In wet, tropical regions, heavy rain beats on the leaves of the tall trees of the dense forest, reaching the ground as a fine spray which then sinks into the absorbent ground without damaging the soil.

When the vegetation is stripped away, the soil is exposed to the sun, the wind and torrential rain. Men armed with ploughs tear out the roots of plants and churn up the surface layers of the soil, reducing its stability. They plant cultivated crops which, if grown and removed year after year, rob the soil of its fertility. The

1 This farm in Arizona was abandoned after grazing and intensive agriculture removed the vegetation and the soil was blown away.
2 When the trees on this hillside in Tennessee were felled, deep gullies developed and the soil threatened to silt up a reservoir.

particles of soil lose their tendency to stick together in grains and are then likely to be washed away by water or, in dry regions, blown away by the wind. The first soil particles to be removed are the finest and often the richest in plant nutrients. This is the beginning of soil erosion which accelerates as more and more rain flows along the surface in rills and rivulets instead of sinking into the

ground. On steep slopes, the rivulets may gather into destructive streams which, armed with eroded material, wear out deep gullies, scarring the surface of the land.

In the past, soil erosion caused by the destruction of natural vegetation and mismanagement of the land sped the downfall of such great civilizations as those of North China and Mesopotamia. In more recent times, European pioneers have colonized large parts of the world. They introduced European methods of agriculture, which had been developed over hundreds of years and worked well in Europe's climate. These methods proved unsuitable in regions with quite different climates and caused the destruction or serious damage of the soil over great areas.

Man-made desert

Pioneers in the United States largely accepted the idea that the natural resources and fertile soils of their great country were inexhaustible. They tore down forests, ploughed up or overgrazed the grassy prairies and burnt large areas of natural vegetation, without realizing that their interference with nature might result in turning fertile lands into soilless deserts. Since the economic depression of the 1930s, the American public has been alerted to the danger. But soil scientists estimate that, in barely 100 years, some 60 per cent of the country has been more or less seriously affected by Man-induced soil erosion.

Many early European settlers viewed African cultivators with scorn. Africans living in the forests practised shifting cultivation. They cleared a small patch of trees, grew crops in the clearing, and

moved on when the fertility of the land began to decline. Such farms were generally covered with weeds even when cultivated, and after the departure of the farmers, forest growth began to reassert itself. This method was certainly inefficient and gave small returns for great labour, but it did help to preserve the soil and maintain its fertility. Even the tangle of weeds protected the soil and prevented erosion, although it often lowered the crop yield. The introduction of ploughing and weed-free farms exposed the soil and caused serious erosion in many African countries.

Many Africans of the savanna regions are livestock owners, whose flocks and herds were limited in number in the past by disease. But the European introduction of *prophylactics* (treatments to prevent disease) led to a sharp increase in the livestock population, which in turn caused serious overgrazing of many grasslands. Stripped bare of vegetation, erosion became a serious problem.

Goats and sheep have also caused great devastation in many areas. Goats, which voraciously tear down leaves and branches of trees, and uproot shrubs and seedlings, have destroyed much of the natural vegetation in Mediterranean lands. Some authorities argue that the goat is such a menace that it should be exterminated in many regions. They cite such examples as the introduction of goats into the island of St Helena, in the Atlantic Ocean, after it was discovered in the sixteenth century. In about 200 years, the vegetation of this formerly forested island was destroyed by the goats. In 1810, too late, every goat on the island was killed: most of the island's fertile soil had been washed into the sea.

Geographers distinguish between natural or geological erosion and soil erosion. Natural erosion occurs all the time. When a new land mass is uplifted, weathering, running water, glaciers, the wind and the sea are constantly wearing down the

land. But the development of soil and natural vegetation ensure that this process is generally extremely slow. When grains of surface soil lose their fertility, they are washed or blown away, but in natural conditions the soil is constantly renewed by the slow weathering of the underlying rock. Soil erosion occurs when Man interrupts the natural cycle of erosion and greatly accelerates the process by his misuse of the land. A layer of soil which took thousands of years to develop can be lost in a few years and it cannot be replaced. Soil scientists on an experimental farm in North Carolina in the United States discovered that 0·002 ton of soil is lost each year in an area where the natural vegetation is undisturbed. In a similar area, where cotton had been planted year after year, the annual soil loss was 31 tons from every acre.

Power-packed raindrops

Soil erosion is caused by rainwater and, in arid areas, by the wind. Raindrops strike the exposed soil with a considerable impact (causing a miniature explosion) and loosen the surface grains. The splash of a raindrop can lift soil particles some two feet into the air and displace them horizontally by as much as five feet. Water erosion is most effective on sloping land, and the longer and steeper the slope, the more effective the erosion. The most destructive form of soil erosion caused by rainwater is *sheet erosion,* which in its early stages often passes unnoticed. As the name implies, sheet erosion is sometimes the removal of an even thin film of soil from the surface but, more commonly the water collects into thousands of rills and channels so tiny that they are erased when the land is ploughed. Eventually, however, sheet erosion becomes noticeable when the subsoil begins to show through on the steeper slopes and the crop yields on such slopes begin to decline.

More spectacular than sheet erosion is gully erosion. A chasm in Georgia in

On the island of Gran Canaria, the ancient method of increasing cultivable land by terracing along the contours of the mountains, holds the soil and prevents it from being washed away.

the United States began to develop when water dripped off a barn roof. Forty years later, the chasm was 200 feet deep and covered an area of 3,000 acres. These ugly gashes in the land are caused whenever rainwater collects into channels which extend over exposed soil. A gully may have its origin in a furrow, a cattle track or a wheel-rut. Once started, gullies grow quickly. Coarse sediment swept along the gully sometimes buries fertile soils on adjacent lands. Deep steep-sided gullies often divide agricultural land into irregular units, making the use of farm machinery impossible.

Wind erosion occurs in broadly flat, dry areas. Where the vegetation has been removed and reckless farming has lowered the fertility of the soil, and where the annual rainfall is generally less than 20 inches, wind erosion is a serious menace. Inches of top soil may be lifted away by strong winds and a former grassland transformed into a desert. Especially during prolonged droughts, dust storms may carry fine soil for miles, choking men and animals, and uncovering the roots of plants which then die. Larger particles of soil are rolled along the ground, destroying or burying small plants. Such extensive erosion has hit broad plains in Africa, Australia and North America, where the best known example is the Dust Bowl of the Middle West of the United States. Wind erosion has not occurred throughout the world on the same scale as water erosion, because semi-arid plains are generally less attractive to human settlement than more humid regions.

In areas affected by erosion, more rainwater flows on the surface and less sinks into the ground. As a result, the permanent water level falls, and springs and wells

1 Trees and grass cling to the soil which is being rapidly undermined by massive gully erosion on the Loldaika Hills in Kenya.

2 The soil of the once green and fertile hills of Greece was washed away after farming, goats and sheep removed the natural vegetation.

3 When grasslands are grazed by too many animals the grass cover is reduced. Sharp hoofs kill the roots, exposing the soil to erosion.

4 On St Helena goats destroyed the vegetation and most of the island's soil was washed into the sea, exposing the underlying rock.

dry up. Although the rainfall is unchanged, such an area becomes progressively dry and desiccated. The soil is eventually washed into rivers, and fish are often killed by the muddy water. The sediment silts up river beds, impedes navigation and causes serious flooding hundreds of miles away. Silt also accumulates in reservoirs and lakes, reducing their storage capacity, and river harbours must be constantly dredged to keep them open.

In the last 30 years, the dangers of soil erosion have been widely appreciated, especially as the world's population is expanding quickly and the demand for increased food supplies has become more urgent. Agriculturists have devised a great variety of methods for conserving soil, the world's most important natural resource. Most of a plant's requirements are supplied by water and by carbon dioxide from the air. A small but essential part of the plant's food, however, comes from chemicals in the soil. Cultivated crops extract the chemicals they need, and when the crops are harvested the chemicals are removed with them. In zones of undisturbed vegetation the chemicals are returned to the soil as humus when the plant dies. Plants use a variety of chemicals, but the greatest problems to the farmers are caused by deficiencies in calcium, phosphorus, potassium and nitrogen. Intensive farming, particularly of the same crop year after year, rapidly exhausts the soil. Fortunately fertility

223

1

2

1 When the trees were cut down and this hillside in the United States cultivated, rainwater carved deep gullies in the slope.
2 Contour ploughing and strip cropping on a slope conserve the soil, help to retain rainwater and break its erosive power.
3 In Jordan, where continual cropping has reduced the fertility of the soil, the wind carries it away in a choking cloud of dust.

subject to erosion, such as on long, steep slopes, cultivation should be at a minimum, and where possible the original vegetation should be restored by reafforestation or by restoring a permanent grass cover.

The cultivation of sloping land offers the most challenging problem to farmers and conservationists. The oldest method used in ancient civilizations in Asia and South America is terracing. People in areas where there was a shortage of level land, laboriously built a series of steps, called *bench-type terraces,* down steep slopes, each terrace being supported by a rock wall or a steep, vegetation-covered mound. On less steep slopes, *broad based terraces,* low broad mounds of earth, are thrown up along the contour. By breaking long slopes into a series of short ones, the surface water never attains much eroding power and most of the soil is held in the flat terrace. Far more widely practised is contour ploughing, which can reduce erosion by half, and combined with other techniques such as strip cropping along the contour, is effective in combating erosion. The roots of the crops help to hold the soil together and the furrows check rainwater running downhill.

Co-operation and control

No system or method can really be successful, however, unless it is related to all the local conditions, including social and economic factors. Traditional methods, where successful, must not be supplanted by methods alien to a region, even if the local methods appear inefficient. For example, shifting cultivation in Africa might well be adapted along the lines of an experiment conducted in the Congo (Kinshasa). Instead of haphazard clearance of forest, cultivation and eventual abandonment, the forest was cleared in long corridors. Regular rotation of crops was enforced to prevent soil exhaustion, but the corridor was reafforested as soon as it was abandoned. Similarly in the Far East, governments have encouraged farmers to cultivate areas of newly-felled teak forest, providing that they plant young teak trees at the same time. By the time the farmers move on, a new teak plantation is established.

Such examples demonstrate that government direction and the education of farmers is needed before soil erosion can be effectively controlled. Sometimes an area affected by erosion cuts across state boundaries and because piecemeal conservation is of little value, peoples of different allegiances must co-operate to prevent the destruction of their land. It is vital that political factors should not stand in the way of the preservation of a national and international asset as basic and essential as soil.

can be restored by fertilizers and crop rotation reduces the drain on the soil's resources.

The restoration of fertility does not, however, solve the problem of shielding the soil from the destructive impact of raindrops. One partial solution is provided by using such crops as clover in a crop rotation. Clover can be ploughed back into the soil as a fertilizer, but while it is growing it covers and protects the soil. The best crops on partly eroded land are those which cover the surface, spreading fibrous roots throughout the soil, binding together. Such plants include grasses, lucerne and some legumes. Strip cropping, a system of alternating inter-tilled crops with others which conserve soil, is a useful technique in stemming erosion. Another method of protecting the surface is by spreading vegetable waste over the soil, leaving it to decompose as humus. This effective but costly technique also helps to retain moisture. In regions highly

3

The disappearing forest

Demands for timber throughout the centuries caused whole forests to be felled, changing the landscape. Only careful preservation can save the remaining few and the wild life they shelter.

1 Vast mixed forests of larch, cedar, birch, pitch pine and alder stretch across the Eastern Sayan Mountains of the Siberian taiga.
2 Groves of gnarled olive trees have replaced the original forests of evergreen oaks, conifers and cork in many Mediterranean countries.

THE EARLY EXPLORERS of the New World, in search of timber to repair their ships, were awe-struck by the vast, luxuriant forests which blanketed eastern North America. Stretching from the St Lawrence River in the north to the Gulf of Mexico in the south and westwards beyond the Mississippi, they were inhabited by a huge variety of plant, bird and animal wild life. The wild turkey roamed in great numbers; eaten by the Pilgrim Fathers, it has become the traditional main dish for dinner on Thanksgiving Day in America. The common forest animals included black bears, woodland bison, deer, mountain lions, martens and wolves. These ancient forests consisted of many species of hardwood, oak, elm, beech, maple, willow and sycamore: *deciduous* trees, which shed their leaves every year at the onset of the colder winter temperatures. To the north and south the deciduous trees were mixed with coniferous evergreens.

Before the axe

In the forests lived the Indians, who were hunters and farmers. Such groups as the Iroquois nation cut clearings for their villages and small plots for cultivation. They used the timber for wooden weapons, canoes and firewood, and made medicines from tree roots. But their inroads were generally slight and when the Pilgrim Fathers arrived, the eastern forests were largely untouched and undisturbed.

Now they are gone. In the last 300 years the original forest has been almost completely destroyed and only a few small pockets survive as reminders of the former beauty of this vast region. Settlers cut down trees for fuel and building, and cleared the trees and undergrowth of large areas for sheep farms, even high up mountain slopes. The discovery of iron ore in the Appalachians created a great demand for charcoal.

As the forests shrank, so the wild animals of the forest dwindled in number with the loss of their natural habitat. Birds and deer were shot for food – some types of wild turkey are now extinct. Carnivorous animals were a threat to livestock and were systematically eliminated. The fashion for beaver hats once threatened the survival of the beaver, but fortunately the craze died down before their total extinction. Today the animal life of the eastern United States is drastically reduced and the main surviving forests

225

are in national parks. The largest and most impressive is the unspoiled Great Smoky National Park of Tennessee with its wild life and 130 different native trees, a greater number than in Europe.

Stretching right across the northern part of North America is another forest, a broad belt of largely coniferous trees, which has to a great extent survived the impact of European immigration. Called the *boreal* (northern) forest, it stretches from Alaska in the west to the Atlantic Ocean in the east, with tongues extending southwards down the western Pacific coast and the Rocky Mountain range. This vast belt extends to the northernmost limit of tree growth and is almost as big as the similar boreal forest of northern Europe and Siberia. In the northern parts of the forest, the trees become more stunted and widely spaced until the cold climate prevents their growth altogether in the barren and bleak northern tundra.

Hunted forest-dwellers

The animal life in the eastern forest was less varied but it provided a rich source of income for many early pioneers. Among the animals that roamed the cold, boreal forest were the ermine, otter, mink and wolverine. These animals were hunted and trapped for their dark, thick furs and their numbers considerably depleted. Among the larger animals were bears, bull moose and herds of caribou, which spent the summer grazing in the tundra but migrated to the forests in winter. Bird and insect life is plentiful in summer, but most birds migrate southwards in winter. Although the boreal forest of North America has survived to a much greater extent than the primeval forests to the south, the more accessible areas have been cut, forest fires have laid waste to some areas, and roads and railways have been built through the boreal forest. When a geographer writes of *natural vegetation regions,* such as the cool temperate deciduous forests, mixed deciduous-coniferous forests, and boreal forests, he is often referring not to the actual vegetation but to the vegetation that occurred before it was disturbed by Man.

Physical factors governing the natural vegetation of a region include climate, soil and land features, and of these climate, particularly rainfall and temperature, is the most important. Rainfall determines the existence of forests, and in temperate latitudes it must be at least 14 inches a year. For example, the westward limit of the temperate deciduous and mixed forests of the eastern United States occurs where the rainfall is below the minimum required for tree growth. The trees become less frequent until they disappear altogether and grasslands or prairie take over. But temperature greatly affects the actual

1 Coniferous forests cover large tracts of British Columbia. Thick bark protects the trees during the cold winters and the conical shape prevents snow from piling up on the branches.
2 Most of England's deciduous forests were cut down centuries ago but many woods remain. This beech wood in Gloucestershire displays all the autumn colours before the leaves fall.

1 Over half of Sweden is covered by forests, mostly of pine, where bears, wolves, wolverines and lynx live in remote areas. The rivers are used to float logs to saw-mills.

2 Herds of red deer haunt the pine forests of Scotland, where four national forest parks have been established. This magnificent stag is watching his herd in a clearing.

trees that dominate the landscape of many regions. To maintain growth, trees must usually have at least three successive months with minimum temperatures above 43 °F. This minimum period governs the limit of poleward and mountain tree growth. Extremes of temperature are also important because some plants are killed by temperatures below freezing-point.

Leaf-shedding trees

Most deciduous trees need at least six months with temperatures above the minimum for tree growth, and growth almost ceases during winter. The shedding of leaves greatly reduces *transpiration* (loss of water vapour), so that the trees do not lose too much moisture during the period when the ground is cold and moisture not easily available. Apart from the shedding of their thin, delicate leaves, most deciduous trees are recognizable by their rounded crowns, supported by low *boles* (the part of the trunk below the lowest branches). Thick bark often covers the trunks and branches to protect the trees from frost damage. The undergrowth in deciduous forests includes small trees, shrubs, plants and mosses. Sometimes luxuriant, it is never as dense, rich and varied as in tropical forests. The development of the undergrowth depends on the amount of sunlight that penetrates to the lower levels of the forest during the growing season. For this reason, undergrowth is better developed in areas where trees

are widely spaced. Some plants, however, flower at the start of the growing season before the broad leaves on the trees open, shading the ground.

The annual fall of leaves that covers the ground, decomposes into *humus* enriching the soil. After the trees are cleared, the land is fertile farmland. Deciduous forests vary greatly in appearance from season to season. Spring is a time of reawakening and flowering; summer, a period of green and shade; autumn, a season of colour when the leaves of some trees turn red, yellow or orange; and winter, the time when the trees are gaunt and bare.

No such seasonal variety occurs in coniferous forests where the trees are evergreen. Conifers are distinguished from other trees by their seeds which are not enclosed in seed cases. These trees are specially adapted to cold conditions. Their leaves are generally hard, narrow and needle-like, and transpiration ceases almost completely in winter. The leaves, by remaining on the tree throughout the year, permit transpiration and *photosynthesis* (the process which uses sunlight to make plant food) to begin almost as soon as the weather is warm enough. Conifers often have thick barks which protect them against the cold, and shallow roots which enable them to grow in shallow soils, making it possible for the trees to absorb moisture from the top layers of soil even if the subsoil remains frozen. These features which make coni-

fers resistant to cold, assist their growth in sandy soils, which do not hold much moisture, and in warm, arid lands where droughts are common.

Conifers are generally conical in appearance; their branches are usually short, getting shorter near the apex. Their shape protects them against winds, and prevents snow piling up on the branches. Their rate of growth varies according to the climate. For example, in southern Finland, it takes about 50 years for a tree to mature, but four times as long in the centre of the country, a factor that discourages the development of a forest industry in that area. The undergrowth in northern coniferous forests is generally thin, partly because of the permanent shade cast by the evergreen trees, and partly because the blanket of needle leaves on the ground makes it difficult for plants to grow. Conifers are often called *softwoods* as opposed to deciduous *hardwoods,* but these terms are somewhat misleading because some conifers have much harder wood than some deciduous varieties.

In the cold north

The boreal forests begin around latitude 50 °N., where other types of vegetation are replaced by forests dominated by larch, pine, fir and spruce, with some deciduous trees such as aspen. This largely unexploited forest is also called *sub-arctic,* and *taiga,* a Siberian name. But taiga is also used for the northernmost part of the forest which has an open, park-like character where the trees grow so slowly that they are only a few feet high although of great age. Except in its southern extremities, the climate is unsuitable for agriculture. Forest industries are carried on in accessible areas such as in the St Lawrence Valley in North America and around the Baltic Sea in Europe. Soils are generally poor and of glacial origin. Soils often determine the type of tree in a particular spot. Pines flourish on dry, sandy soils – some types are planted in southern European sand dunes to bind the loose, shifting dunes. On damper soils, large numbers of spruce often grow, whereas larch favours deep soils. Firs are generally widespread in their distribution. Although most of the

Lassen Volcanic National Park in California, with its blanket of pine forest, is a refuge for wild life, such as mule and black-tailed deer, bear and smaller mammals.

forest is evergreen, the forest that lies farthest north, reaching 72° 50'N. in central Siberia, is made up of Dahurian larch, a needle-leafed tree which sheds its leaves annually.

In the south, the boreal forests of Eurasia and North America merge into the deciduous forests. Throughout the boreal forest, species vary from region to region. The Scots pine is the *dominant plant* (the tallest plant in a particular plant community) of the western European boreal forest but, to the east, it is replaced by the Norway spruce and further still by the Siberian spruce, larch, fir and stone-pine. White spruce and balsam fir are dominant in many parts of North America. Along the Pacific coast of the United States from British Columbia to northern California, the climate is warmer and the rainfall heavy. In the coniferous forests of this region, some of the world's tallest and oldest trees grow, reaching heights of over 300 feet in their life span of more than 4,000 years. In 1965 the highest known living tree was a Californian redwood of 368 feet. The only rivals to these giants are some eucalyptus trees in Australia.

Inroads of agriculture

South of the boreal forests lie belts of mixed coniferous-deciduous forest and the cool temperate deciduous forest. The climate of these belts is far more favourable to plant growth. The winter becomes shorter the further south one goes, although the winter months are still often fairly cold. But longer, warmer summers make agriculture possible and so these vegetation zones are attractive to Man and cover regions where advanced civilizations have developed. In China, Korea and Japan, the forests of this type are far less disturbed and are major timber reserves.

In the European cool temperate deciduous forests, common trees include oak and beech. The oakwoods generally occur on brown earths, soils that are particularly favourable for farming, and which remain generally moist throughout the year. Beech forests thrive on drier, sandy soils and tend not to occur in poorly drained areas. Other trees of this zone in Europe include the ash, chestnut, elm, hornbeam and sycamore; alders, aspens and willows grow in the less favourable places. The North American cool temperate deciduous forest contains a much greater variety of trees than that of Europe, possibly because many European species did not survive the Pleistocene Ice Age. The more luxuriant North American forest also contains such trees as hickory, magnolia, maple and walnut and, in the undergrowth, such colourful shrubs as azaleas, fuchsias and rhododendrons.

Separating the cool temperate lands from the sub-tropical regions are the warm temperate zones, where rain is plentiful throughout the year. The warm temperate rain forests are similar in appearance to cool temperate forests but they consist largely of evergreens, including the evergreen oak. Pines also occur in soils too sandy to retain much moisture. Such forests occur in parts of southern Africa, Australia, China and New Zealand, and in southern Japan, and south-western South America.

Natives displaced by invaders

The Mediterranean zone is also warm and temperate but it has a summer drought and a cool, moist winter. These conditions also occur in California, parts of Australia and South Africa and central Chile. The original forests of the Mediterranean area included evergreen oaks, cork, and conifers, such as pines, firs, cypresses and cedars. Little of the original forest remains, having been replaced by such characteristic plants as figs, olives, vines, and imported plants, such as citrus fruits. In some areas, dense thickets up to ten feet high called *maquis* in France and *chaparral* in California have replaced the natural forests.

In those parts of the world where the original vegetation has been destroyed, a new pattern of land use has been superimposed on the landscape, including roads, railways and towns. The new vegetation must be capable of thriving in the same natural conditions as the original. Agriculturists have done much to adapt natural conditions by drainage and irrigation, the use of fertilizers and the development of new varieties of plants and trees.

The forests of cedars in Lebanon were felled to build Phoenician ships and Solomon's huge temple. Only a few trees, which grow up to 200 feet, still stand on the bare hills.

228

Winning land from Nature's wastes

Only about one tenth of the Earth's surface is farmed. All over the world, swamps, marshes, sand dunes, deserts and coastlands are being reclaimed and turned into productive agricultural land.

THE RAPID and accelerating increase of the world's population has made the control and development of natural resources, both on the land and in the oceans, a matter of great urgency. In the past, exploitation of natural resources has often been reckless and destructive, without regard for the future. Large forests have been cleared and grasslands overgrazed or ploughed up. Intensively cultivated soil has quickly lost its fertility, causing soil erosion. Today, the rich topsoil of many once fertile lands has been scattered by the wind or swept by rivers into the sea.

Disregard for the future was largely based upon the misconception that the Earth's resources were limitless. But today, in our increasingly overcrowded world, we are much more aware of the dangers involved in the wilful over-exploitation of the land. Dry land covers less than 30 per cent of the Earth's surface, and of this area only about 10 per cent is farmed. Ice and snow blanket vast regions, and even in places where the snow melts for a brief season, the subsoil remains permanently frozen. The growing season in many cold regions is too short for crops useful to Man; rugged mountains and high, icy plateaux make farming impossible and there are vast tracts of sandy and rocky desert which are too dry for most plants. More than half of the world's population earn their living from farming the limited part of the Earth's surface where physical and climatic conditions are favourable to agriculture. Within this limited area, much of the potentially cultivable land is already farmed and, in some regions, soil erosion has reduced the crop yield.

Land beneath the sea

Not all farming has, however, been destructive. Some regions have been faced with a shortage of cultivable land for centuries. The Dutch have painstakingly reclaimed land from the sea, using windmills to pump the water up to sea-level. Great civilizations grew up in southwestern Asia and Egypt where the people laboured hard to bring water to arid land. Considerable tracts of swamp and desert remain a challenge and an opportunity for new farming land in the future.

Swamp and marshland, when drained, can provide excellent agricultural land. The Fens of eastern England were drained in the second half of the seventeenth century, providing about 500,000 acres of fertile, level land. But the area is still subject to flooding because after it was drained the drying peat shrank and wind erosion removed surface soil. As a result, the land in places is now about ten feet below the level of the coastal belt. The drainage of the Pontine Marshes and parts

of the Po Valley in Italy created agricultural lands which now support large populations. The reclamation of the former Zuider Zee in the Netherlands, begun in 1920, continues and the drainage of the fourth of the five *polders* (reclaimed areas) was completed in 1968, providing thousands of acres of fertile land for farming. In tropical areas, swamp drainage has created new farmland and cleared mosquito-breeding swamps in many countries, such as Guyana and Malaysia.

Reclamation of coastal swamps has provided a large part of the region's cultivated land in Guyana and its neighbour Surinam. Dams and *dykes* (banks of earth and stone) enclose narrow, rectangular polders. Sea or river dams protect the polders from

1 In the Netherlands, work goes on unceasingly to reclaim more land from the sea. The Oosterpolder dyke, the first stage of a new project, reaches out into the Zuider Zee.
2 Many small farms, guarded by a long dyke, stand on the Noord Oost Polder of the Zuider Zee. Now good agricultural land, this area was covered by the sea until reclaimed in 1942.

inundation by the sea, and a back dam prevents flooding from the water of the adjacent swamp. The long sides of the polders, called *middle-walks* in Guyana, provide footpaths between the dams. Where the reclaimed land is above sea-level, even if only at low tide, the excess water drains away naturally along ditches through sluices. Pumping, a costly process, is only necessary where the polders lie below sea-level.

In the reclamation of all coastal swamps, farmers face the problem of removing salt from the soil. Newly reclaimed polders are usually left for perhaps two years before the first planting. Rainwater beats on the exposed surface and dissolves much of the salt. Sometimes the farmers flood the polders with fresh river water, which also flushes salt out of the soil.

This type of swamp reclamation can probably be applied in large areas in the tropics, especially around the mouths of the Amazon and Orinoco rivers in South America, and in similar swamps surrounding the mouths of the great rivers of West Africa. Large areas of inland swamp, such as the *sudd* region of the upper Nile, could also be drained if the river channels were straightened and deepened. The Gezira cotton region of the Sudan was formerly a derelict swamp lying between the two arms of the Nile. But some of the inland swamps of western and eastern Africa are so vast that the cost of reclamation would be prohibitive. Drainage of swamps around major cities, such as Kampala in Uganda, which lies on Lake Victoria, provides land for new residential areas and destroys the breeding grounds of disease-carrying insects.

Reclamation of swamps, however, may lower the level of water underlying adjacent areas and so damage the natural vegetation, perhaps causing soil erosion on sloping land. In some cases, swamps and marshland may usefully be left undrained, because their value as recreational areas for hunting and fishing, and the breeding grounds of fur-bearing animals, fish and birds exceeds their value as agricultural land. On the other hand, many drained areas are flat and fertile and can be farmed efficiently with modern machinery. Fairly intensive farming with a high yield per acre can be carried on without much fear of extensive soil erosion.

Water in the deserts

The problem involved in reclaiming semiarid and desert regions is finding enough water to irrigate dry soils. Farming in many parts of the world is in fact only made possible by extensive irrigation, involving the storage of water, the diversion of rivers, and often the extraction of underground water reserves. In temperate zones, the lowest rainfall for plant growth is ten inches a year, whereas in the tropics, where the evaporation is much greater, some 20 inches is needed. Where the rainfall is below these limits, irrigation is necessary. Land reclamation by irrigation is an ancient farming technique.

Water control and irrigation in the Nile Valley probably began between 4,500 and 5,000 years ago and has continued up to the present, when it is planned that the waters held back by the newly constructed Aswan High Dam will transform about 2,000 square miles of desert into fertile farmland and raise productivity on more than 1,000 square miles of already cultivated land. In South America and China, large irrigation works were built before the birth of Christ. Today, more than a third of Asia's farmland is irrigated. Extensive tracts of irrigated land also occur in many other countries including the United States where some 85 per cent of all crops grown in California depend on irrigation.

One of the most dramatic land reclamation programmes in arid regions is taking place in Israel. Long before the state was established in 1948, Zionist pioneers had begun to reclaim badly eroded and neglected lands. Since 1948, the pace of reclamation has been increased and the area of farmland has been more than trebled. In areas where soil erosion is likely to occur, farmers carefully plough along the contours to reduce surface run-off of rain. On steep slopes, earth terraces, sometimes supported by rock walls, are built along the contours, and parallel lines of trees break the force of the wind, reducing both erosion of the soil and evaporation of moisture. Gullies which have scarred the land are generally filled in, but some are straightened and planted with eucalyptus trees and grasses. They

1 Household refuse and rubble is used in Essex to raise the level of low-lying waterlogged land. Such areas can then be used for building, recreation or covered with soil and farmed.

2 The Fens in eastern England, where drainage began in the seventeenth century, now provide thousands of acres of fertile land, some as much as ten feet below sea-level.

provide drainage channels in which erosion is prevented by the vegetation cover. Trees are also planted on drifting dunes to anchor the loose sand.

The main problem in Israel is the maintenance of water supply. Of the rain that falls, an average of some 60 per cent evaporates in the air or on the ground, and another five per cent flows away as surface run-off. Of the remainder, much is lost through underground drainage. Such figures vary greatly from year to year. The amount of surface run-off increases during violent downpours, whereas fine rain leads

to greater evaporation. In the past, people conserved water by trapping rain in stone cisterns, collecting spring water, and digging shallow wells. In this century, deep wells have been dug and long pipelines convey water hundreds of miles to desert areas.

Perhaps the most impressive reclamation schemes are in the Negev, Israel's southern desert where the annual average rainfall is as low as one inch. A pipeline conveys water from the Sea of Galilee to the Negev. The most visionary plan of all, to establish a great regional reclamation

1 In Les Landes in France, the invading wind-blown coastal sand dunes were halted when a reclamation project stabilized the dunes with flourishing forests of pine trees.

2 Traditional transport and modern mechanization work side by side in the Gezira desert of the Sudan. Cotton and other crops are irrigated with water from Senna dam on the Blue Nile.

3 Young eucalyptus trees now grow in the Libyan desert where the sand dunes have been sprayed with oil to stabilize them. The desert will, in time, yield harvests from this experiment.

project, has not been achieved because of frontier problems between Israel and its Arab neighbours. For example, the entire waters of the River Jordan could be utilized if Israel and Jordan could reach an agreement. Political conflict has unfortunately hindered the development of the entire region, in Israeli and Arab territory alike.

Irrigation and reclamation are best operated within a large framework of a natural region, across which frontiers often run. As Theodore Roosevelt (President of the United States 1901–1909) observed: 'Every river system, from its headwaters in the forest to its mouth at the coast is a simple unit and should be treated as such.'

One of the main problems involved in irrigation is the salinity of the water that is available. Lands once fertile may be irrigated by water with a high salt content and soon become infertile. Sea-water contains between 33 and 37 parts of salt per 1,000 parts of water. Underground water or inland brackish lakes may contain only 0·5 to 2 parts of salt per 1,000 parts of water, but such water can seriously damage farmland. However, if the land is well drained, a salinity of 6 to 8 parts of salt per 1,000 can be safely used, because the salt is constantly washed out. It has been estimated that 30 per cent of irrigated land in the Soviet Union needs to be reclaimed once again, this time to remove the salts brought into the soil by irrigation water. The problem also occurs in such places as northeastern Brazil, California, Iraq and the Indus plain of Pakistan.

Desalination is a costly process and the decisive factor is the supply of cheap power, such as an atomic plant or, as some scientists claim, the development of power from the sun. Until desalination is made less expensive, water with a high salt content cannot be used, and water containing comparatively little salt must be mixed with fresh water before it can be safely used. Another possibility for the future lies in the experiments of scientists who are trying to produce useful crops which can grow in salty soils. A problem still awaiting a solution is the loss of water in reservoirs through evaporation. Experiments have been tried covering water areas with a film of such substances as cetyl alcohol, which would reflect the sun's rays and reduce evaporation of the water.

Invading sand dunes

Coastal sand dunes in temperate zones are blown by the wind inland, destroying farmland, burying villages, and blocking the channels of streams and causing swamps. A major reclamation project achieved great success in the dunes of the Landes region of France. The dunes were stabilized by forests of pine and by hardy plants whose maze of roots bound the loose sand grains together. Branches and other plant waste were spread over the surface and covered by a layer of sand. After decomposing, this organic matter provided nutrients for plants and helped to create a cohesive soil. Once desolate, the Landes is now a flourishing region.

In Libya, experiments are under way to stabilize sand dunes by spraying them with oil. A year after planting the dunes with acacia and eucalyptus seedlings, seedlings had grown into six-foot-high healthy trees. Their shed leaves provide humus and help to retain moisture. In time, this part of the reclaimed desert can be used to grow crops.

During wartime, a country which usually imports food supplies faces a national emergency if those food supplies

1 A cloud of dust hangs over the heaps and spoils of an opencast coal mine which scars the English landscape near Newcastle.
2 The same landscape, but the mine has been filled in and levelled, showing what can be done where the demand for land justifies the expense.

Fertilizers spread from planes on the steep hill pastures of North Island, New Zealand, have increased crop yields and turned scrub land into productive grazing.

are cut off. Farmers then turn their attention to cultivating so-called *marginal lands,* which under normal conditions are too infertile, inaccessible or badly drained for economic agriculture. In a country such as Britain, most of these marginal lands lie in hill or upland country, where the soils are shallow and their top layers often infertile, providing poor conditions even for the growth of pasture crops. To convert areas of gorse and bracken into good grazing land requires considerable capital outlay. Reclamation includes careful fertilization and reseeding, and the cost is not justified if level and more fertile land is available. Apart from hill country, marginal lands include areas of light, sandy soils which do not retain moisture, cold, heavy soils which retain too much, and flat marshland. Such areas are only reclaimed if the need for land is sufficiently urgent.

In industrialized countries, many areas become derelict through misuse, and the landscape is often defaced by such unsightly features as slag heaps, quarries

and open-cast mines. Many such excrescences are relics of the Industrial Revolution, but recently in many countries people have become aware of the need to preserve the beauty of the countryside. Reclamation projects have transformed derelict sites. Piles of industrial waste may be completely sterile but they can be levelled down to provide building areas. Where soils exist, they can be fertilized and derelict sites can become recreation grounds, forest plantations, or even be restored as farmland. Gravel pits and quarries can be filled with dredgings from rivers and canals or landscaped as boating lakes and caravan sites. Humus from sewage, and waste organic matter such as brewery and sugar beet wastes, can be ploughed into the surface to develop a topsoil.

Reclamation of swamps, deserts and marginal land will become increasingly important as the world's population expands and the amount of agricultural land per head decreases. But as land reclamation is always more costly than the farming of land which does not require special techniques its future will continue to be largely governed not by what is possible, but what is economically possible.

Making the deserts bloom

For thousands of years, farmers of the Earth's dry regions have grown crops by irrigating their land. The spread of this technique gives hope for feeding the world's increasing population.

THROUGHOUT THE WORLD, millions of acres of former desert and wasteland are now covered by prosperous, productive farms. This has been made possible by *irrigation,* artificial watering. In areas where the rainfall is just sufficient for farming (over 10 inches) but is spasmodic or falls at only one time of year, irrigation can avert crop failure and increase yields. It is also used in regions of moderate or even heavy rainfall for crops, such as rice, which need much moisture.

Early civilizations in the Old World owed much to irrigation, which was a Neolithic innovation, quite as important as the domestication of animals or the invention of pottery and weaving. The earliest towns were often founded near tracts of fertile, irrigated land which produced enough food for several hundreds, or even thousands, of people. Jericho, probably the world's oldest town, stands in the hot, dry Jordan valley beneath the rugged eastern escarpment of the Judean plateau. In one of the gorges, reaching the valley close to Jericho, are several large perennial springs, which are really rivers emerging from underground courses in the massive limestone plateau. These streams supply water to the flourishing orange, date and banana groves which occupy land that has been continuously cultivated for about 10,000 years, longer than anywhere else in the world.

In Mesopotamia, irrigated land supported the first pre-Sumerian urban communities. Here, the Tigris, Euphrates and their tributaries flow across a plain of silty

A shaduf, one of the ancient devices which raises water from shallow wells to water crops, is used by a Vietnamese farmer.

Farmers in the Szechuan Province of China pedal a primitive waterwheel to lift water from a river to flood a ricefield.

alluvium, formed from fine sand and clay particles borne from the mountains of Persia and eastern Turkey during their spring floods. The earliest cultivators probably sowed grain on flooded land when the water was drying up in early summer. They soon realized that better and more certain harvests could be assured by embanking plots and admitting water at regular intervals from canals filled by the natural rise of the rivers during the flood season. In this system of irrigation, the main canals are called

inundation canals. They become clogged with silt and must be cleared during the season of low water. Considerable organization is needed to dig and maintain canals and to ensure that the distribution of water is fair and methodical. Law, police and expert officials are needed: in other words, a state. It is thought that the earliest states were created to build, administer and defend early irrigation systems. Sumeria and similar early states (such as those in the Indus valley and northern China) have been called *hydraulic civilizations.*

Tapping underground water

Some rivers in Arabia and elsewhere flow only intermittently after occasional heavy summer rainfall. The flood water is diverted on to suitable land which, after soaking, is ploughed and sown. This method of irrigation is usually called *flush irrigation.* Cotton is produced near Kassala and Tokar in Sudan by this system.

These methods of irrigation utilize water flowing over the surface in rivers, but so great are the gains from watering land in the dry climates of the Near East that much ingenuity and toil has been expended to obtain underground water and to distribute it to crops. In Persia, thousands of *qanats,* sloping tunnels dug into gravelly or sandy deposits at the foot of mountain ranges, emerge at a point where an area of a few hundred acres can be commanded. Water infiltrates into the tunnel and gives a steady supply to the crops being grown. From Persia (where, it

A huge irrigation canal provides water for thousands of acres of fertile farmland on the Canterbury Plains in New Zealand.

is believed, the *qanat* was invented) this method of utilizing underground water has spread throughout the dry lands of the Old World from northern India and central Asia to Morocco.

Wells are also dug to reach water stored underground; many devices, operated by labourers or domestic animals such as oxen or mules, lift the water to the surface. The two commonest ancient devices used in the Near East are the *shaduf* and the Persian water wheel. Both the shaduf and the Persian water wheel can be used to lift water from canals or rivers, especially during any season when the water level is low, or during the flood season, to land that is too high to be commanded by *gravity* or *flow irrigation*.

Chinese ricefields

The Chinese have been adept at irrigation since they began to use iron tools early in the first millennium BC. Their first irrigation systems were in two tributary valleys of the Hwang-Ho, the Wei and the Fen. Their increasing numbers enabled them to undertake large works along the lower Hwang-ho, where it flows across the Great Plain, and in Szechuan where, during the second and first centuries BC, they diverted the Min River so that the plain of Chengtu could be irrigated. Later, when they expanded southwards, they dug canals to divert water from the Yangtze-Kiang and its major tributaries, where they cross lowlands, and so were able to convert great tracts of level land into ricefields. Further south, where the land is hilly, slopes were terraced and canals followed the contours to convey water to the crops.

The first large modern irrigation schemes were designed and built in India. The British engineers were inspired, and to some extent instructed, by some large medieval works, which had fallen into disrepair. These older works included the Western and Eastern Jumna canals, not far from Delhi, which were originally built in the fourteenth century and restored between 1820 and 1830. In 1836 Colonel Proby Cautley, who had worked on the Eastern Jumna canal, began surveys for an entirely new and much bigger scheme: the Ganges canal which followed the central line of the *doab* (gently sloping tongue of alluvium) between the Ganges and Jumna rivers. This *doab* is 300 miles long, and near the intake from the Ganges at Hardwar, the canal is 200 feet wide. Its capacity is 6,750 cubic feet per second (cusecs). To obtain command at the head of the *doab,* Cautley had to locate the headworks in the Himalayan foothills and had to plan and build some works which, for the period, were both brilliant and gigantic. The Ganges canal was eventually completed in 1862. It banished poverty and the recurrent famines caused by the failure of the fickle monsoon rains.

Soon afterwards, about 1875, the modern works in Punjab, on the Chenab, were begun and these culminated in the Triple Project (1905–17), which harnessed the waters of the Jhelum, Chenab and Ravi in an integrated scheme. The last of the great British works in India was also in

1 Hoover Dam, one of the largest in the world, supplies water for irrigation schemes in California, Arizona and Nevada.

2 Along the banks of the Nile, near the Sahara, crops growing in the fertile alluvial soil are watered by irrigation channels.

the Indus valley, at Sukkur, where a barrage nearly a mile long was built between 1925 and 1932, to command more than 5 million acres in Sind. The supply diverted into the main canals 46,000 cusecs of water between June and September. The Indus plains in Punjab and Sind received so little rainfall that before the construction of these modern works they were largely uninhabited. When irrigation began, the land was settled under government supervision by peasants who moved from overcrowded districts elsewhere. Villages, towns, roads, railways, minor irrigation canals and rich crops of wheat and cotton appeared on formerly empty semi-desert. The upper Chenab canals, built between 1889 and 1898 to irrigate over a million acres, enabled the population to increase in the watered area from 8,000 to 800,000 in a decade.

These irrigation works are the economic foundation of West Pakistan. Without

them, it is doubtful whether a Moslem state could have been created in the subcontinent by partition in 1947 when the Indian Empire was broken up. Sind, however, is an example of an irrigation scheme that has been adversely affected by salt. The source of the salt is not so much the irrigation water as the subsoil. Under irrigation, the *water-table* (the level of underground water) rises and saline water is drawn up into the soil, where it evaporates, leaving its salt behind. During and after the Second World War, a good deal of land was abandoned because crops could no longer be grown. The only cure is drainage in deep ditches so that the level of water in the subsoil can be kept well below the depth of the roots of crops. This is very expensive, because pumping is usually required, as well as the excavation and maintenance of a canal system almost as elaborate as the irrigation system itself. However, this is now being undertaken by the Pakistan government with the help of loans from the International Bank and other lending agencies.

Whilst these and other great works were being designed and constructed in India, European emigrants had been settling in the dry West of the United States, in Australia and in South Africa. In all of these countries, dams have been constructed to store water and to supply distribution systems. The irrigation schemes of the Murray valley in Australia are particularly noteworthy and the system of reservoirs, tunnels and diversions in the Snowy mountains since the Second World War provide not only more water for irrigation but also generate power. Another complex system has been evolved in California, where power, the urban water supplies of Los Angeles, and extensive orange groves, vineyards and *truck* (vegetable) farms in the Great Valley are supplied.

Lands of the Nile

The Nile, the second longest river in the world, illustrates both ancient and modern irrigation practices. In Egypt, which consists of a narrow strip of alluvium 400 miles long, hemmed in by desert cliffs and ending in a delta, the Nile rises in August and September, when its water is reddened by volcanic silt washed from the mountains of Ethiopia into the Blue Nile. The ancient Egyptians divided the alluvium into large embanked fields, called basins, into which flood water was admitted and allowed to deposit its silt. In October, when the river level falls, surplus clear water was drained from these basins, which could then be ploughed and sown to wheat, barley or clover. From the harvest time in March or April until after the next flood, the land was fallow, apart from small plots watered from wells or the river.

In the nineteenth century, this traditional or *basin* method of irrigation was converted to *perennial* irrigation so that

cotton, sugar, rice, millet or maize could be grown during the former fallow period. To raise the level of the river artificially when it is naturally low between March and July, barrages were constructed at the head of the delta just below Cairo. However, at this season, there is usually insufficient water flowing in the river to irrigate all the cultivated land commanded by the distribution canals. Two storage dams were therefore built, at Aswan in 1902, and raised in 1912 and again in 1933

1 A well is dug in Morocco to tap the precious underground water, vital to men, animals and crops in a region where little rain falls.
2 A Persian waterwheel raises water from a deep well. Jars tied to a continuous rope on a wooden wheel dip into the water as it is rotated by an ox walking round and round. The jars empty into a tank, from which an acre or two of land can be watered.
3 Near Bangkok, in Thailand, a farmer and his wife scoop water from an irrigation channel on to a field of water melons.

Spray irrigation, useful on sloping land and during droughts, waters young plants in Bedfordshire to promote growth.

and on the White Nile just above Khartoum at Jebel Auliya in 1938. These store surplus water towards the end of the flood season and are operated to release it between April and the end of June, when Egypt's need of water for the summer crops is most critical and the Nile is at its lowest. Since 1956, with financial and technical help from the U.S.S.R., the Egyptian government is building a new, very large dam at Aswan, called the High Dam (*Saad al-A'ali*). The water stored behind this structure will flood the Nile valley far into northern Sudan, and will not only permit irrigated agriculture to be extended in Egypt but will be used to generate electric power.

So great is the discharge of the Nile during its flood that a good deal of water is surplus to Egypt's requirements. This has enabled the Sudan government to construct irrigation schemes on the extensive clay plains adjoining the confluence of the Blue and White Niles. A dam was built at Sennar on the Blue Nile between 1921 and 1927. This can be used to divert water from the Blue Nile into the Gezira main canal from mid-July until mid-January, and enables many tenant farmers to grow cotton, millet and clover. From mid-January onwards, all the natural flow of the Nile is allowed to flow downstream because it is needed for the Egyptian spring and summer crops. The Egyptian prior right to the entire flow of the river during this 'timely season' was written into agreements with the Sudan in 1927 and 1959. Since 1959, the Sudan government has greatly extended the area under irrigation by the Manaqil scheme and has constructed another dam at Roseires, near the Ethiopian frontier. The cotton grown on the irrigated tracts of the Gezira plain in northern Sudan since 1930 has brought the Sudan government much revenue and foreign exchange. Here, as in West Pakistan, irrigation is the foundation of independence.

These forms of irrigation all require level land, so that water can flow readily over the surface from the distribution canals. In the present century, however, a new method of watering growing crops on sloping land has been invented. A rotating sprinkler (often used for lawns or gardens) distributes water. The water is brought by a series of light metal pipes, usually made of an aluminium alloy, and laid across the fields. The pressure needed to keep the sprays working is provided at a central station or by small electric motors or diesel engines.

This technique is now being widely used in Israel. About 70 years ago, Jewish colonists in Palestine relied mainly upon wells and small pumps to irrigate their orange groves on the sandy coastal plain. After the state of Israel was founded in 1947, the new government laid a trunk main southwards from the large, reliable

One of the barrages built on the Nile near Cairo to retain water for irrigation when the river is low during the dry season.

springs at Rosh Ha'ayin in the Yarqon valley (northeast of Tel Aviv) to carry water to a dry area near Lakhish where, on a large settlement scheme, many Jewish immigrants were trained as co-operative farmers. Later, an even larger water main was laid from the Sea of Galilee (Lake Kinneret) across the hills of southern Galilee and Mount Carmel to the coastal plain. Powerful pumping stations raise water from the lake (which is more than 600 feet below the level of the Mediterranean), and the new supply, besides being used in towns, has permitted a further expansion of spray irrigation and contributed to Israel's economic progress.

Spray irrigation is not confined only to countries with a dry, hot summer. It is proving very useful on intensively producing farms in southeastern England where, despite the frequent rainfall, droughts in spring and early summer sometimes cause crops to do badly or even to fail altogether. Growers of small fruits and vegetables find that even if they use their spray equipment only once in three or four years, the costs of installation are repaid. Truck farmers near the industrial cities of the United States measure daily rainfall and use formulae to ascertain how much water should be sprayed on to their fields in dry weather to maintain crop growth. Since its primary object is to increase food production, irrigation will be a vital weapon in the struggle to feed the increasing population of the world. Spray irrigation is likely to spread in intensively-farmed temperate countries where the rainfall is light or moderate.

In Africa, where the traditional cultivator is completely ignorant of water conservation and irrigation, there is great potential. To obtain the fullest benefit from irrigated agriculture, much research and technical education is needed to ensure that the soil is properly managed, pests are controlled, the most suitable varieties of crops are grown and the farmer is instructed and capable.

Husbanding the riches of the Earth

Land has many uses, from the production of food to enjoyment of the scenery. Man is now learning to strike a balance between these conflicting demands on Nature's gifts.

THE RAPID INCREASE in the world's population over the last 100 years has led to a great increase on the acreage of land under cultivation. In the future, as the population growth accelerates, the demand for farmland will increase. The clearance of forests, the reclamation of deserts, and the drainage of swamps will be demanded. Sites will be needed for new towns and factories and urban areas will encroach further into the countryside.

In the past 40 years, however, scientists have warned that over-exploitation or misuse of the land and its resources can turn pleasant lands into deserts. To the European colonizers of the last few hundred years, the virgin territory in the Americas, Africa and Australasia offered enormous wealth. Land was practically free. Forests, a nuisance to the farmer, were cut down or burned. Grasslands were either ploughed up or stocked with huge numbers of cattle and sheep.

Lethal farming methods

The original vegetation was destroyed and the wildlife, deprived of food and cover, declined rapidly in numbers. Animals were ruthlessly hunted for their meat or their skins. The introduction of farm machinery proved fatal to many small creatures and pesticides, sprayed over the land to improve the crop yields, were lethal poisons to many birds and other species of wildlife. Although the attitude of early colonizers is understandable, their descendants learned that quick returns from the land often led to disaster. Overgrazed and over-cultivated soils lost their fertility and stability. Crop yields fell as the wind and rain stripped away the unprotected soil, until only a barren wilderness remained. Rivers, once teeming with fish, were made lifeless, polluted by silt from the eroded land, by industrial waste from factories, and by sewage from sprawling cities.

Today, scientists advise caution to avoid repeating the mistakes of the past. More people throughout the world now realize that they have a responsibility to conserve the land and its resources for future generations. Man has other needs than food alone. In industrial countries, holidays are getting longer and the working week is gradually getting shorter. Recreational facilities, especially out-of-doors, are required by more and more people every year. This trend is very evident in the United States where millions of people flock from the cities to enjoy the countryside, to hunt and fish, to boat on reservoirs and lakes, to swim in the sea, and to ski on mountain slopes. The magnificent Great Smoky Mountains National Park in Tennessee had 15,000 visitors in 1934 when it first opened, but, in 1955, more than

When the Kariba Dam was built in Rhodesia game wardens saved thousands of animals and birds from the rising water. This duiker doe was rescued from a rapidly drowning island.

2,500,000 people passed through its gates. In 1967 there were about 10 million cars on the roads in Britain, but it is estimated that, by 1980, the figure will reach 20 million. The exodus from cities and towns to beauty-spots in the countryside and to the coast will reach enormous proportions. Parks, woodlands, nature reserves, and coastal areas must be conserved and provided with facilities, such as roads and hotels, so that people can enjoy their visits.

The idea of conservation is not new. Marco Polo reported that Kublai Khan was a conservationist who protected the plant and animal life of several beauty-spots in the Mongol Empire. Royal decrees from early times and through the Middle Ages forbade the killing of certain animals, protected eagles and hawks for falconry and reserved large areas for hunting by nobles. These feudal measures maintained some preserves for centuries and saved many species of wildlife in Europe. Norman kings of England set aside the New Forest in Hampshire so that the king could always hunt there. An early English law recognized the danger of fire and established that anyone who let fire spread into his neighbour's trees would be heavily fined, because 'fire is a thief'. But it was not until the twentieth century that most European countries established parks and reserves on a national scale. By 1960 almost every country had set aside areas of scenic beauty and to protect wildlife. Switzerland has the longest tradition of conservation; the first game preserve was set up in 1542.

One of the great tragedies of recent times has been the destruction of much of the immensely varied and abundant wildlife of Africa. The opening up and exploitation of Africa has led to the extinction of several species and others are in danger. Sometimes wild animals were killed for food; others were regarded as dangerous and were slaughtered. The leopard which preyed on domestic animals was considered a menace and became practically extinct in some areas. Unfortunately, however, baboons and wild pigs, the leopard's prey, multiplied rapidly and caused serious damage to farm crops. To upset the balance of nature without understanding and research causes serious problems. Even as menacing a creature as the crocodile serves a role by feeding on sick fish which might otherwise spread disease and seriously deplete the quantity of the fish in rivers.

Probably more serious than hunting in the reduction of African wildlife has been the reckless destruction of the animals' habitats (the cover of which enables them to escape predators) and their sources of food. To protect the survivors, great national parks and reserves have been established where the animals can be studied at close quarters – a source of great pleasure and interest to visitors. In a continent where many people suffer from a lack of meat and animal food products, it is understandable that support for conservation of wildlife is by no means unanimous, and poaching in the parks is

1 Yellowstone Park in Wyoming was opened in 1872, the first of America's national parks. Lower Falls on Yellowstone River drops 319 feet.
2 Deer feed in Nara Park in Japan where 19 parks have been set up to protect unusual wildlife, forests, shrines and scenic beauty.
3 In Australia constant watch is kept from tree-top lookouts for summer fires which can destroy thousands of acres of valuable forest.

The Grand Canyon in northwest Arizona reaches a depth of 5,500 feet and varies from two to 18 miles wide. In 1919 105 miles of its 200-mile extent was set aside as a national park.

still a serious problem. But conservation of wildlife can be beneficial to African countries; in Kenya tourism has become the country's largest single source of income. Further, in national parks and reserves, some animals breed quickly and exhaust their available food supplies. Selective slaughter, called culling, a fairly new practice, can benefit the herd as a whole and prevent starvation. Regulated culling of over-large herds also guarantees meat supplies for town-dwellers often from lands which are quite unsuitable for domestic animals.

The Kruger National Park of South Africa, which covers 8,000 square miles, was established in 1898. Here visitors can see elephants, lions, giraffes, hippopotamuses, many species of antelope and other animals in their natural environment. Scientists believe that parks should be greatly increased in number if the wildlife is to be saved. But the expense of establishing and maintaining parks in developing countries is very considerable.

Throughout the world, prompt government action has saved many species of animals and birds from extinction. In New Zealand a flightless bird called the notornis, thought to be extinct since 1878, was found in 1948 in a remote valley on South Island. The New Zealand government made the whole area a national park and introduced penalties for anyone killing the bird or taking its eggs.

Saved from extinction

In Scotland ospreys nested regularly until the end of the nineteenth century. Now they are breeding there again, protected by law and a continuous watch that guards them from egg-stealers. The musk-ox, which once roamed over Alaska, Northern Canada and Greenland was saved from extinction by the Canadian government which set aside 15,000 square miles as a sanctuary. In 1962 the World Wild Life Fund was established to finance action to save wildlife all over the world.

When the Kariba Dam was built on the Zambezi River in Rhodesia between 1956 and 1960, it created the world's largest artificial lake, drowning 2,000 square miles and endangering wildlife. A massive effort, called 'Operation Noah' was mounted by game wardens to rescue thousands of animals and birds from islands and tree-tops where they had been driven by the rising water. Once captured, by using nets and tranquillizers, the animals were released on dry land, after being tagged to aid the study of their migration.

National parks and forests now exist in most parts of the world. The first national park, the Yellowstone Park of Wyoming, was opened in 1872, and by the 1960s the United States had 32 parks. Within them forest and game are protected against fire or human destruction. The parks are refuges for some species that are close to extinction and other parks preserve great natural features, such as the Grand Canyon. Most of the parks contain hotels, camping grounds and other forms of accommodation, together with good roads and trails for walkers and horsemen. Covering an area more than ten times as great as the national parks are the national forests. Other recreational areas include state parks for outings and picnics and national monuments, including battlefields and other historic sites. Canada soon followed the United States in setting up a national parks system and established many wildlife sanctuaries.

The U.S.S.R. has some 60 nature reserves ranging from those in the north where reindeer and elk are protected to the desert reserves in the south. Stocks of beaver, which were nearly exterminated in the Soviet Union, have been restored by work in the reserves. Britain has ten national parks, where the natural scenery is safeguarded, and other strictly supervised nature reserves where scientists can conserve and study animal and bird life in their natural habitats.

Last Java rhinoceroses

In Japan, in spite of the great shortage of agricultural land, a national parks law was passed in 1931. There are now many parks which protect unusual wildlife, as well as forests, areas of scenic beauty and national shrines such as the volcanic cone of Mount Fuji. In Indonesia, which has over 100 nature preserves, a park called the Oedjong Koelon contains the last few surviving rhinoceroses of Java. The male rhinoceroses were hunted for their single horns which were believed to have aphrodisiacal powers. The Kasiranga Reserve in India protects the few remaining Indian species of this rhinoceros.

Over-fishing in the oceans has led to international agreements to protect sea life. Several countries, including Canada, Japan, the United States, and the U.S.S.R. have agreed a treaty restricting the over-hunting of seals in the North Pacific. The threat to fish life in inland waters is also great as a result of Man's misuse of natural resources. Many fish, such as trout, cannot live in muddy streams characteristic of badly eroded regions. Silt also smothers spawning beds and blocks the sunlight required by aquatic plants. In many cities another source of

pollution, sewage, is now treated and made harmless before it is pumped into rivers and lakes. Laws in many countries restrict the dumping of industrial wastes into rivers and lakes because they often contain materials poisonous to fish. But treatment of industrial wastes to render them harmless is expensive.

The drainage of lakes and other wet areas is often justified because new farmland is created. But with the increasing demand for recreation, the popularity of water sports, and the growing awareness that areas must be conserved for lakeside wildlife, such projects are now examined critically before reclamation is embarked upon. In far too many cases in the past, areas have been drained at great expense only to produce poor agricultural land. Five attempts, four of which were unsuccessful, were made to drain a lake in central Sweden. In 1931, the project was finally completed, but since that date the land has been constantly subject to flooding and farming has proved less profitable than the fishing which once took place there. The drainage also caused a general lowering of the *water table* (the underground water-level), reducing the water power capacity of nearby hydro-electric plants.

Rivers and lakes are an integral part of the land and water supplies and must be considered as part of any national conservation programme. As the standard of living of the people of any country rises, so the consumption of fresh water increases to meet domestic, industrial and agricultural demands. In Britain, the consumption of water will probably double over the next 20 years. Some densely populated areas, such as the city of Manchester, face particularly difficult problems and some bold solutions have been proposed. The successful dam built across the outlet of the Zuider Zee and

the creation of a freshwater lake behind the dam has inspired engineers to propose similar dams and lakes round the coast of Britain. A dam across Morecambe Bay would hold back a freshwater lake to supply Manchester. Similar dams have been suggested for the Solway Firth in Scotland and the Wash in eastern England. Advocates of these projects argue that the lakes would also become recreational areas but, apart from the immense engineering problems involved, the cost of these schemes would be enormous. One alternative, of course, is to create more inland reservoirs. There are valleys in Britain which are thinly-populated and which could be dammed. But the flooding of even a few small villages is controversial, involving the loss of valuable agricultural land, the transfer of the people to another area, and creating difficult human problems.

Thought for the future

The attraction of sea coasts for holidays has led to building and other developments which has marred the beauty of many areas. The situation is serious in Britain where only nine per cent of the coastline of England and Wales is protected within the national parks. But the government has recently designated several Areas of Outstanding Natural Beauty which contain a much larger area of coastline. It has published a report which recognizes the disastrous results of unplanned development and the need for control.

Even in countries where conservation is generally accepted, there are still people who damage land for personal gain or vandals who start forest fires. The future of conservation depends very much on education. Children must be taught that their lives are closely related to their environment. They possess a rich natural inheritance which can easily be destroyed but, by careful conservation, they can live harmoniously with their surroundings and pass on to later generations a world worth living in.

1 In the Soviet Union 60 nature reserves have been established. These egrets and white spoonbills are protected in the Astrakhan Reserve on the lower reaches of the Volga.

2 Britain has many reserves and sanctuaries for the preservation and study of wildlife. At Abbotsbury in Dorset swans, protected by law, nest at the huge breeding ground.

Index

Figures in *italics* indicate an illustration of that subject. The letters a, b and c indicate the first, second and third columns of the page respectively.

M

"Mackerel" sky *138b-c*
Magellan, 85
Magma 29b
Magnetic variation 79a
Mahogany tree, felling of *197b*
Maize *152c*
  flour, preparation of *152c, 185b*
  influence on South American
  culture 81a
Mammoth *141c*
Mammoth Cave, Kentucky *30b-c*
Manganese 206b
Man-made fibres 196c
Mantle, of the Earth 17b; *23a-b*
Map(s) *See also* Atlas(es)
  cartography, ancient 73a
  Babylonian, on clay *73b*
  clay 73a; *73b*
  Este 85a
  flat 109a
  of the world, from Ptolemy's
  Geographica 74-75
  papyrus 73a
  projections 109a
    of Mercator 80b
  scales in 110c, 111
  topographical 112c
Marginal lands, cultivation 232b
Manioc, processing of *187a*
Market gardening 169
Marshland, reclamation of 229a
Masai people 168c
Matterhorn 23b-c
Maya Empire 81b
Mercator, Gerhard, work of 88a
  map projection of 80b
Mesa 32a
Metamorphic rocks 30a
Meteorology 145
Mica 207a
Mid-oceanic ridges 18a, 19 *(map)*
Milk delivery, Spanish *155b-c*
  production 155c
  transport of, from farm *156b-c*
Milking, techniques *156*
Millet 152c
  harvest *151a*
Mimi spirit-man, Aborigine,
  rock-painting of *123a-b*
Mine disaster, Yugoslavia *209b-c*
Minerals 205
  from the oceans 179c
Mining. *See under specific*
  commodity
Mitla, stonework in *82c*
Mixed farm, Ontario *153b-c*
Mohair 196b
Monsoon *140*
  forests 203a
Monte Alban, Mexico, site of
  Zapotec remains *84b-c*
Moors, in Spain and Portugal 82b
Mountains 21
  Alps *21b-c*
  block 23
  effect on climate 144a
  erosion of 24b
  Etna *27*

Everest *24b-c*
  fold 21b
  formation of *23a-b*
  Fujiyama *22b-c*
  Himalayas 19a; *18a-b*
  Kanchenjunga *18a-b*
  Kilimanjaro *94a-b*
  Matterhorn *23b-c*
  Pelée, volcanic eruption of 25a
  Snowdon *30b-c*
  Table Mountain, Cape Town
  66a-b
  Vesuvius 26a
  volcanic 22a
Mud flows 35c, 36a
  soil, cracking *60b*

N

Nansen 104b
Nara Park, Japan, deer in *238a-b*
National Parks 239c
Natural gas. *See* Gas, natural
Natural vegetation. *See* Vegetation,
  natural
Nature, man's impact on 217a
  reserve, U.S.S.R. 240a
Nautilus, sub-polar journey of 102c
Navigation 77
  ancient 78b
Navigator at work *87a-b*
  17th century *80a*
Nebraska homestead 27a-b
Netherlands, The *41(map)*
  land reclamation in *217b-c,*
  229b-c
New Zealand, climate of 128a
Niagara Falls *55a-b*
Nile, delta, marshland in 43a-b
  fertile banks of *234b-c*
  irrigation 235a; *236b-c*
Nimbus, satellite *147a-b*
Noah's Ark *13*
Nodules, mineral, of the oceans
  179c
North Sea gas 216c
  rig *178b-c, 215b-c*
Nuee ardente 25b
Núñez de Balboa, conquest of
  South America *84a-b*

O

Oasis, Moroccan *62b-c*
Oats 152; *149b-c*
Ocean, currents 51
  depths 50*(diagram)*
    exploration of 49; *50b-c*
  farming of 177
  floor of 49b
    structure of 17a

life in 52a
  salinity 52a
Oil *See also* Petroleum
  derricks, Venezuela *214b-c*
  desert *130a-b*
  Libyan, searching for *216a-b*
  rig, Persian Gulf *215b-c*
  shales 215a
  springs, Trinidad *213b-c*
  vegetable, uses for 189a-b *(table)*
Oil palm 191a
  nuts *192a-b*
    pounding of *191b-c*
Old Faithful geyser, Wyoming
  122b-c
Olive groves *225b-c*
Olympic National Park, Washington
  220a-b
Opencast coal mine, Newcastle
  232a-c
Orange crop, frost protection for
  129b-c
Oranges, cultivation 163a
  harvest *162c, 163b-c*
  market, Jerusalem *161b-c*
Ore deposits 205c
Ore, geological searching for 208c
Orogenic forces 22a
Over-fishing 240a
Over-grazing, in soil erosion 222a;
  223
Oyster fishing 173b

P

Palaeoclimatology 141
Pamir Plateau *65b-c*
Papyrus maps 73a
Park, Mungo 95a
Pea harvesting, Kent *172b-c*
Pear tree, pruning *164a-b*
Peary, Robert *104c*
Peat, precursor of coal 209c
  transport of *212b-c*
Pedology 57a
Pelorus compass *78c*
Penguins, emperor *106a-b*
Pentinger Table *76b-c*
Petroleum 213
  New Guinea *213a-b*
  overland pipes *216b*
  recoverable reserves of 214b
  refinery, Jeddah *214-215*
Phosphates 207a; *208a-b*
Photo-mosaic, in surveying *120b-c*
Photography, aerial 119a
Phytogeography 218a
Pineapple *162b*
  cultivation 176a; *162a*
Pit ponies *211*
Pizarro, conquest of South America
  84a
Plains, coastal 43c
  flood 42a
  glacial 44b
Plane table surveying 116a; *113*
Plankton 173
Plans 114a
Plant life, climatic effects on 218a
  patterns of 218a

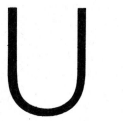